D1682769

MINI GRAPHICS 2

MINI GRAPHICS 2

Maximum impact in a mini format
Un maximum d'impact dans un mini format.
Máximo impacto en formato mini.
Massimo impatto in formato mini

Translators of the foreword: French / Spanish / Italian translator:
Satèl·lit bcn - François Schapochnikoff / Reyes Bermejo Mozo /
Arrigo Frisano-Paulon

First published in 2012 by Sandu Publishing

Copyright © 2012 by Sandu Publishing Co., Limited
Copyright © 2012 English language edition by
Promopress for sale in Europe and America.

PROMOPRESS is a commercial brand of:
Promotora de Prensa Internacional S.A.
C/ Ausiàs March, 124
08013 Barcelona, Spain
Phone: +34 93 245 14 64
Fax: +34 93 265 48 83
info@promopress.es
www.promopress.info

Sponsored by: Design 360° – Concept and Design Magazine
Chief Editor: Wang Shaoqiang
Executive Editor: Daniela Huang
Chief Designer: Wang Shaoqiang
Book Designer: Leo Cheung
www.sandu360.com

ISBN: 978-84-92810-40-6

All rights reserved. No part of this publication may be reproduced or transmitted in any form or by any means, electronic or mechanical, including photocopy or any storage and retrieval system, without permission in writing from the publishers.

Tous droits réservés. La reproduction ou la transmission intégrale ou partielle du présent ouvrage ainsi que son stockage sur un système informatique, par quelque procédé que ce soit, électronique ou mécanique, ou par photocopie, téléchargement, enregistrement ou autre, faite sans le consentement écrit du détenteur du droit d'auteur est illicite.

Todos los derechos reservados. Esta publicación no puede reproducirse ni transmitirse en todo ni en parte, de ninguna forma ni por ningún medio, electrónico o mecánico, incluyendo fotocopia, grabación o cualquier sistema de almacenamiento, sin el permiso previo escrito del editor.

Tutti i diritti riservati. Questa pubblicazione non può essere riprodotta o trasmessa in tutto o in parte, in qualsiasi forma e con qualsiasi mezzo, elettronico o meccanico, incluse fotocopie, registrazioni o qualsiasi altro sistema di storage, senza il permesso scritto dell'editore.

Printed in China

CONTENTS

Preface   004
Project   013
Interview   330
Biography   373
Acknowledgements 384

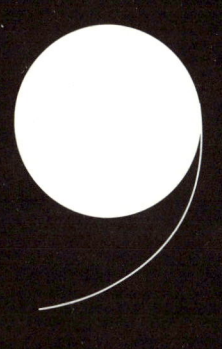

Scale is a funny thing, especially given the contemporary context — more and more designers probably can't imagine working for a big bloated company or agency as something desirable beyond a means for health insurance or a steady pay check. I used to think like that, but I've had a real dearth of decent bosses every time I've worked for a bigger agency[1].

More and more, beyond being what is available to most, freelance life is becoming the most appealing option[2]. Independence alone is attractive — no clocks to punch, no weird unwanted co-workers, (theoretically) fewer concessions to design decisions, more autonomy... Being freelance is the maverick Wild West lone gunman image of today. The strange thing is that "the dream" is not merely attainable anymore, but more and more the norm. Post-industrial society has increasingly dismantled former employment structures, such as design studios and advertising agencies. I know this first-hand — it's what has guided my career so far. I could never get salaried positions at agencies when I was starting out and learned quickly to find my own clients and supplement them with contract gigs, both in-house and remote alike.

And this is where scale comes in — most freelance people I know lean on others who freelance to take on larger projects — I do this all the time. No matter how varied your skill set, one person cannot do everything. I've been running a design studio in Tokyo for the past seven years and have kept myself and a programmer employed full-time, bugging 3D animators, SEO specialists and others with highly focused capabilities when needed.

I've had a few chances to take it to the next level — to open a legitimate office, sign leases, take out loans, and essentially sign away the freedom that being small-scale brings. I have continually said "no thank you" to this opportunity — economies perennially feel too shaky in the world at large, clients are too flaky, and debt is already very much a factor[3]. I'd rather work with talented friends on the projects requiring a specific body of skills and save the hassle of structuring an office, a printer, an accountant, salaries, insurance, health insurance, et al.

And that's how most folks I know and work with in graphic design operate — keep things small. Keep it all reasonable. And beyond that, keep everything in perspective. We all have slow months, even those with offices and employees. We all have rent and bills and loans and mouths to feed. Sometimes it's boom, sometimes it's bust, but you keep your overhead low and your eyes on the prize.

I like the "mini" in "mini graphics": it's something we can take in and understand, both aesthetically and socio-economically. To take on projects that are "smaller in scale" is process-oriented. One can obtain a grander sense of scope and scale through taking ownership of aspects of a project rather than having a slice of a project delegated unto one. For example: the logo leads to the typographic palette, which leads to the color palette, which leads to the stationery, which wholly informs the website, which leads to the motion element, which informs the branding-out. Each project helps us gain a sense of what we are doing and who we, in essence, are as design practitioners. Small, in essence, equals control.

And that is the beauty of scale — you start small and wind up often able to contribute so much more than folks working for larger entities. Give me a small company's identity over a component of a component of a multinational corporation's ad campaign any day — the client's budget will get stretched further and they'll be infinitely more pleased than the corporate creative director... and they'll tell their friends. And one'll get more work. And things will keep rolling on the small scale in a way that Google and Nike will never understand. You'll have the pay, the friends, the ever-important street cred, and the wiggle

Ian Lynam is a graphic designer and writer living in Tokyo. He runs a multidisciplinary design studio that focuses on pan-cultural identity design, motion graphics, and editorial design. He is a graduate of Portland State University (B.S. Graphic Design) and California Institute of the Arts (M.F.A. Graphic Design). His most recent book is Design of Manga, Anime & Light Novels. An Asia Pacific Design Award winner, he writes regularly for Idea Magazine, Slanted Magazine, Néojaponisme, and a host of design books.

Ian Lynam
Keeping it mini

room that your classmate stuck in a high-rise churning out work for the big boys will never have. Sure, they'll have the mortgage and the kids and the eco-friendly car, but they won't be able to drop it all and head to Malaysia for some beach time and amazing curry when the dreaded slow month rears its ugly head... and the reality is that they won't have the enterprising spirit to knuckle down and find some more small stuff when the going gets rough — they'll just find a lesser agency and downgrade to prop up a lifestyle that must be fed. "Mini" doesn't need much food or gas. It thrives on craft, quality and camaraderie. It doesn't advertise its side-projects as implicitly or charge for drinks at the corporate holiday party. It moves the world, but at its own pace and in its own time.

And when I say "mini", what I really mean are the independent designers making his or her way sans corporate design job. The most stressed, but the happiest. The ones with options. The ones tapping this out on an iPad at 3:30 in the morning with deadlines intact, a drink (or two) in the gullet and a happy partner because our time is flexible.

For those keeping it small, I salute you!

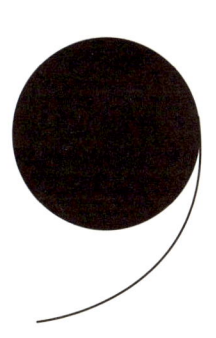

---

[1] Which was always in the capacity of being a contract worker: to date, I've only ever been salaried as a design educator – never a designer working for a firm full-time.

[2] Though I do wonder at times: a recent overview of waiters and waitresses in the U.S. showed that they'd rather take their chances on the tipping-based system rather than a salaried existence. I think the hopeful nature of freelancers is very much in line with American wait staff – we are all folks holding out for the big tip in lieu of proper careers and healthcare... Or maybe we just don't like bosses so much – it's the catch-22 of contemporary selfishness.

[3] Thanks, graduate school – you were the best decision I ever made and the reason I pay $500 a month to stay above water.

La taille d'une compagnie est un facteur étrange, surtout si l'on tient compte du contexte actuel – de plus en plus de designers ne s'imaginent pas et ne souhaitent sûrement pas travailler pour une agence ou une compagnie gigantesque à moins de vouloir une bonne mutuelle et un salaire régulier. C'est ce que je pensais auparavant, mais j'ai connu une véritable pénurie de patrons décents chaque fois que j'ai travaillé pour une agence importante[1].

Être free-lance est l'option qui est de plus en plus offerte à la plupart et c'est aussi la plus attractive[2]. L'indépendance en elle même suffit à séduire – plus de pointeuse, plus de collègues bizarres qu'on n'a pas choisis, moins de concessions (en théorie) quant aux décisions concernant le design, plus d'autonomie... Un cavalier du Far West, solitaire et indépendant, telle est l'image du free-lance aujourd'hui. Le plus étrange est que ce « rêve » n'est plus seulement accessible, mais est de plus en plus devenu la norme. La société post-industrielle a conduit au démantèlement des structures qui recrutent – bureaux d'études et agences de publicité. Je l'ai appris de première main – c'est ce qui a guidé ma carrière jusqu'à présent. Je n'arrivais jamais à obtenir un poste en tant que salarié lorsque j'ai débuté et j'ai rapidement appris à trouver ma propre clientèle et je lui proposais des contrats à durée déterminée en travaillant sur place ou à distance.

Et c'est là que la question de la taille entre en jeu – la plupart des free-lances s'appuient sur d'autres free-lances pour faire face à des projets plus importants – je le fais tout le temps. Peu importe l'étendu de vos compétences, une seule personne ne peut pas tout faire. Depuis les sept dernières années je dirige un bureau de design à Tokyo et j'emploie à temps plein, en plus de moi-même, un programmateur et je collabore avec des animateurs 3D, des spécialistes SEO et d'autres personnes aux capacités très ciblées quand cela est nécessaire.

J'ai eu à plusieurs reprises l'occasion de passer au stade supérieur – ouvrir un bureau traditionnel, signer des baux, faire des emprunts, et renoncer, finalement, à cette liberté qu'une petite structure apporte. A cette perspective j'ai toujours dit « non merci » – Dans ce monde, l'économie semble toujours être trop instable[3], les clients inconstants et l'endettement un facteur d'une importance non négligeable. Je préfère travailler avec des amis de grand talent sur des projets qui nécessitent certains types de compétences et m'éviter les tracas de la gestion d'un bureau, d'une imprimante, d'un comptable, de salariés, d'assurances, de mutuelle santé, etc …

Et c'est ainsi que beaucoup de personnes que je connais et avec qui je travaille procèdent dans le design – rester petit. Rester raisonnable. Et par dessus tout, garder le sens des proportions. Nous connaissons tous les mois creux, même ceux avec des bureaux et des employés. Nous payons tous un loyer, des factures, des emprunts, et nous avons tous des bouches à nourrir. Parfois c'est l'essor, parfois c'est l'échec mais on maintient nos frais généraux au minimum et on ne perd pas de vue nos objectifs.

J'aime le mot « mini » dans « mini graphic » c'est un concept que l'on intègre et que l'on comprend tant sur le plan esthétique que socio-économique. Se charger de projets de petite envergure c'est être axé sur la procédure. On a une meilleure vue d'ensemble lorsqu'on prend en charge les différentes étapes d'un procédé plutôt que de ne s'occuper que d'une partie. Par exemple; le logo mène à la palette typographique, qui conduit à la palette des couleurs, qui à son tour amène à la papeterie et son design. Ensuite entre en jeu le graphisme du site internet, qui amène aux animations graphiques, ce qui conduit au branding. Chaque projet nous apporte une meilleure compréhension de ce que nous faisons et de qui nous sommes, nous, en tant que professionnels du design. Petit veut essentiellement dire maîtrise.

Graphiste et auteur Ian Lynam vit au Japon. Il dirige un bureau pluridisciplinaire en design et se focalise sur l'identité visuelle interculturelle, l'animation graphique, et le graphisme éditorial. Il est diplômé de l'université d'état de Portland (Licence – graphisme) et de l'institut des Arts de Californie (Master – graphisme). Design of Manga, Anime & Light Novels est son ouvrage le plus récent. Lauréat du Asia Pasific Design Award, il collabore régulièrement à Idea Magazine, Slanted Magazine, Néojaponisme et une multitude de livres sur le design.

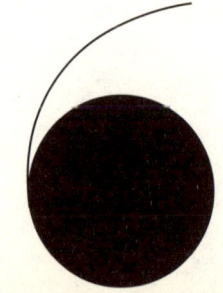

De Ian Lynam
Rester «mini»

Et c'est là la beauté des petites structures, vous commencez petit et vous finissez souvent par apporter bien plus que ceux qui travaillent pour des entités plus importantes. Je préfère de loin m'occuper de l'identité visuelle d'une petite boîte, plutôt que d'être un maillon, d'un maillon du maillon de la campagne publicitaire d'une multinationale — le budget du client s'agrandira et il sera bien plus satisfait que le directeur de création d'une société, et il en parlera à ses amis. Et on aura plus de travail. Et cela continuera à petite échelle d'une façon que Google et Nike ne comprendront jamais. Vous aurez la paie, les amis, une crédibilité indispensable, et la marge de manœuvre que vos camarades, coincés dans leur tour et travaillant à la chaîne pour leur boss, n'auront jamais. Bien sûr ils auront un emprunt immobilier, des enfants, et une voiture écologique, mais ils ne pourront pas tout plaquer et partir en Malaisie pour la plage et un délicieux curry quand le mois creux montrera son horrible tête. Et la vérité est qu'il leur manquera cet esprit d'entreprise nécessaire pour s'y mettre et chercher quelques contrats quand les temps se compliquent, ils se limiteront à trouver un poste moins important dans une agence plus petite afin de maintenir un style de vie qui doit être alimenté. « Mini » n'a pas besoin de beaucoup de nourriture ou d'essence. Il fonctionne aux compétences, à la qualité et à la camaraderie. Il n'informe pas des projets parallèles aussi implicitement, ou il ne facture pas les boissons des fêtes organisées au bureau. Il change le monde, mais en prenant son temps, à son rythme.

Et quand je dis « mini », ce que j'entends vraiment par là c'est un ou une designer indépendant(e) qui fait son chemin sans un job dans une grosse entreprise. Les plus stressés, mais les plus heureux. Ceux qui ont le choix. Ceux qui à 3h30 du matin travaillent sur leur iPad et respectent les délais, avec un ou deux verres dans le gosier, et un partenaire heureux parce que notre temps est flexible.

A vous qui restez mini, je vous tire mon chapeau!

---

[1] À ce jour j'ai seulement été salarié en tant que professeur de graphisme – jamais en tant que designer engagé à temps plein pour une entreprise.

[2] Bien que parfois je m'interroge : une récente étude qui avait pour sujet les serveurs et serveuses aux Etats-Unis a révélé qu'ils préféraient les risques d'un système basé sur la rémunération au pourboire plutôt que de vivre d'un salaire fixe. Je pense que la nature optimiste des free-lances est identique à celle des serveurs américains. Nous sommes tous des gens qui espérons le gros pourboire à la place d'une carrière classique et d'une mutuelle. Ou alors nous n'aimons peut-être simplement pas tant que ça les patrons. C'est la situation inextricable de l'égoïsme moderne.

[3] Merci, licence et master! Vous êtes les meilleures décisions que je n'ai jamais prises et les 500 dollars que je paie par mois pour garder la tête hors de l'eau.

La escala es algo curioso, especialmente en el contexto actual. Probablemente, para la mayoría de los diseñadores la idea de trabajar para una empresa o una agencia enorme solo resulta atractiva como una forma de obtener el seguro médico o unos ingresos regulares. Yo solía pensar así, pero cuando he trabajado para agencias grandes, apenas he tenido jefes decentes[1].

Cada vez más, la vida del freelance es la alternativa más accesible y se está convirtiendo también en la más atractiva[2]. La independencia ya es interesante en sí misma: sin horario fijo, sin tener que aguantar compañeros de trabajo raritos, sin tener que hacer (en teoría) tantas concesiones en el diseño, con una mayor autonomía, ... La imagen de los trabajadores independientes actuales es la del llanero solitario e inconformista del Lejano Oeste. Lo extraño es que «el sueño» va dejando de ser algo difícilmente alcanzable para convertirse en la norma. La sociedad postindustrial ha provocado la disolución de las estructuras laborales anteriores: los estudios de diseño y las agencias de publicidad. Lo sé de primera mano, porque es lo que ha guiado mi carrera hasta ahora. Como no podía acceder a puestos en plantilla en las agencias para las que trabajaba cuando empecé, pronto aprendí a buscar mis propios clientes y a compaginar esos trabajos con encargos puntuales en las propias empresas o desde casa.

Y aquí es donde la escala viene al caso: la mayoría de los trabajadores independientes que conozco colaboran con otros autónomos para aceptar proyectos más grandes. Yo lo hago constantemente. Por muchas habilidades que uno tenga, una sola persona no puede hacerlo todo. Llevo siete años dirigiendo un estudio de diseño en Tokio en el que hemos estado contratados a tiempo completo un programador y yo, y hemos contado con la colaboración de los animadores 3D, con su tabarra habitual, o con especialistas en posicionamiento web o en otros campos cuando nos ha hecho falta.

A lo largo de estos años, se me han presentado oportunidades para llevarlo más allá y montar una empresa en toda regla, firmar contratos de arrendamiento, pedir préstamos y renunciar a la libertad que supone el trabajar a pequeña escala. En esas ocasiones mi respuesta ha sido siempre: «Gracias, pero no.» En este mundo, las economías parecen tener una inestabilidad constante, con clientes demasiado volubles y la deuda como un factor fundamental[3]. Prefiero trabajar con amigos con talento en los proyectos en los que hacen falta especialistas de distintos ámbitos y ahorrarme el lío de montar una oficina con una impresora, un contable, varios sueldos, los seguros, el seguro médico y demás.

Así es como trabaja la mayoría de los colegas que conozco y con los que colaboro en esto del diseño gráfico: a pequeña escala, dentro de unos límites razonables y, sobre todo, relativizando las cosas. Todos tenemos meses flojos, incluso quienes tienen oficinas y empleados. Y alquileres, facturas y préstamos y bocas que alimentar. A veces estás hasta arriba y otras, de brazos cruzados, pero basta con contener el gasto y no desviarse del objetivo.

Ian Lynam es un diseñador gráfico y escritor afincado en Tokio. Dirige un estudio multidisciplinar dedicado al diseño y centrado en la creación de imagen corporativa basada en un enfoque multicultural, y en el grafismo animado y el diseño editorial. Es licenciado en diseño gráfico por la Universidad de Portland State y tiene un máster en Bellas Artes del California Institute of the Arts. Su último libro es Design of Manga, Anime & Light Novels. Ha sido galardonado con el premio al diseño Asia Pacific Design y colabora en varias publicaciones, como Idea Magazine, Slanted Magazine, Néojaponisme, y en un gran número de libros sobre diseño.

Ian Lynam
Hazlo «mini»

Me gusta el «mini» de los gráficos que presiden este libro, es algo muy fácil de entender y asimilar, tanto en el sentido estético como en el socioeconómico. Asumir proyectos a pequeña escala es algo centrado en el proceso. Uno capta mejor el alcance y la escala de un proyecto al llevar las riendas de algunos aspectos del trabajo que al serle asignada una parte aislada. Por ejemplo, el logotipo determina la paleta tipográfica que, a su vez, establece la paleta de colores. Ésta marca el diseño de la papelería, que está estrechamente relacionado con el diseño web y el grafismo animado y conforma finalmente la imagen de marca. Cada uno de los proyectos nos ayuda a entender lo que hacemos y lo que somos, en esencia, al dedicarnos al diseño. Moverse a pequeña escala equivale a controlar.

Y precisamente eso es lo bueno de la escala: empiezas por lo pequeño y muchas veces acabas pudiendo hacer mucho más que quienes trabajan para clientes más grandes. Prefiero encargarme de la imagen de una empresa pequeña que del componente de un componente de un componente de la campaña de publicidad de una multinacional: el presupuesto del cliente se irá estirando y quedará mucho más satisfecho que el director creativo de una empresa, y correrá la voz. Y de ahí saldrá más trabajo. Y las cosas se irán encadenando a pequeña escala de una forma que Google y Nike nunca entenderían. Tendrás los ingresos, los amigos, la importantísima reputación y la libertad de acción que ya querría para sí tu compañero de facultad, que ha quedado atrapado en un puesto para una gran compañía, haciendo trabajos como churros desde la oficina de cualquier rascacielos. Sin duda, tendrá su hipoteca, sus niños y su coche ecológico, pero ninguna posibilidad de dejarlo todo para pasar unos días de playa en Malasia, disfrutando de un fantástico curry, cuando los proyectos empiecen a escasear... y lo cierto es que tampoco tendrá el espíritu emprendedor suficiente para remangarse y buscar algún encargo pequeño cuando las cosas se pongan difíciles. Se limitará a buscar un puesto menor en una agencia menos importante para mantener el estilo de vida que lleva. Lo «mini» no exige demasiados recursos. Se alimenta del saber hacer, la calidad y el compañerismo. No tiene que promocionar sus proyectos paralelos de forma implícita o financiarse con las bebidas de la fiesta de empresa. Mueve el mundo, pero a su ritmo y a su debido tiempo.

Y cuando digo «mini», a lo que me refiero es a ser un diseñador independiente labrándose una carrera sin tener un puesto en una empresa. Los más estresados, pero también los más felices. Los que tienen alternativas. Los que pueden estar redactando esto a las 3:30 de la madrugada en el iPad, sin dejar de cumplir los plazos de entrega, habiéndose tomado una copa (o dos) y bien avenido con su pareja porque tienen un horario flexible.

Desde aquí, presento mis respetos a todos los que están en lo «mini».

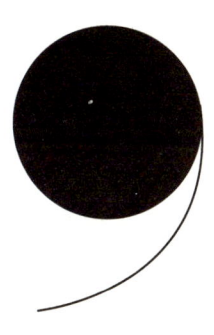

---

1 Siempre en calidad de trabajador independiente contratado por obra. Hasta la fecha, solo he trabajado en plantilla como profesor de diseño, no como diseñador para una firma a tiempo completo.

2 Aunque a veces uno duda: en un estudio reciente sobre los camareros en Estados Unidos se ha demostrado que prefieren arriesgarse a depender de las propinas que tener un sueldo fijo. Creo que la naturaleza optimista de los trabajadores independientes tiene mucho que ver con los camareros de Estados Unidos: todos tenemos la esperanza de que nos den una buena propina en lugar de contar con un trabajo en condiciones y un seguro médico... O tal vez sea simplemente que no nos gusta demasiado tener jefes; es la trampa 22, la trampa lógica, del egoísmo contemporáneo.

3 ¡Bendito posgrado! Porque fue la mejor decisión que tomé y por los 500 dólares mensuales que tengo que pagar para seguir a flote.

Le dimensioni sono una cosa strana, specialmente se inquadrate nel contesto della vita contemporanea: sono sempre di più i designer che probabilmente non riescono a immaginare che lavorare per un'azienda o un'agenzia grande e grossa, e ben gonfia, possa essere desiderabile, al di là di un mezzo per avere le ferie e le malattie pagate o una busta paga fissa. Questa era anche la mia idea, eppure ho avuto a che fare con ben pochi capiufficio decenti nelle mie esperienze con grandi agenzie[1].

La vita freelance sta diventando una possibilità per un numero sempre crescente di persone, e anzi in molti casi rappresenta l'opzione più attraente[2]. L'indipendenza di per sé è allettante: niente cartellini da timbrare, nessun collega balordo da sopportare, meno concessioni alle decisioni sul design (almeno teoricamente), una maggiore autonomia — l'immagine del freelance oggi è quella del pistolero solitario e ribelle del Far West. Per quanto possa sembrare strano, «il sogno» non è più solo raggiungibile, ma sta rappresentando sempre di più la norma. La società postindustriale ha portato con sé un crescente smantellamento delle antiche strutture aziendali — gli studi di design e le agenzie pubblicitarie. L'ho provato sulla mia pelle, essendo ciò che ha guidato finora la mia carriera. All'inizio non riuscivo mai a farmi assumere da nessuna agenzia, così ho dovuto imparare rapidamente a trovarmi i clienti da solo e curare i loro progetti, fossero in sede o a distanza.

E qui entra in gioco la dimensione: la maggior parte dei freelance che conosco si appoggia su altri freelance per gestire i progetti più consistenti, e io stesso lo faccio continuamente. Si può anche essere bravi a fare un sacco di cose, ma nessuno può fare tutto da solo. Da sette anni gestisco uno studio di design a Tokyo in cui gli unici dipendenti sono me stesso e un programmatore, racimolando animatori 3D, specialisti SEO e altre figure professionali altamente specifiche quando necessario.

Mi è capitato di trovarmi di fronte alla possibilità di fare il passo successivo: aprire un ufficio come si deve, sottoscrivere contratti d'affitto, ricorrere a prestiti, e in fin dei conti firmare la condanna a morte la libertà, legata alla dimensione su piccola scala. Ho sempre risposto «no, grazie» — l'economia sembrava sempre troppo traballante su scala globale, i clienti troppo imprevedibili, e i debiti già anche troppo presenti[3]. Preferisco lavorare con amici di talento su progetti che richiedano un bagaglio specifico di competenze e risparmiarmi la seccatura di dove mettere in piedi un ufficio con una stampante, un commercialista, stipendi, assicurazioni, contributi e tutto il resto.

Così opera anche la maggior parte di quelli che conosco e con i quali collaboro nel design e nella grafica: su scala ridotta. Mantenendo tutto a dimensioni ragionevoli, e per di più, sempre nella giusta prospettiva. Un mese storto capita a tutti, anche a quelli con un ufficio e relativi dipendenti. Tutti dobbiamo pagare un affitto, le bollette, magari un'ipoteca, e tutti abbiamo delle bocche da sfamare. Ci saranno sempre alti e bassi, ma basta non esagerare con le pretese e rimanere coerenti con i propri obiettivi.

Sono d'accordo con il «mini» nella »mini grafica», è qualcosa che possiamo comprendere e metabolizzare, in senso sia estetico sia socio-economico. Occupandoci di progetti di dimensioni minori, non perdiamo di vista l'orientamento al processo stesso. È più facile cogliere al meglio il senso, la portata e le dimensioni di un progetto incaricandosi di tutti i suoi aspetti, anziché occupandosi di una sola porzione delegata di un progetto più grande. Ad esempio: dal logo si passa alla paletta tipografica, poi alla paletta dei colori, quindi alla cancelleria, da qui all'intera impostazione del sito internet, che determina gli elementi in movimento, da cui segue il branding out. Ogni progetto ci aiuta ad acquisire il senso di ciò che facciamo e in sostanza di ciò che siamo come professionisti del design. In sostanza, piccolo significa controllabile.

Ian Lynam è un designer grafico e scrittore. Vive a Tokyo e dirige uno studio di design multidisciplinare specializzato nel design di identità multiculturale, nella grafica in movimento e nel design editoriale. Ha studiato alla Portland State University (Laurea in Design Grafico) e al California Institute of the Arts (Master in Design Grafico). La sua opera più recente è Design di Manga, Anime e Romanzi Leggeri. Già vincitore del Premio Asia Pacific Design, scrive regolarmente per Idea Magazine, Slanted Magazine, Néojaponisme e un sacco di pubblicazioni sul design.

di Ian Lynam
Perché mini è meglio

Questo è il vero fascino della dimensione — si parte dal piccolo e spesso si finisce per poter dare molto di più di chi lavora per grosse aziende. Se fosse per me, sceglierei sempre l'identità di una piccola impresa piuttosto che una parte di una parte di una parte della campagna pubblicitaria di una multinazionale — il cliente sarà più elastico con il preventivo e infinitamente più soddisfatto rispetto al direttore creativo della grossa azienda... e spargerà la voce. E arriveranno altri lavori. E le cose continueranno a muoversi su piccola scala in un modo che Google e Nike non comprenderanno mai. Arriveranno risultati economici, molti amici, una solida reputazione (sempre indispensabile) e uno spazio di manovra che il nostro vecchio compagno di classe lanciato in carriera a sputare lavoro per le grosse case non può neanche sognare. D'accordo, a lui restano l'ipoteca e i figli e l'auto ecologica, ma di certo non potrà mai mollare tutto e farsi una settimana in spiaggia in Malaysia a mangiare un fantastico pollo al curry, approfittando del tanto temuto «mese storto»... e la realtà è che gli mancherà lo spirito imprenditoriale necessario a rimboccarsi le maniche e arrangiarsi in qualche modo nei momenti duri — finirà per trovare un'agenzia meno importante, adattandosi per mantenere uno stile di vita che in qualche modo deve essere sostenuto. «Mini» significa meno spese per il cibo o la benzina, è un concetto che si alimenta di mestiere, qualità e cameratismo. Non strombazza i propri sottoprogetti in modo tanto subliminale, né mette in conto le bevande alle cene natalizie aziendali. Muove il mondo, ma al suo ritmo e con i suoi tempi.

E quando dico «mini», ciò che intendo veramente è il designer indipendente che va avanti a modo suo, senza il bisogno di essere assunto da un'azienda di design. Il più stressato ma il più felice. Quello con più possibilità di scelta. Quello che scrive articoli come questo alle 3.30 di notte sul suo iPad e riesce a rispettare tutte le scadenze, con un bicchiere (o due) nello stomaco e una persona al mio fianco felice perché il nostro tempo è flessibile.

Perché mini è meglio... alla nostra!

1 situazione sempre legata alla condizione di lavoratore a contratto – la mia unica esperienza come dipendente rimane quella di istruttore nel design, e non ho mai lavorato come designer a tempo pieno per un'azienda.

2 eppure a volte rifletto sul fatto che un recente sondaggio tra i camerieri e le cameriere negli Stati Uniti ha rivelato che preferiscono giocare sul sistema delle mance piuttosto che accettare una vita da dipendente; credo che la natura ottimista dei freelance sia perfettamente in linea con i camerieri americani — in entrambi i casi ci affidiamo a una grossa mancia anziché a una carriera vera e propria con contributi pagati... o forse non ci piacciono proprio i capi! È il Comma 22 dell'egoismo contemporaneo.

3 grazie, master post-laurea, per essere la migliore decisione che ho preso in vita mia e allo stesso tempo i 500 dollari che pago ogni mese per stare a galla.

Brilliant design is not necessarily highly visible wall graphics or eye-catching packaging.

Surprise is more than often from the creativity embodied in a palm-sized card, an out-of-the-ordinary mailer or a piece of tactile print work. You never know as your name card is dressed with special materials and decorated with special types, it may help you impress the dealer and find collaborators. You can't imagine what a jaw-dropping moment it is when you are holding a bleeding rubber "heart" invite for an exhibition. You have no idea what's in the gift box until it is opened. Creative minds can blossom anywhere you can think of.

Herein, Mini Graphics 2 will lead you to adventures in a mini wonderland.

It is not about size. It is all about ideas and hearts.

Mini Wonderland

BIRTHDAY RING

Agency:
TT:NT
Work Type:
Greeting Card

It is believed that birth month flowers originated in the Roman Empire.

January-Carnation, February-Violet, March-Jonquil, April-Daisy, May-Hawthorn, June-Rose, July-Tulip, August-Poppy, September-Morning Glory, October-Cosmos, November-Chrysanthemum, December-Orchid.

A range of fold-out paper jewellery. The collection consists of twelve ring designs which are laser-cut and engraved from 200g/m2 textured white paper come with engraved recycled brown envelope.

'Birthday ring' collection is a paper card that folds into a flower-shaped ring resembling the birth flower for each calendar month.

They are special birthday presents for the special day.

014

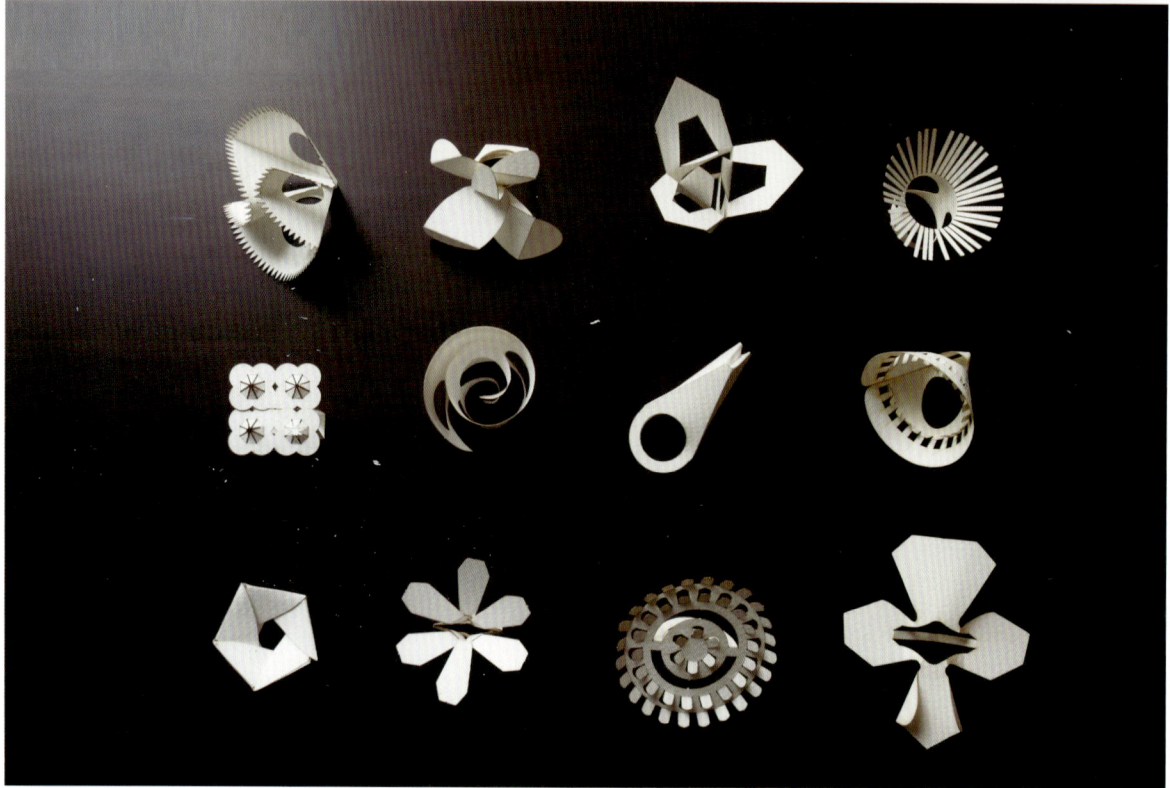

Birthday Ring

Birthday Ring
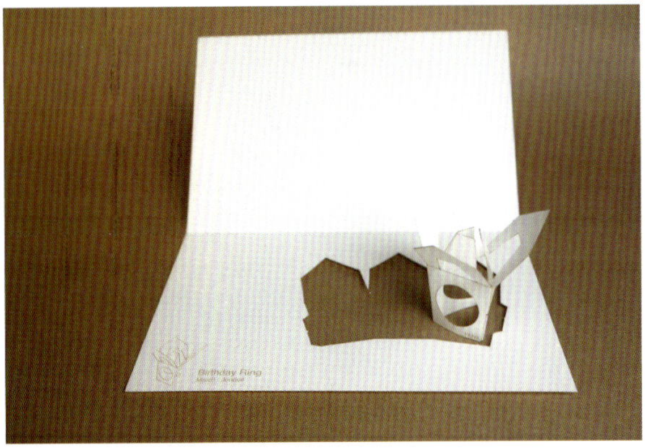
Birthday Ring
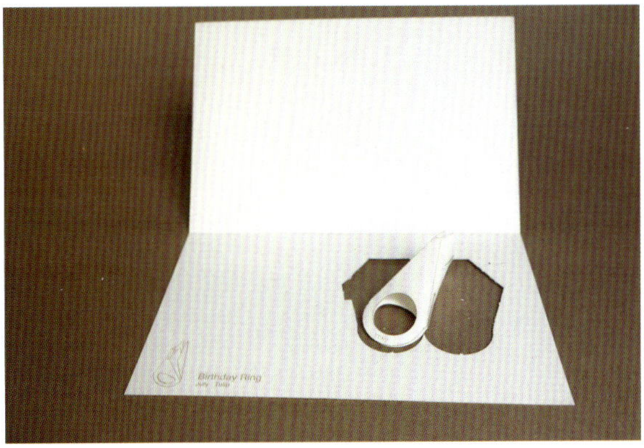
Birthday Ring

Birthday Ring
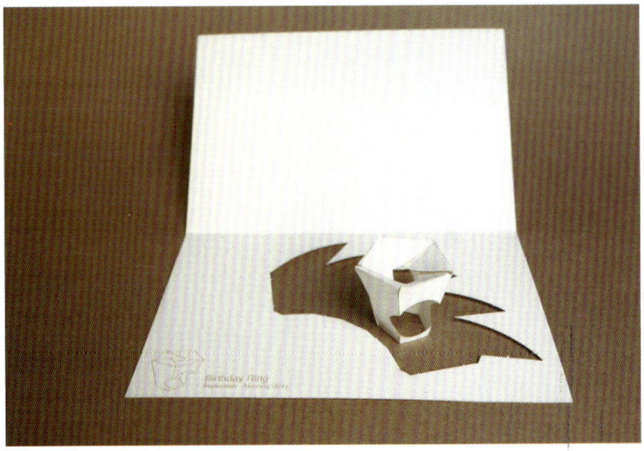
Birthday Ring
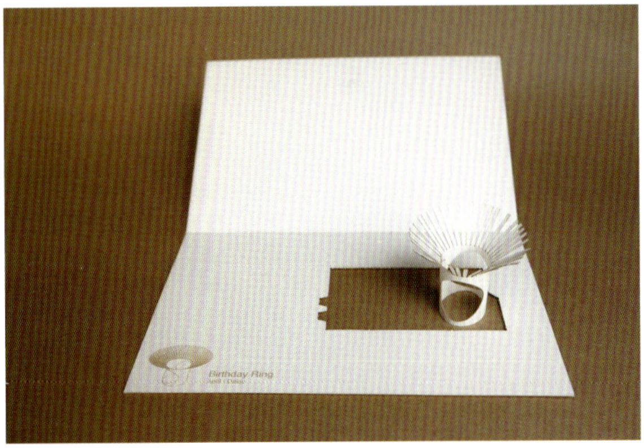
Birthday Ring
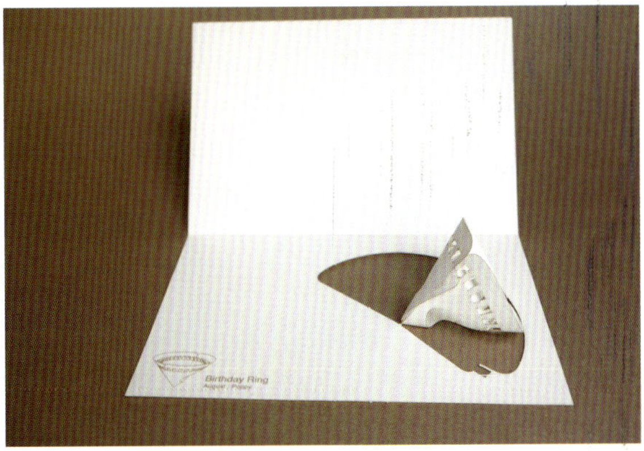
Birthday Ring

INBEING

Agency:
Bejing Woowe Design Co., ltd
Designer:
David Yang
Work Type:
Invitation

Invitation design for Inbeing, a jewelry brand in Beijing, China.

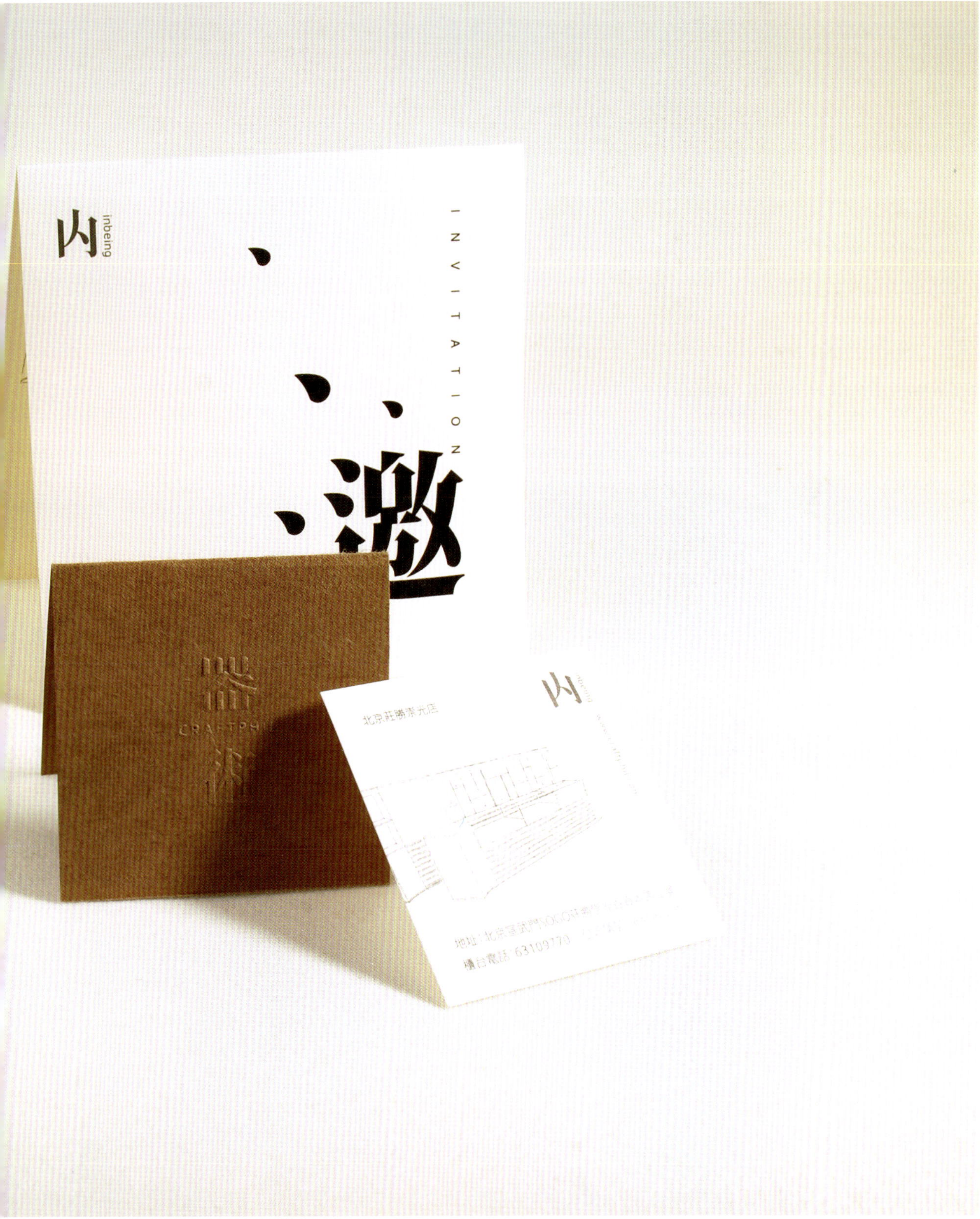
内
inbeing
INVITATION
邀
北京莊勝崇光店
櫃台電話 63109770

2412-DIE WEIHNACHTS-ZAHLEN-GAZETTE

Designer:
Alex Ketzer
Work Type:
Greeting Card

"2412 - Die Weihnachts-Zahlen-Gazette" was the studio's Christmas gift in 2010 for family, friends, colleagues and clients. The newspaper-like magazine is giving information and statistics to the holy feast, including a CD with funky beats for hours of dance beneath the Christmas tree. Let's start the X-Mas-dance-party…

ich wünsche ☐ Dir / ☐ Euch / ☐ Ihnen ein frohes Weihnachtsfest und hoffe, dass der Weihnachtsmann all ☐ Deine / ☐ Eure / ☐ Ihre Wünsche erfüllt!

Vielen lieben Dank für die

☐ gute Zusammenarbeit
☐ vielen Biere, Grasbowlen und Gin Tonics
☐ kurzweiligen Gespräche und Telefonate
☐ tiefen Einblicke in die Psyche der Frauen
☐ prima Musik-Empfehlungen
☐ tollen Musik-Frigge-Sessions
☐ spannenden und aufregenden Projekte
☐ guten Links im Netz und die App-Store-Tipps
☐ leider zu wenigen Treffen (davon mehr in 2011)

im Jahr 2010, mit den besten Wünschen, dass es im Jahr 2011 genau so weitergeht!

In diesem Sinne

☐ guten Rutsch und ein frohes neues Jahr
☐ nicht lang schnacken, Kopf in Nacken!
☐ Tschaikowski und Bis Domerri

☐ Dein
☐ Euer
☐ Ihr **Alex**

24I2
DIE WEIHNACHTS-ZAHLEN-GAZETTE

Alles, was Sie schon immer über das Weihnachtsfest wissen wollten, sich jedoch nie zu fragen getraut haben, erfahren sie hier schwarz auf weiß. Aber Vorsicht: Die pure Wahrheit über das Fest der Feste ist vielleicht nicht so schön, wie Sie denken…

XUE XUE INSTITUTE
4TH ANNIVERSARY
INVITATION

Designer:
Wang Zhi Hong
Work Type:
Invitation

Turning the two-dimensional
invitation cards we commonly
see into a "message box,"
showing the extra thoughts
and depth put into its
content.

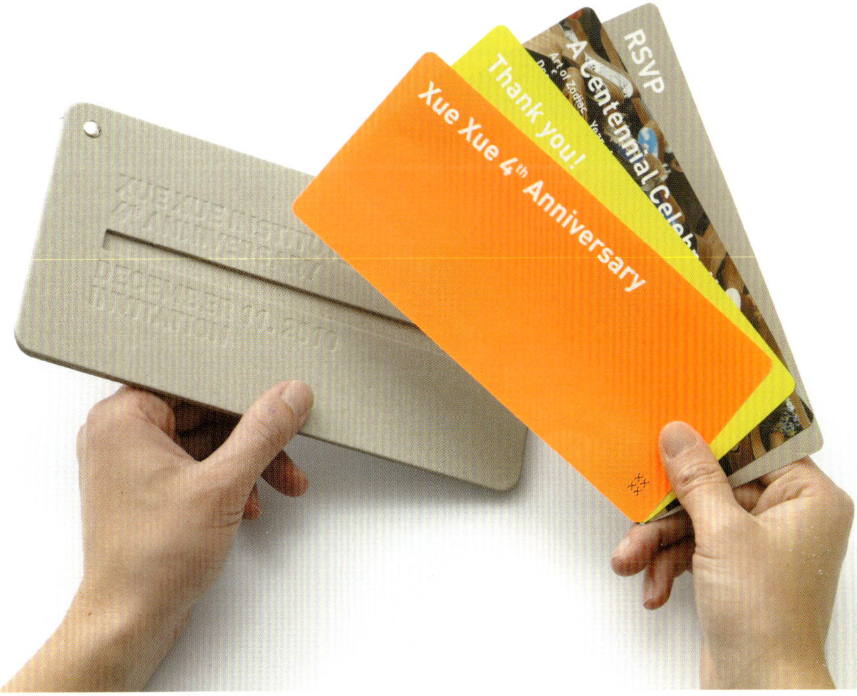
RSVP
Thank you!
Xue Xue 4th Anniversary

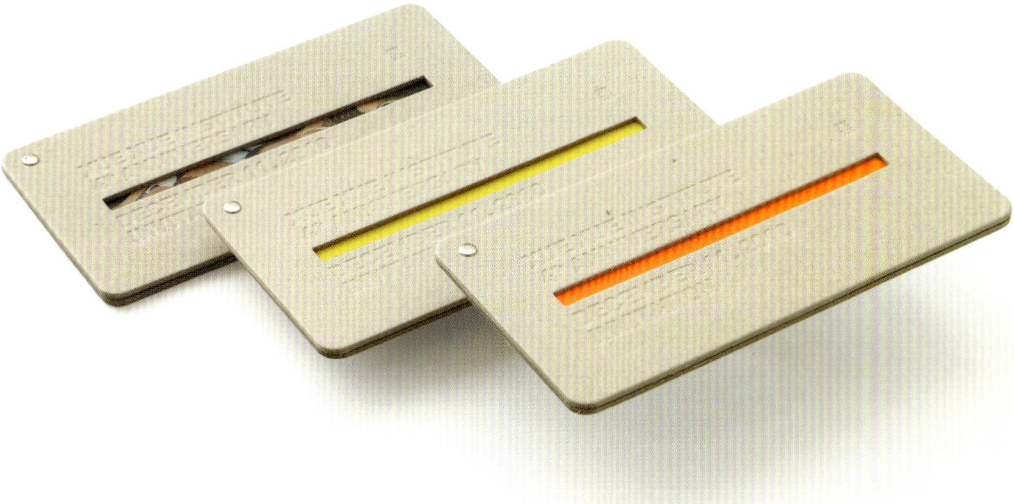

IMAGINE 8

Agency:
BLOW
Designer:
Ken Lo, Crystal Cheung
Work Type:
Identity

Imagine 8 is a production studio for video production, DJ and event management. BLOW were asked to create a new identity design for Imagine 8 to enhance the overall image and create strong association with video production industry.

They have used the TV test signal as a graphic element to design the identity for Imagine 8. With different color combinations, the identity provides strong visual impact and variety to signify the diversity of Imagine 8's offerings.

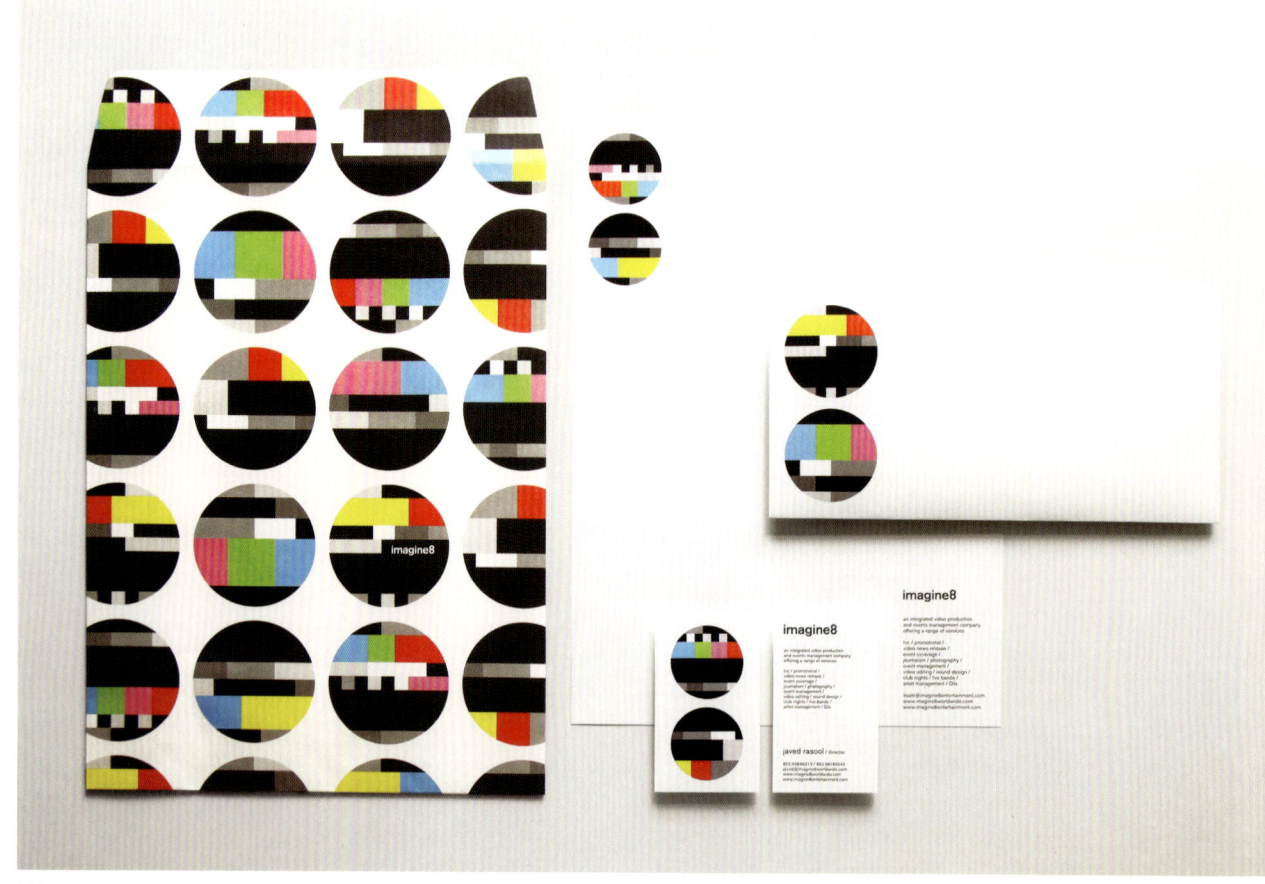

ADJUST YOUR SET

Agency:
This is Real Art
Work Type:
Identity

Identity for a digital
content creation company,
referencing a traditional
television test card
graphic pattern.

NATALIE EBNET

Agency:
Mattson Creative
Designer:
Ty Mattson
Work Type:
Identity

Television editor, Natalie Ebnet has worked on shows for networks including NBC, CBS and Discovery Channel. She needed a unique identity to distinguish her brand and demonstrate her services. We worked together to design a logo that's as smart as it is simple.

IDIOLALIA

Agency:
idiolalia
Designer:
Edward Dessaso
Photography:
Edward Dessaso
Work Type:
Identity

Following the definition of the word idiolalia, the direction in which the design of the business cards took focused on a minimal theme involving the sole use of foil stamping. This was chosen due to the ability to incorporate the use of a holographic foil, providing a parallel between the material's ability to fluctuate in color with the identity's methodology of adaptability. Stamped upon a bleached white card, the foil blocking incorporates a subdued yet radiant atmosphere to catch and imprint the cards message to the viewer's curiosity.

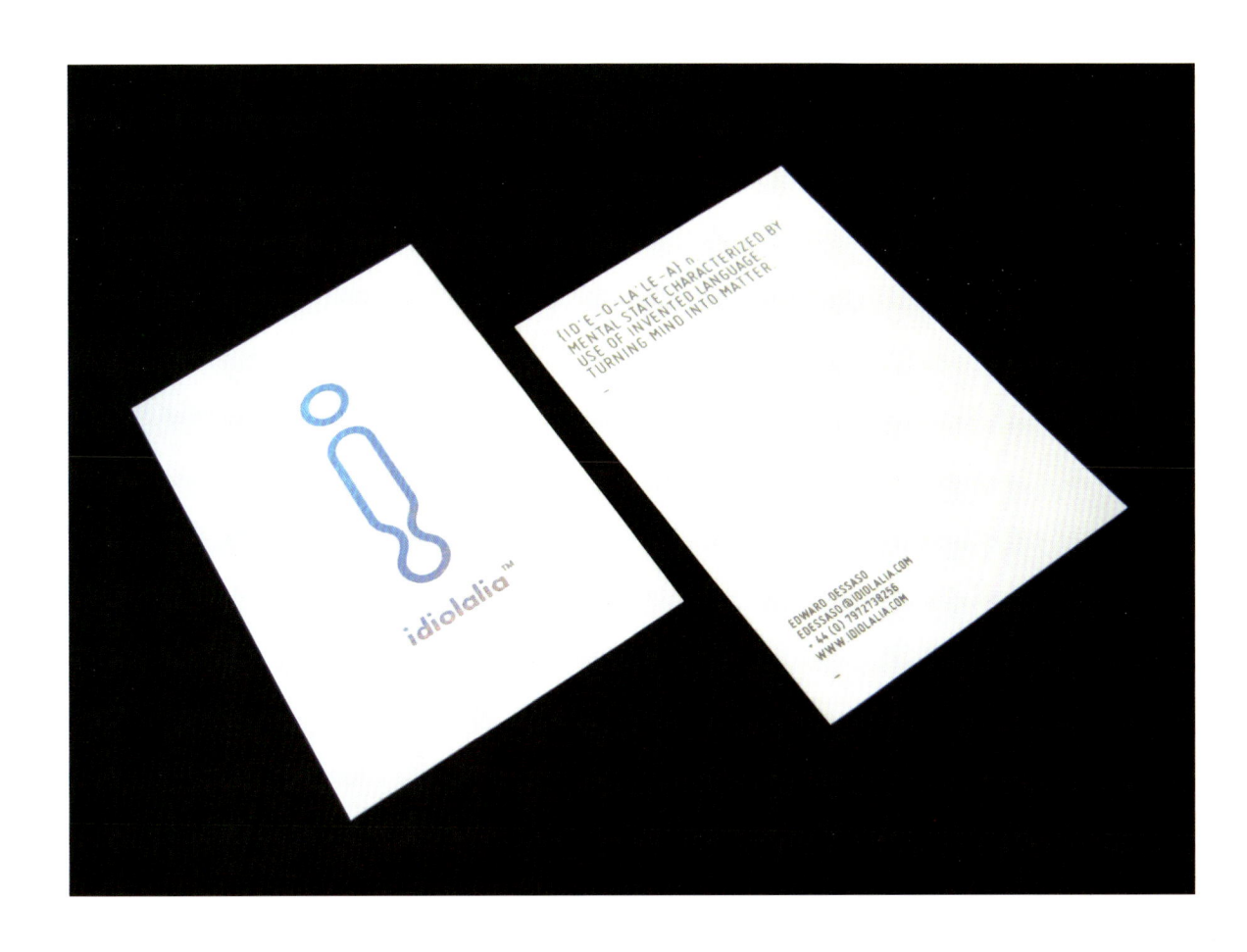

UNITED BAMBOO F/W
2011 INVITES

Agency:
Studio Lin
Designer:
Alex Lin
Work Type:
Invitation

The second in a series of
invitations for United
Bamboo's fashion show.
Using the exact same
graphics and size as the
last season, Studio Lin
produced this invitation
as a die-cut refrigerator
magnet. The color scheme
and materiality reflected
the collection's cool and
masculine inspirations.

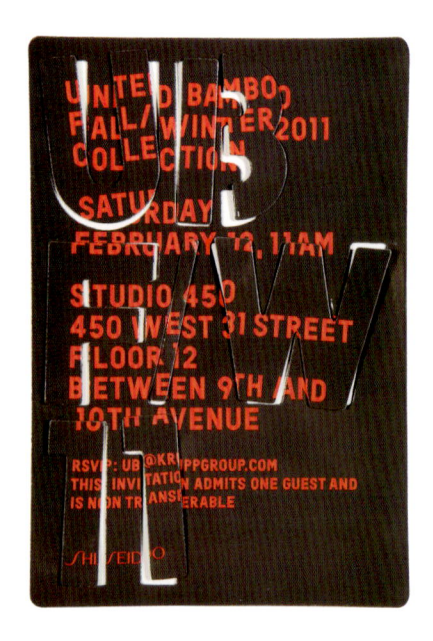

026

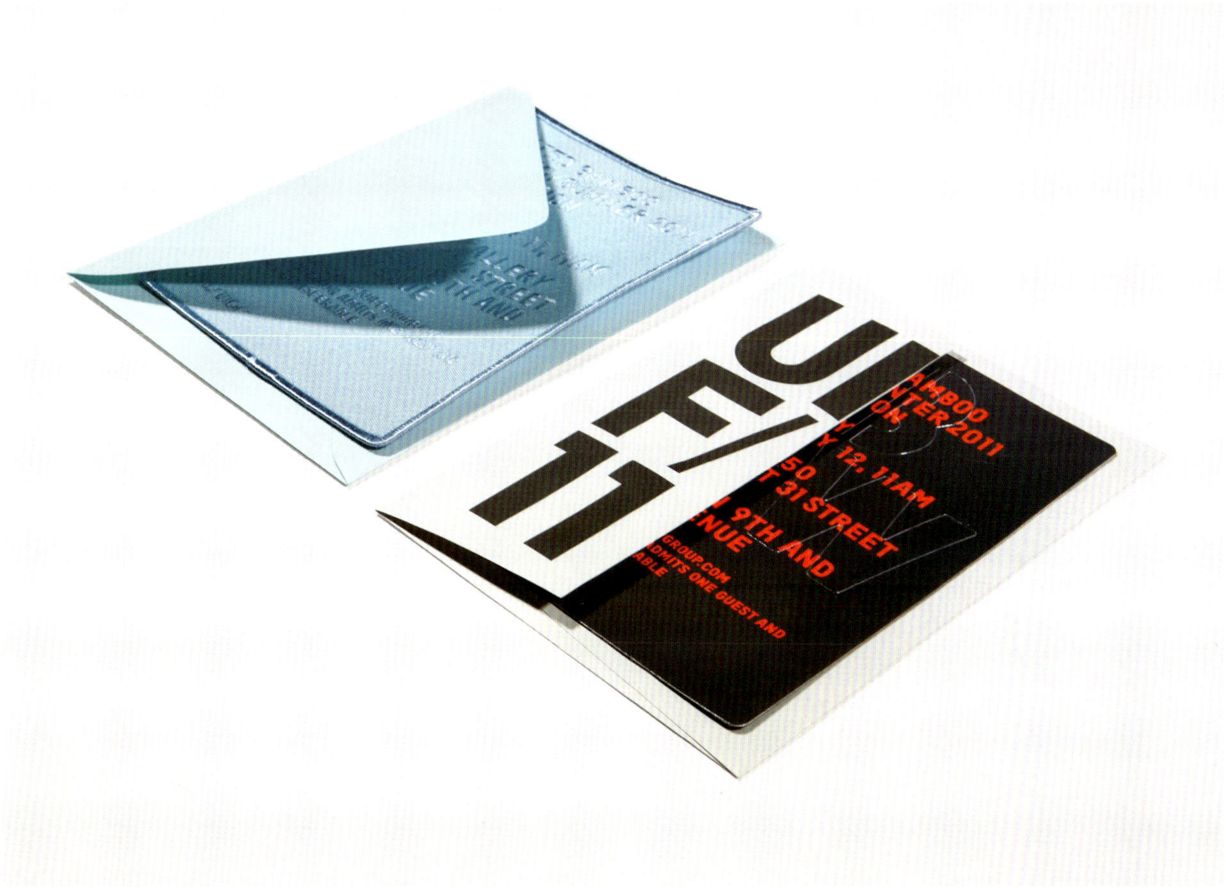

UNITED BAMBOO
FALL/WINTER 20
COLLECTION
SATURDAY
FEBRUARY 12, 11
STUDIO 450
450 WEST 31 ST
FLOOR 12
BETWEEN 9TH A
10TH AVENUE
RSVP: UB@KRUPPGROUP.COM
THIS INVITATION ADMITS ONE G
IS NON TRANSFERABLE
SHISEIDO

ZOE PAWLAK

Agency:
Glasfurd & Walker
Work Type:
Identity

Identity, stationery and website styling for contemporary Vancouver artist & curator Zoe Pawlak.

NOVANET

Agency:
Neue Design Studio
Photography:
Thomas Brun
Work Type:
Identity

Novanet is an IT company consisting of senior consultants that specialize within dynamic solutions and .NET technology. The ASCII visuals are used throughout the profile as a symbol for the company's focus on sharing knowledge, simultaneously putting emphasis on close-customer relations.

NIKLAUS STOECKLIN
Designer:
Aleksandar Savic
Work Type:
Identity

It is a self-initiated project for an imaginary client, Nicklaus Stoecklin, psychologist from Finland. The aim was to create something that would clearly present the way he can get you out of the mess in your head (presented by labyrinth). Aleksandar Savic came with the final concept in pretty early stages of design, but the real problem was how to calculate the square perforations on the outer envelope, which took me approximately 10 days to resolve. But, it payed out eventually.

NIKLAUS
STOECKLIN
PSYCHOLOGIST

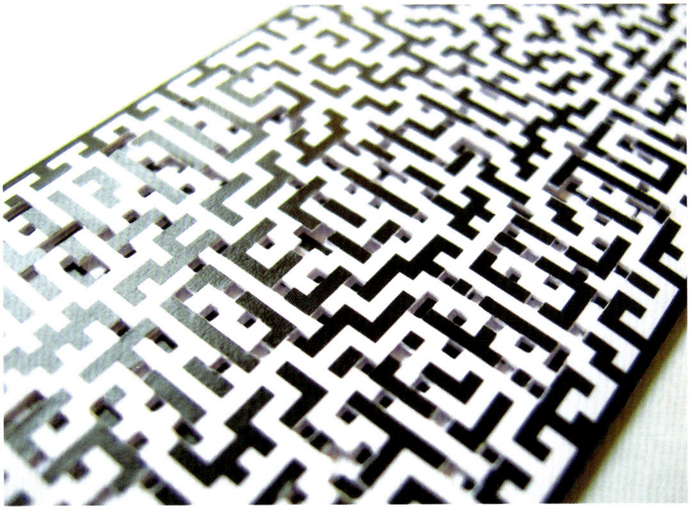

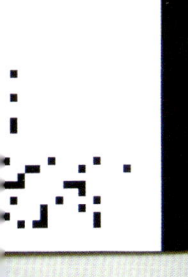

POPULAR FRONT

Agency:
Cue
Designer:
Nathan Hinz
Work Type:
Identity

In recent years, the lines between traditional and new media agencies have become increasingly blurred. As Popular Front has become more immersed in this changing creative world, the company realized it needed a better way to reflect how it's positioned within an increasingly competitive creative landscape. Cue helped Popular Front evolve its platform and created a new identity system that reflects the spirit of the creative company.

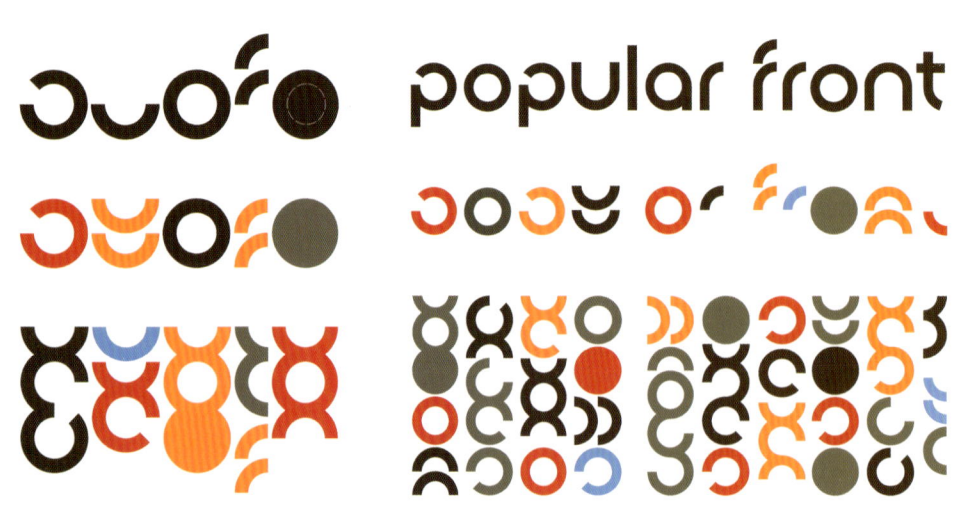

032

popular front

popular front
JASON ULRICH
PRESIDENT
JULRICH@POPULARFRONT.COM
612 767 8406 PHONE
555 FIRST AVE NE MPLS MN 55413
612 362 0900
POPULARFRONT.COM

popular front

HORTIART

Agency:
Bunch
Work Type:
Greeting Card

A range of Christmas material produced for IPF comprising of a Christmas card, receipt holder, stickers and posters. The colourful illustrations added to the festive feel of the applications. The posters were created in a limited edition especially for Christmas.

Hortiart
Zvonimirova 20
Zagreb 10000
Croatia
T/F +385 1 4824 032
info@hortiart.hr
www.hortiart.hr

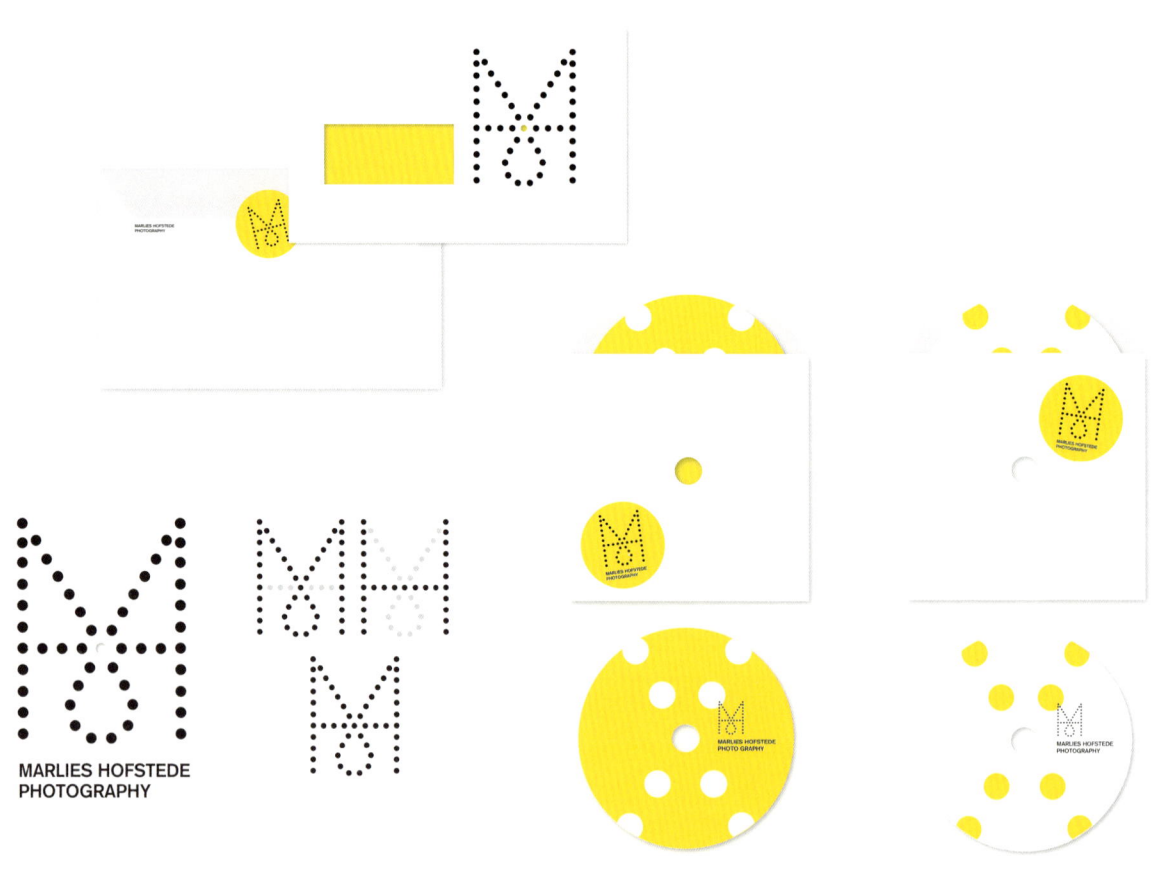

MARLIES HOFSTEDE

Agency:
Trapped in Suburbia
Work Type:
Identity

Marlies is a female photographer who does travel shoots, life style photo and fashion. She wanted to focus more on fashion, so we gave her an edgy look. The logo is the base for the whole identity and forms a monogram of the letters M & H.

MARLIES HOFSTEDE
PHOTOGRAPHY

Van Loostraat 119
2582 XC Den Haag
06 26 10 26 23
info@marlieshofstede.nl
www.marlieshofstede.nl

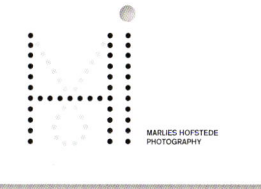

MARLIES HOFSTEDE
PHOTOGRAPHY

ABBILDUNG ÄHNLICH
Designer:
Alexander Lis
Photography:
Christiane Feser
Work Type:
Invitation

Invite for an exhibition by Christiane Feser, Marcus Grundling, Yasuaki Kitagawa, Jean-Baptiste Maitre, Yasuaki Kitagawa, Peter Müller & Adrian Nießler.

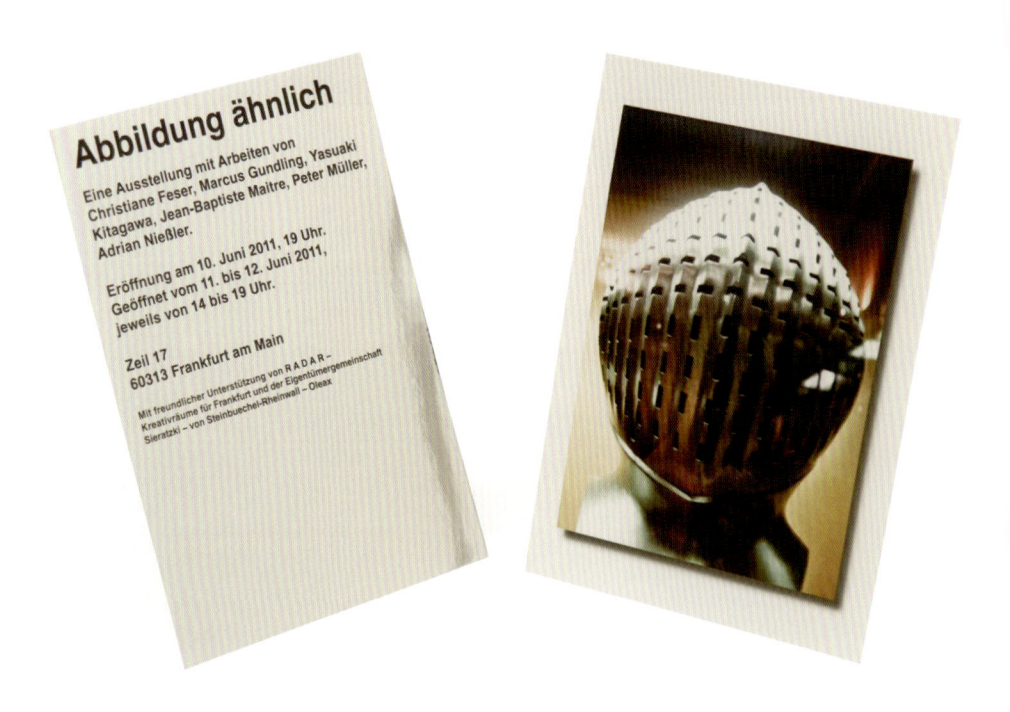

I TRAMONTI DELLA
MARILENA

Agency:
Studio Filippo Nostri
Work Type:
Invitation

Invite designed for a
photography workshop.
The idea was to give the
impression of a book: the
A4 sheet folded to A5 with
photograph glued.

PAST/PRESENT/FUTURE

Agency:
KentLyons
Work Type:
Greeting Card

For our 2009 Christmas card a 50 cm² twelve pointed Moravian star, hand carved from ice was left to melt over 15 hours. We documented this process with Polaroid film and sent the results out as cards to our friends. We also created a stop-frame animation of that process that can be seen.

A limited edition Merry
Christmas from KentLyons.
Featuring a 50cm³ twelve
___/225
Past/Present/Future
KentLyons
Past/Present/Future
star after your snapshot
was taken by visiting
www.kentlyons.com for
a short stop-motion film.

Past/Present/Future

Past/Present/Future

CORA HILLEBRAND

Agency:
Lundgren+Lindqvist
Photography:
Cora Hillebrand
Work Type:
Identity

Mini portfolio business cards for Swedish photographer Cora Hillebrand comprising a die-cut Polaroid-shaped envelope with several different image inserts. On the envelope, Cora's contact details are printed, much in line with a traditional business card. The insides of the envelopes were printed in bright blue. We selected nine different images from a range of projects by Cora which were printed on cardboard and perforated for easy detachment. This allows Cora to compose various mini portfolios customized for different client types. We also perforated printer friendly paper for quick updates.

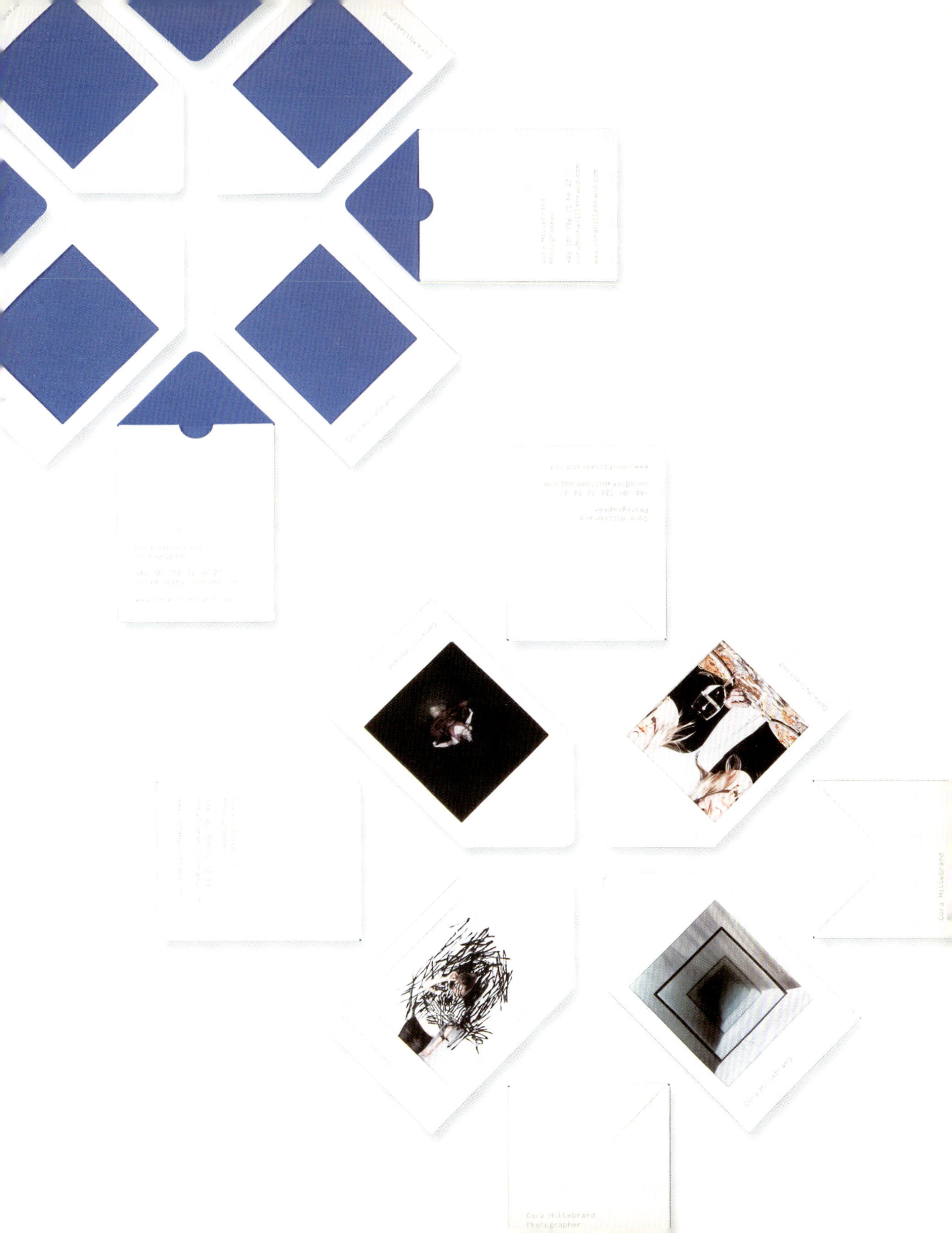
Cora Hillebrand
Photographer

THE NIGHT OF VICTORY
Agency:
JOYN:VISCOM
Work Type:
Invitation

Invitation proposal for
The Night of Victory
celebration in Olympics
2008.

NIKE TRAIN TO BE
STRONG

Agency:
Exposure
Work Type:
Invitation

Invites designed and
produced for Nike Women
Train To Be Strong Media
presentations in Miami and
Los Angeles.

NEW YEAR'S GREETING
CARDS

Agency:
Coba & Associates
Designer:
Jana Orsolic
Copywriter:
Jana Orsolic
Work Type:
Greeting Card

We wanted to give a go to our new corporate identity with New Year greeting card. Reviewing our efforts from the previous year we gave the clear perspective of what we are planning for the next one.

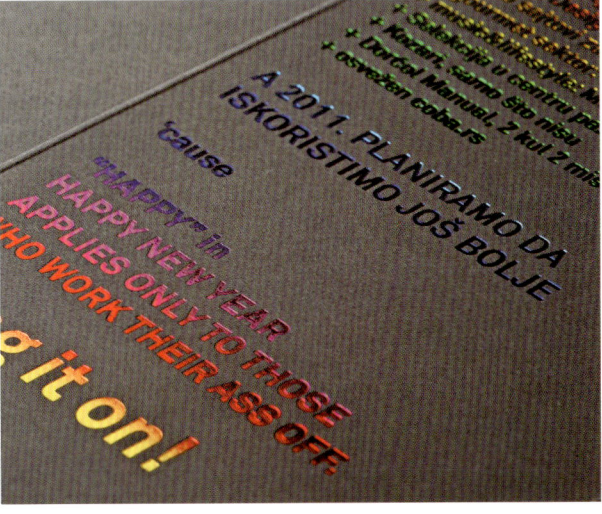

Coba&associates
SUMMA SUMMARUM
2010

+ Designed.rs osvojio nagradu na web festu
+ Packtivity, konferencija o dizajnu pakovanja
+ C&a i Designed na Mikseru
+ web sajtovi za pbf, apc, erpim
+ gourmet sektor: Culinaria, Sogani, Bistro
+ music&lifestyle: Miedpot, Mint, Plastic
+ Selekcija u centru pažnje, Maple, Moxi
+ Kozeri, samo što nisu
+ Dorćol Manual, 2 kul 2 mis
+ osvežen coba.rs

A 2011. PLANIRAMO DA ISKORISTIMO JOŠ BOLJE

'cause

"HAPPY" in HAPPY NEW YEAR APPLIES ONLY TO THOSE WHO WORK THEIR ASS OFF.

Bring it on!

SHU

Agency:
Clutch Design
Designer:
Yasutaka Akagi, Clutch Design
Copywriter:
Batistuta Bazooka
Work Type:
Identity

These are envelopes created as a brand development of the production company. When the company moved, old envelopes were transformed to new envelopes by stamping foil on the old envelopes. There is a beautiful contrast between the natural texture and rich color of Tant paper and the texture and vivid color radiating from foil printing. This artwork won the Gold Lion in the 58th Cannes Lions International Festival of Creativity.

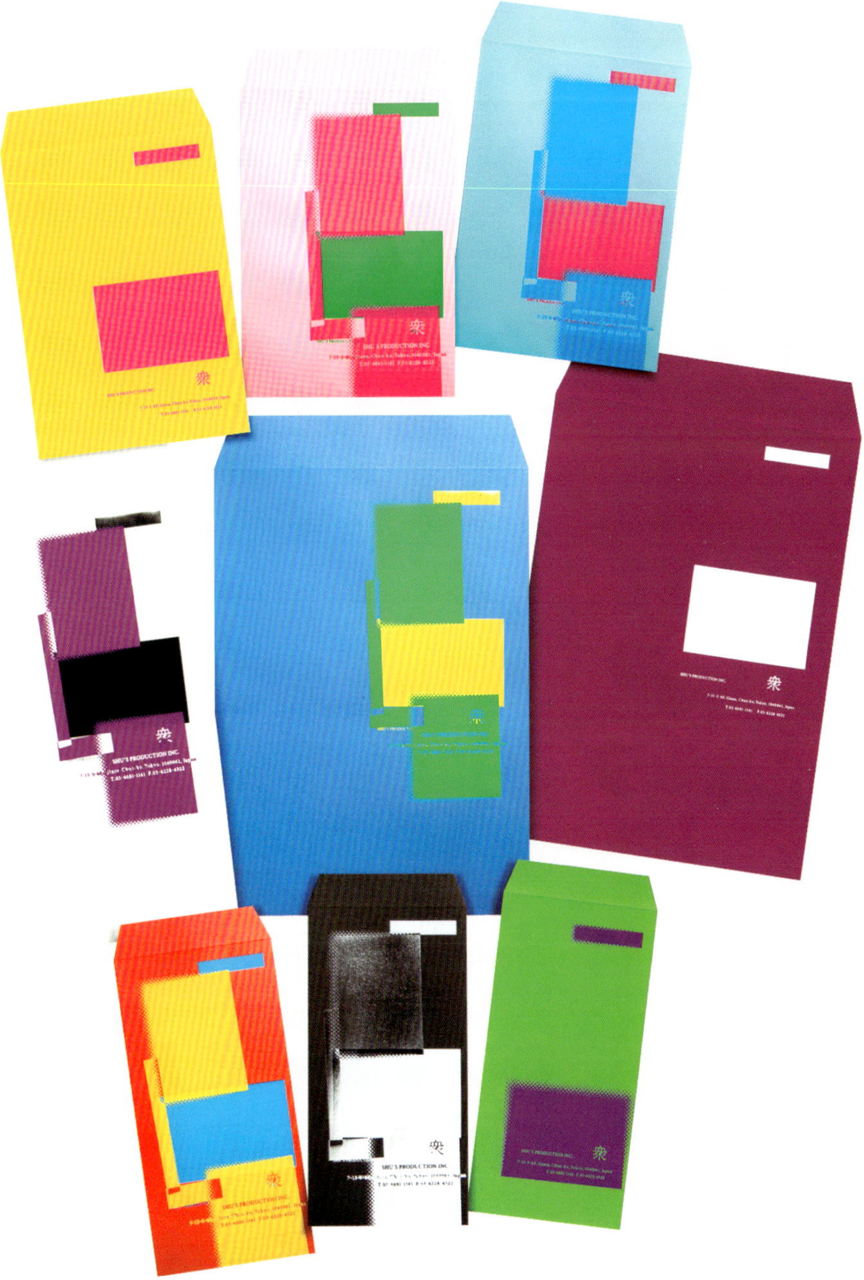
SHU'S PRODUCTION INC.
衆

ESTORIL FASHION ART
FESTIVAL

Agency:
MusaWorkLab
Work Type:
Identity

Corporate identity,
brand system and visual
development for Estoril Art
and Fashion annual festival
2010, organized by Moda
Lisboa to promote tourism
in the Estoril coast.

ACESSO
ESTORIL FASHIONART FESTIVAL
SPECIAL GUEST
www.estorilfashionartfestival.com
SHOWCASE TRANS-MISSION PT+ES
ESTORIL FASHIONART FESTIVAL
30 JUN / 4 JUL '10
Este livre trânsito é pessoal e intransmissível.
O seu uso indevido implica a sua imediata anulação.
Cascais
estoril
MODALISBOA

JOSÉ MANUEL FERRATER
EUGENIO RECUENCO
DANIEL RIERA
DAVID URBANO
1 JULHO
19H00
SHOWCASE TRANS-MISSION PT+ES
ESTORIL FASHIONART FESTIVAL

ETERNA
É A NOITE
1 JULHO
MARINA DE CASCAIS
21H00
SHOWCASE TRANS-MISSION PT+ES
ESTORIL FASHIONART FESTIVAL

EXPOSIÇÃO
BOOM SHIRT
PENSAR
INTERVIR
ENVIAR
SHOWCASE TRANS-MISSION PT+ES
ESTORIL FASHIONART FESTIVAL
150 ARTISTAS CRUZAM-SE PARA RESOLVER 50 CAMISAS ALVAS NUM PROJECTO DE INTERCÂMBIO.
DAÍ RESULTAM CERCA DE 50 PEÇAS INATACÁVEIS.
AS REGRAS FORAM TRÊS: PENSAR NO QUE SE QUER, INTERVIR ONDE FOR PRECISO, ENVIAR PARA QUEM MAIS APETECER.

DESFILE
SPORTIVE
DESPORTOS QUE MARCAM A COSTA DO ESTORIL REVISITADOS PELA MODA
4 JULHO
MARINA DE CASCAIS
19H00
SHOWCASE TRANS-MISSION PT+ES
ESTORIL FASHIONART FESTIVAL
30 JUN / 4 JUL '10
Cascais
estoril
MODALISBOA
www.estorilfashionartfestival.com

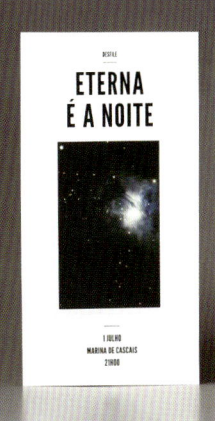

ARQWARE

Agency:
Savvy Studio
Work Type:
Identity

Arqware is a firm of architects based in Monterrey, Mexico. For this branding project Savvy developed a main concept based in the Scientific Method and its phases that represent the way the firm works, and created a visual system with images and words based in the mood and beliefs of the brand.

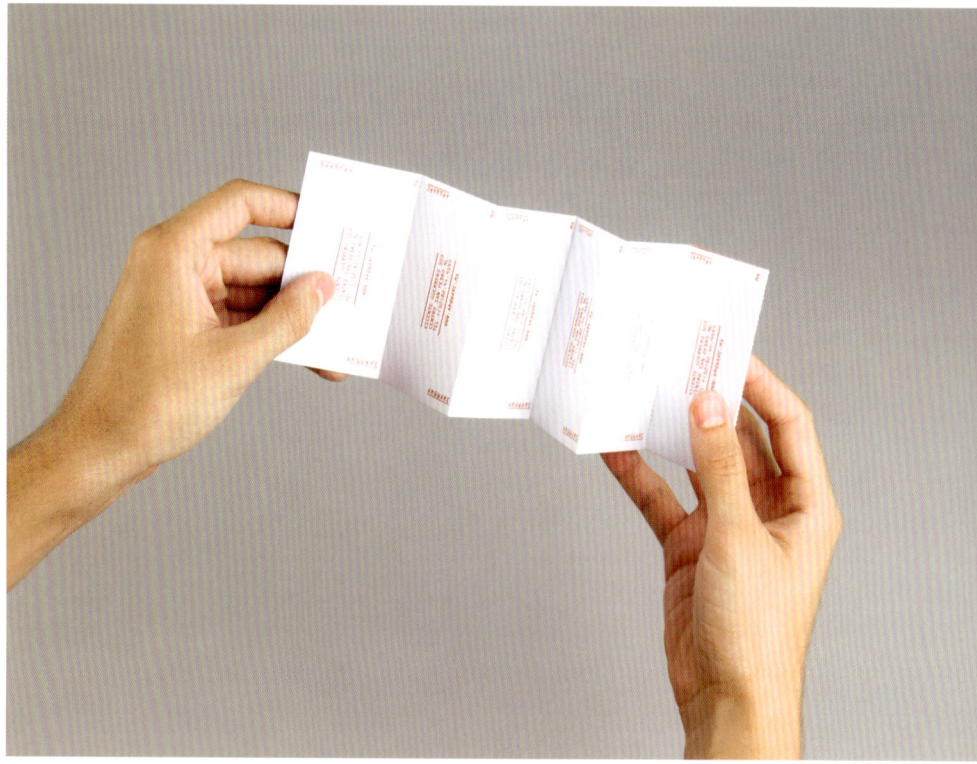

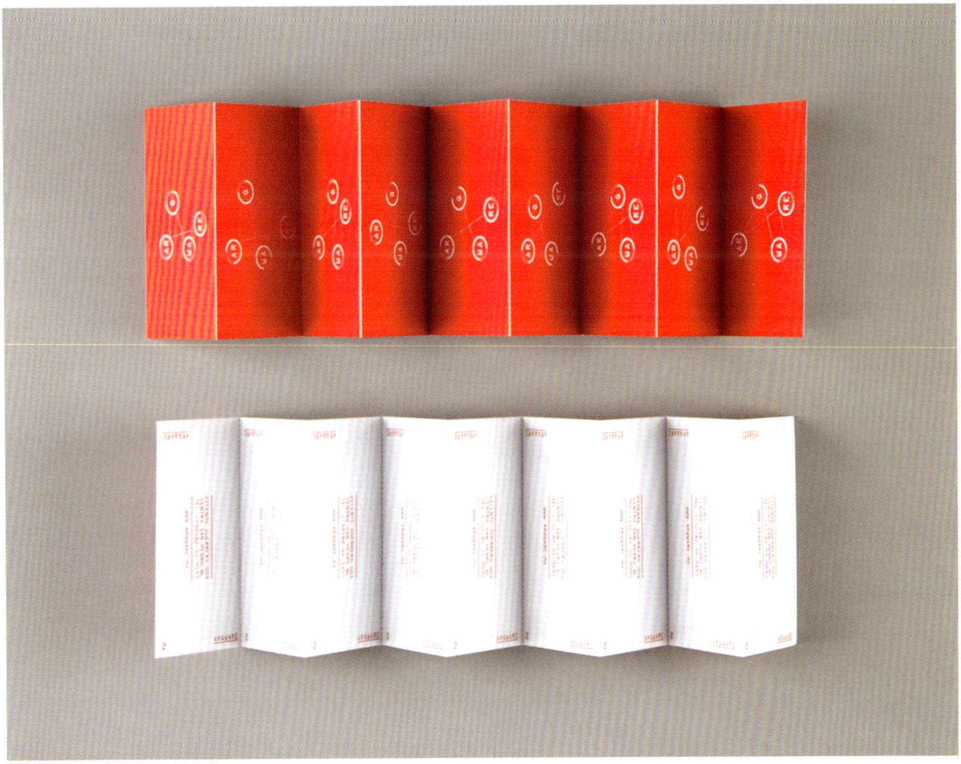

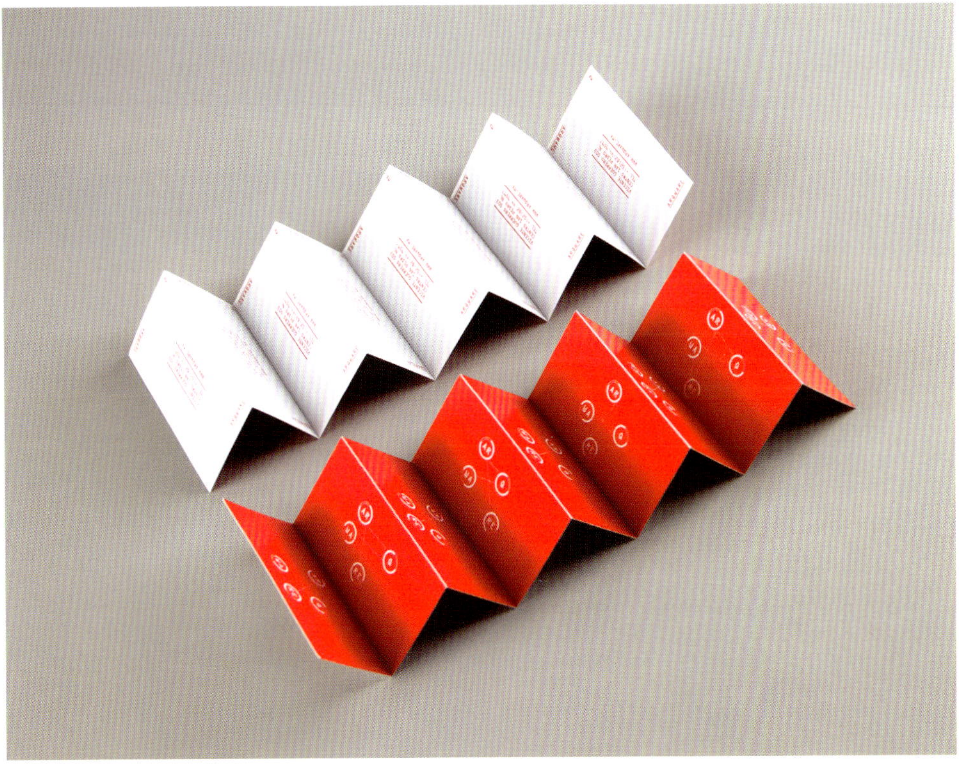

HESSEN DESIGN

Agency:
Heine/Lenz/Zizka
Work Type:
Identity

The core element of this new corporate design for the German design center Hessen Design is an adhesive label which is attached to each medium by hand. Due to its flexibility the sticker does not interfere with the specific medium but rather interacts with it. This concept makes the branding as strong as easy.

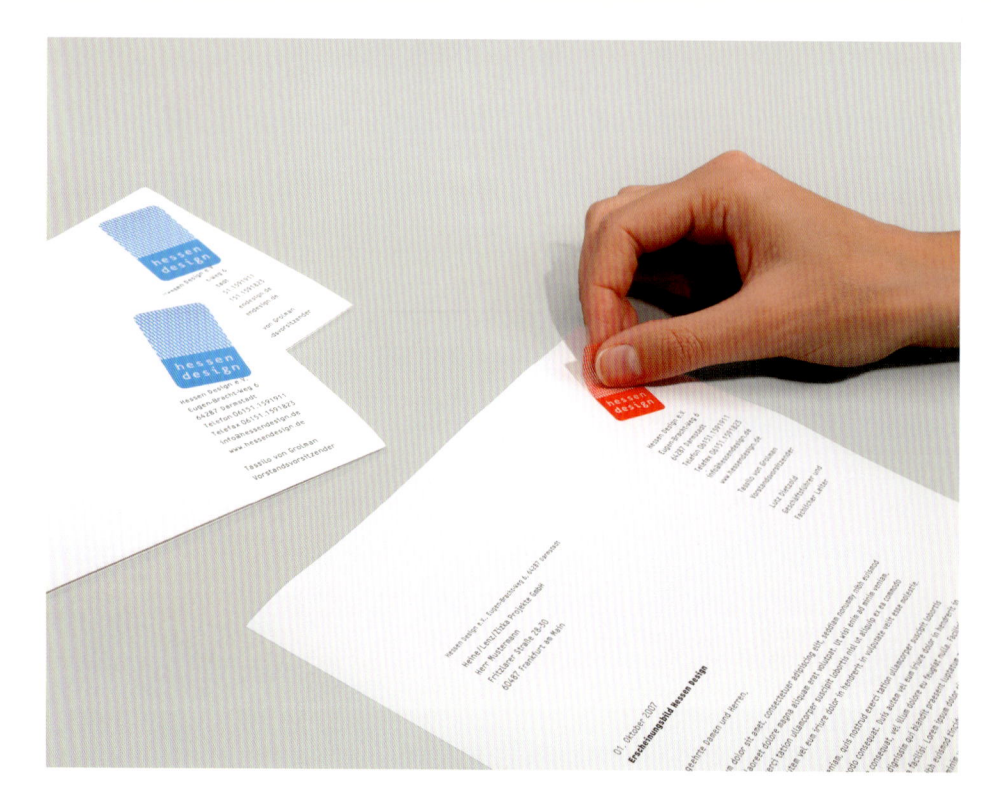

ESPAÇO B

Agency:
MusaWorkLab
Work Type:
Invitation

Invitation for the opening store "Espaço B", a boutique of fashion, design and lifestyle. The whole shop is based only in black and white, both interior and all the products. The aim was to create an invitation to the image of the store, and so the monochrome and the materials were chosen to detail. The invitation shiny black acrylic with white silkscreen, and an envelope matte white PVC, create a unique piece that level scored by its impact.

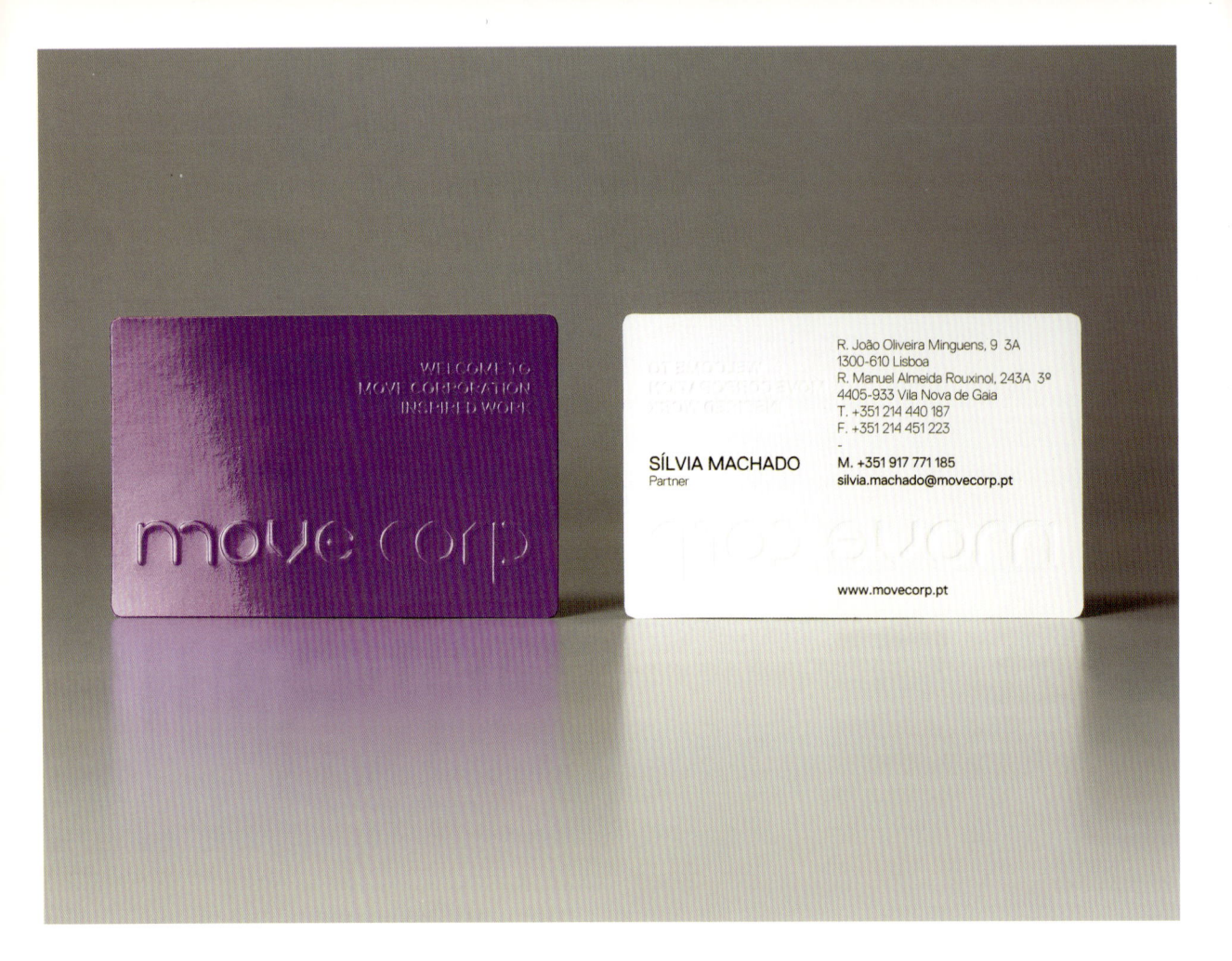

MOVE CORP

Agency:
MusaWorkLab
Work Type:
Identity

Move Corp is a management company. With this values we build the corporate identity and stationery. We tried to create a single and simple typeface, consisting of parts or pieces that represent the various parts of the management processes. The glossy color and finish of the cards give the company the direction wanted.

QUBE STUDIO

Agency:
Qube Studio
Work Type:
Identity

A business card is a rather small space in which to incorporate key information and three printing techniques, yet that is exactly what we did --offset, silkscreen and debossing being represented. The paper stock, although expensive, is key to the success of the business card. Too thin and the item feels cheap, too heavy and the item appears overbearing.

MESSY DESIGN SELF-
PROMO

Agency:
Messy Design
Designer:
Corrie Anderson
Copywriter:
Jason Yagan
Photography:
Paul Mason
Work Type:
Promotion

Messy created this self promotional piece to raise awareness about the importance of good typography in design. The package contained a sealed booklet which folded out to reveal four altered images of our own faces, demonstrating basic typography rules in a humorous and engaging way.

You wouldn't do it to your face, so why would you do it to a typeface?

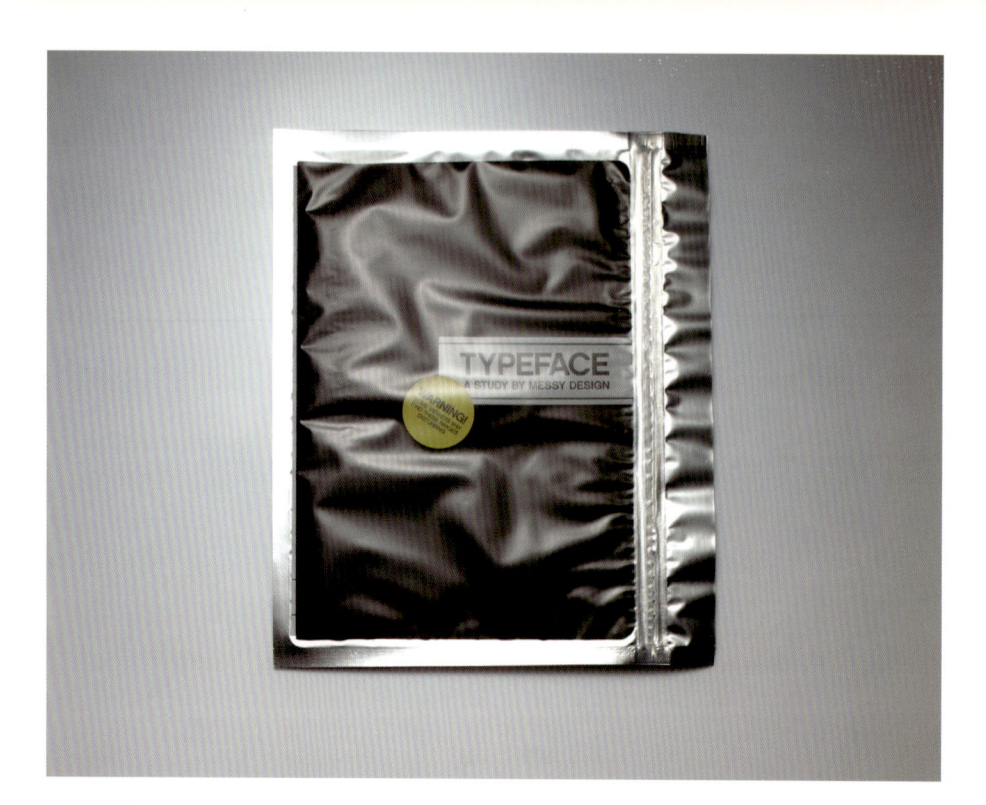

STRETCHING A TYPEFACE LOOKS UNNATURAL

Stretching Typefaces: Stretching or compressing typefaces ruins their integrity

We ensure type isn't stretched so you don't have to. messy.com.au

COMIC SANS CAN MAKE YOU LOOK SILLY

Typeface Selection: Choosing an inappropriate typeface conveys the wrong message

We use the right typeface for the job so you don't have to. messy.com.au

INCOMPATIBLE TYPEFACES CAN LOOK UGLY

Mixing Typefaces: Mixing incompatible typefaces together can confuse your message

We know how to use compatible typefaces so you don't have to. messy.com.au

BAD KERNING CAN RUIN A GOOD TYPEFACE

Kerning: The adjustment of space between individual letters for a visually appealing result

We make type appealing so you don't have to. messy.com.au

FER AND NORA WEDDING
INVITATION

Agency:
La caja de tipos
Work Type:
Invitation

What Fer and Nora wanted for their wedding was to be a big party where all guests have fun with them. We have several ideas but the one that fits better was an invitation that the guests themselves have to finish. It has two parts, the lower with the event data and instructions in order that everyone know what to do and top with a series of micro-perforated circles with laser that can be separated as each guest wants and draw various elements regarding the wedding such as a heart, rings, a shrimp…. These leftover circles become confetti.

FER & NORA

MANUSCRIPT RECORDS

Designer:
kissmiklos
Work Type:
Identity

The brand identity is a reflection of the company's name and the industry it is in. The pattern is the result of hand drawing, which looks like the surface of a disc. This idea was further developed into many more variations. The finalized brand identity is a complex reflection of the record publishing company's area of operation, and at the same time presents the possibility of going even further. The design was not purchased due to insufficient finances.

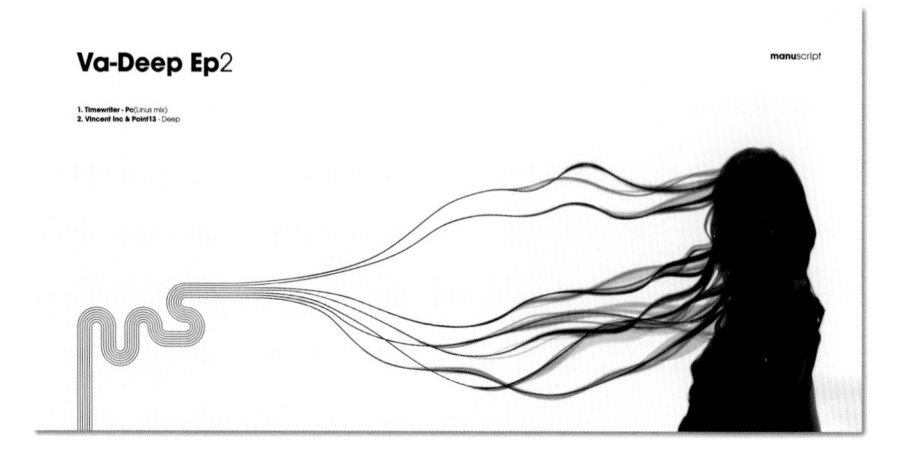

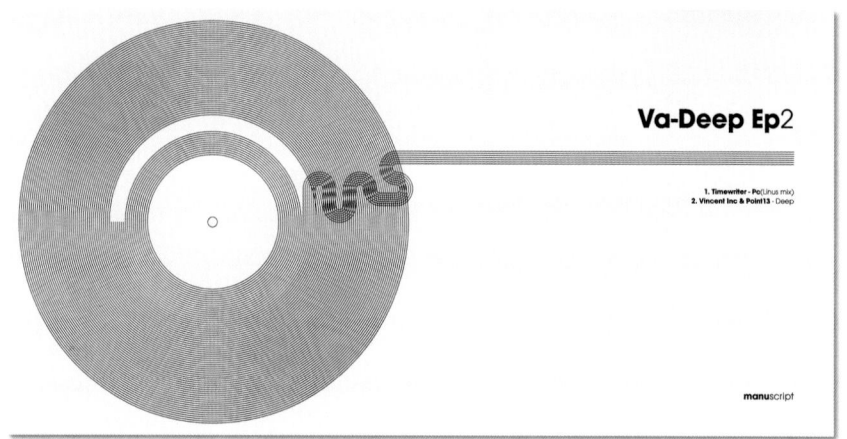

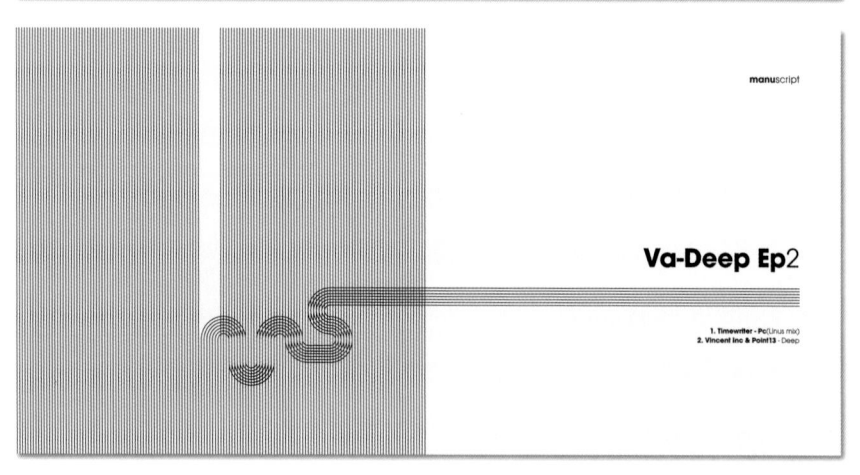

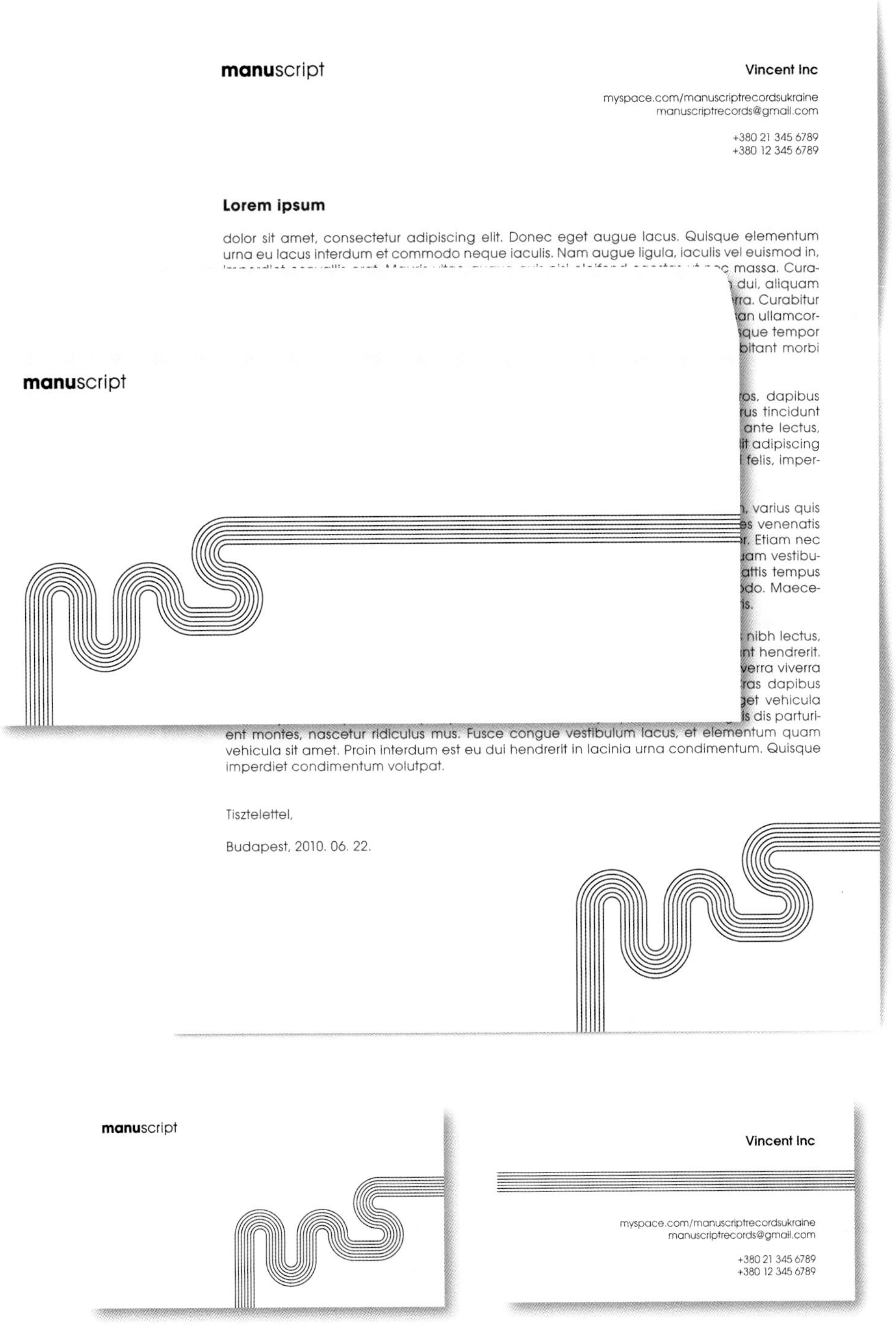

manuscript

Vincent Inc

myspace.com/manuscriptrecordsukraine
manuscriptrecords@gmail.com

+380 21 345 6789
+380 12 345 6789

Lorem ipsum

dolor sit amet, consectetur adipiscing elit. Donec eget augue lacus. Quisque elementum urna eu lacus interdum et commodo neque iaculis. Nam augue ligula, iaculis vel euismod in,

manuscript

dui, aliquam
rra. Curabitur
an ullamcor-
que tempor
bitant morbi

os, dapibus
us tincidunt
ante lectus,
it adipiscing
felis, imper-

, varius quis
es venenatis
. Etiam nec
am vestibu-
attis tempus
do. Maece-

nibh lectus,
nt hendrerit.
erra viverra
as dapibus
get vehicula
dis parturi-

ent montes, nascetur ridiculus mus. Fusce congue vestibulum lacus, et elementum quam vehicula sit amet. Proin interdum est eu dui hendrerit in lacinia urna condimentum. Quisque imperdiet condimentum volutpat.

Tisztelettel,

Budapest, 2010. 06. 22.

manuscript

Vincent Inc

myspace.com/manuscriptrecordsukraine
manuscriptrecords@gmail.com

+380 21 345 6789
+380 12 345 6789

INSITU BRANDING
Agency:
Qube Konstrukt
Work Type:
Identity

Insitu approached us to re-brand their existing business. The brief was to create a unique and bold identity that stood out from its competitors. It also needed to reflect their shift towards specifying top-of-the-line European and Australian contemporary furniture. The final identity is a combination of distinct colour and exaggerated form, reflective of the style of furniture they carry. Insitu is now recognised nationally as a leader in the commercial and hospitality furniture industry and their identity has stood the test of time.

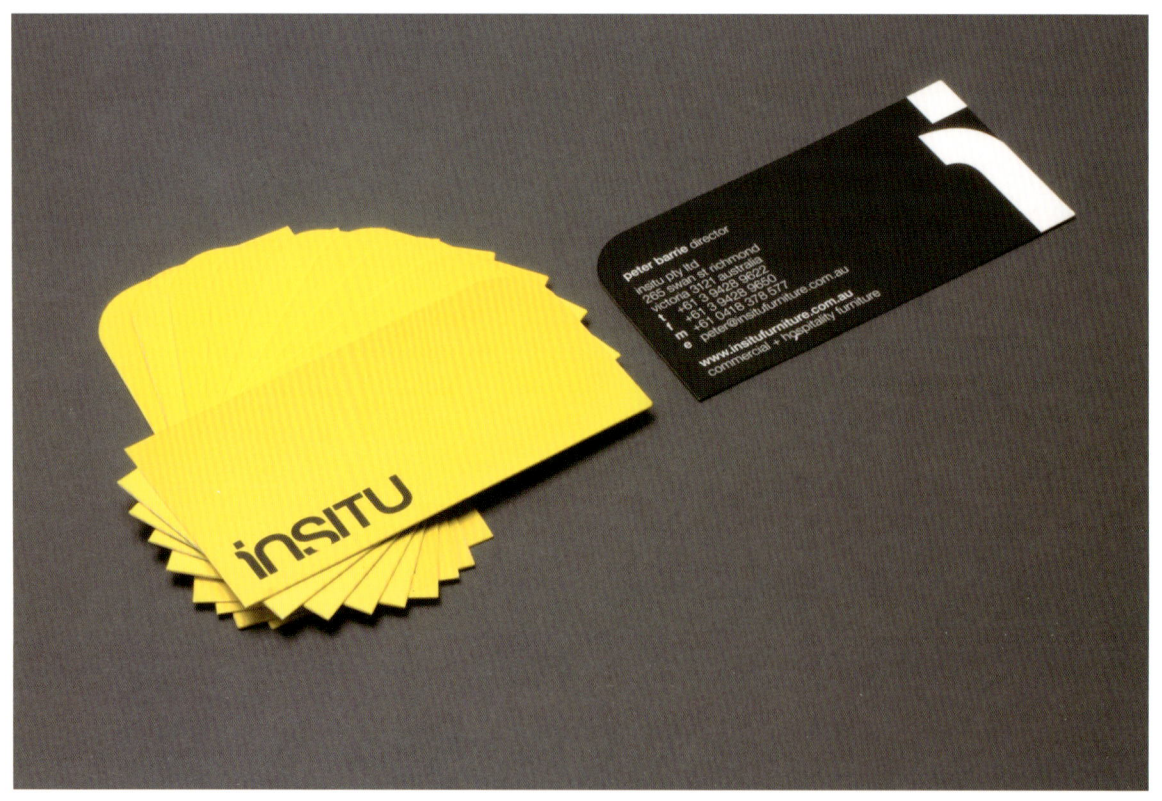

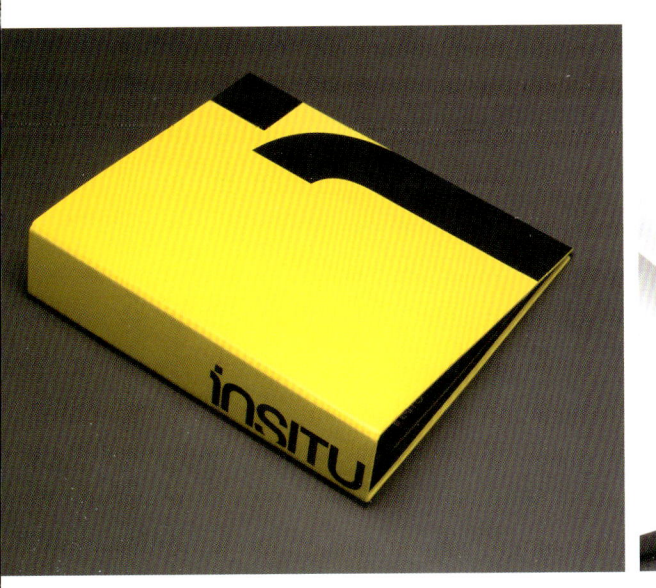

jennifer webster
insitu pty ltd
265 swan st richmond
victoria 3121 australia
t +61 3 9428 9622
f +61 3 9428 9650
m 0425 748 987
e jennifer@insitufurniture.com.au
www.insitufurniture.com.au
commercial + hospitality furniture

A-SIDE / B-SIDE

Designer:
Larissa Kasper & Rosario Florio
Work Type:
Promotion

A7 flyer announcing a party where two different music genres coincide. Printed on yellow translucent paper to make the different information readable on both sides.

066

LAFORET FLOOR GUIDE

Agency:
HAKUHODO INC.
Designer:
Rikako Nagashima
Work Type:
Promotion

This is the floor guide for Laforet Harajuku, a fashion mecca at the forefront of fashion in Japan.

The previous floor guide design was a bit frou-frou and girly, but in recent years men's stores had been increasing as tenants and the target age range had become older, so I changed the appearance with a more solid and unisex font design and color scheme.

The color schemes change with the four seasons.

SALON NEMETZ

Agency:
Designliga
Work type:
Identity

Christina Nemetz is the ringmaster of Munich's hair fashion scene. Disarming, spontaneous and a polarizing force, she brings the full extent of her passion, expert advice and craftsmanship to each individual client. Clients at her salon come away with not only a new hairstyle, but also an insight into the avant-garde pulse of the city.

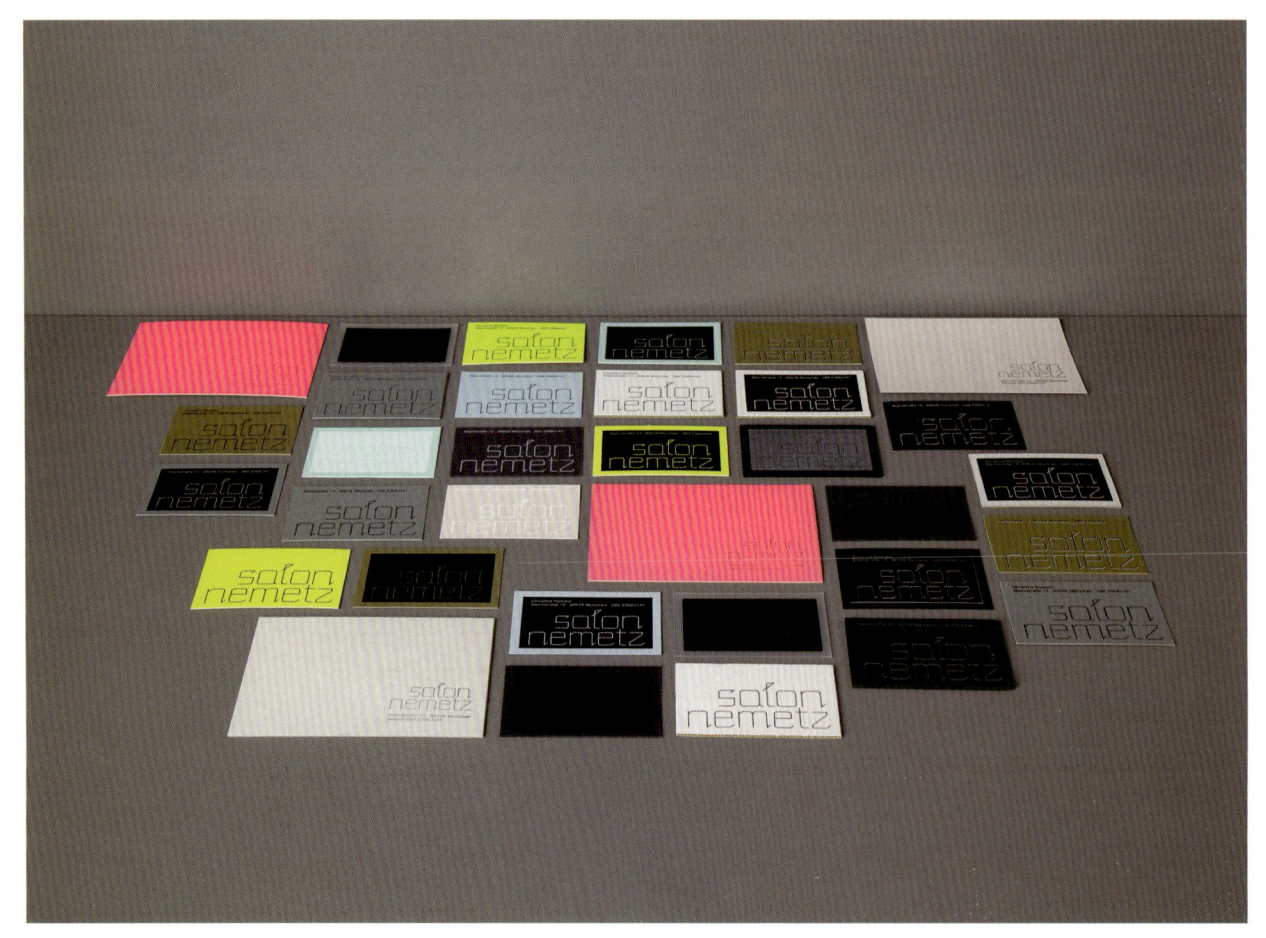

salon
nemetz

Christina Nemetz
Sternstraße 13 . 80538 München . 089 23684141
salon
nemetz

SELO

Agency:
Quinta-feira
Work Type:
Identity

Visual Identity and business cards for SELO, a company that works with artists management and production in Brasil. The logo uses the physical perforated dots and cut-out mail stamp form because SELO means mail stamp in Portuguese.

HUA DESIGN OFFICE
INC.
Designer:
Huarong Chen
Work Type:
Identity

Identity design for Hua
Design Office Inc.

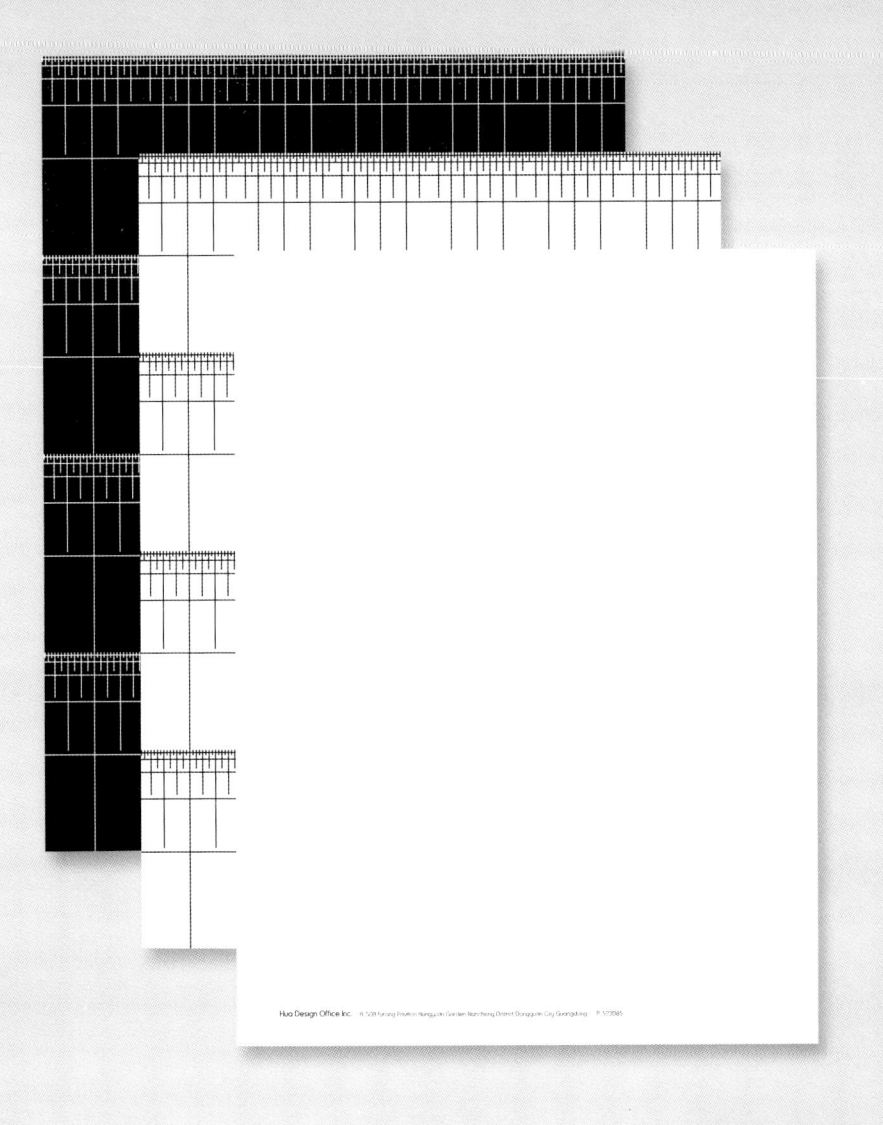

TENOVERSIX

Agency:
RoAndCo
Designer:
Roanne Adams
Work Type:
Identity

TenOverSix is a boutique and gallery-like installation space in Los Angeles offering high-concept designer accessories. The boutique was named after the price tag for "10/6" (10 pounds 6 shillings) on the Mad Hatter's hat in Alice In Wonderland. We used the vernacular of contemporary price tags, borrowed the color palette from Monopoly money, and repurposed gold "discount" stickers as the brand's signature symbol.

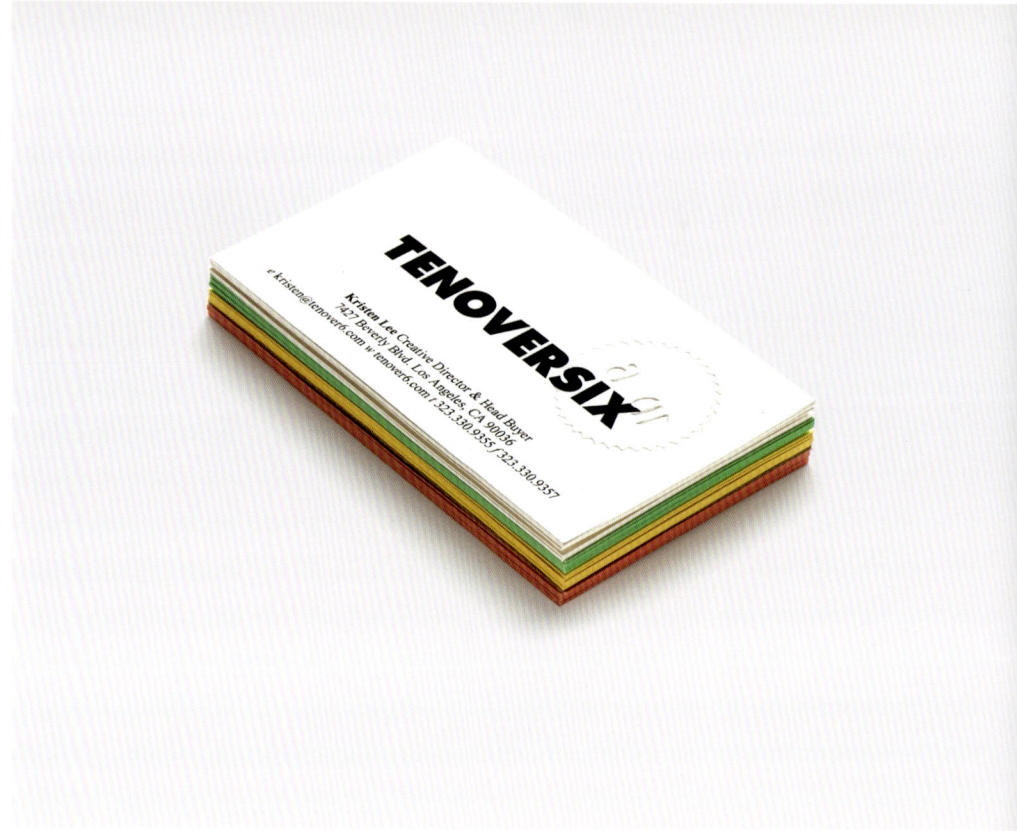

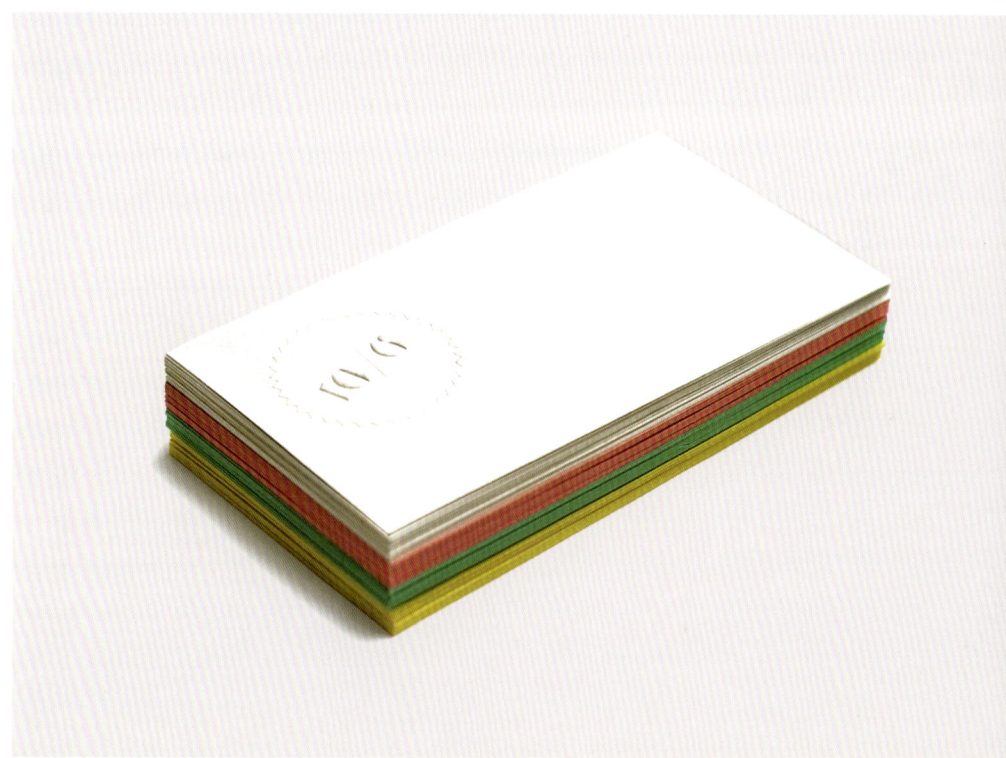

TENOVERSIX

CORDIALLY INVITES YOU TO OUR
PRIVATE LABEL FALL '09
PRESENTATION & COCKTAIL PARTY

DESIGNED BY
BRADY CUNNINGHAM & KRISTEN LEE
FRIDAY, MARCH 20TH 7-9PM

AT TENOVERSIX
7427 BEVERLY BLVD. LOS ANGELES, CA 90036
RSVP@TENOVER6.COM

10/6

MARTINI DOLCE & GABBANA

Agency:
MusaWorkLab
Work Type:
Invitation

This invitation to the launch of Martini-Gold is composed of two parts. A black wrap involved golden interior with information of the party. The wrap opened form a poster inside. The whole piece is based on the colors of the product (Black and Gold), as well as in the contrast between the high-glossy paper in the exterior, with the matte gold invitation referring to the materials inside the bottle.

TNOP™ 2009 BUSINESS
CARD
Agency:
TNOP™ DESIGN
Work Type:
Identity

"Don't Judge Me By The Look
Of My Card, Do It By The
Content Of Its Design."
We're asking people who
received this card to focus
on the thought process
as well as the production
process that we put into
creating the card rather
than the styling of it. We
also wanted to showcase
traditional printing
methods like, letterpress
printing and edge painting
that represent the craft
quality in TNOP's work.

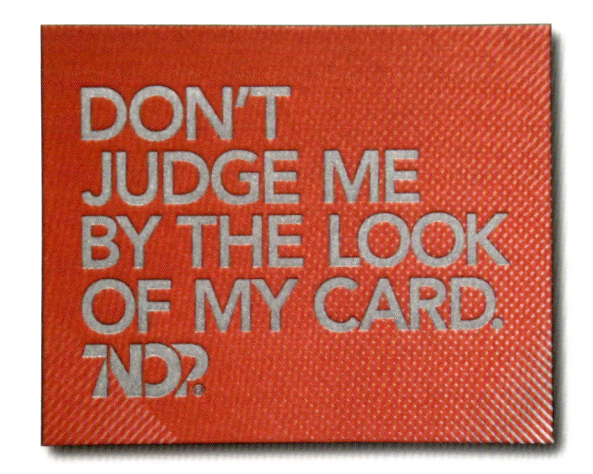

G & S BRANDING

Agency:
Takt Studio
Designer:
Tait Oosthuizen
Photography:
James Newman
Work Type:
Identity

Brand created for 3D visualization and styling company specializing in the property development industry. The brand needed to look current but have the flexibility to outlast the latest trends. The brand identity is simple, communicating the partners' names on a strong foundation with the clean and direct typeface reinforcing strength. Printed materials was rolled out on spicers paper's `Stephen spicy white', providing a textural softness and unique tone that intentionally counters the heaviness of the identity. Business cards were letter-presses and gilded adding that little something special.

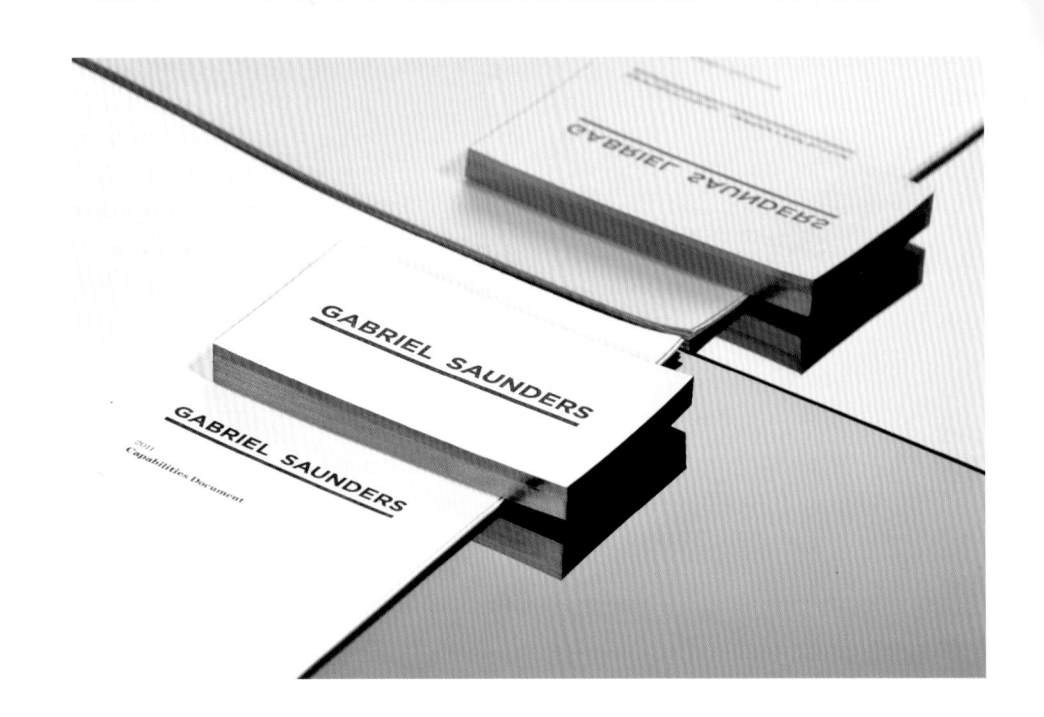

SKYLER S. LEWIS
Designer:
Marissa Rivera
Work Type:
Invitation

The inspiration for the cowhide posters came when I was asked to participate in a show that looked at how humans constantly reconstruct nature and their environment according to their aesthetics. Artist Skyler S. Lewis makes cowhide sculptures out of colorful sequins. I knew I wanted to illustrate the type so that it was structured yet decorative. That's when the idea to shape the posters so that they mimicked the contour of the sculptures and then print the posters on gold and silver paper became apparent. Ultimately, we felt that the posters succeeded in causing intrigue with their unusual shape and lead to a prosperous opening night.

Sprawl

AN ART SHOW FEATURING
THE WORK OF
SKYLER S. LEWIS

OPENING RECEPTION
OCTOBER 5, 2010
5:00 - 8:00 PM

SHOW DATES
OCTOBER 4TH THRU
OCTOBER 15TH

HERITAGE ART GALLERY
AZUSA PACIFIC UNIVERSITY
701 E. FOOTHILL BLVD.
AZUSA, CA 91702

TOP SHELF

Designer:
Ben Jennings
Work Type:
Identity

Top Shelf is a newly-established bookbindery that specialises in creating products uniting traditional bookbinding methods with modern flair. The client requested a bespoke identity that communicated the same care and attention to detail demonstrated by their products.

078

Top
Shelf

Bobbie Casiano
Bookbinder
Available Fri–Mon
0401 412 927
www.top-shelf.com.au
info@top-shelf.com.au

SALLY RICHARDSON

Agency:
Studio Equator
Designer:
Liam Delaney
Photography:
Wuttke Photography
Work Type:
Identity

Sally Richardson is a renowned Australian make-up artist who runs her own very successful hair and makeup business, but her business had always been entirely through word of mouth. Sally came to Studio Equator in 2011 to gain help in actively promoting herself and her business.

Studio Equator designed a logo and visual identity that reflects Sally's high profile celebrity work. Our logo design is a simple and elegant composite of scissors, eyelashes and the 'S' of Sally's name, and is complemented by customised typography.

SALLY
RICHARDSON
HAIR & MAKEUP

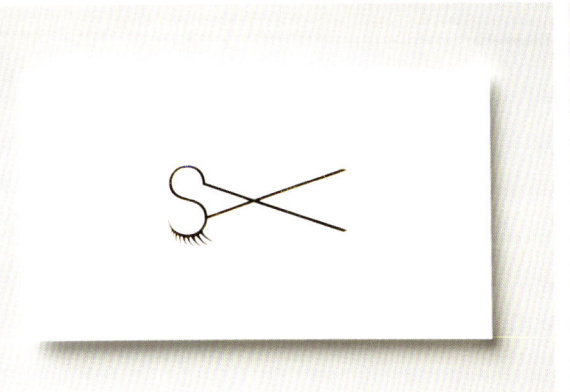

m. 0405 629 583
e. sally@sallyrichardson.com.au † www.sallyrichardson.com.au

ITO SOKEN
Agency:
HAKUHODO INC.
Designer:
Rikako Nagashima
Work Type:
Identity

These are business cards for a freelance editor called Ito Soken. The tool of his trade is his perspective. His product is the things he sets his eyes on. For this reason, his business cards have illustrations of eyes and perspectives on them. And at the other end of his gaze, the thing he is after (hearts).

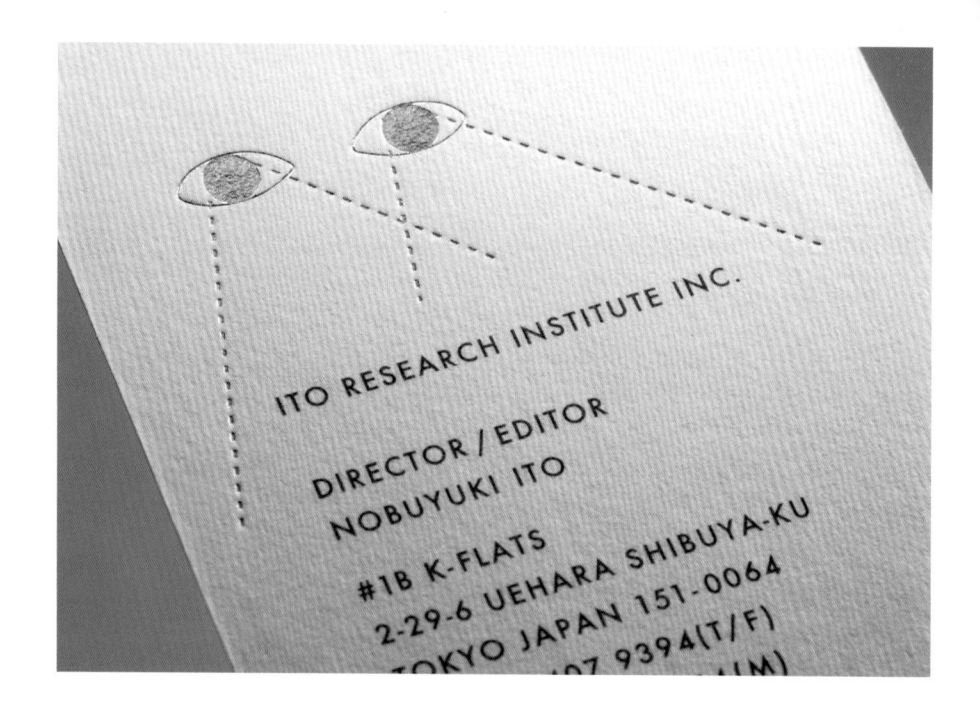

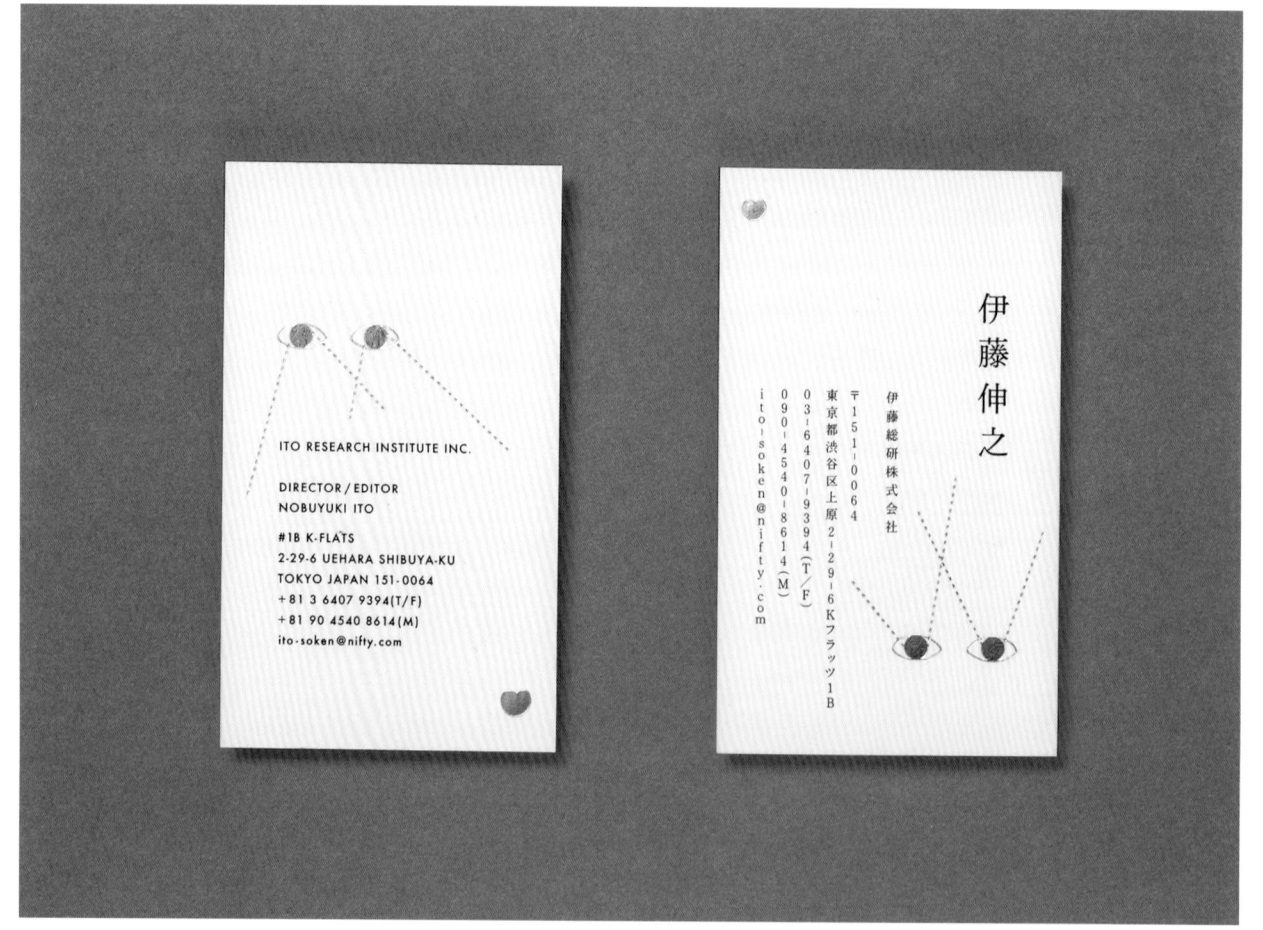

CHARLES CAMPBELL
BESPOKE TAILORING

Agency:
Teacake
Designer:
Graham Sykes / Rob Walmsley
Illustration:
Ilyanna Kerr
Work Type:
Identity

Every man needs a tailor and every bespoke tailor needs a bespoke identity to promote their traditional craft to a modern and sophisticated audience. It was our job to do just this and with the help of the very talented illustrator Ilyanna Kerr we created this logo using a traditional serif typeface and traditional line drawing of a master tailor's most important tool. So far we have produced a set of hand pressed business cards on stunning lilac Colorplan in a robust 540g. Packaging and a full website are underway including carrier bags, shirt boxes and silk tie envelopes for their new showroom.

YIEWTOPIA INVITE

Designer:
Ghazaal Vojdani & Alice Stein
Work Type:
Invitation

Yiewsley and West Drayton was one of the places in Greater London to be hit the hardest during the recession, causing the high street shops to close their doors. Thomas More's utopian alphabet has been used for the invitation of the launch party of the shop "Yiewtopia" (Yiewsley+ Yiewtopia), which aimed to re-establish a sense of community by workshops and community projects for the duration of 6 months.

In August 2009 Yiewsley was named 'worst hit town by the recession in the whole of London'.
Despite its rich heritage and cultural assets the area is neglected and suffers from poor identity and lack of social pride.
   A group of Central Saint Martins students are joining forces with the council and local community to revive the highstreets of Yiewsley West Drayton through a series of participatory, creative projects.
   In addition transforming vacant retail spaces into open and welcoming hubs for the community focusing on conducting ongoing research, running workshops, discussion groups & events.

Please come and celebrate the opening of our first shop and the official launch of the project.
   You are invited to bring a recipe to go in the community cookbook. Or you could bring something else you would like to share. It could be a record for us to play, some food for us to eat, something broken for us to fix or simply your ideas! We hope to see you there!

* THOMAS MORE'S UTOPIAN LANGUAGE 1516

You are
cordially
invited to the
official launch
party of 'Yiewtopia'

6–9pm Saturday 24th
April 2010 9 New
Parade Yiewsley
West Drayton
UB7 7QR

IF ARCHITECTURE

Agency:
Seesaw
Work Type:
Identity

IF Architecture is a
dynamic interdisciplinary
practice, which aims to
respond to the social,
cultural, political,
technological and
environmental conditions
of modern life through
critical investigation
design and research,
producing ambitious
and innovative urban
environments, buildings and
interiors. Each project
is conceived in its own
right and IF's bespoke
approach was represented in
the visual brand and the
resulting business cards.

IF ARCHITECTURE
IVA FOSCHIA
+61 418 123 299
PO BOX 3158
SOUTH YARRA VIC 3141
IF@IFARCHITECTURE.COM.AU
WWW.IFARCHITECTURE.COM.AU

MEMPHIS MENSWEAR
Designer:
Ghazaal Vojdani & David Weller
Work Type:
Invitation

An invitation designed for a collaborative exhibition between the Italian Trade Commission and the Central Saint Martins Fashion menswear course. The theme of the exhibition was the post-modernist design movement, Memphis. Our graphic output also took a greta deal of inspiration form the concepts within their work, including the use of symmetry, contrasting and replicating materials and decoration as an integral aspect within the design.

CREATIVE SPACE

Agency:
RoAndCo
Designer:
Tadeu Magalhães, Cynthia Ratsabouth
Work Type:
Identity

Creative Space is a brokerage firm based in LA whose mission is to connect unconventional spaces to creative companies. With a 360 degree approach to real estate, they are the people who match tenants with not only an office space, but also expert contractors, consultants, designers, and vendors. Our approach to branding was based on the concept of space and how what is put into it changes it fundamentally. The "creative spaces" are reflected throughout the branding system -- from their business cards to their website, playing with the idea of vacant space as a space to be filled.

PEDRO GARCÍA

Agency:
Clase bcn
Work Type:
Identity

The new brand identity Pedro García shoe based on the development of a graphics system created exclusively from the typeface Caslon 540. The texts are composed by basic rules of implementation which gives a very distinctive personality. The typography is always applied in black and white flag made in cash left, and sensitive. The game is completed with the highlight of the salient points of each piece based on playing with different bodies of Caslon. The logo thus becomes a block of text that includes the full address and details of the company and shares the same rules as the rest of the information. Also this has been implemented throughout the corporate typeface of the company computer system so that the composition of letters, texts, and bills are also applied to the same rules.

pedro garcía/store
c/ jorge juan, 14
callejón, local 3
28001 madrid/españa
tel/fax+34 91 575 34 41
info@pedrogarcia.com
www.pedrogarcia.com

pedro garcía

pedro garcía
pol.campo alto, c/italia 46
03600 elda, alicante/españa
tel +34 96 539 90 07
fax +34 96 539 48 46
info@pedrogarcia.com
www.pedrogarcia.com

pedro garcía
pol.campo alto, c/italia 46
03600 elda, alicante/españa
tel +34 96 539 90 07
fax +34 96 539 48 46
info@pedrogarcia.com
www.pedrogarcia.com

TAYLOR BLACK

Agency:
Interabang
Designer:
Adam Giles, Ian McLean
Work Type:
Identity

Handmade in London by designer-maker Philippa Black, Taylor Black's jewellery is characterised by its contemporary take on classic jewellery such as solid perfume lockets and charms, all with a signature rose clasp. The signature rose became the key to the identity, reflected in the crown emblem and imagery. The vintage feel was highlighted through the use of original Victorian botanical illustrations, which were intensely cropped to give them a contemporary edge.

092

TAYLOR BLACK
LONDON

Philippa Black

philippa.black
@taylorblack.co.uk

23 Merchants House
Greenwich
London SE10 9LX
+44 (0)7703 310 832

taylorblack.co.uk

ETIENNE BOILARD
Creative Director:
Karim Charlebois-Zariffa
Designer:
Lea Behr
Work Type:
Identity

Business card for the DOP (director of photography) Etienne Boilard. Card with no ink, only laser cut holes. The goal was to use only light and shadow like he does in his work. This was a project executed by my intern : Lea Behr. Laser cut by Furni. Great, simple and efficient concept. Concept by Lea Behr and Karim Charlebois-Zariffa.

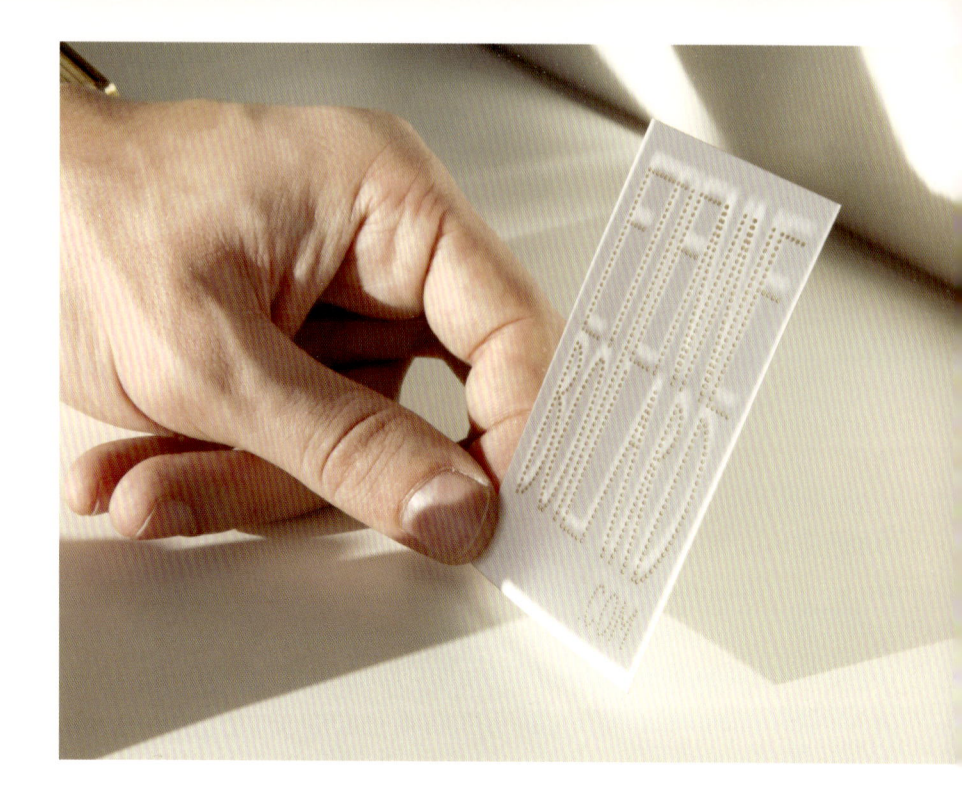

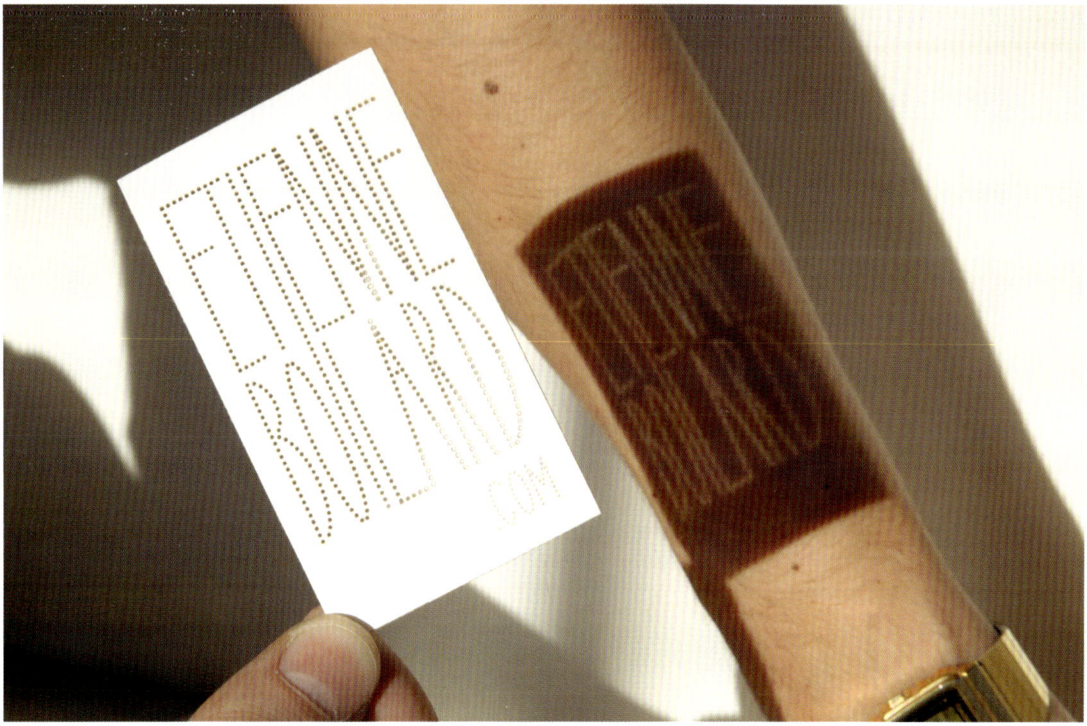
ETIENNE
BOILARD
.COM

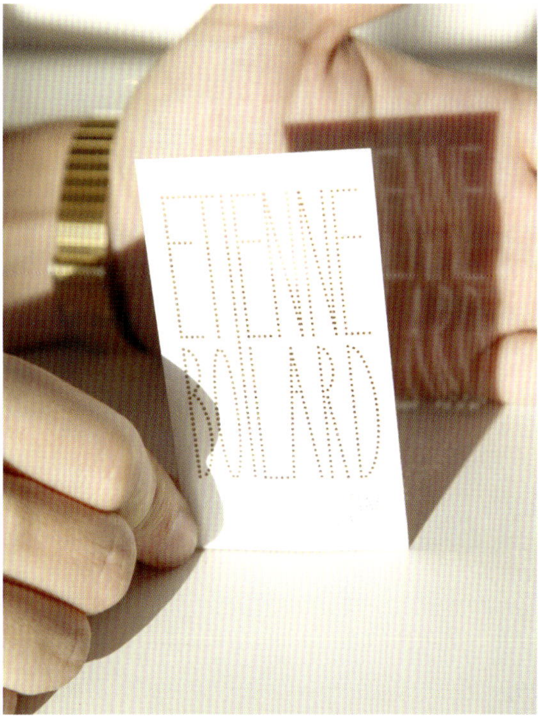
ETIENNE
BOILARD

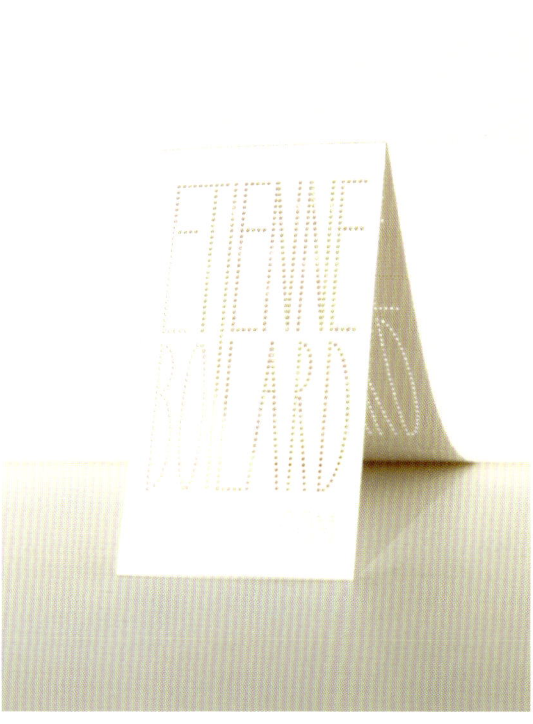
ETIENNE
BOILARD

POSITIVE POSTERS
STATIONERY

Agency:
Motherbird
Work Type:
Identity

Business cards for
'international feel-
good' project, Positive
Posters. The cards are
hand-stamped to generate an
approachable, tangible and
low-fi feeling.

096

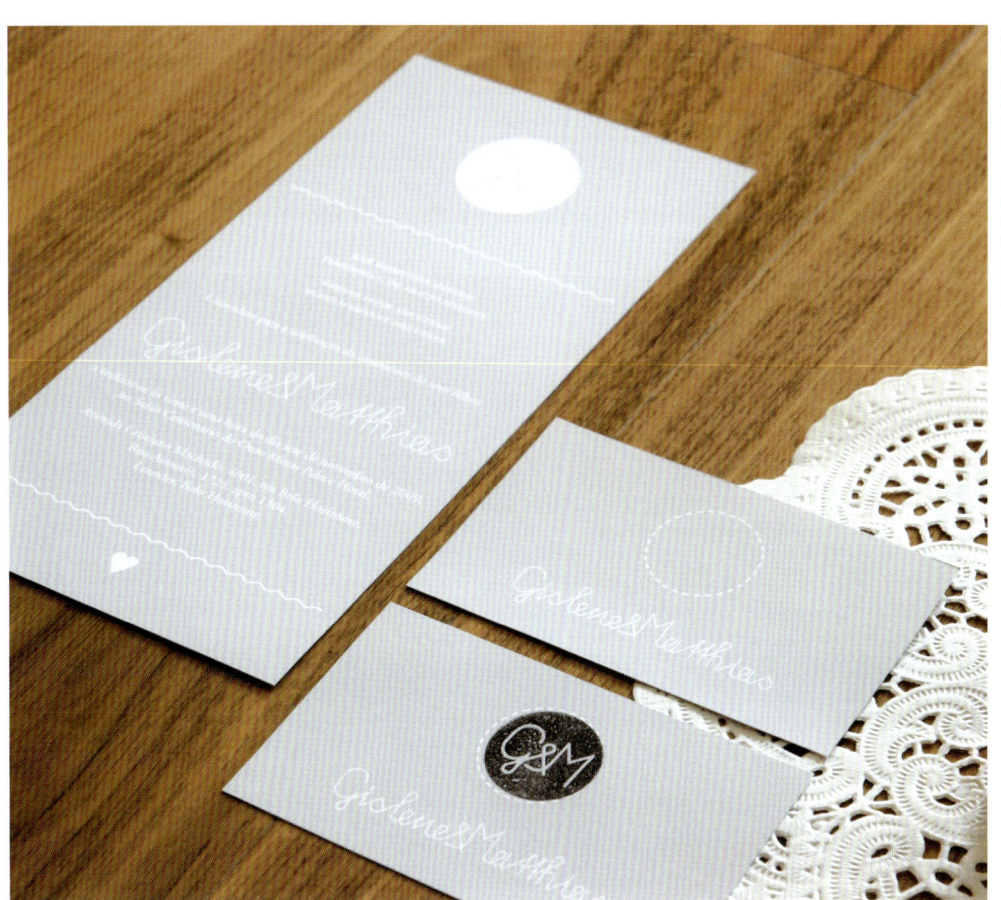

MATTHIAS MEUTZNER'S
WEDDING STATIONERIES
Designer:
Ulrike Meutzner
Work Type:
Invitation

My brother was getting married. For this eventful occasion I created a logo, a font and the invitation.

The ampersand connects the initials of the names of the happy couple.

ENGAGEMENT INVITE

Agency:
Mark Pernice / Matic
Work Type:
Invitation

Two pieces of cardstock, blind embossed on one side and gold foil stamped on the other then riveted together. In the middle is a piece of thread that falls out and hangs to reveal a message. "To love and to be loved is to feel the sun from both sides." Also, included was an ink strip. Invitees were asked to include their thumbprints and that of their guests. Later, each place card was individualized with a unique design made from the two. Some guests got creative including messages, toes, entire fingers and a cats paw.

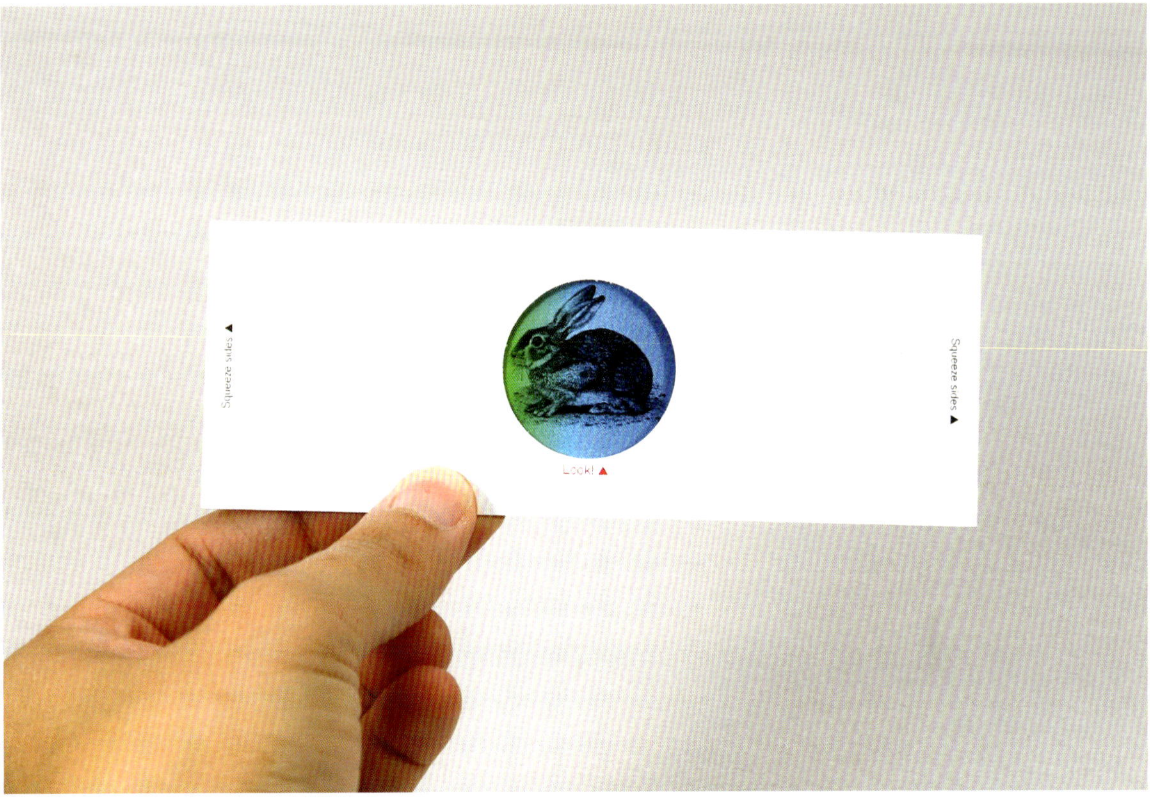
Squeeze sides ▲
Squeeze sides ▲
Look! ▲

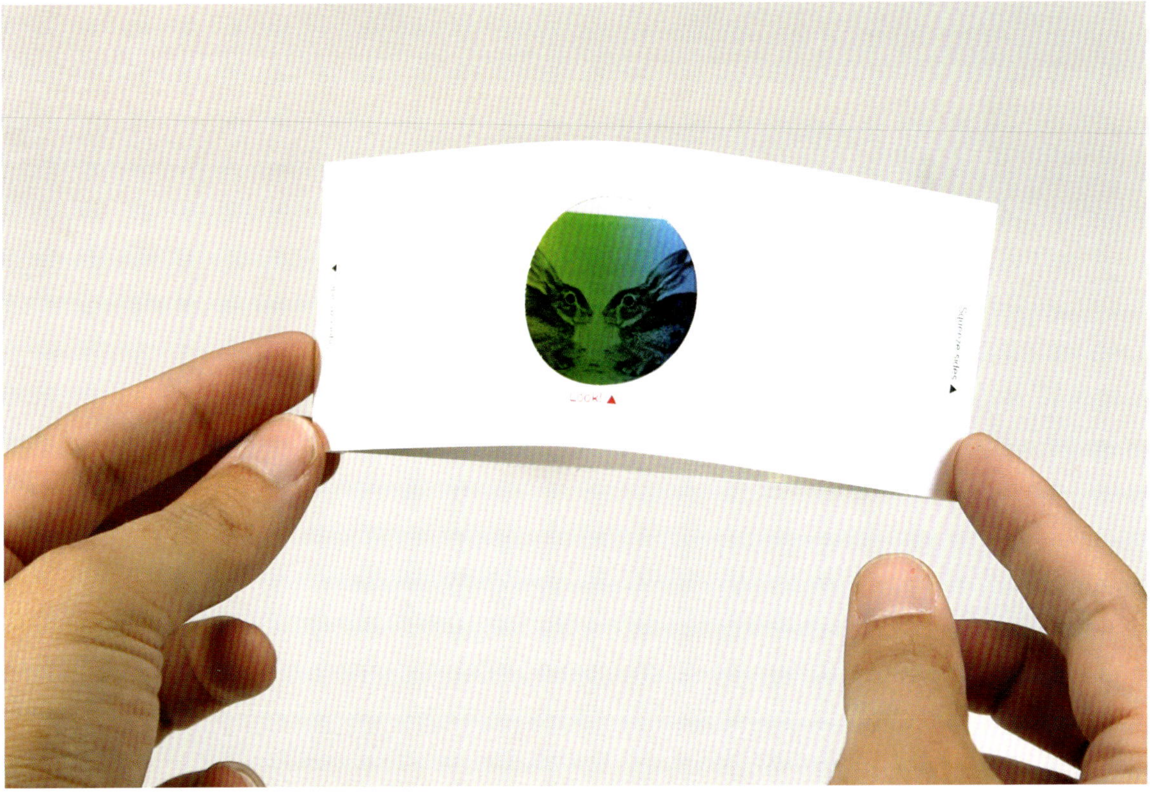
Squeeze sides ▲
Look! ▲

DENIS GUILLOMO
Designer:
Alex Ketzer
Illustration:
Denis Guillomo
Work Type:
Identity

To point out the detailed segmentation of Denis Guillomo's artworks in his name cards, big cardboards were individually painted by the French artist. Finally they were cut in card size and stamped with name and website. Every piece of the whole is therefore a piece of art and a unique work.

DENIS GUILLOMO

info@denisguillomo.de
www.denisguillomo.de

NAOMI & AL

Designer:
Luci Everett
Work Type:
Invitation

Naomi and Al approached Luci in need of a wedding invitation design which was untraditional, personal and most importantly had a handmade feel. Luci worked closely with the couple in creating the hand-drawn elements, using paper collage, coloured pencil and felt-tipped pen. The pieces included an A6 invitation and A5 folded map, which not only contained the wedding location but also locations which were meaningful to the couple's story. The pieces were printed on creamy, slightly textured paper.

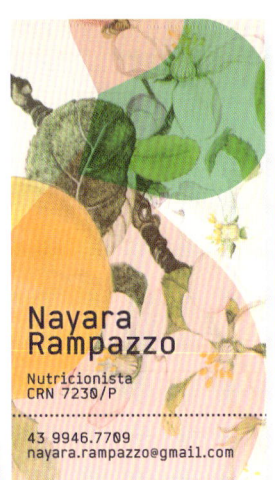

NAYARA RAMPAZZO

Designer:
Lucas Rampazzo
Work Type:
Identity

A series of business card
for a nutritionist using
healthy food illustration.

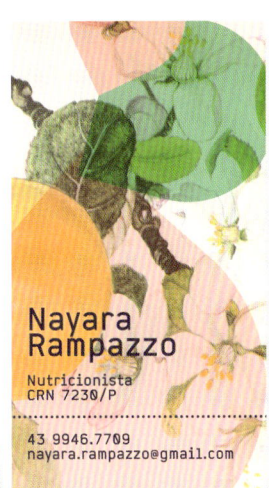

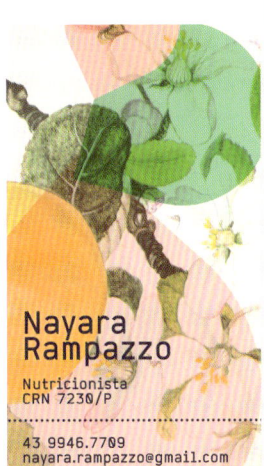

ACO HUD / NATUVIVE

Agency:
Dalston Creative
Designer:
Magnus Polbratt & Sofia Leverbeck
Work Type:
Invitation

Invite produced for a press event for the launch of a new anti-age cream by Natuvive. It was produced for the healthcare company ACO Hud. The aim was to create a modern, vibrant and green invite. This was produced in collaboration with Patriksson PR.

SKÖNHETSVÅRD
INSPIRERAD AV
NATUREN

JUST B. INVITATION SS 09

Agency:
Smel
Work Type:
Invitation

Smel has been the design partner for Dutch fashion brand Just B. since 2007, and in this role has developed an integral brand concept. Seasonal invitations and a teasing campaign are sent to clients and retailers to invite them to the fashion fairs where the new collections are being presented.

The concept of each invitation contains a detail or image that is related to the upcoming collection. An autonomous and intriguing design which is born from the love for fashion and influences of art by Just B. and Smel.

The combination of a relatively simple design with a more complex folding or printing technique results in a surprisingly clean and powerful product. Our goal is to create invitations that have a personal, humoristic and nostalgic feel, are stylish and perfectly executed, and turns a smile upon the recipients face.

106

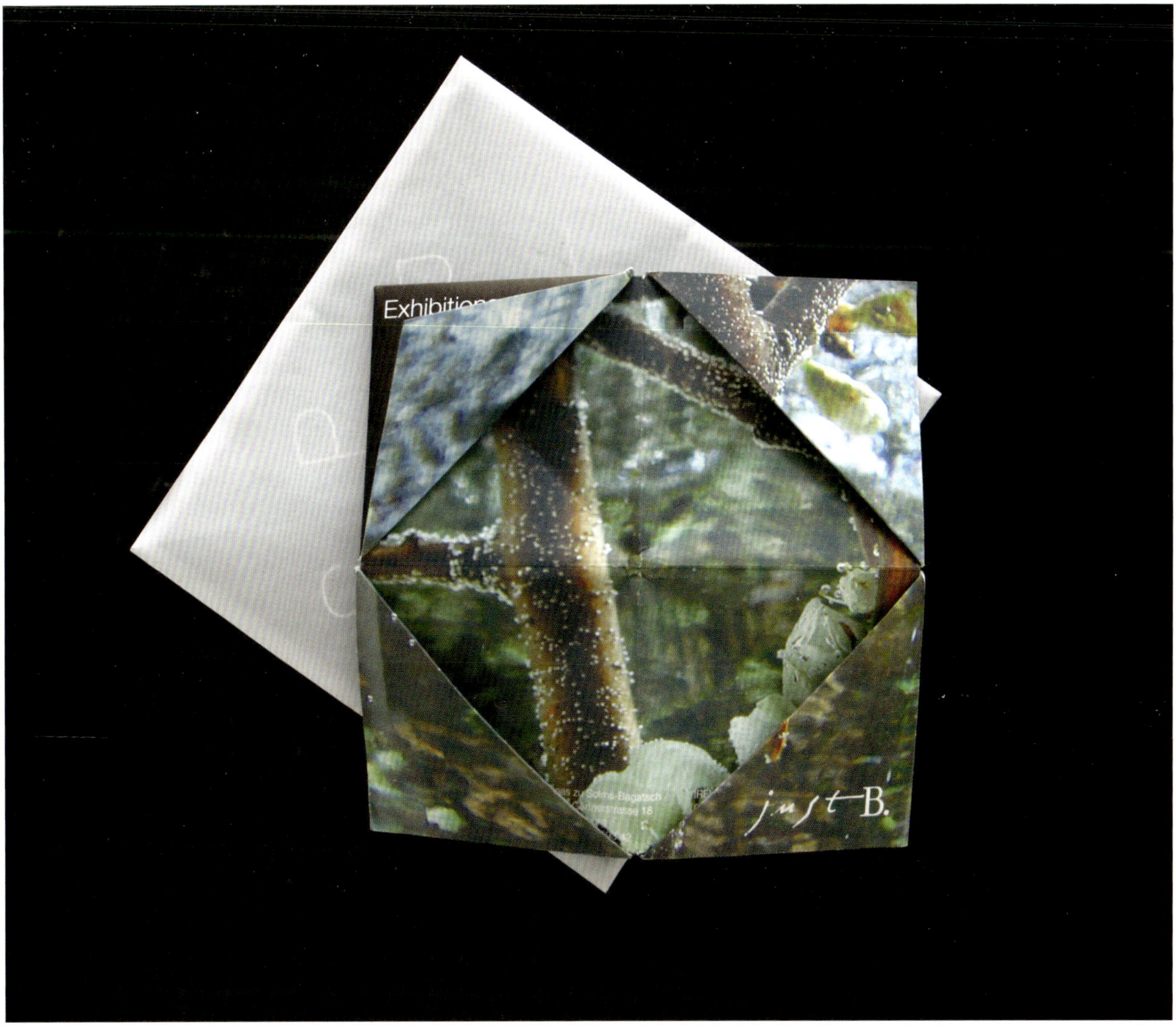
Exhibitions
just B.

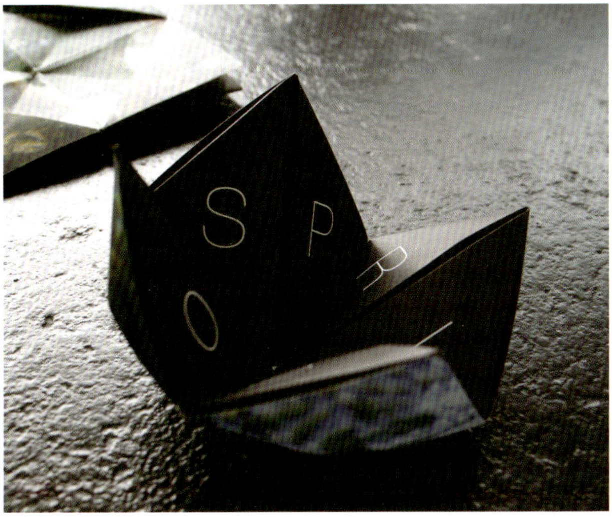
S P
O

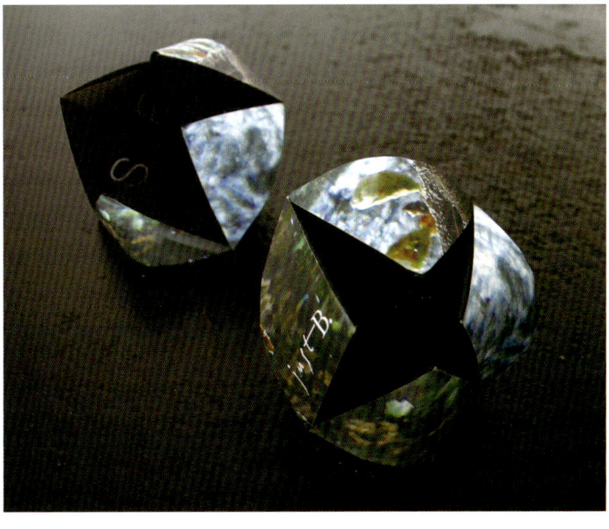
just B.

THE VIRIDI-ANNE
2012 SS COLLECTION
INVITATION

Agency:
NIGN Company Limited
Designer:
Kenichiro Ohara
Work Type:
Invitation

The Viridi-anne is a fashion brand, initiated and produced by Tomoaki Okaniwa. The brand holds two collections in Paris every year and 2012 Spring/Summer Collection's theme was incomplete. The invitation card expressed the theme with totally incomplete expression — an invitation card is folded unevenly and all the characters were handwritten. The typography on the back also reflects the concept of incompleteness.

DEVOA 2009-2010 AW
COLLECTION INVITATION

Agency:
NIGN Company Limited
Designer:
Kenichiro Ohara
Work Type:
Invitation

DEVOA is a Japanese fashion brand, initiated by Daiske Nishida, a designer with a unique background of sports physiology. To integrate his background on the collection, 2009-2010 AW collection's theme was set as "materiality and stereoscopic". The invitation card took in the essences of the theme with a solidity of the invitation's form, which was initially shrink-wrapped. The wrapping process was done manually and each card was rolled and packed in a way that gold parts, which happens to be the typeface, emerges on the front. Once the package is opened and the card is spread, its organic texture reminds of the body parts - an essence of physiology.

分図
09
DEVOA
Chart
17 Tue.
Exhibition
Thu. February 2009
FOR PRESS &
Fri. February 2009
DEVOA
2-24-14
KYU BUS 01 (To Ookayama Elementary School)
Station—Himonya 2chome
OFFICE
2-24-14 Meguro-honcho
Meguro-ku Tokyo
Phone: +81(0)3 57 68 52
Facsimile: +81(0)3 57
E-mail: info@devoa.jp
devoa.jp

DEUTSCHE & JAPANER

Agency:
DEUTSCHE & JAPANER
Work Type:
Identity

The new printed matters for DEUTSCHE & JAPANER, following the colours of Japanese and German national flags.

DEUTSCHE & JAPANER
CREATIVE STUDIO

DEUTSCHE & JAPANER
Ina Yamaguchi
+49 621 32674360
iy@deutscheundjapaner.com
Weylstraße 4
68167 Mannheim
Germany
DEUTSCHE & JAPANER
CREATIVE STUDIO

HONOR SS 2011
PRESENTATION
COLLATERAL

Agency:
RoAndCo
Designer:
Tadeu Magalhães
Photography:
KT Auleta
Work Type:
Promotion

Honor, a high-end women's luxury brand, wanted to create something unique and luxurious for the launch of their brand. We pulled inspiration from 1960's French films, Le Ballon Rouge and Belle Du Jour, to help establish Honor's collection image. Inspired by all things Parisian, the show invitation came in a box along with gourmet macarons, which created a buzz in the fashion community and a large turnout at the show.

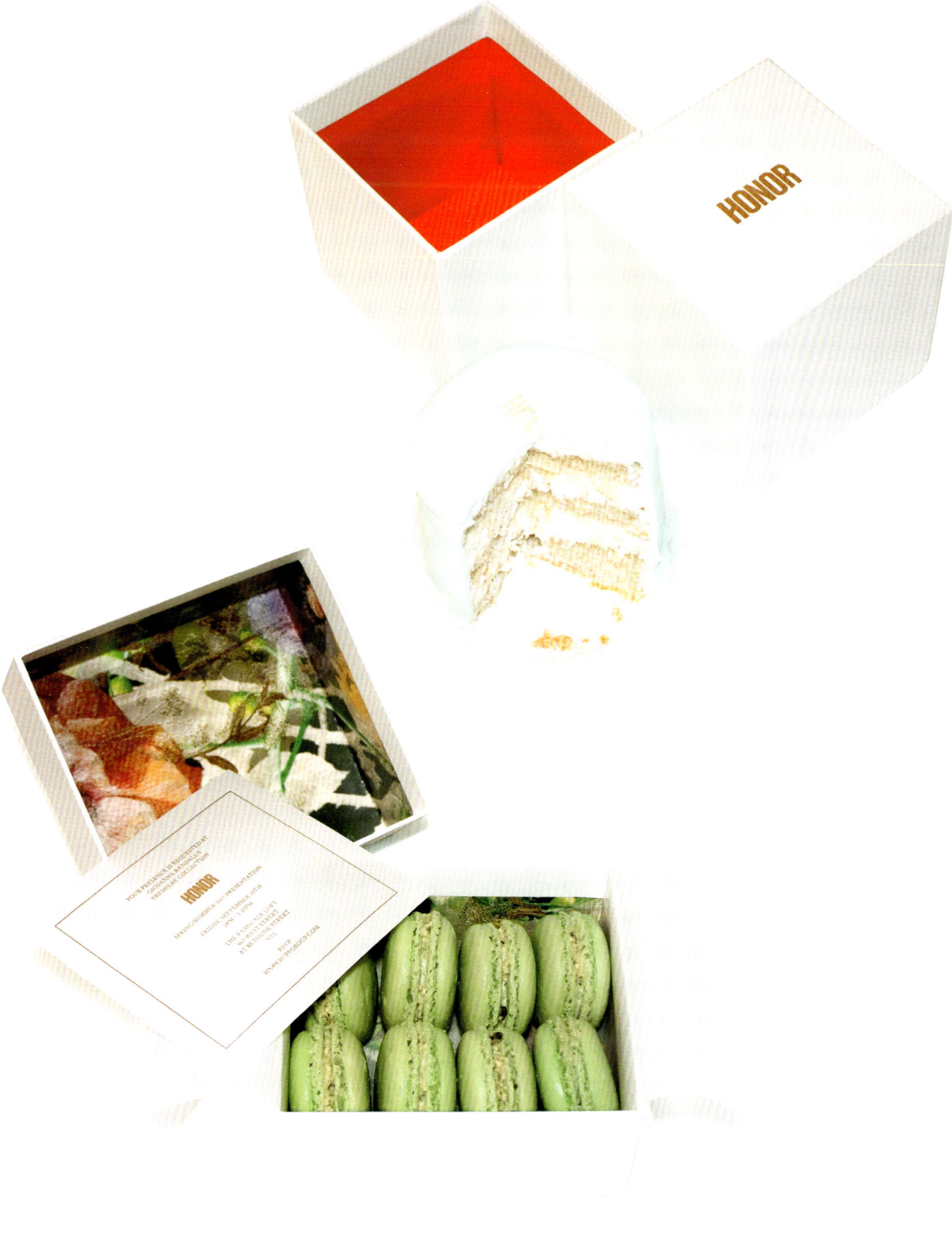

HONOR BRANDING
Agency:
RoAndCo
Work Type:
Identity

Honor is a high end women's
luxury brand by designer
Giovanna Randall. We
were hired to design a
branding aesthetic that
is sophisticated and
straightforward, tailored
to the line's primary
buyer: modern, smart women.
By infusing historic
elements with bold, clean
fundamentals, the Honor
brand identity embodies the
line's main inspiration: a
heritage of fearless women,
past and present.

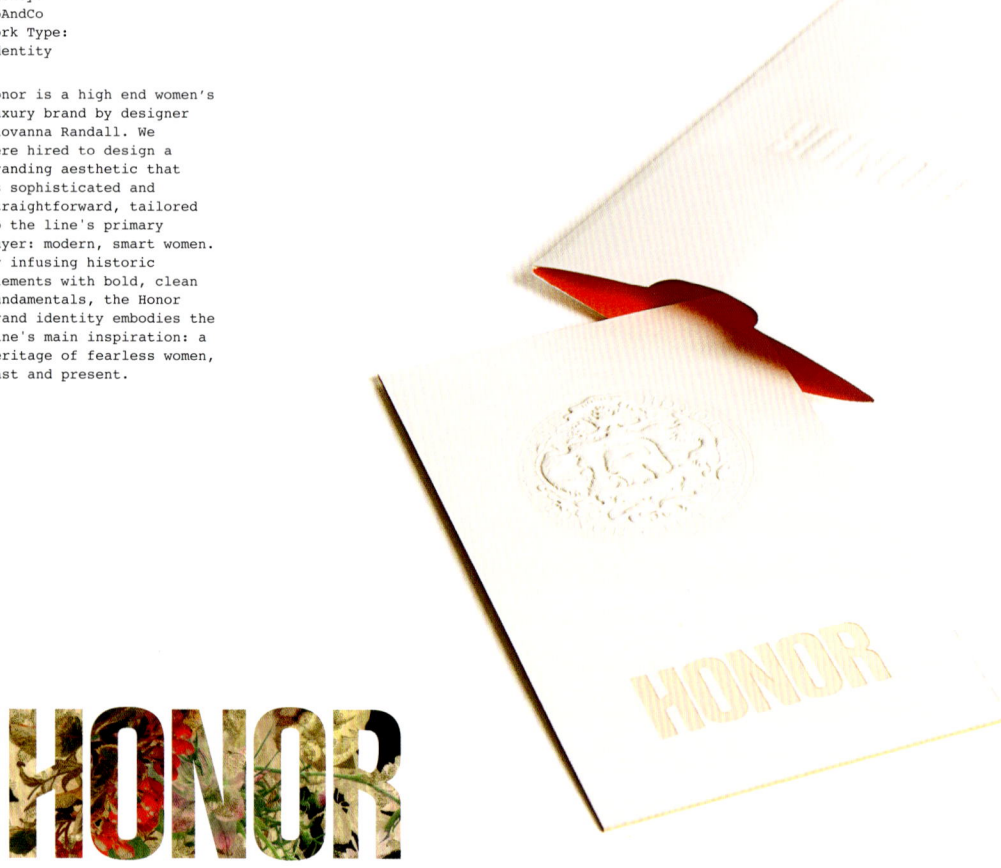

HONOR 2011
DEBUT COLLECTION

THIS GARMENT WAS MADE WITH EPICUREAN
MATERIALS IN NEW YORK CITY.
IT IS MEANT TO LAST A LIFETIME AND BEYOND.
WEAR IT WITH LOVE.
XOXO
GIOVANNA

HONOR

WWW.HONORNYC.COM

HONOR 2010 HOLIDAY
CARD

Agency:
RoAndCo
Work Type:
Greeting Card

Honor is a high end women's luxury brand headed up by designer, Giovanna Randall. With Honor's logo intricately laser-cut in a lace pattern on the front and text reading "Ho Ho Honor" on the inside, our approach to this holiday card was to create a piece that would be both elegant and light-hearted.

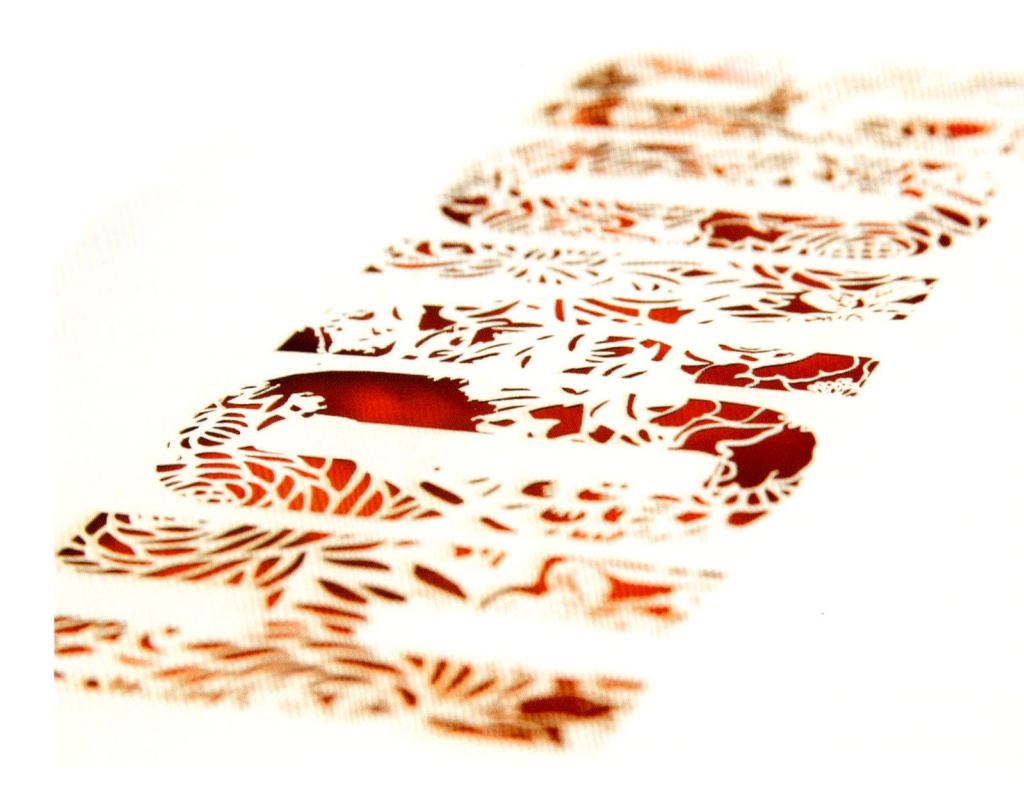

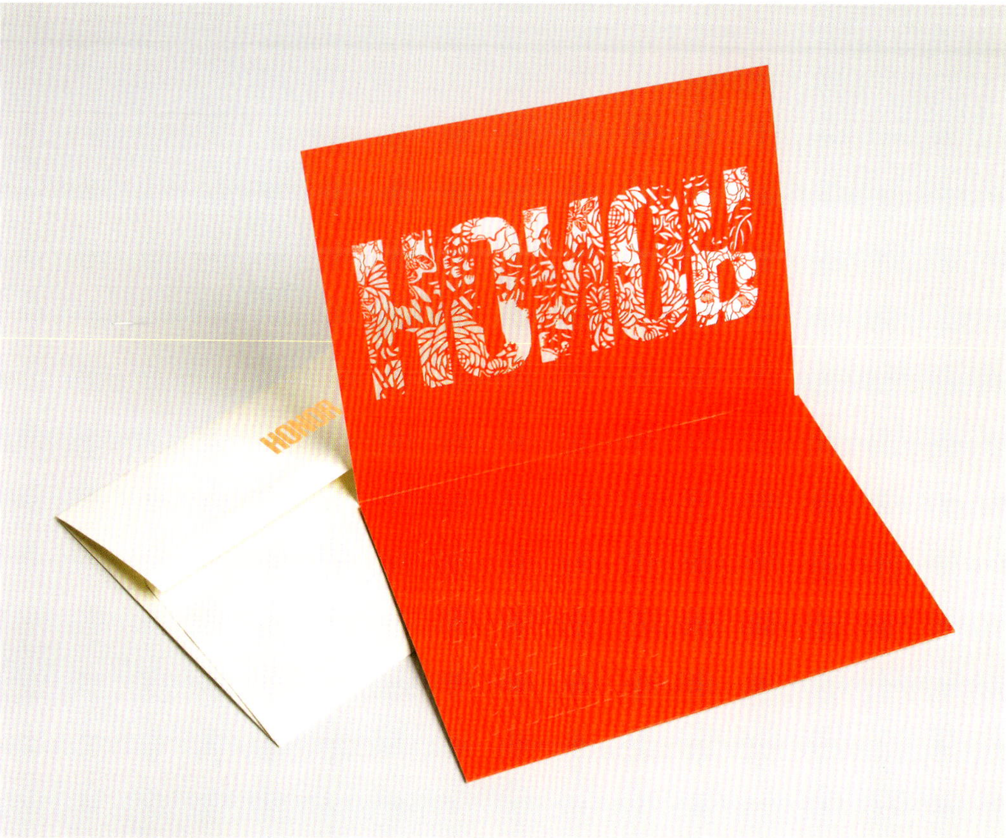
HONOR
HONOR

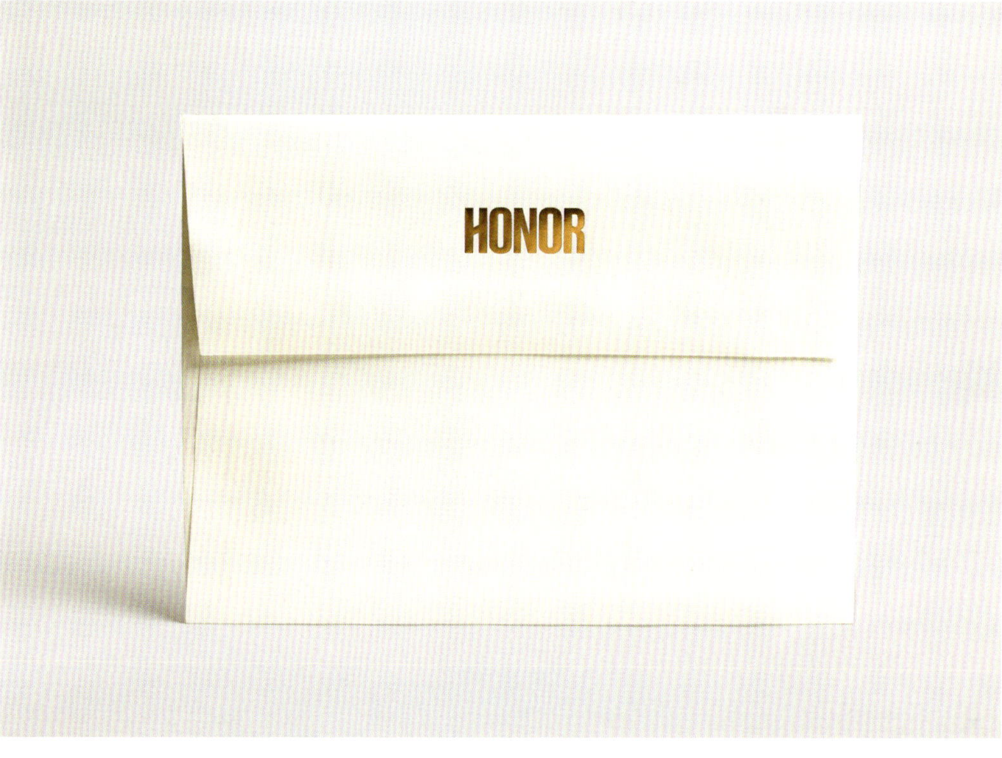
HONOR

MUSEUM OF FINE ART OF
CAEN
Agency:
Murmure
Work Type:
Invitation

Invitations for the event
and installation "the Night
of the Museums". These
greeting cards are semi
transparent polypropylene
boards, printed with
serigraphy, put in a black
envelop pierced through and
through randomly, imitating
the luminous mushroom of
the art installation it
promotes. It was attached
to luminous balloon, filled
with enough Helium so
the whole remains on the
ground. The assembly is
scattered in the city few
nights before the event,
free to move.

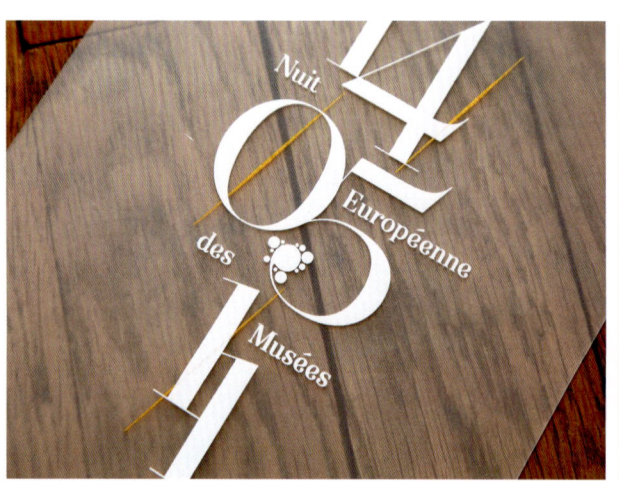

Musée des Beaux-Arts de Caen

14/05
Nuit Européenne des Musées

INVITATION / MURMURE
à la nuit tombée...

CONTENDER KAPITAL

Agency:
Planet Creative
Work Type:
Invitation

Big-league investment funds call for a big-league graphic design. And with a target group that is accustomed to luxury and flair, the graphic design needs a look and feel of quality and elegance.

VÄLKOMMEN TILL INFORMATIONSKVÄLL
OM STELLA POLARIS TISDAG 27 APRIL
Grand Hôtel – Stockholm
STELLA POLARIS
STELLA POLARIS
STELLA POLARIS

Contender
HY2 Ltd
INVESTMENT MEMORANDUM
CONTENDER

DUCK DUCK GOOSE

Agency:
Gardens&co.
Work Type:
Identity

We were asked to develop a new logo and visual identity for the European furniture company. A unique typeface and visual language were created to represent the Art-Deco style of the furniture. The re-branding project included stationery, product brochure (a set of postcards), in-store posters, swing tag and product label.

DUCK
DUCK
GOOSE

Mobile +61 0430 344 135
Email wm.mo@au-ddg.com
Tel. +61 3 9040 2010   Fax +61 3 9040 2011
31-37 Artemis Lane QV Melbourne VIC 3000

DUCK
DUCK
GOOSE

DUCK
DUCK
GOOSE

THE NORTH FACE

Agency:
Hatos, Normalization
Designer:
Kamikene
Work Type:
Invitation

Invitation of an opening preview of THE NORTH FACE Kyoto store.

The position of the store was described in the map of the wide range so that the atmosphere of a town called Kyoto might also be felt.

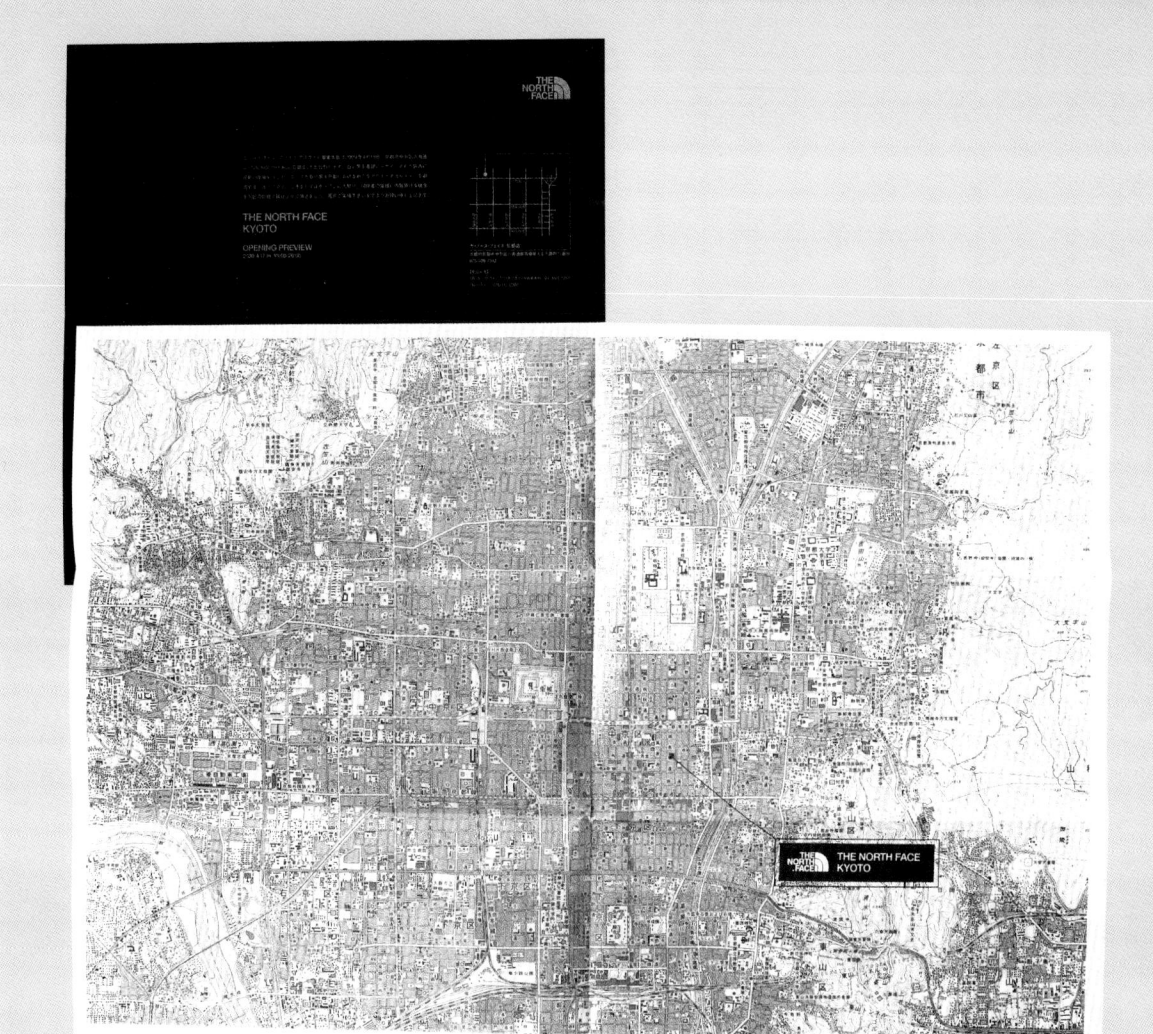

THE NORTH FACE
KYOTO

OPENING PREVIEW

BOUVARDIA'S 2010
AUTUMN COLLECTION
INVITATION

Agency:
GRAPHITICA
Work Type:
Invitation

GRAPHITICA designed this exhibition invitation for clothing brand "Bourvadia's 2010 Autumn Collection". The theme of "Black + XXX = Your Color" inspired the use of high gloss UV printing technolgy to create a design that shines and shimmers.

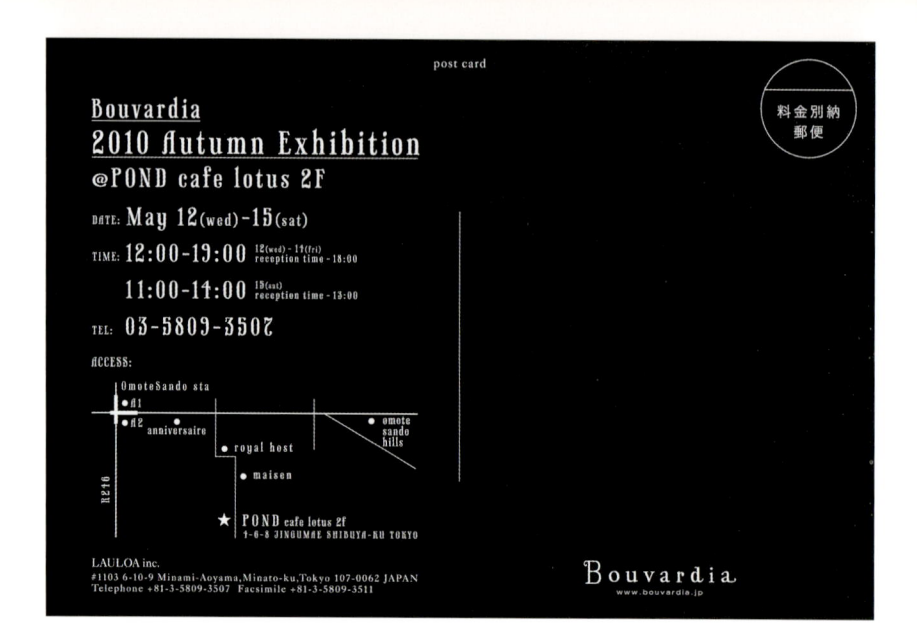

BOUVARDIA'S 2009-2010
WINTER COLLECTION
INVITATION

Agency:
GRAPHITICA
Work Type:
Invitation

GRAPHITICA designed this exhibition invitation for clothing brand "Bouvardia's 2009-2010 Winter Collection". The three-piece pack included a champagne gold printed information sheet, featuring a textile inspired watermark, a VIP card style invitation and a 1 inch badge, comprising three alternate designs — all based around the theme of Paris at Night.

INSTITUT PARFUMEUR
FLORES
Agency:
Bunch
Work Type:
Greeting Card

A range of Christmas material produced for IPF comprising of a Christmas card, receipt holder, stickers and posters. The colourful illustrations added to the festive feel of the applications. The posters were created in a limited edition especially for Christmas.

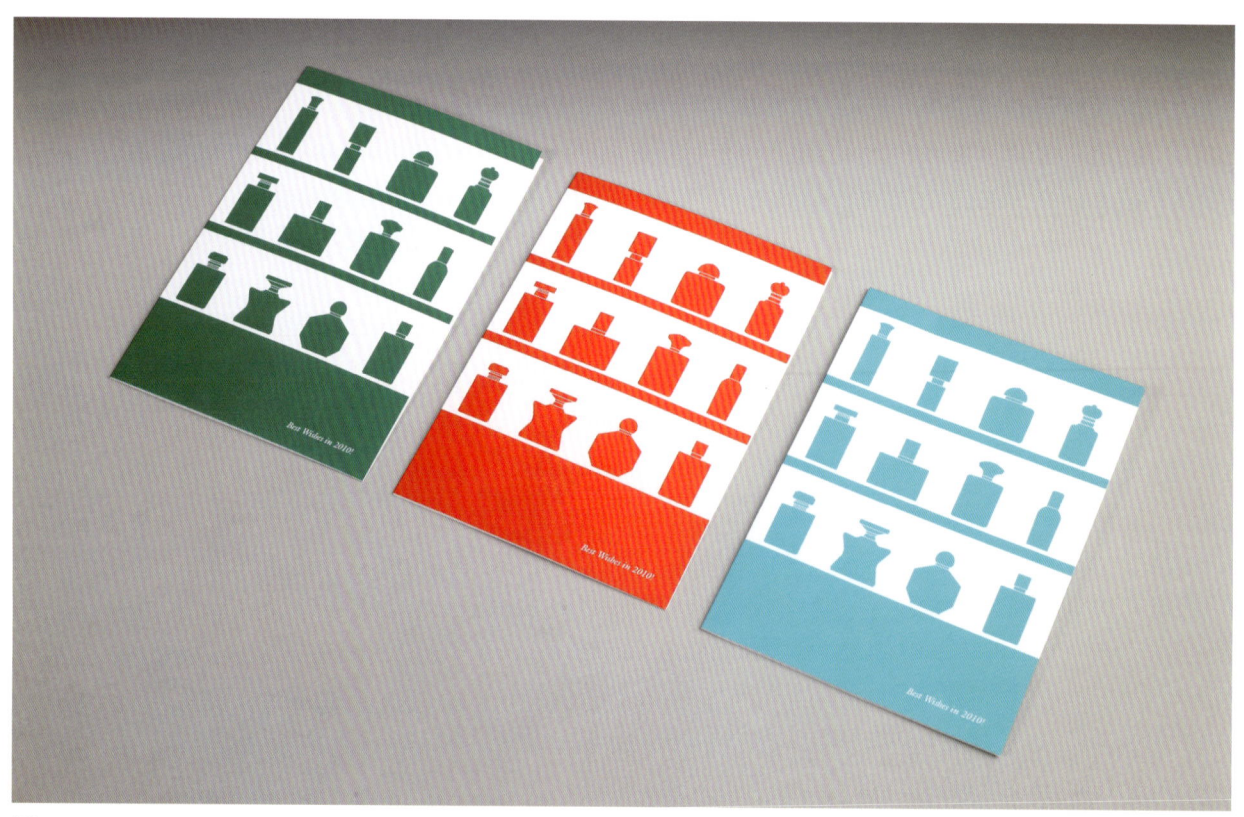

INSTITUT
PARFUMEUR
FLORES

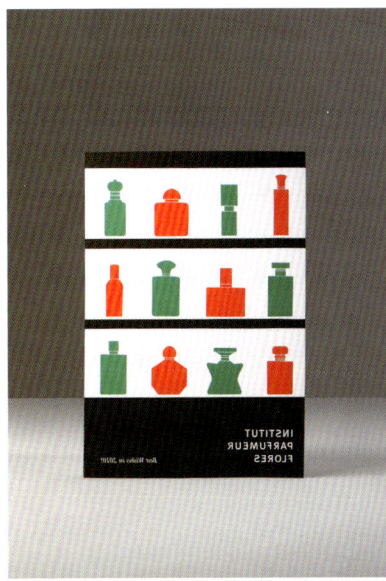

THE VIRIDI-ANNE
2010 SS COLLECTION
INVITATION

Agency:
NIGN Company Limited
Designer:
Kenichiro Ohara
Work Type:
Invitation

The Viridi-anne is a fashion brand, initiated and produced by Tomoaki Okaniwa. The brand holds two collections in Paris every year and 2010 Spring/Summer Collection's theme was ecdysis. The invitation card expressed the theme by portraying the process of opening an envelope as ecdysis.

OPEN

& Summer Collection
POST OFFICE
TOKYO JAPAN
POSTAGE PAID
by AIRMAIL

OPEN

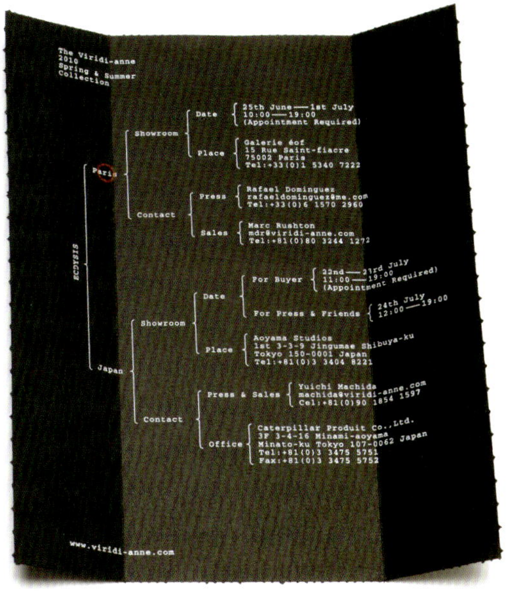
The Viridi-anne
2010
Spring & Summer
Collection
ECDYSIS
Paris
Showroom
Date
25th June —— 1st July
10:00 —— 19:00
(Appointment Required)
Place
Galerie éof
15 Rue Saint-fiacre
75002 Paris
Tel:+33(0)1 5340 7222
Contact
Press
Rafael Dominguez
rafaeldominguez@me.com
Tel:+33(0)6 1570 2960
Sales
Marc Rushton
mdr@viridi-anne.com
Tel:+81(0)80 3244 1272
Japan
Showroom
Date
For Buyer
11:00 —— 19:00
(Appointment Required)
For Press & Friends
24th July
12:00 —— 19:00
Place
Aoyama Studios
1st 3-3-9 Jingumae Shibuya-ku
Tokyo 150-0001 Japan
Tel:+81(0)3 3404 8221
Contact
Press & Sales
Yuichi Machida
machida@viridi-anne.com
Cel:+81(0)90 1854 1597
Office
Caterpillar Produit Co.,Ltd.
3F 3-4-16 Minami-aoyama
Minato-ku Tokyo 107-0062 Japan
Tel:+81(0)3 3475 5751
Fax:+81(0)3 3475 5752
www.viridi-anne.com

THE VIRIDI-ANNE 2010-
2011 AW COLLECTION
INVITATION

Agency:
NIGN Company Limited
Designer:
Kenichiro Ohara
Work Type:
Invitation

The Viridi-anne is a fashion brand, initiated and produced by Tomoaki Okaniwa. The brand holds two collections in Paris every year and 2010-2011 Autumn/Winter Collection's theme was symbiosis. The invitation card expressed the theme by showing how microprobes parasite while co-existing with its mother nature.

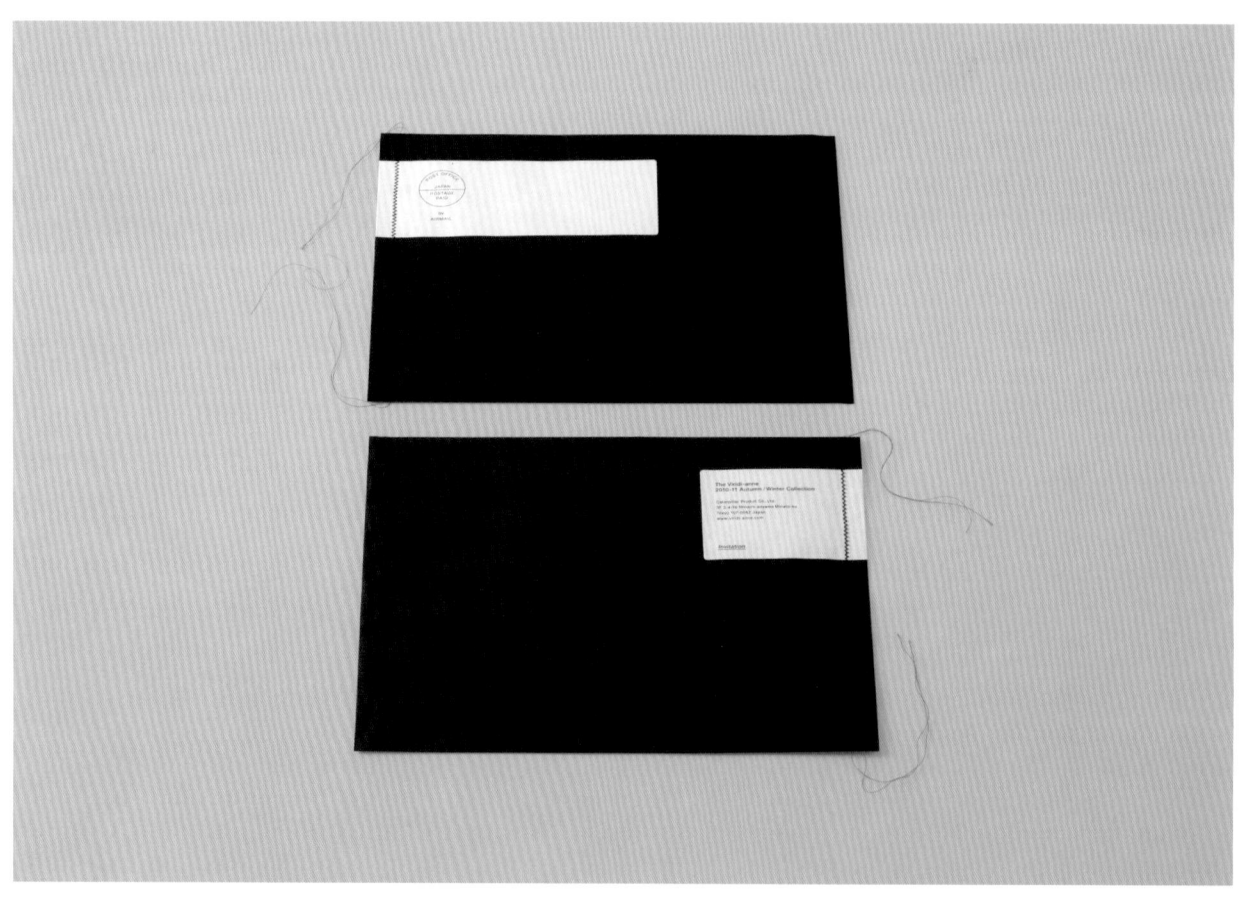

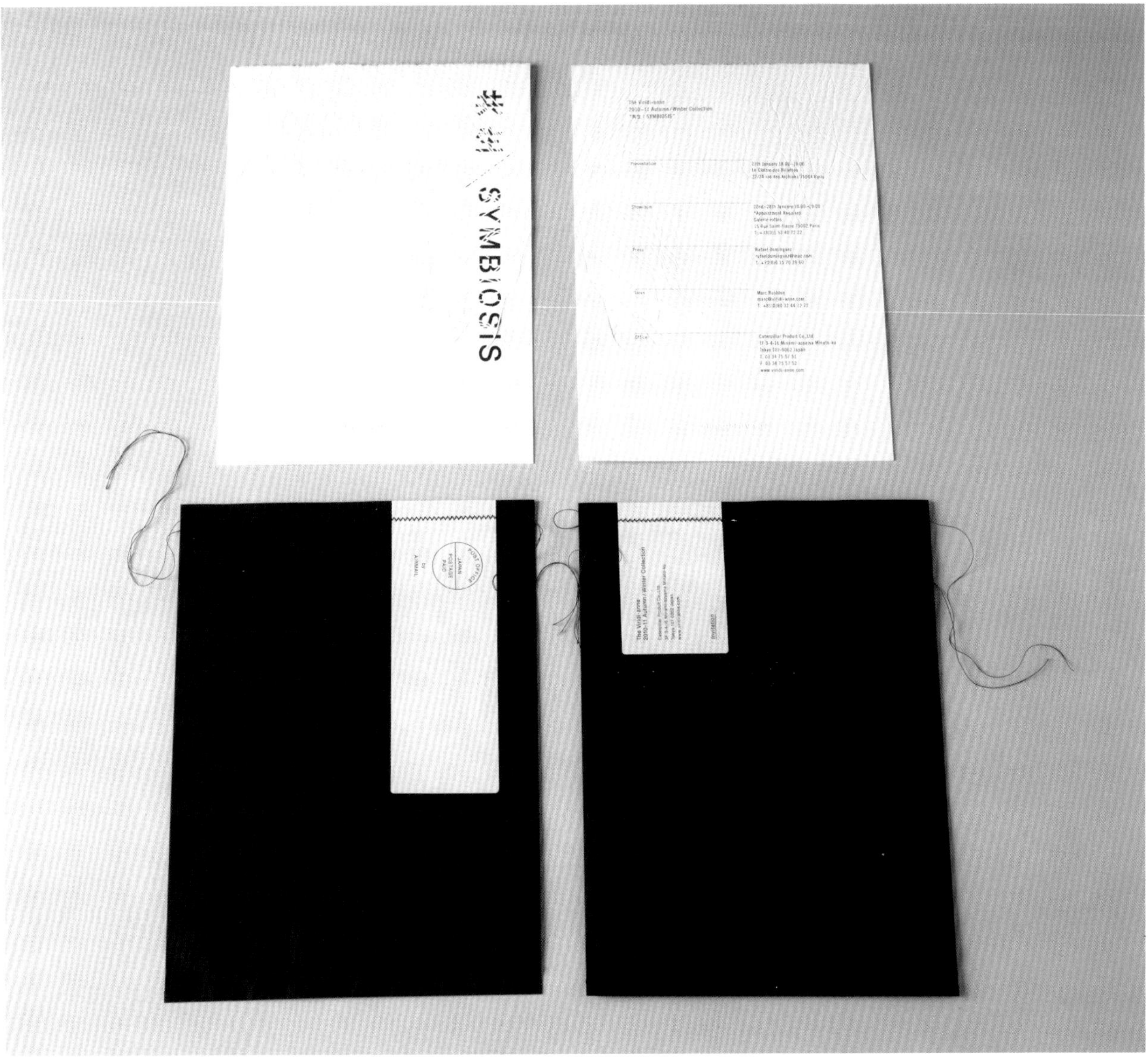
SYMBIOSIS

THE VIRIDI-ANNE 2009-
2010 AW COLLECTION
INVITATION
Agency:
NIGN Company Limited
Designer:
Kenichiro Ohara
Work Type:
Invitation

The Viridi-anne is a
fashion brand, initiated
and produced by Tomoaki
Okaniwa. The brand holds
two collections in Paris
every year and 2009-2010
Autumn/Winter Collection's
theme was chrysalis.
The invitation card
incorporated essences of
the theme with its form and
material. Three-layered
thin envelopes, treated
with wax and crease finish,
were employed to create a
sense of solidity. A black
card, with a hologram stamp
of an insect, was inserted
in the envelope to visually
express chrysalis.

THE VIRIDI-ANNE
2009-10 AUTUMN & WINTER COLLECTION
"CHRYSALIS"

FOR BUYER: 18TH - 19TH FEBRUARY 11:00 - 19:00
(APPOINTMENT REQUIRED)

FOR PRESS & FRIENDS: 20TH FEBRUARY 12:00 - 19:00

AT SPACE EDGE (SPACE A)
3-26-7 SHIBUYA SHIBUYA-KU
TOKYO 150-0002 JAPAN

BY AIRMAIL

POST OFFICE
JAPAN
POSTAGE
PAID

INVITATION

CLOE & MARK WEDDING STATIONERY

Agency:
Sage
Work Type:
Invitation

The key concept or feature piece of this wedding stationery is an interactive invite that literally brings the bride and groom together. The special day was held in the Barossa Valley wine region. To convey this location, we replaced the traditional image of confetti (or rice) above the couples heads with vine leaves. Each item was digitally printed in a palette of 4 colours.

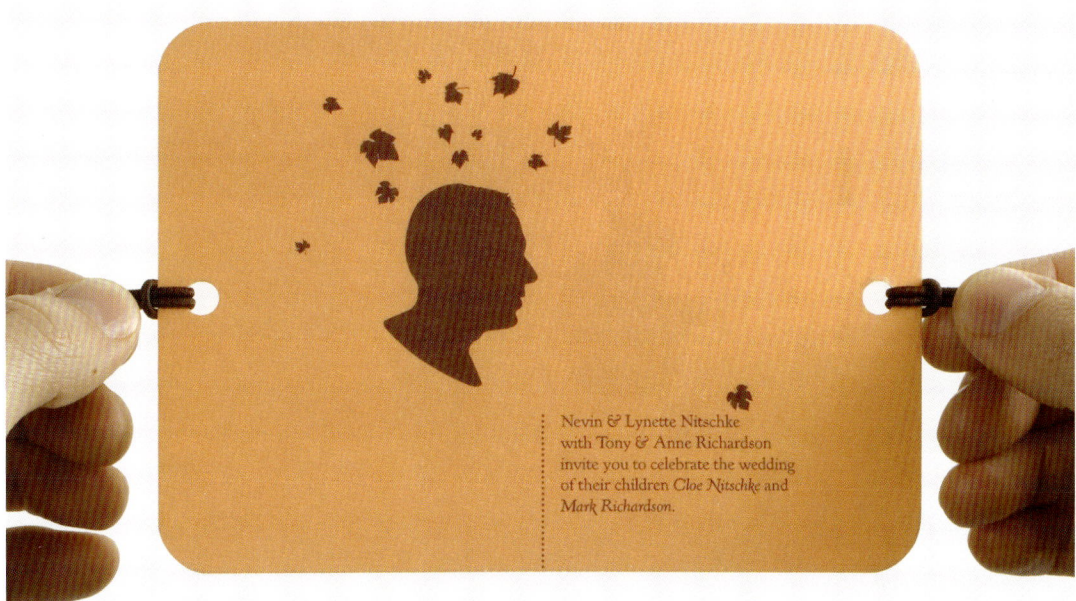

Saturday 23 January 2010
CEREMONY 3pm, Langmeil Church,
7 Maria St, Tanunda SA 5352
RECEPTION 6.30pm, Langmeil Winery, Cnr
Langmeil & Para Roads, Tanunda SA 5352

Nevin & Lynette Nitschke
with Tony & Anne Richardson
invite you to celebrate the wedding
of their children *Cloe Nitschke* and
Mark Richardson.

TIMO WEILAND

Agency:
RoAndCo
Designer:
Tadeu Magalhães, Cynthia Ratsabouth
Work Type:
Identity

Timo Weiland, an up-and-coming designer, wanted to take his brand from a relatively unknown line to an established Men's and Women's ready-to-wear collection. Inspired by Timo's love of classic tailoring, unisex accessories and modern elegance, we combined ideas of refined classicism, quirky details and contemporary street-style to create a uniquely "Timo" identity. We art directed and designed the collateral for Timo's debut Spring `10 and subsequent Fall `10 presentations.

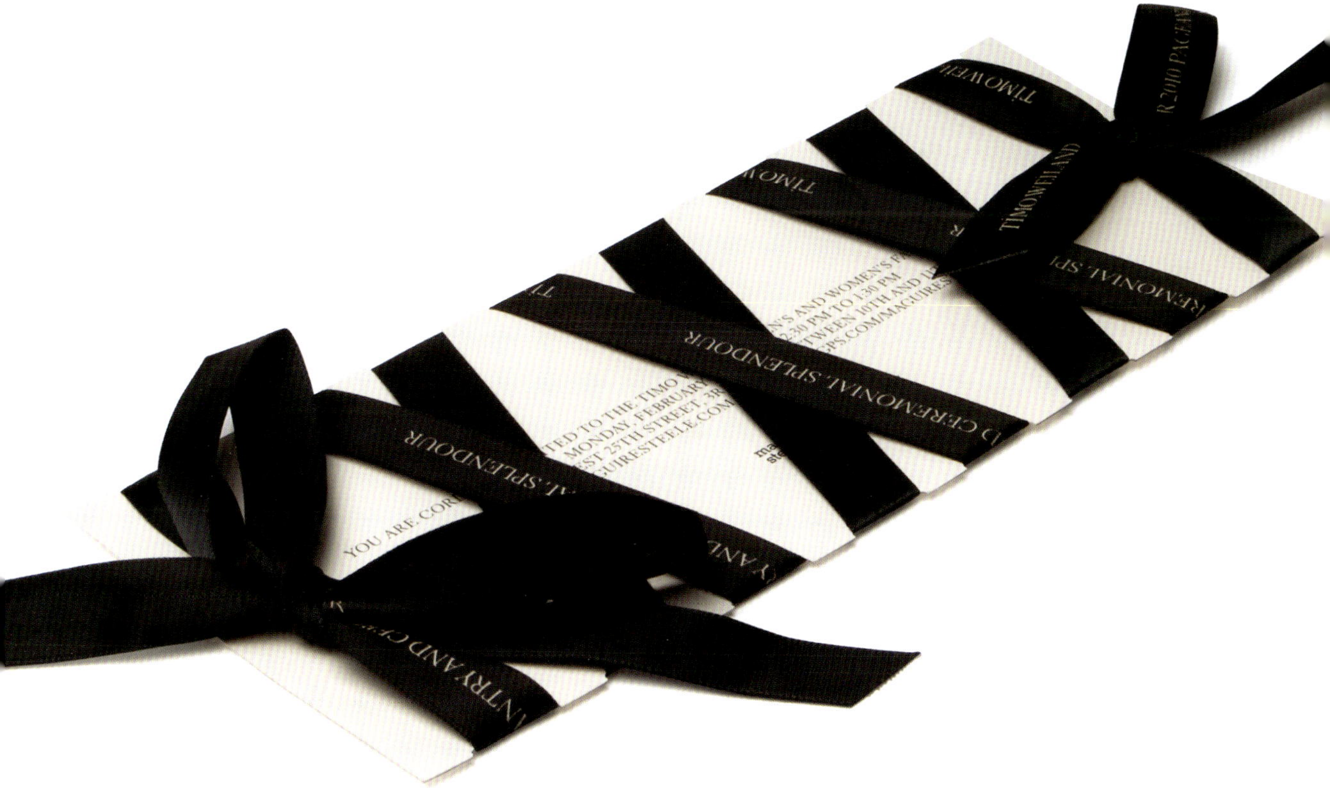
CEREMONIAL SPLENDOUR
TIMOWEILAND

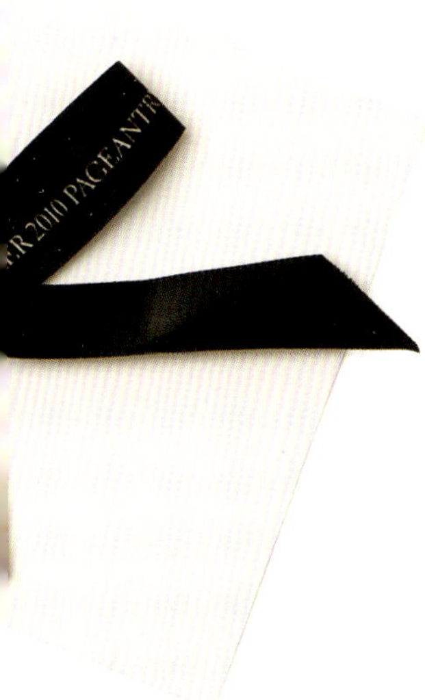

KLAUS
Agency:
Blok Design
Work Type:
Identity

Klaus is a high-end, contemporary furniture store renowned for its products. The identity needed to mirror the owner's passion for highly distinctive yet timeless design. To that end, we juxtaposed many elements: contemporary design with the family's history, charcoal gray and black next to pure white, sophisticated lines with low-res imagery.

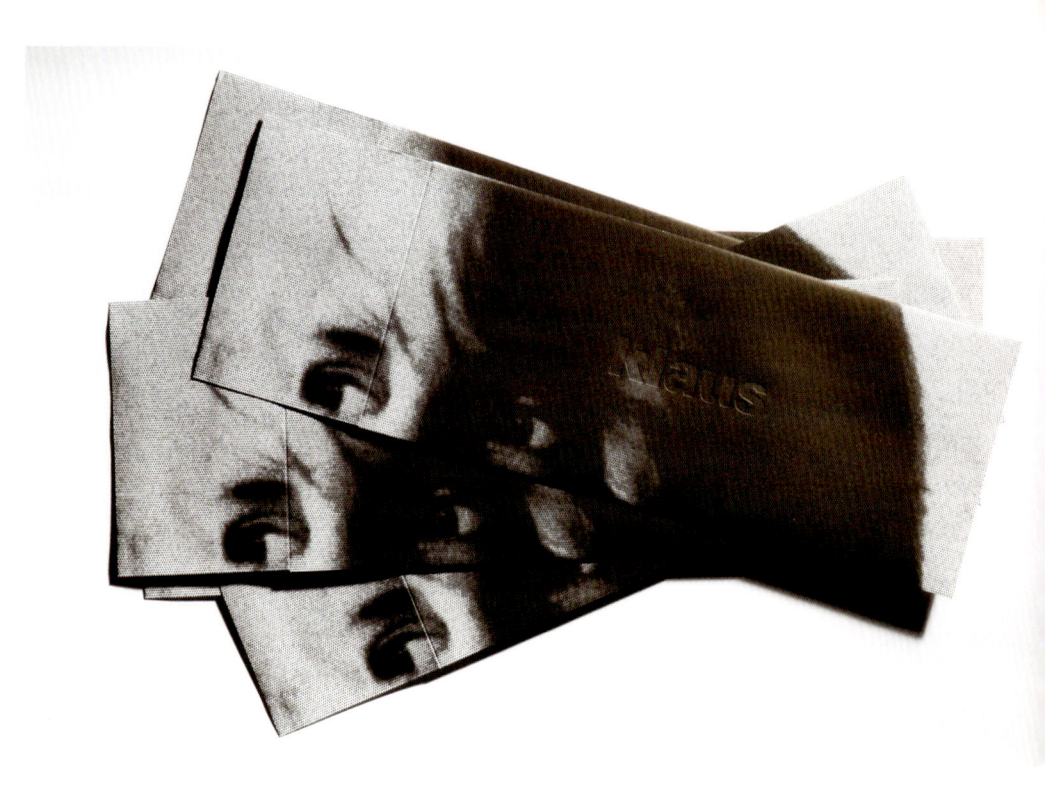

klaus

klaus
300 KING ST. EAST. TORONTO. ON. M5A 1K4
WWW.KLAUSN.COM / TEL. 416 362 3434

TASCHEN POP-UP STORE
Agency:
BLOW
Work Type:
Promotion

Taschen, one of the most illustrated art publishers in the world, was opened their first pop-up store in K11 Design Store. We have designed a poster, a post card as well as the environmental graphics for the Taschen pop-up store.

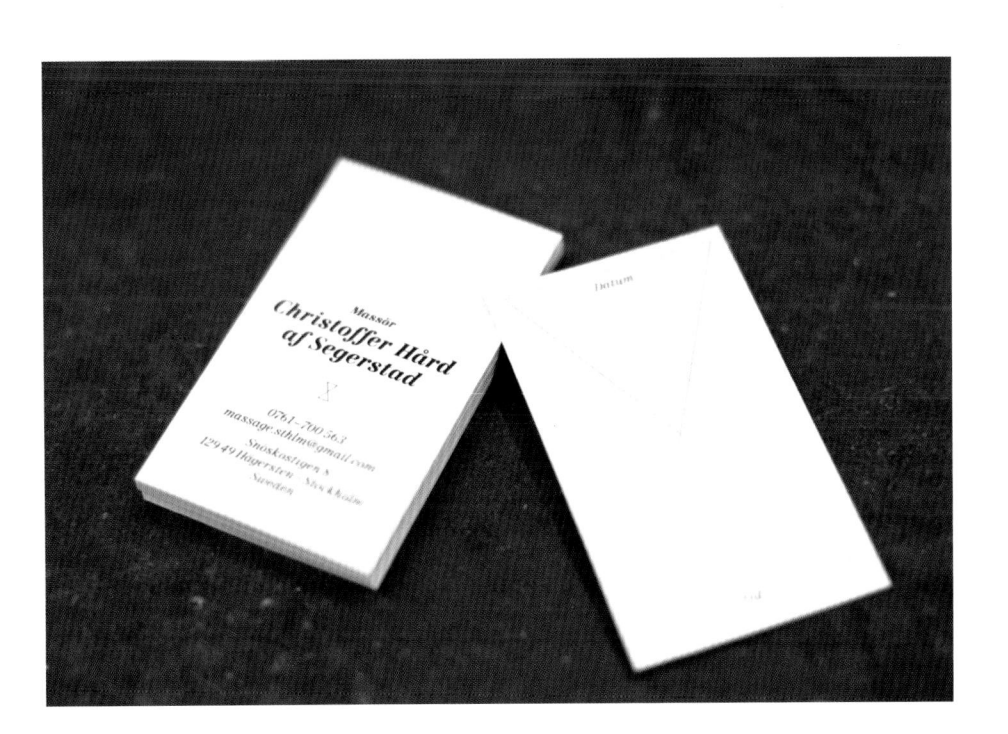

CHRISTOPHER HÅRD

Designer:
Dominic Rechsteiner
Work Type:
Identity

Christopher Hård is a self-employed masseur working in Stockholm. Concept: design of a business card. "Balance" is the key word: it characterized the concept, the typographical design and the paper selection (PLIKE white 330g/m2). The back of the business card can also be used for appointment scheduling.

MARIA VOGEL

Agency:
Anagrama
Work Type:
Identity

Maria Vogel is Latin America's up and coming fashion designer. Our goal for this project was to develop a brand that was convincing, sober, and above all, portrayed Maria's vision, all this without competing with her imposing designs.

MARIA VOGEL

MARIA VOGEL

María Fernanda Vogel.

Virgilio Garza No. 549 Int – 8
Colonia Chepevera
CP 64030 – México

contacto@mariavogel.mx
+ 52 (81) 8347 9524
811 588 0122
mariavogel.blogspot.com
www.mariavogel.mx

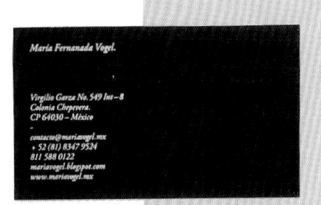

277, 5th Avenue México T + 52 (81) 8366 6666 M + 52 (81) 8366 6666 contacto@mariavogel.com www.mariavogel.com

MARIA VOGEL

ZAHA HADID ARCHITECTS
IDENTITY

Agency:
The Greenspace
Work Type:
Identity

London based agency The Greenspace were briefed to develop a new identity and website for the internationally renowned architectural practice that would support a growing, ambitious, worldwide brand with a visually inspiring design. A solution was needed that would showcase ZHA's avant-garde designs, breadth and depth of their ground-breaking work and the strength of Zaha Hadid, senior partner Patrik Schumacher and their team of world-class architects.

The Greenspace have developed a brand Identity that has a minimal feel. It is inspired by the contemporary material and construction choices employed by ZHA, visualised through the use of varying paper stocks, simple highlight colours and carefully chosen print techniques.

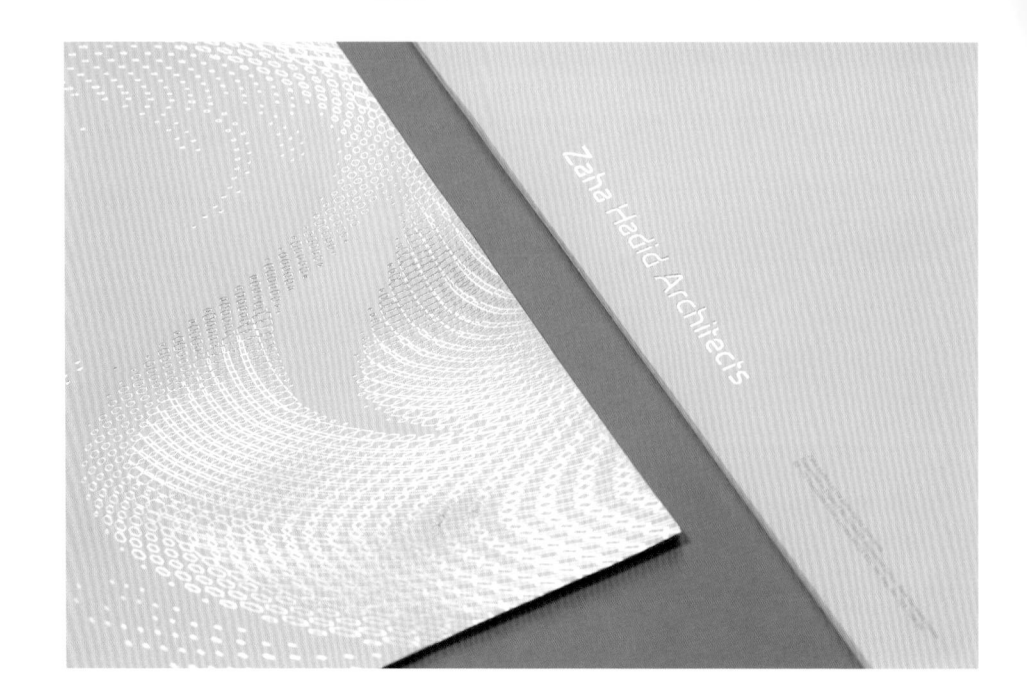

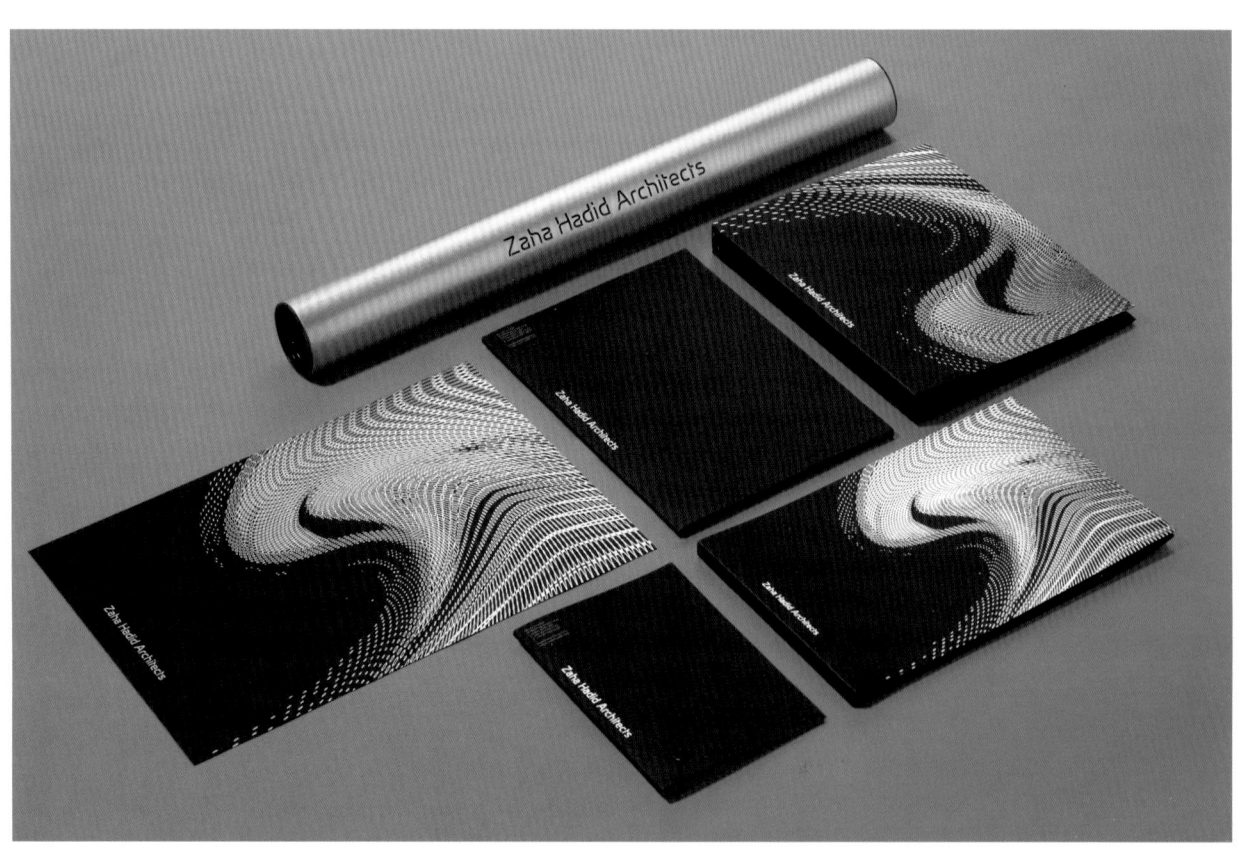

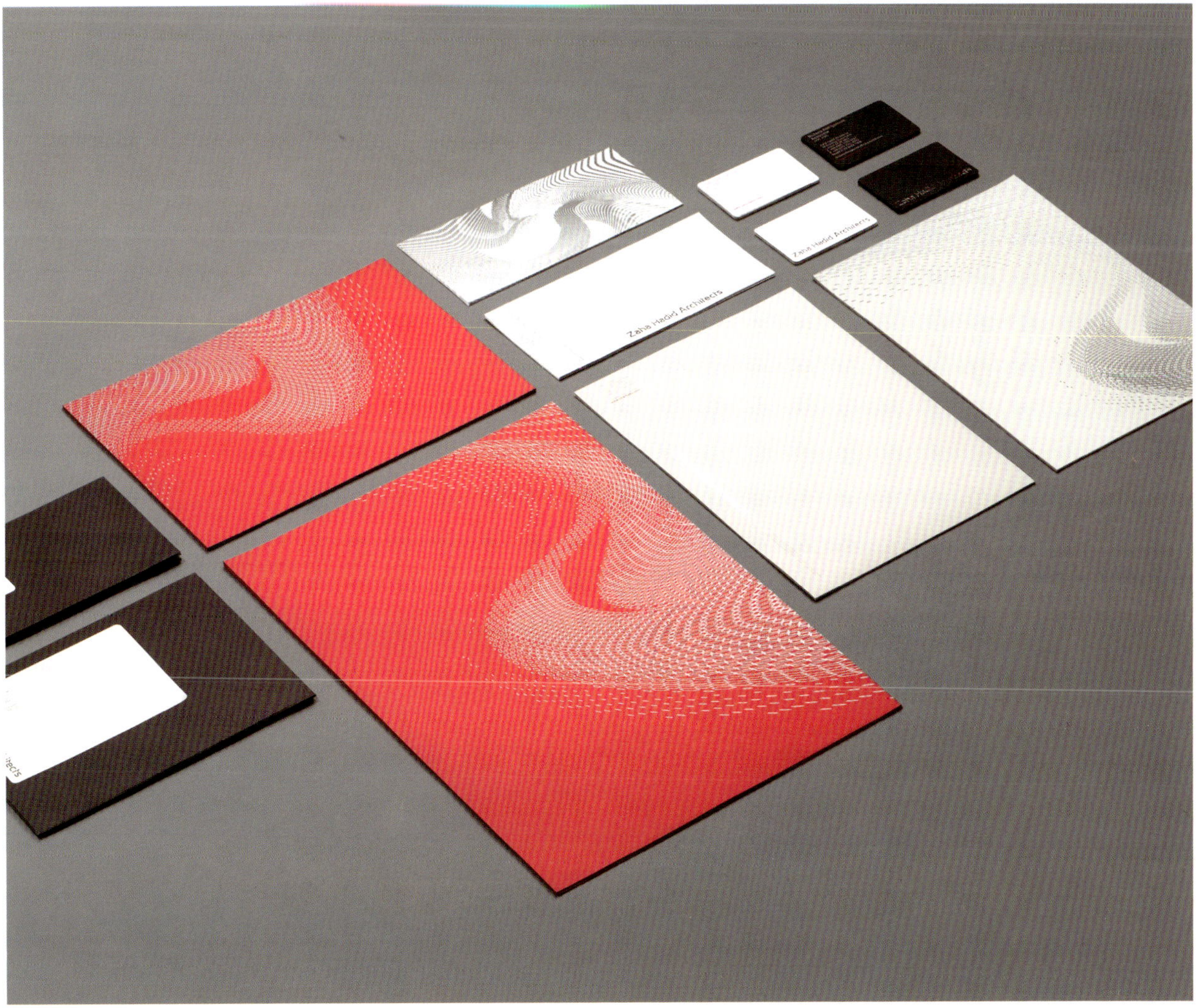
Zaha Hadid Architects

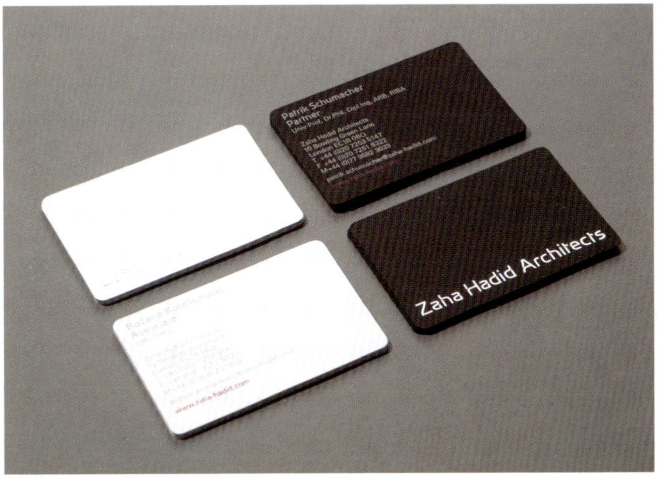
Patrik Schumacher
Partner
Zaha Hadid Architects

AUDIO INVITATIONS

Agency:
filthymedia
Work Type:
Invitation

Audio Brighton turned six years old in 2010 so to celebrate the event, and the launch of Audio Southampton in the same month, we were asked to produce 500 bespoke invitations for each club.

The artwork was influenced by the evening's disco theme, with six abstract, overlapping shapes printed in a dark foil, de-bossed and triplexed by Generation Press.

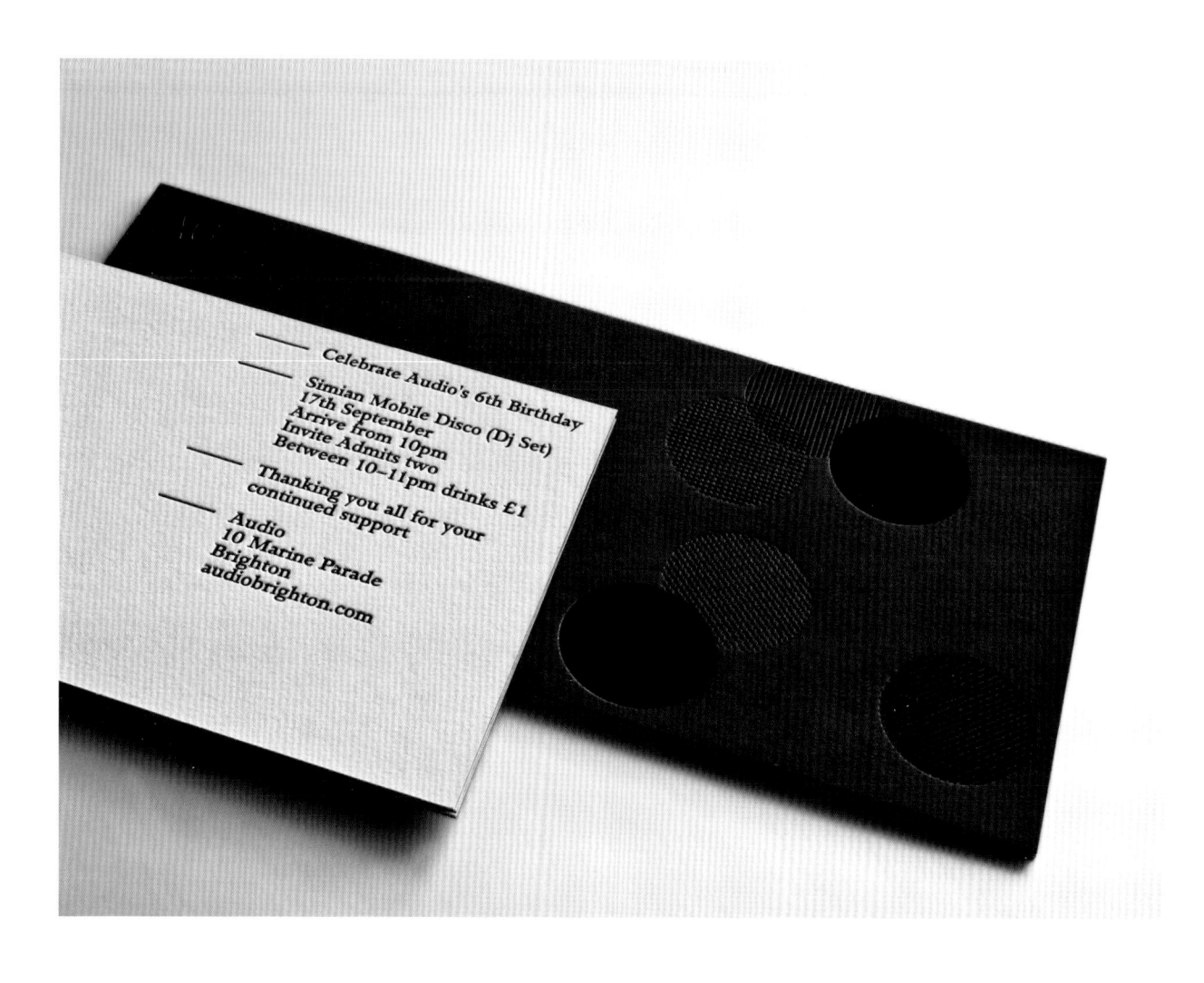

Celebrate Audio's 6th Birthday

Simian Mobile Disco (Dj Set)
17th September
Arrive from 10pm
Invite Admits two
Between 10–11pm drinks £1

Thanking you all for your
continued support

Audio
10 Marine Parade
Brighton
audiobrighton.com

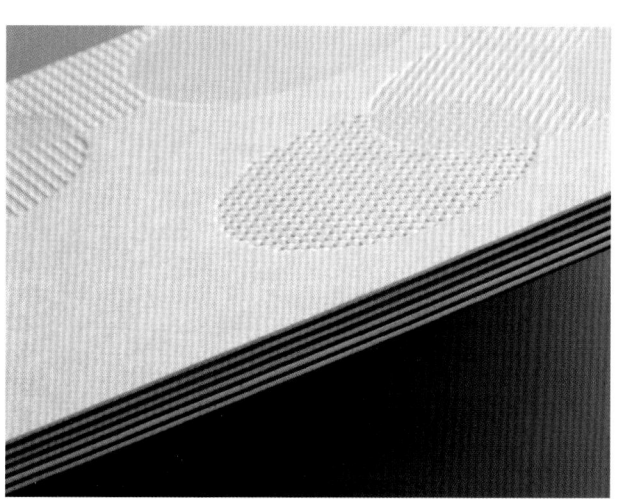

Audio·Launch

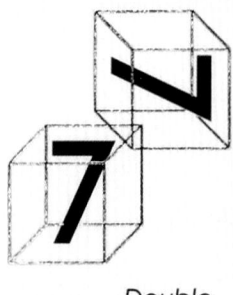

DOUBLE SEVEN

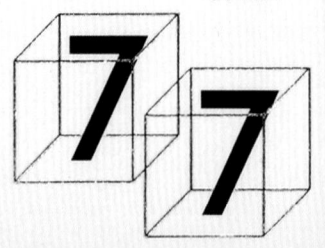

Agency:
HAKUHODO INC.
Designer:
Rikako Nagashima
Work Type:
Identity

This is the business card design for Double Seven, a company comprised of two web planners.

In addition to web planning, the company prides itself on its multi-faceted approach, which includes implementation of associated real events.

The basic logo design is two cubes containing the number 7, but to express the company's unfettered energy, four lively variations were designed.

At times the cubes overlap like alien spaces, expressing the interface between virtual and real spaces.

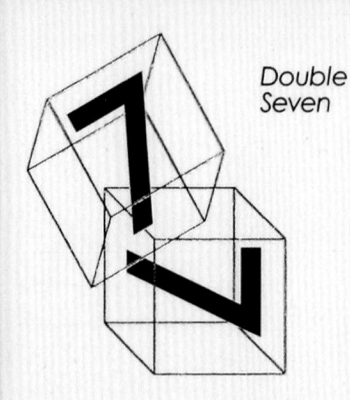

TROIS

Agency:
GRAPHITICA
Work Type:
Identity

GRAPHITICA designed this name card for Trois inc., using traditional letterpress and embossing techniques to create a simple but impressive appearance.

HR

Agency:
Hyperlocaldesign
Designer:
Sandro Bianco
Work Type:
Identity

Reduction of materials such as ink, water and paper reduce carbon emission. Besides, it saves money wasted on mailing . Reducing is the fastest way to reach simplicity. Reduce your printings but with the best quality ever. Founded on these thoughts, Hélio Rosas company graphic identity, the H®, was developed.

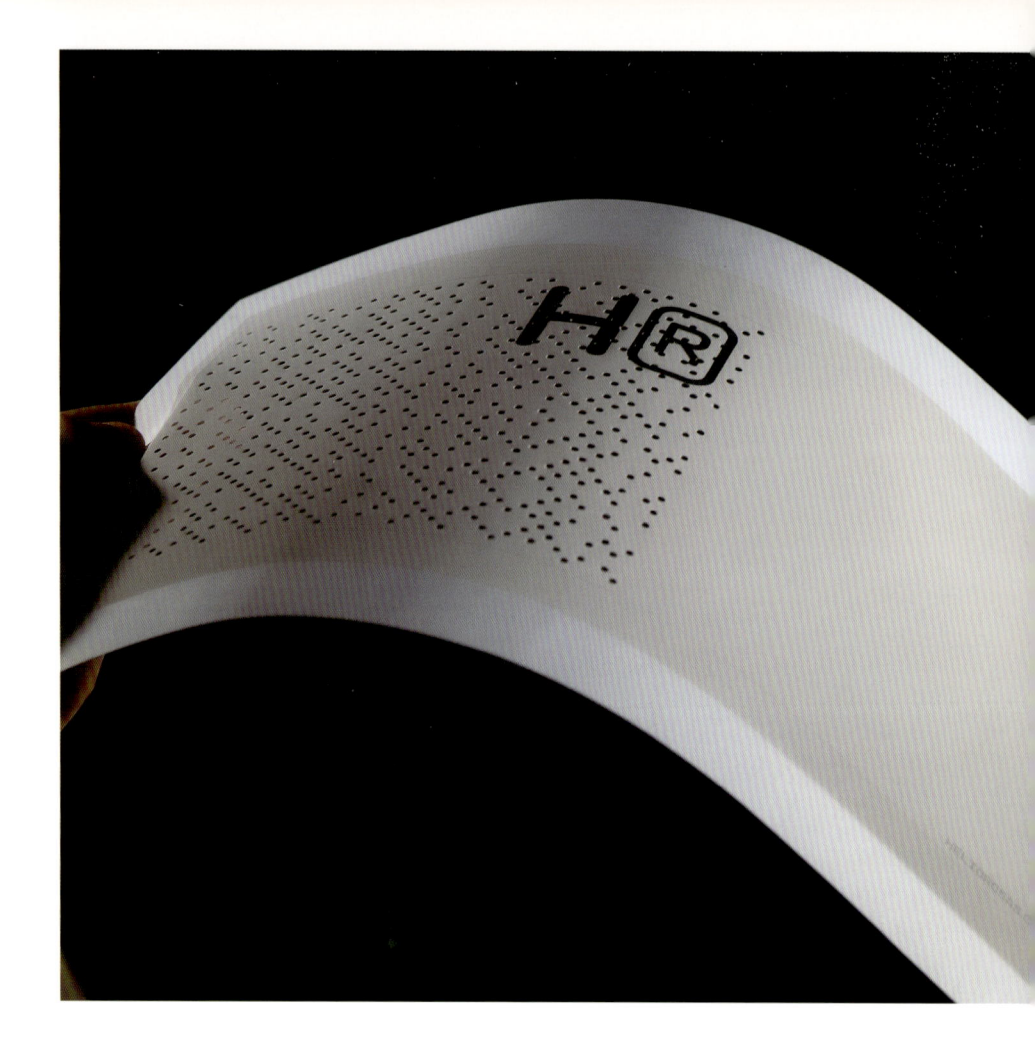

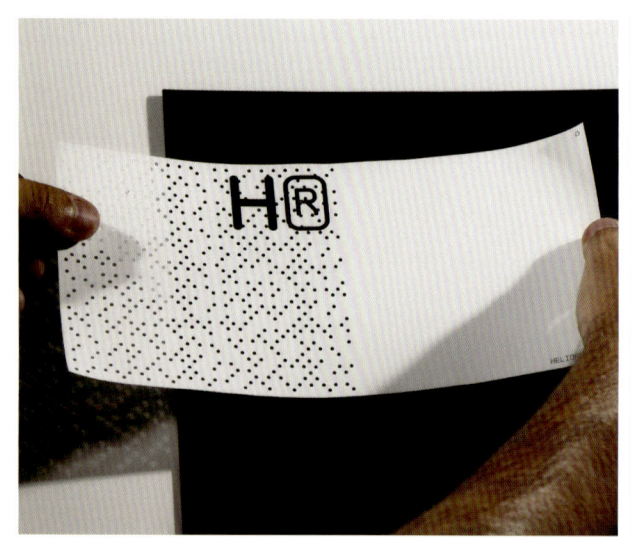

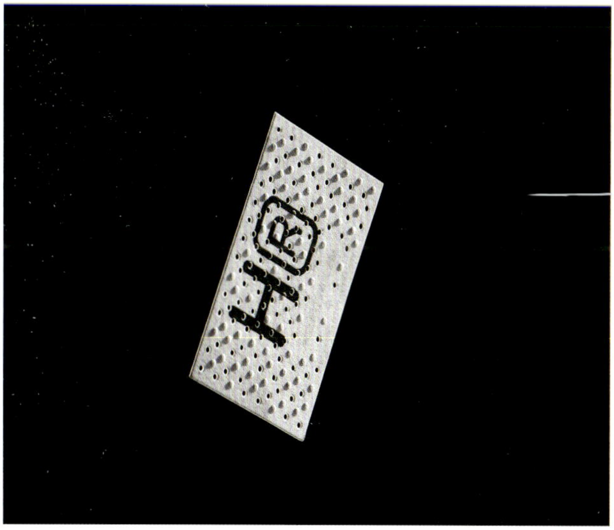
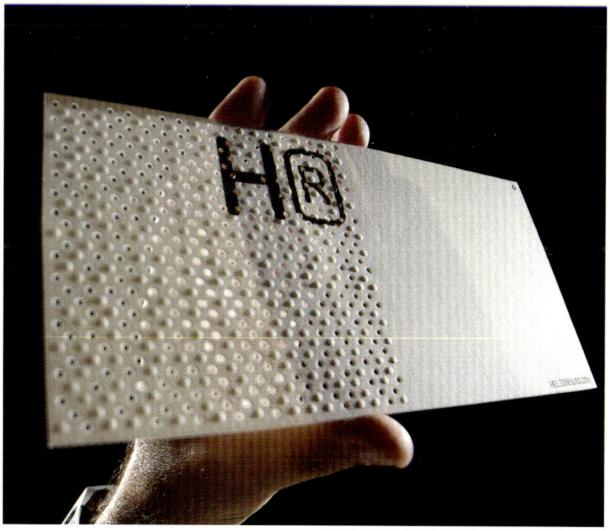
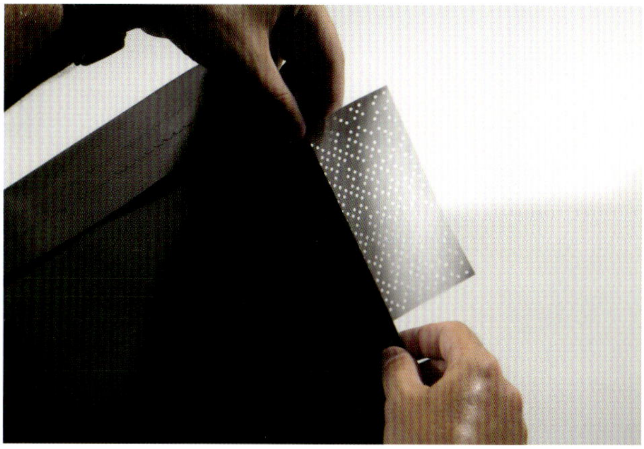
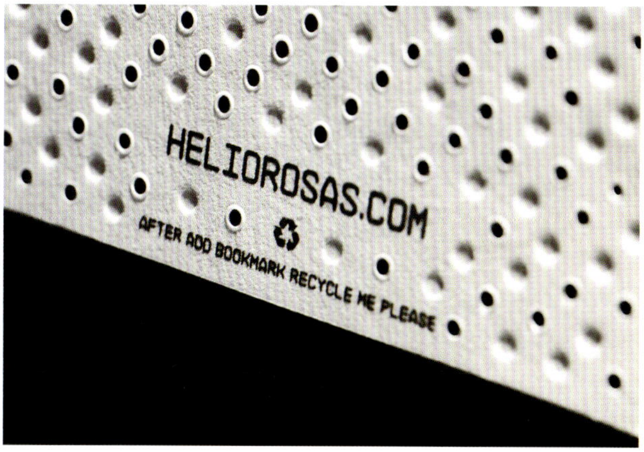
HELIOROSAS.COM
AFTER ADD BOOKMARK RECYCLE ME PLEASE
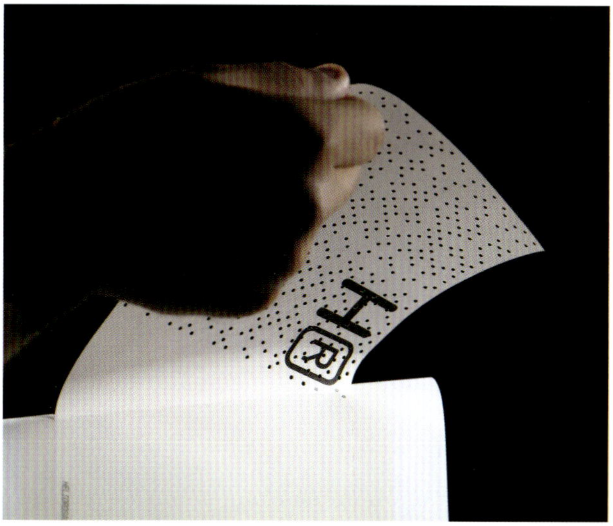
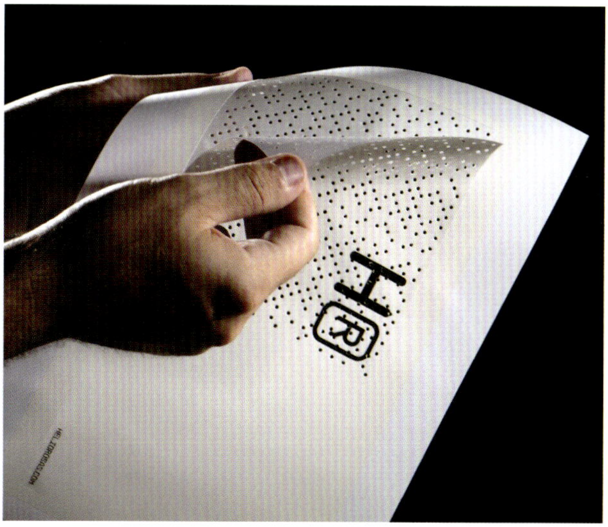

FRIENDS FOR LIFE—
THANK YOU CARD

Agency:
Seven25. Design &
Typography. Inc.
Work Type:
Invitation

Thank You Card design for
Friends For Life.

JACQUELYN POUSSOT
PHOTOGRAPHY
Designer:
J. Kenneth Rothermich
Work Type:
Identity

This business card needed to embody the creative spirit of Jacquelyn's work as a photographer while maintaining a refined look. The die-cut fits perfectly with her field of work, as well as incorporating the viewfinder graphic from her logo. By keeping the design element minimal and the typography elegant, this trick felt less like a gimmick and more like the solution that her identity had been waiting for.

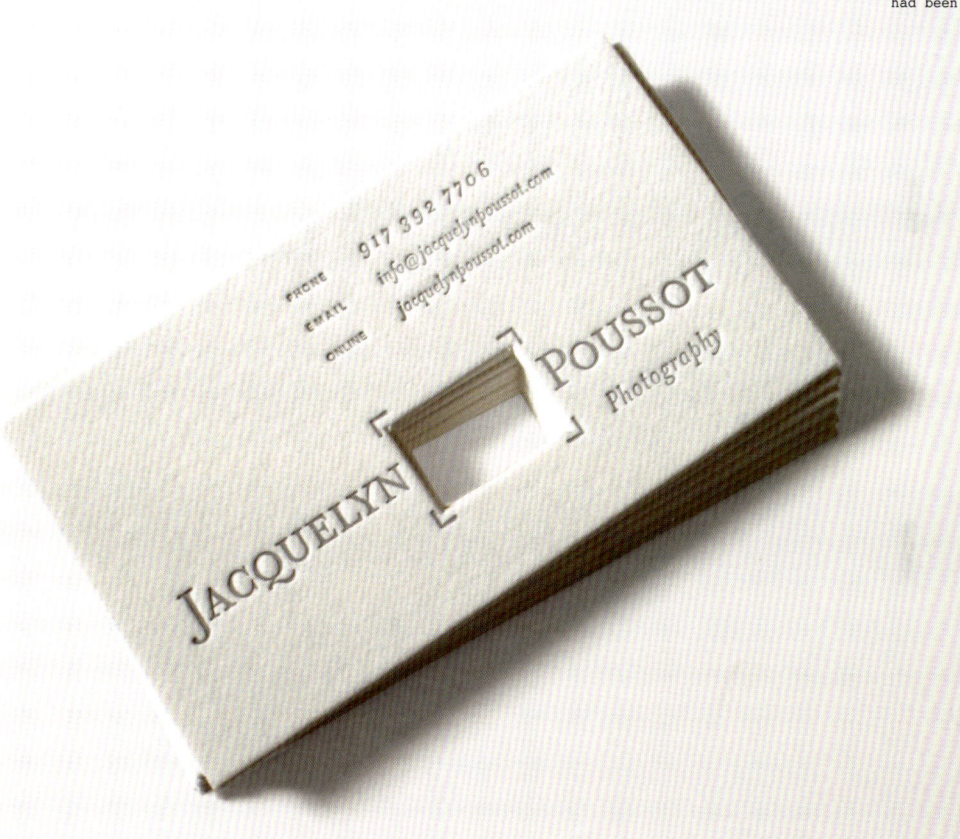

CACHAREL

Agency:
FACETOFACEDESIGN
Work Type:
Invitation

Fashion show invitation and look book for a French brand Cacharel.

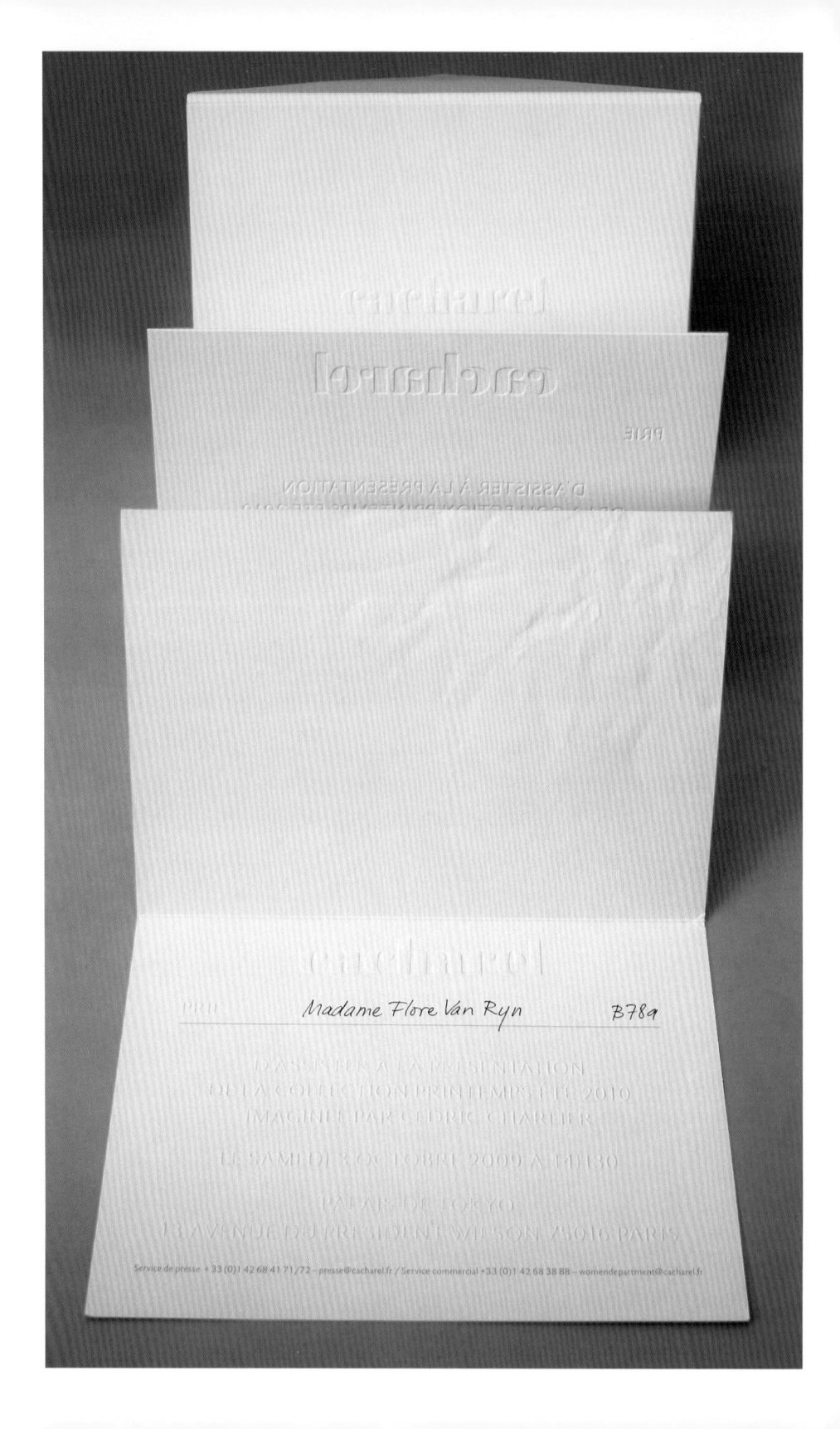

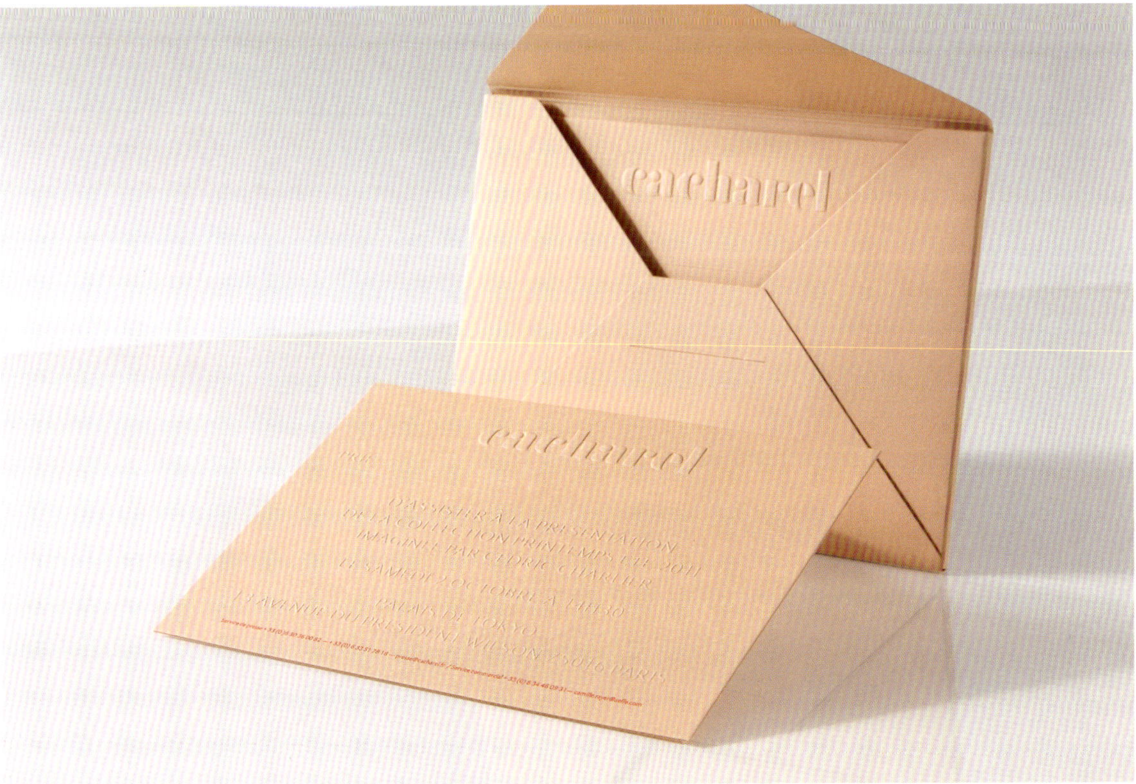
cacharel
cacharel

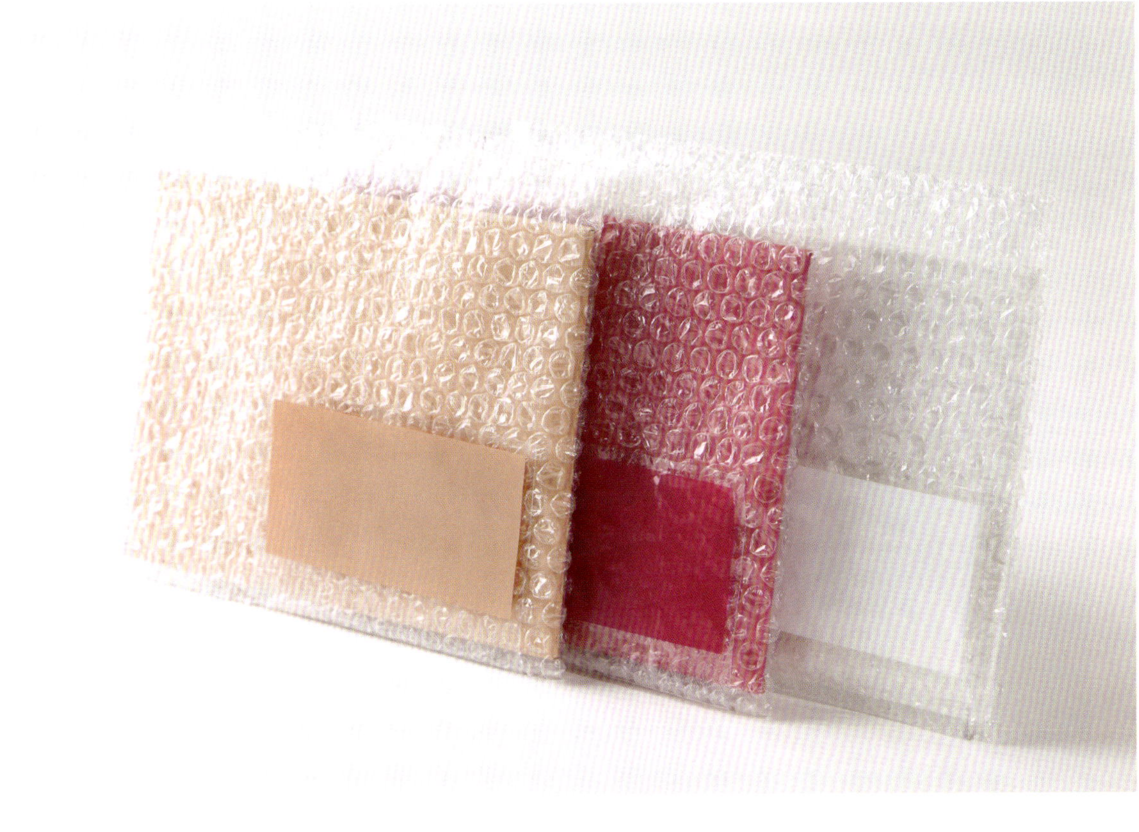

R & K WEDDING
INVITATION

Designer:
J. Kenneth Rothermich
Work Type:
Invitation

This invitation - designed for my own wedding - juxtaposes traditional (if a bit over-the-top) invitation-style flourish and script against big & bold, modernist typography right on top of each other. The production methods were kept simple to let the graphics and typography do their thing while sticking to a budget.

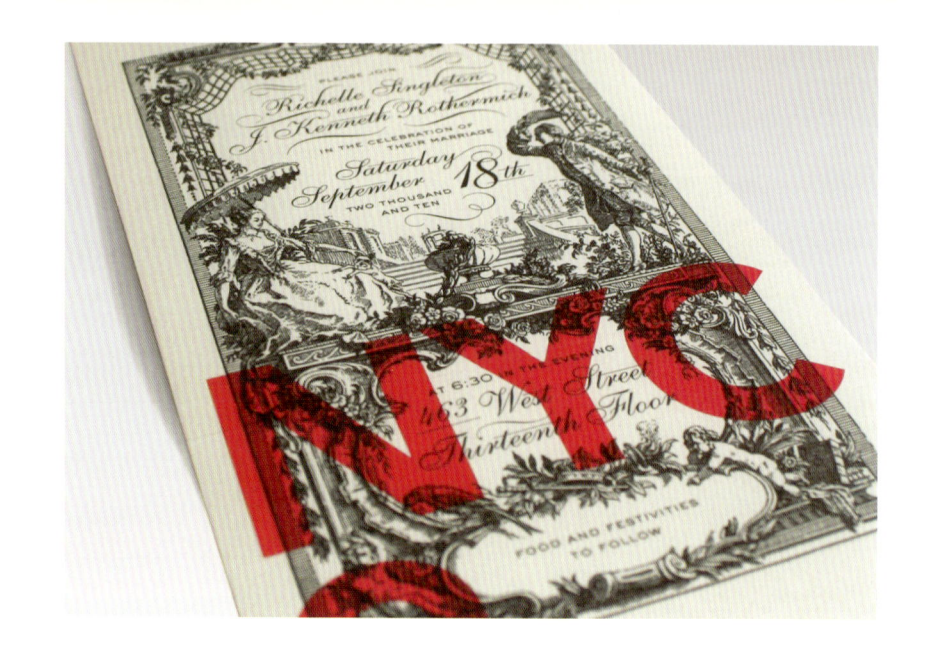

R&K
NYC
9
18
10
ATTENDING
NOT ATTENDING
R 9
& 18
K 10
R&K
AN INVITATION
433 10TH STREET, APT 1 BROOKLYN, NY 11215

LAUNCH

YOU ARE INVITED TO THE LAUNCH OF
ELENBERG FRASER A NEW ARCHITECTURAL PRACTICE
BY PROFESSOR LEON VAN SCHAIK PRO VICE CHANCELLOR
& PROFESSOR OF ARCHITECTURE, RMIT UNIVERSITY
Showroom 374 George Street Fitzroy
Friday 3 May 2002, 6pm–8pm
RSVP Monday 22 April Rulla Asmar
9417 2855 or r.asmar@e-f.com.au

ELENBERG FRASER

ELENBERG FRASER

ELENBERG FRASER
ARCHITECTURE
374 GEORGE STREET FITZROY MELBOURNE VICTORIA 3065
AUSTRALIA
TEL +61 3 9417 2855 FAX +61 3 9417 2866
MAIL@E-F.COM.AU WWW.E-F.COM.AU

ELENBERG FRASER
IDENTITY

Agency:
Fabio Ongatato Design
Work Type:
Identity

Fuelled by a desire to overturn established hierarchies and challenge aesthetic norms, Elenberg Fraser arrived on the architectural scene in 1998. In developing their new corporate identity, our main objective was to help establish the firm as a player in the architectural market. We also wanted to acknowledge the subversive element of the firm's approach to architectural solutions and in particular, to express their commitment to the transformation of form through graphic perception.

The identity subverts 'normal' design hierarchies using elements in random, unexpected ways. The fuzz pattern is the visual concrete: a two-dimensional white noise inspired by patterns that disclose information. In an unusual combination, a bold headline logotype contrasts emphatically with a softer, humanist face. A colour code system highlights the key aspects of the firm's activities: blue for facts about the firm (the team construct their models from blue foam), black for the projects, and soft grey for the abstract thought. This unconventional identity gave Elenberg Fraser a solid base from which to relaunch their business.

TXEMA YESTE WEDDING
INVITATION
Designer:
Juan Areizaga & Marti
Canillas
Work Type:
Invitation

Wedding invitation for the Spanish fashion photographer Txema Yeste. The brief was to create a simple but sophisticated invitation using an informal style and language. The envelope is used down so the backside becomes the front side and it is serigraphy printer. It contains a thick cotton paper card with black hot stamping text. The edges of the card are covered with black aniline.

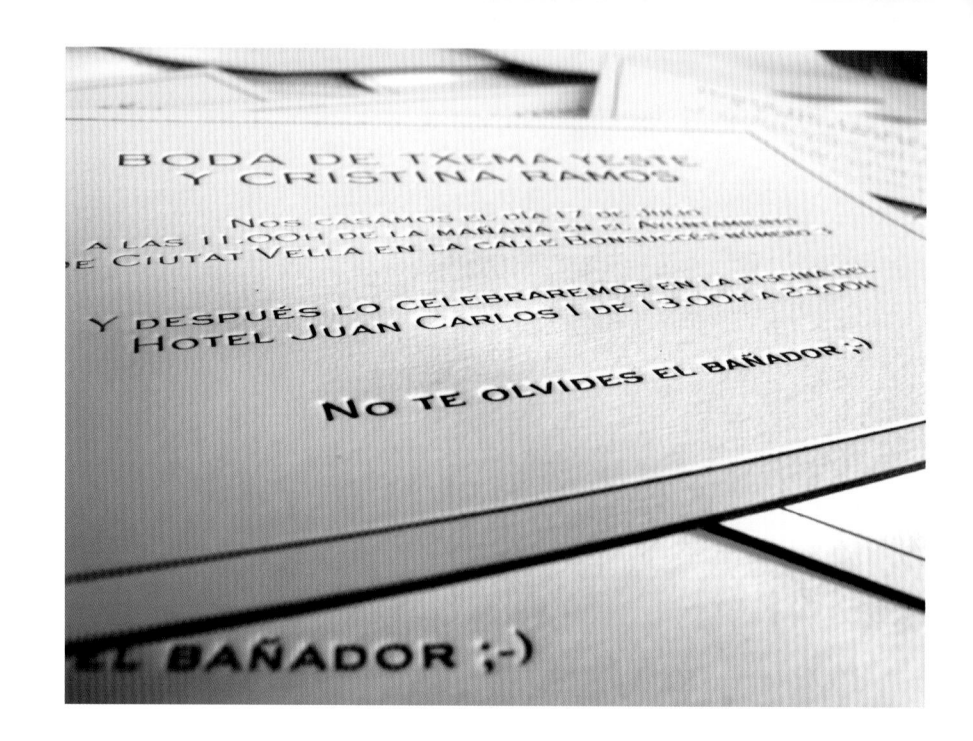

YESTE & CRISTINA
TXEMA
AMOS
17 de Julio del 2010

BODA DE TXEMA
CRISTINA
TXEMA
AMOS
ASAMOS EL DÍA 17 DE
LA MAÑANA EN EL
17 de Julio del 2010

DROP INN HOSTEL

Agency:
Bravo Company
Work Type:
Identity

Drop Inn is a budget hostel. To further emphasis this, the "O" is dropped, making it look neglected and run-down. Everything is printed on recycled gray boards. The flyer is the "O" that dropped off. If you bring the "O" back to the hostel, you get a discount reward.

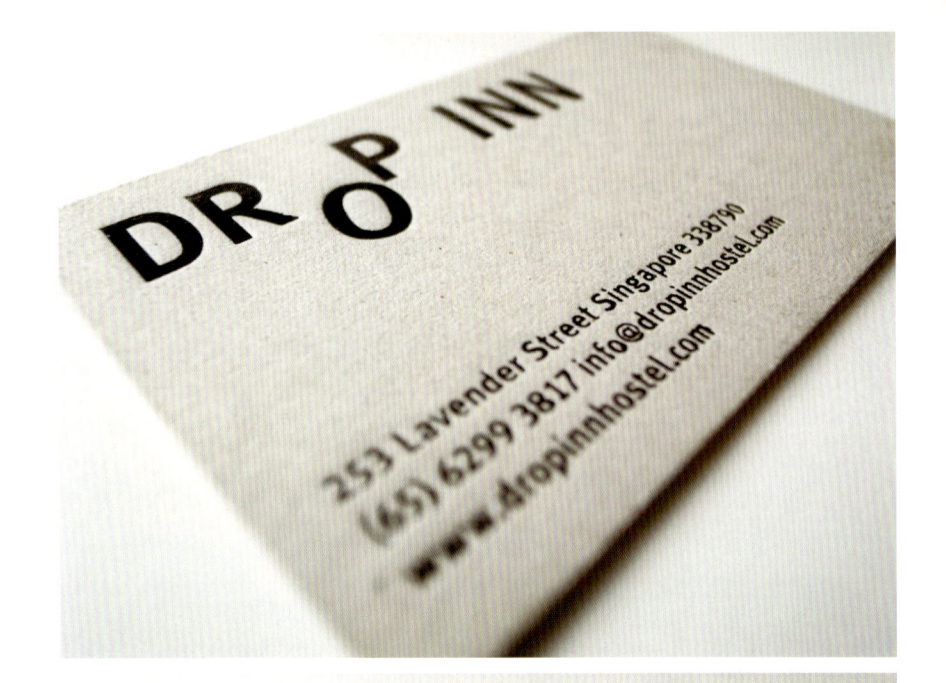

We dropped our 'O'.
Drop Inn and return it to us!*

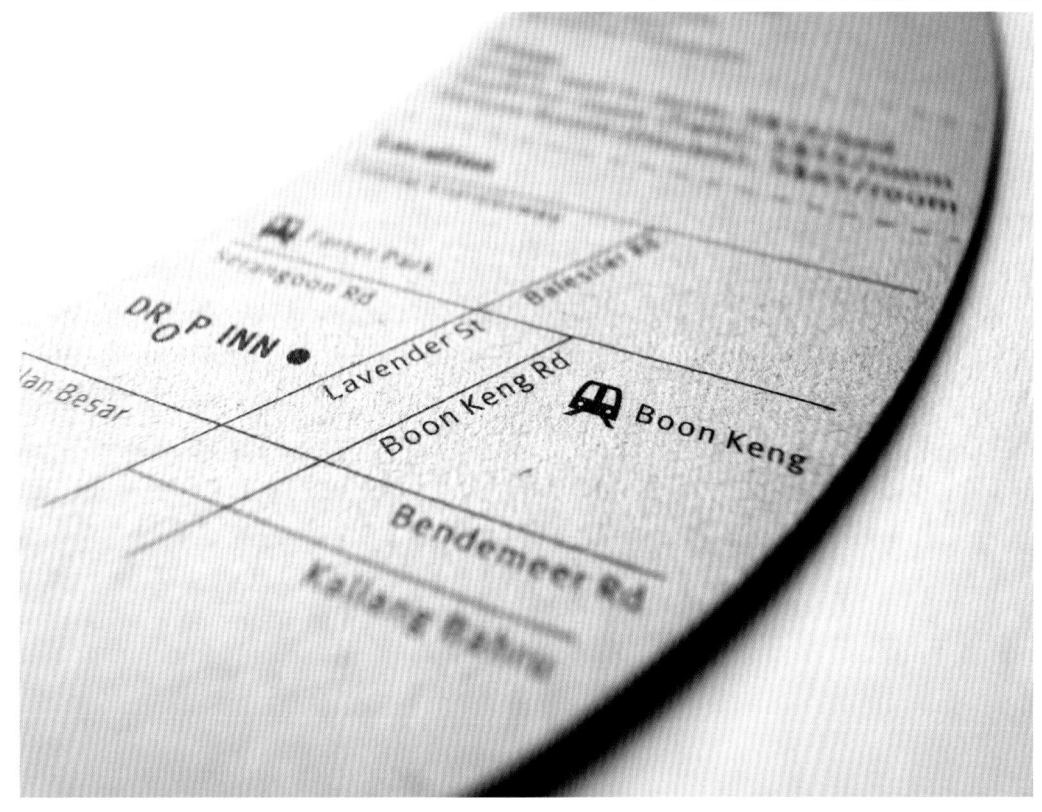

*Enjoy 5% off room rates when you drop in with this flyer.

DR O P INN

NANA

Agency:
Gardens&co.
Work Type:
Identity

Nana Chan, a self-styled epicurean, commissioned us to create an identity for her self-projects: blog, Youtube channel and tea house in Taipei (Coming soon!). From a Lawyer turned to gourmand and travel junkie, she believes the simpler things in life that matter most. We like it so much and, in fact, it is our belief too. We based on her personality and writing, a pure and quiet visual language was created to convey her message. We take "- - - - -" to portray the repeating pattern of our living and Nana shares the little surprises to our lives "- n - a - n - a -". We adapted this system throughout all projects and applications. All photos were taken by Nana.

-n-a-n-a-

NANA

Agency:
Gardens&co.
Work Type:
Identity

Nana Chan, a self-styled epicurean, commissioned us to create an identity for her self-projects: blog, Youtube channel and tea house in Taipei (Coming soon!). From a Lawyer turned to gourmand and travel junkie, she believes the simpler things in life that matter most. We like it so much and, in fact, it is our belief too. We based on her personality and writing, a pure and quiet visual language was created to convey her message. We take "- - - - -" to portray the repeating pattern of our living and Nana shares the little surprises to our lives "- n - a - n - a -". We adapted this system throughout all projects and applications. All photos were taken by Nana.

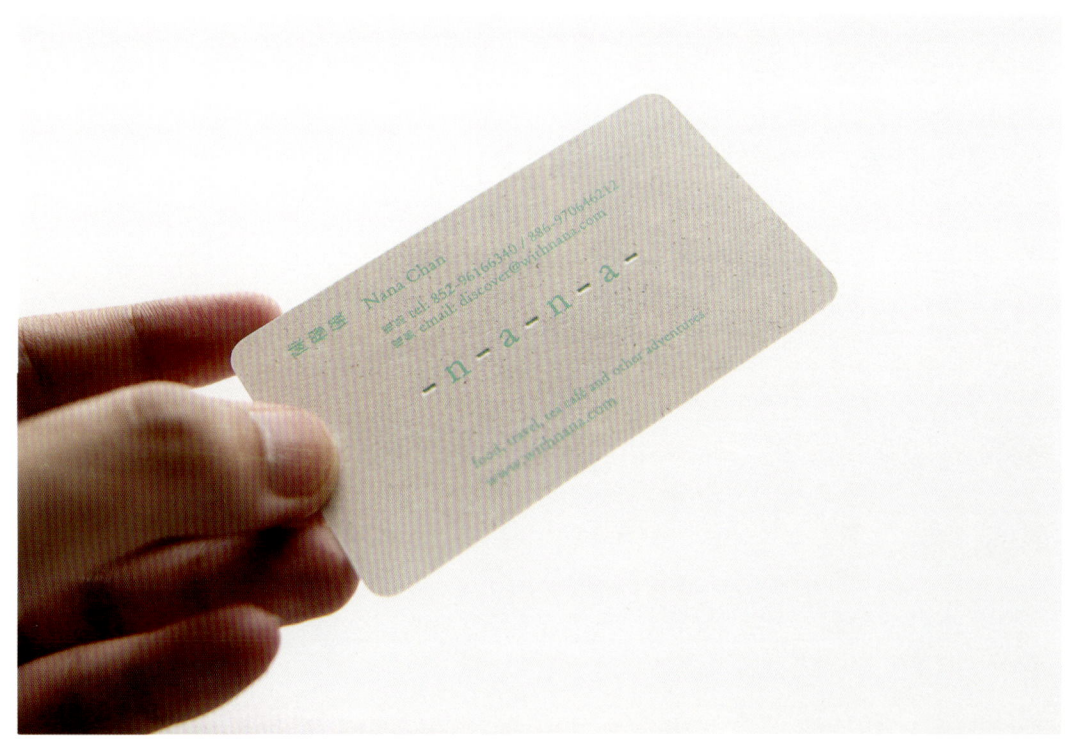

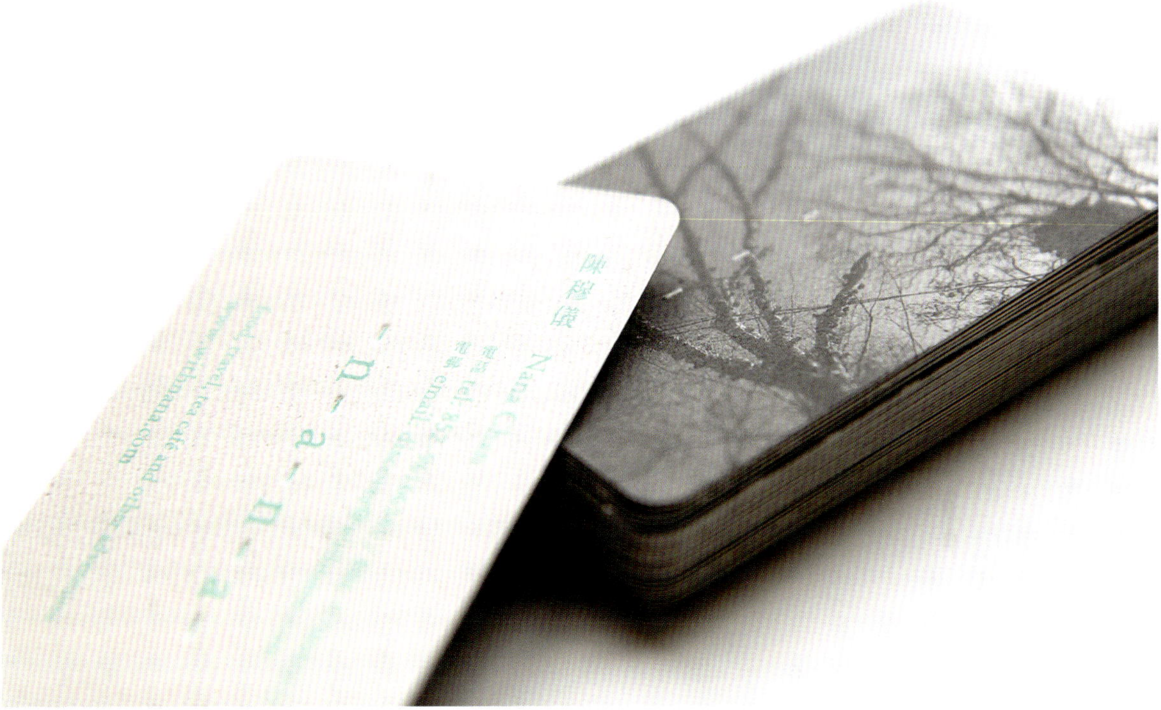

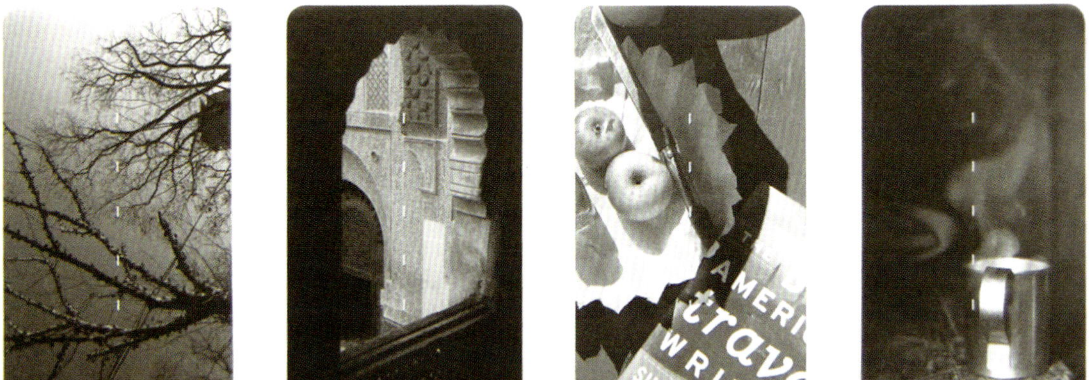

THE BALLET SCHOOL

Agency:
A Beautiful Design
Work Type:
Identity

Namecard design that reflect the nature of ballet teaching.

A ballet teacher is like a puppet master, teaching dancers the precision of the dance movements and how to control every single muscles in the body.

The Ballet School

West Coast Plaza
154 West Coast Road #01-74
Singapore 127371
Tel. & Fax. 6779 3833
enquiries@theballetschool.com.sg
www.theballetschool.com.sg

LAUNCH INVITATION

Agency:
Nomina Design
Work Type:
Invitation

The kimono in the hanger is actually an invitation. It was created by Nomina's team of professionals for the opening of Legas Design's showroom. Made using origami techniques, it's got one more special feature: the little hangers in which each kimono hung were manufactured by Legas Design - a company that provides store equipment - itself! Each hanger is made of paint-coated wire and the invitation uses paper with a hammered finish.

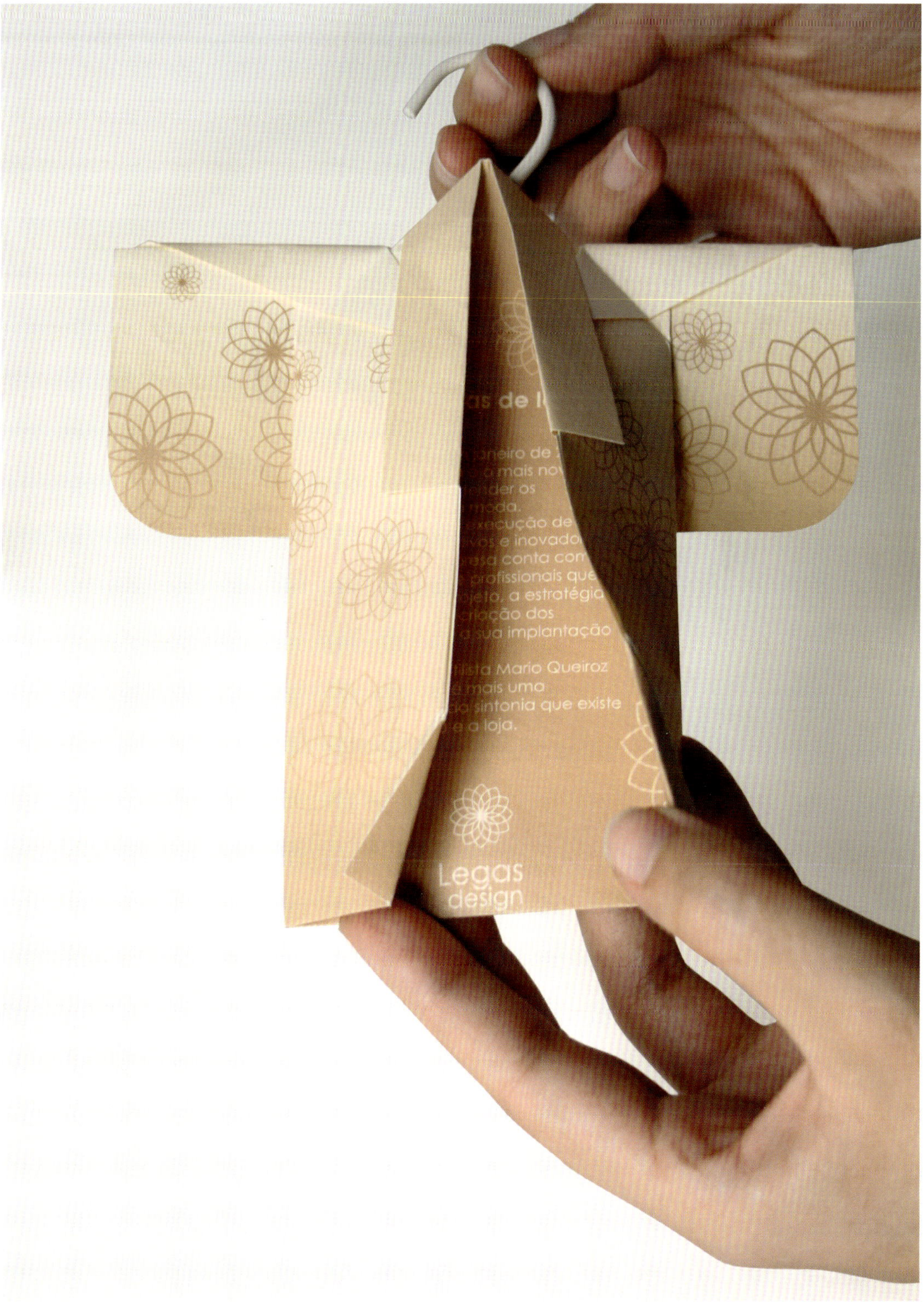
Legas
design

TERUHIRO YANAGIHARA
Agency:
desegno ltd.
Designer:
Haruhiko Taniuchi
Work Type:
Promotion

Portfolio for Interior
Designer Teruhiro
Yanagihara.

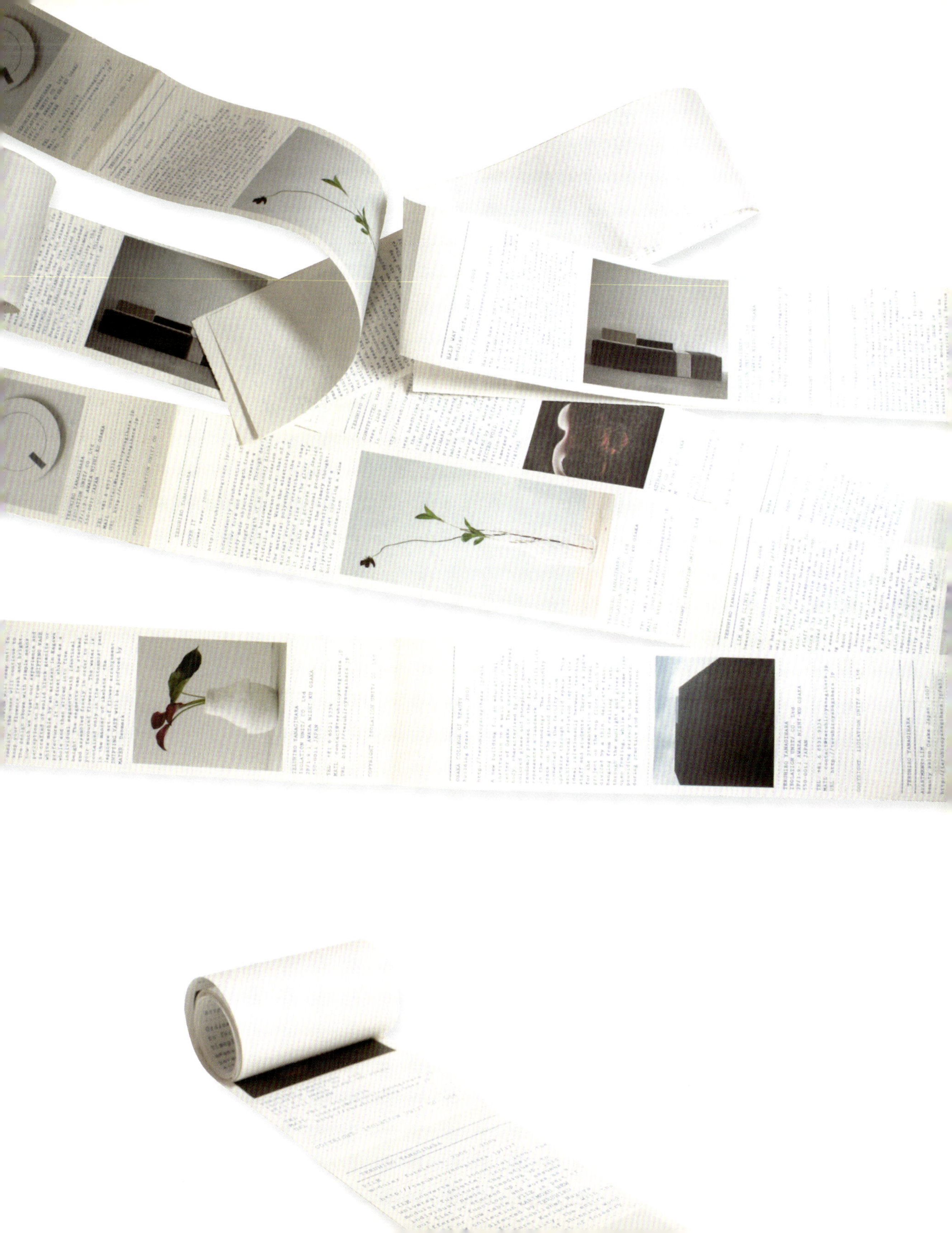

TWIST TO READ

Agency:
Leo Burnett Dubai
Designer:
Kapil Bhimekar
Work Type:
Identity

Number of yoga centers in Beirut were growing rapidly. Danielle Abisaab, a yoga instructor for over 10 years needed to reposition herself.

Most Yoga postures/exercises involve twisting of the body. We adapted this observation on to our business card design. We started by choosing a non-tearable and flexible paper to print our visiting card on. The messaging was then divided into two equal parts. With one half printed on the front and the other half on the back. To read the entire message the user would have to twist the visiting card. Folding lines were printed on both sides of the card to guide the user while twisting the visiting card.

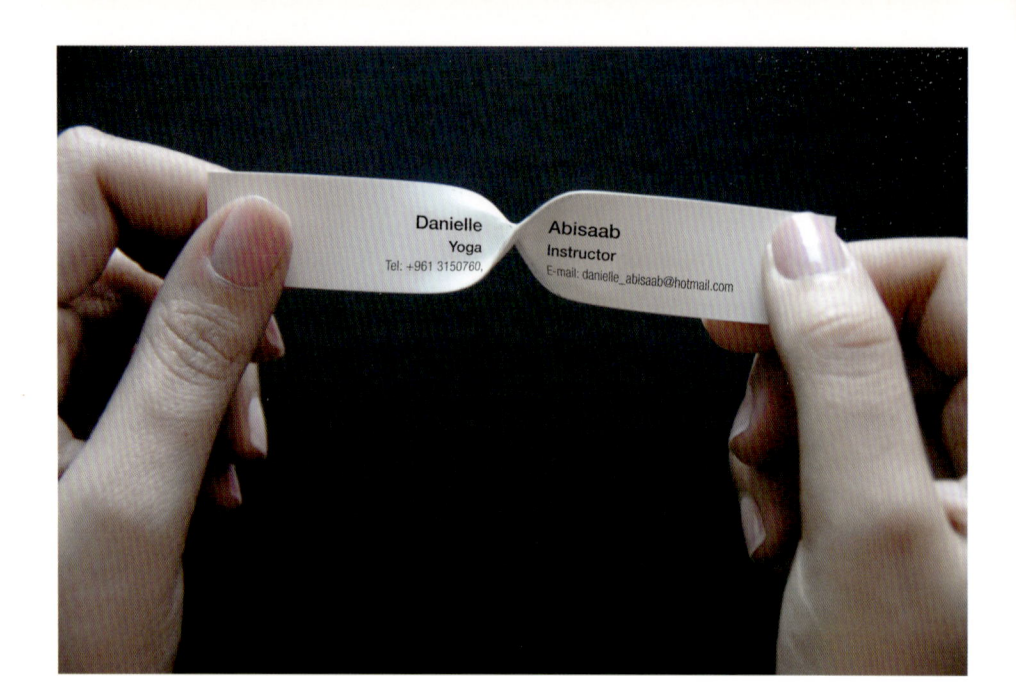

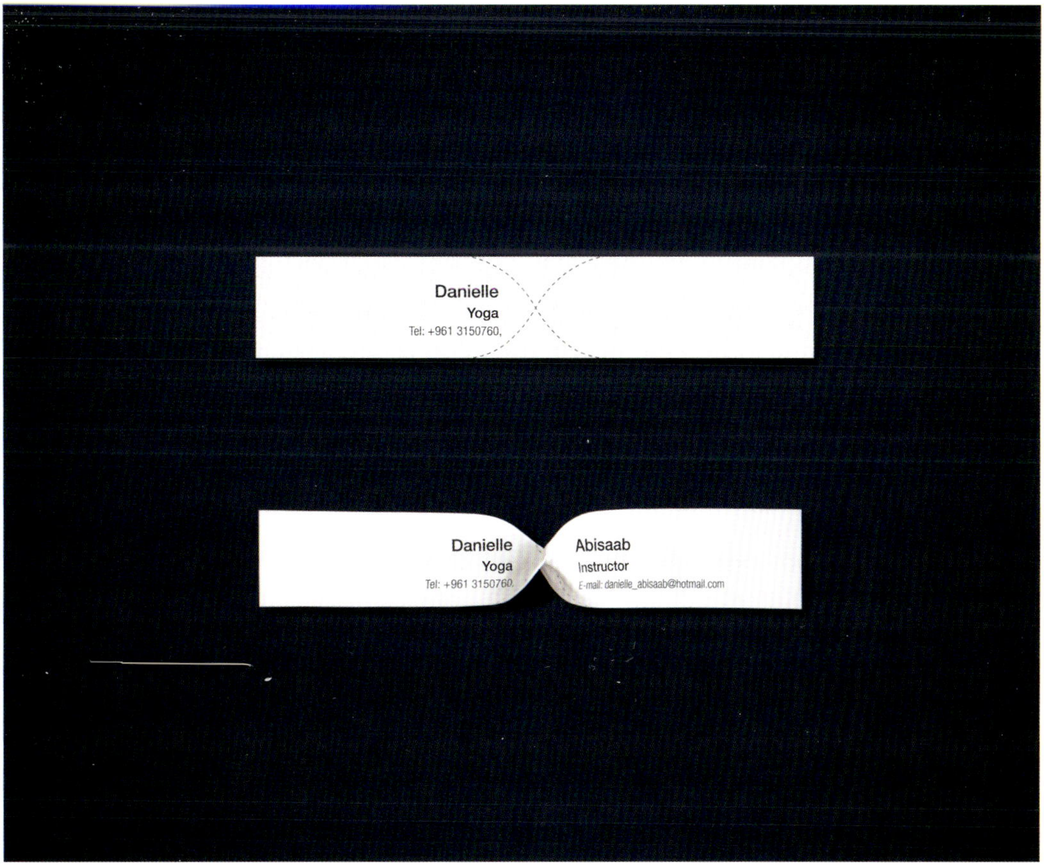
Danielle
Yoga
Tel: +961 3150760,
Danielle
Yoga
Tel: +961 3150760,
Abisaab
Instructor
E-mail: danielle_abisaab@hotmail.com

Danielle
Yoga
Tel: +961 3150760,

LOSE YOUR BELLY

Agency:
Leo Burnett Dubai
Designer:
Kapil Bhimekar
Work Type:
Identity

To design a business card for fitness trainer Zohra Mouhetta that complements the effectiveness of her personal training programmes and makes for a memorable hand out to prospective clients.

To stand out from all the leave-behinds people receive every day, we designed a unique, foldable business card that invites the recipient to interact with it and clearly demonstrates what personal fitness training can do for the body.

Though exact response rates were not available at the time of this submission, the number of inquiries and sign-ups, including corporate clients, increased substantially within a month.

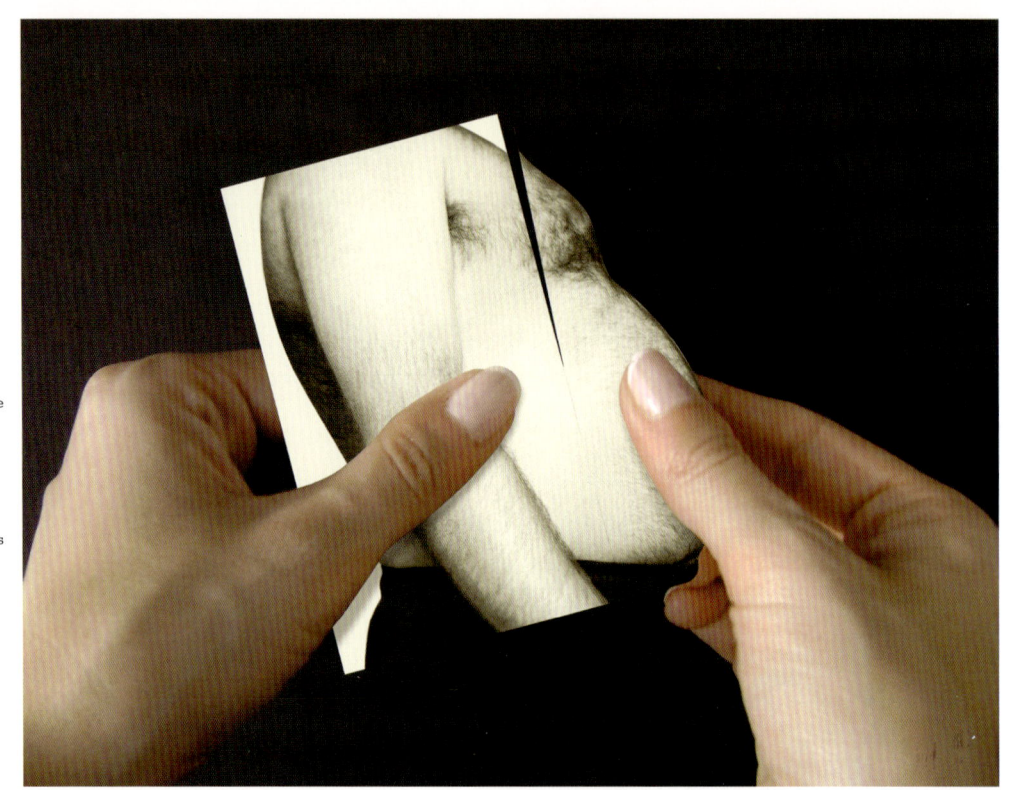

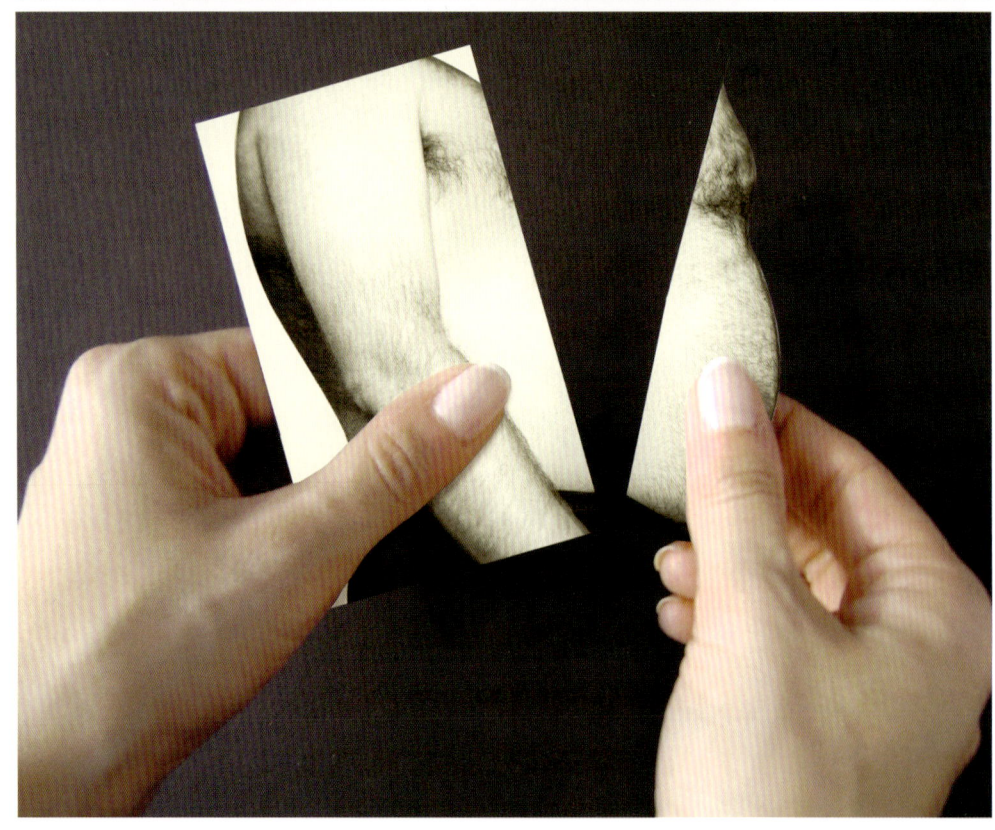

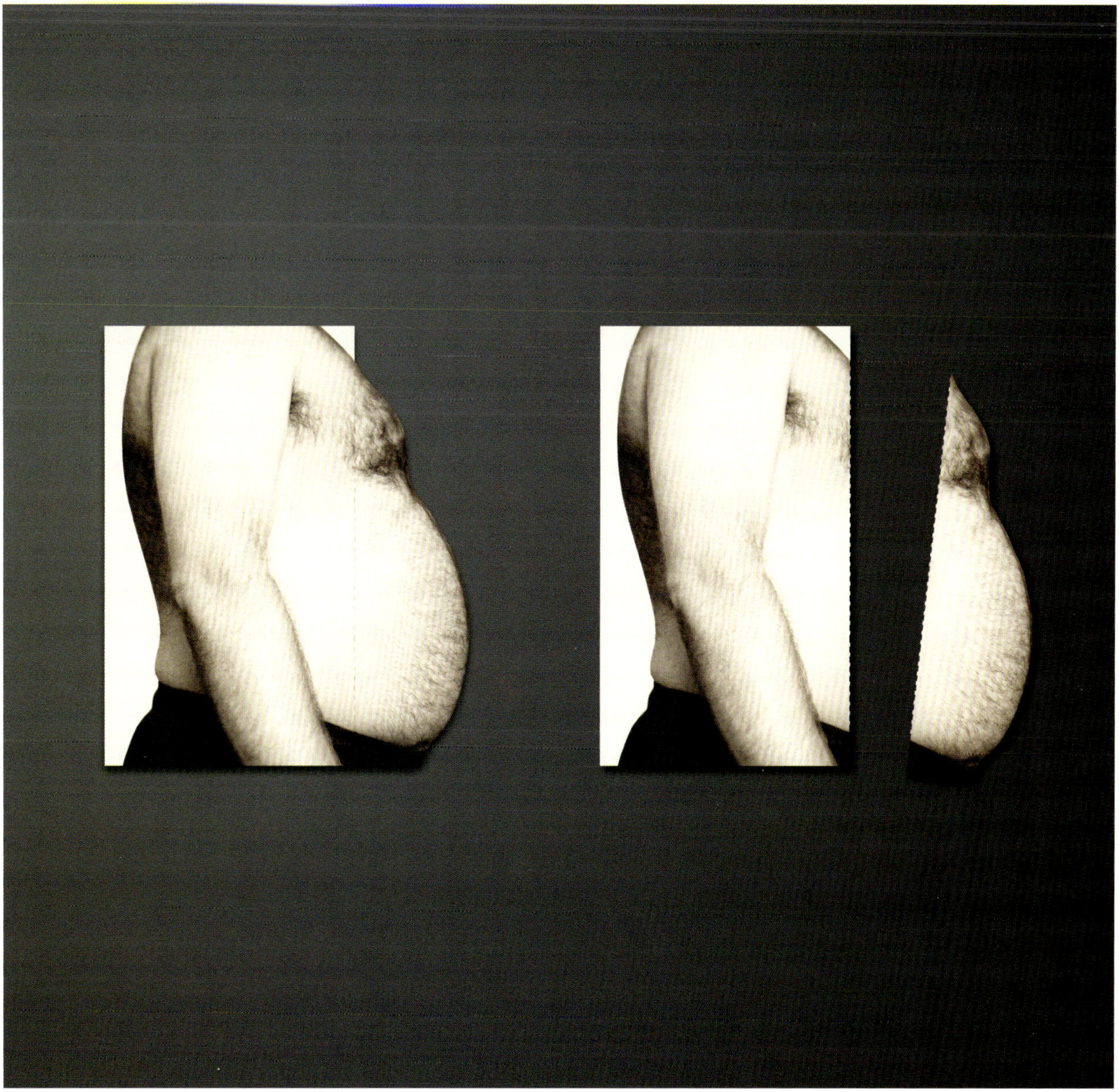

TECHNO STATT ERSTER
AUGUST

Designer:
Dominic Rechsteiner
Work Type:
Promotion

The "Restaurant Schwarzer Engel" is a cooperative which was founded 25 years ago. Besides food and drinks, the customer can enjoy concerts and cultural happenings. Concept: design of a flyer, which shows the antithesis between a quiet place and a techno event. Analog photography emphasizes the naturalness of the image. The typographic design is reduced and decent.

CORPORATION POP CARDS

Agency:
Corporation Pop
Work Type:
Identity

Our business cards are screen printed on to 12mm thick recycled plastic. The plastic is made from confiscated illicit CDs which have been crushed and then dispersed in a pale blue transparent polycarbonate recycled from blue, cold water drinks containers. The cards were cut to size, with radius corners, using a high velocity water jet. The two references to water are deliberate as our name, Corporation Pop, is colloquial English for tap water!

LASER CARD

Designer:
Tim Wan
Work Type:
Identity

Laser cut on fluorescent acrylic self promotional business cards. Limited edition of 50 were made and were given out to visiting professionals or during studio visits whilst I was still a student. The concept was to produce a limited run of high impact business cards that would be a talking point whilst leaving a memorable piece of design for the professionals to keep and remember be by.

NIKE TRAIN TO BE
STRONG

Agency:
Exposure
Work Type:
Invitation

Invites designed and
produced for Nike Women
Train To Be Strong Media
presentations in Miami and
Los Angeles.

BICA DO SAPATO
2009/2010 & 2010/2011

Agency:
Alva
Work Type:
Promotion

Bica do Sapato is located at the Lisbon docks -- serves contemporary twists on Portuguese classics food.

The retro-modern space is well suited to the forward-thinking food.

Every new year, Bica do Sapato celebrates the New Year with a party. These are the menus for the 2009/2010 and 2010/2011 dinners and parties.

The choice for 2009/2010 is abstract graphic forms, mixed with some oil painting and fast motion horse photography.

In 2010/2011 party, we went with the classics. 3 menus are layered classic paintings mixed with some other rich visual elements.

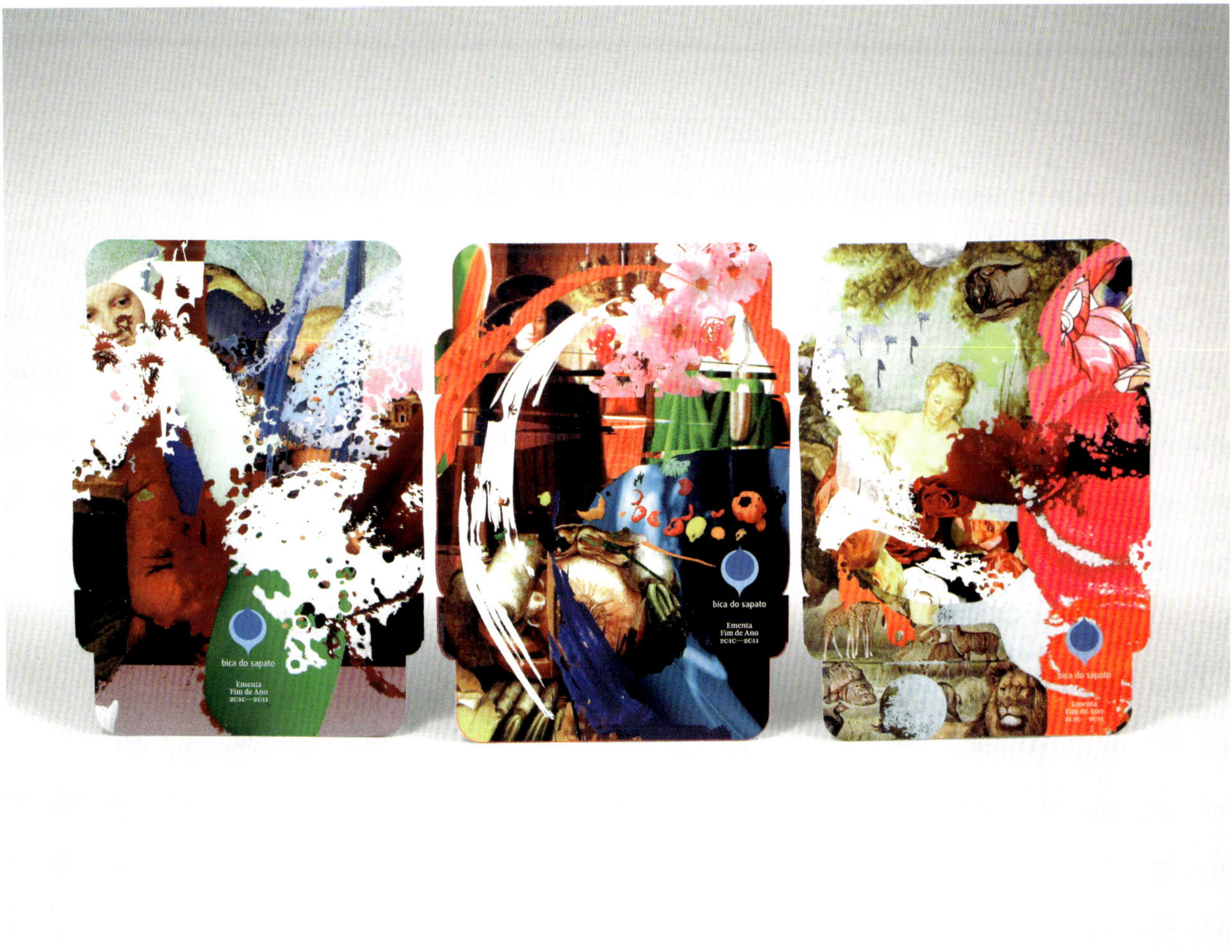

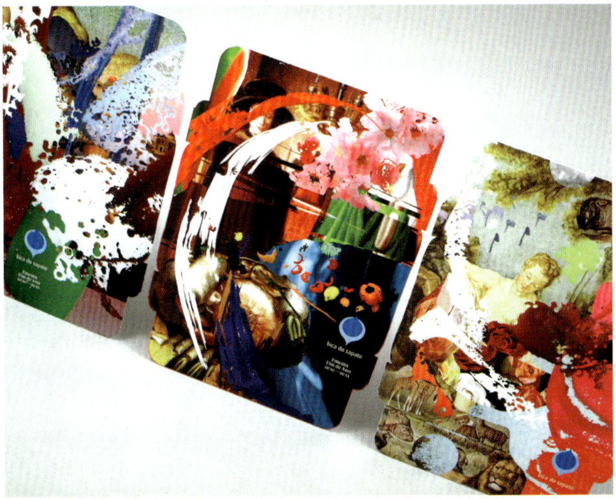

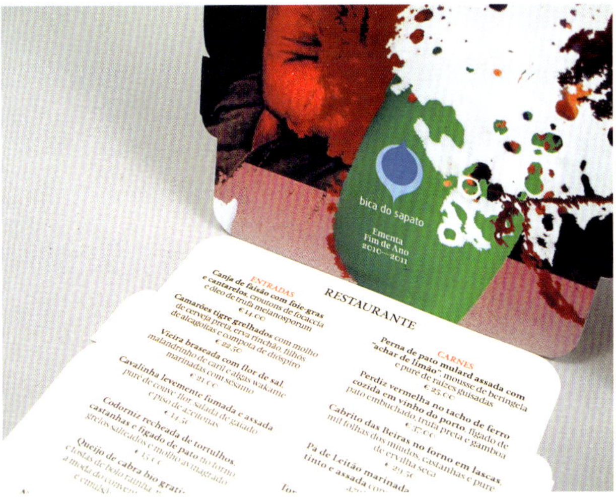

DECHIRE
Agency:
MURMURE
Work Type:
Identity

This set of cards is inspired by the new realism. It's realised from torn posters carefully framed, offering a natural and original design, on the back of which we put a stamp with the information.

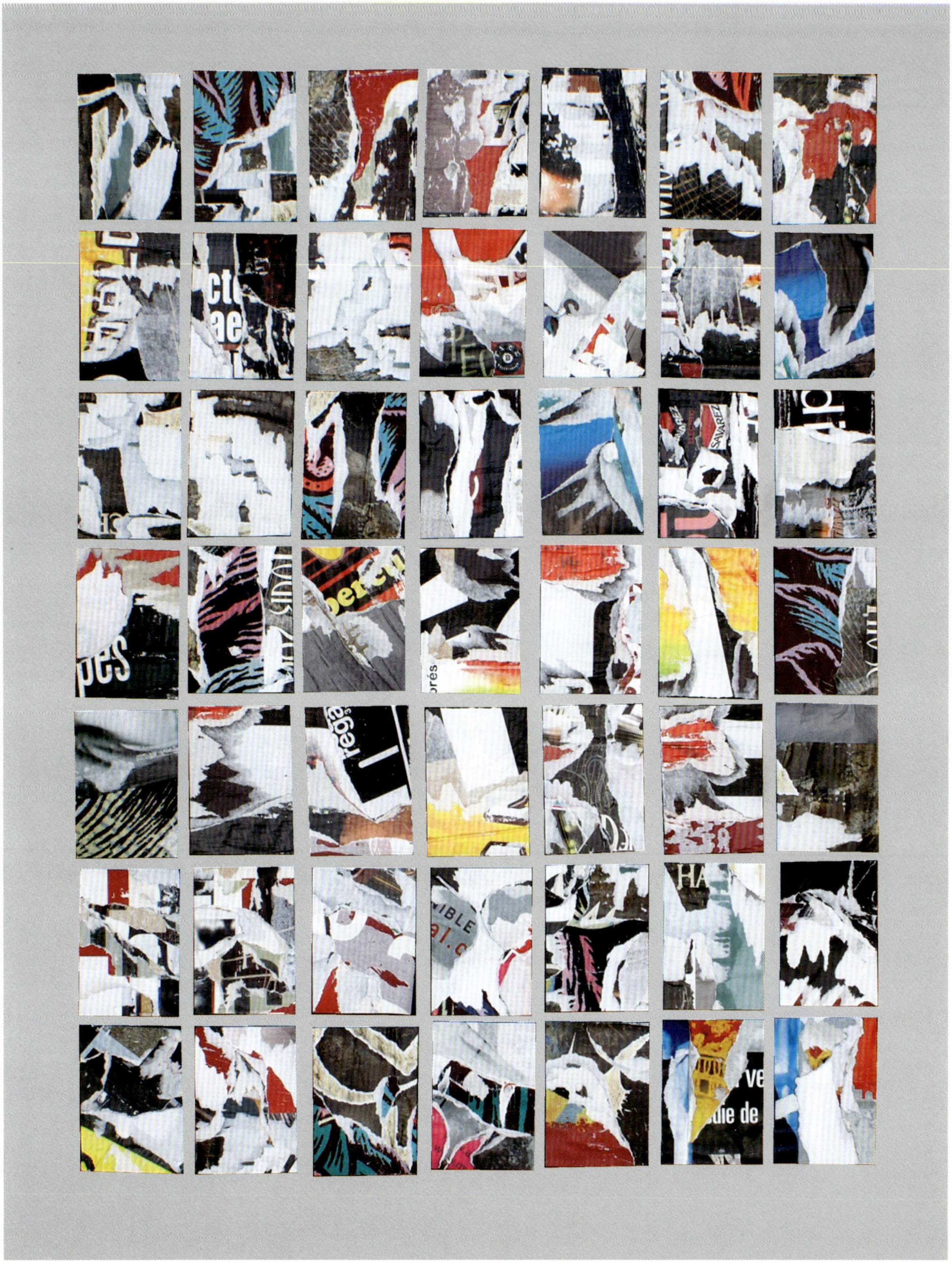

Á ESPERA DE GORETE

Designer:
Paulo Lopes
Work Type:
Promotion

"Á Espera de Gorete" is a Theatre Play, about the actual social situation in Portugal, composed by a series of absurd and hilarious sketches, with the purpose of instilling a very serious sense of vindication.

To fit this aesthetics of the absurd, the graphics were designed as colorful and kitsch as the Play. The promotional materials included several poster formats, and the postcard distributed everywhere in the city of Lisbon.

CLUB DF

Designer:
Mathias Martin & Agustin Zea
Work Type:
Identity

For the new club Club DF, we choose to take one of the painting located in the club, and decline it as a logo.

We choose the circle shape to remember a seal, in order to give an idea of exclusivity and privacy to the place. All the stationery uses a different painting. Also, we used the golden color to epitomize luxury and exclusivity of Club DF. The logo is inspired from a painted portrait located in the club.

RE-BRAND: THE
RESEARCH AGENCY

Designer:
Ant Gatt
Work Type:
Identity

Re-brand for The Research Agency a leading boutique market research company based in New Zealand. The identity combined a reductive colour and typographic palette with a distinctive black and white line drawn illustrations. The illustrations depict scenes of everyday life with brand messages incorporated in the form of typographic signs. The immense level of detail in the illustrations enabled flexibility. This can be seen in the business cards. A myriad of close up details from the larger illustrations where used on the back of the cards - enabling each staff member to have their own unique set.

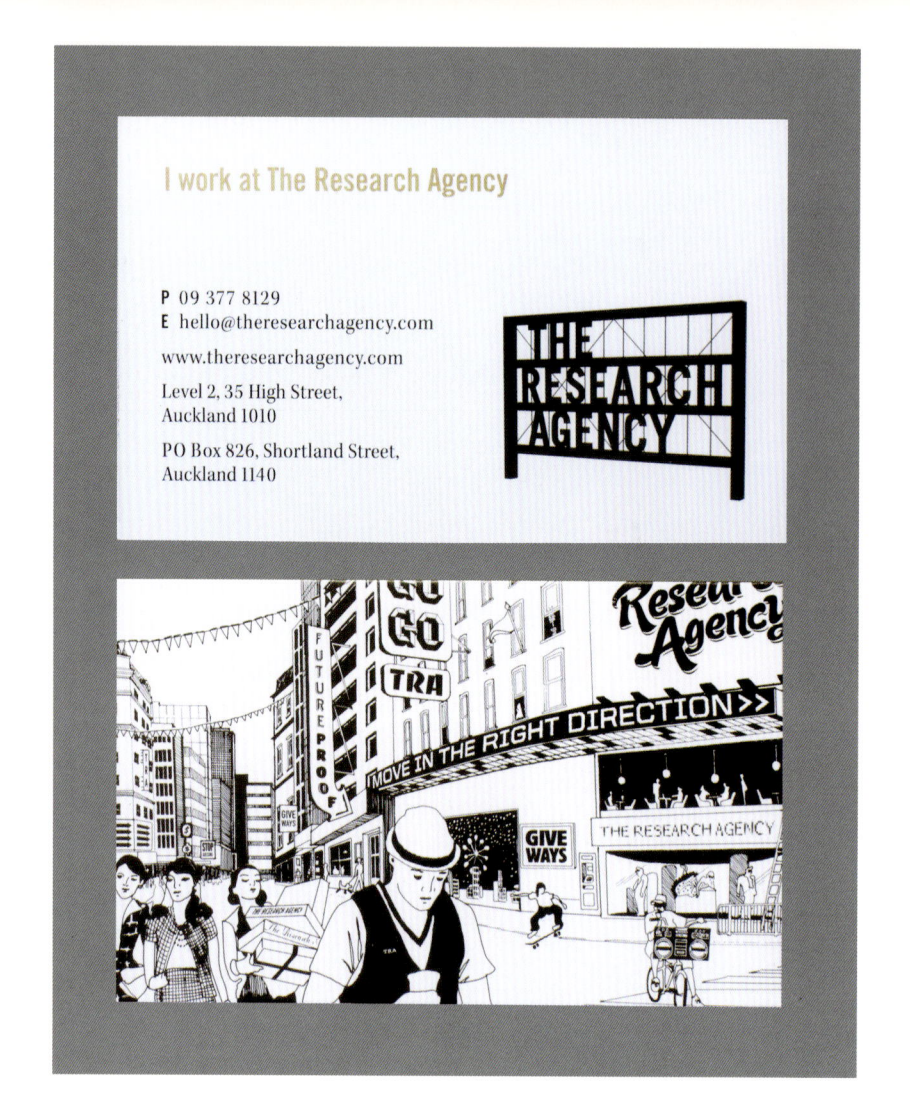

Amber Coulter
Partner
P 09 377 8129
M 021 588 326
E amber@theresearchagency.com
www.theresearchagency.com
Level 2, 35 High Street,
Auckland 1010
PO Box 826, Shortland Street,
Auckland 1140
THE RESEARCH AGENCY
DIRECTION TO GROW
THE RESEARCH AGENCY
STOP GUESSING
GROWTH
This Way
MOVE IN THE RIGHT DIRECTION
GIVE WAYS
GO 4WD

The Research Agency
GO GO GO
TRA
MOVE IN THE RIGHT DIRECTION>>
THE RESEARCH AGENCY
MOVE IN THE RIGHT DIREC
GIVE WAYS
THE RESEARCH AGENCY
GROW
THE RESEARCH AGENCY
STOP GUESSING
GO 4WD
GROW
DIRECTION TO GROW
THE RESEARCH AGENCY

MATIAS FIORI PERSONAL
CARDS

Designer:
Matias Fiori
Work Type:
Identity

My personal cards for 2011 season; simple and rustic, CMYK, 250g white paper, both sides. There are a lot of doodles, basic information, and my logo.

pica!
¡fuck off!
PAPA-RA-PA-PA-PA!

ma-
tías
fiori.
Diseñador Gráfico
099 376 670
www.matiasfiori.com
hola@matiasfiori.com

SELF PROMOTION

Designer:
Alberto Hernandez
Work Type:
Identity

Self promotion is an important tool at postgraduate shows. For this particular occasion I designed some special business cards. These could be unfolded allowing people to see the poster and to tear this apart along the perforated lines in order to separate the little cards with the contact details.

——hi there,
I'm *Alberto Hernández*. I'm a Spanish *graphic designer* based in London. I've just finished my MA Graphic Design at LCC and I'm currently looking for a work placement.

If you are interested in my work, please, feel free to contact me on *075 1656 1613* or email me at *alberto@hereigo.co.uk*. To see more of my stuff, visit *www.hereigo.co.uk*

Thank you so much!

SIMON BEATTIE
STATIONERY

Agency:
Purpose
Work Type:
Identity

Simon Beattie is an Antiquarian bookseller, specialising in European language and culture.

Purpose recently created a suite of catalogues to showcase his rare and interesting collections.

The new stationery set draws upon the rich array of eclectic typefaces and colour in Beattie's books and catalogues. All his correspondence becomes framed with a variety of decorative quotation marks and provides a contrast to the more ordered address details.

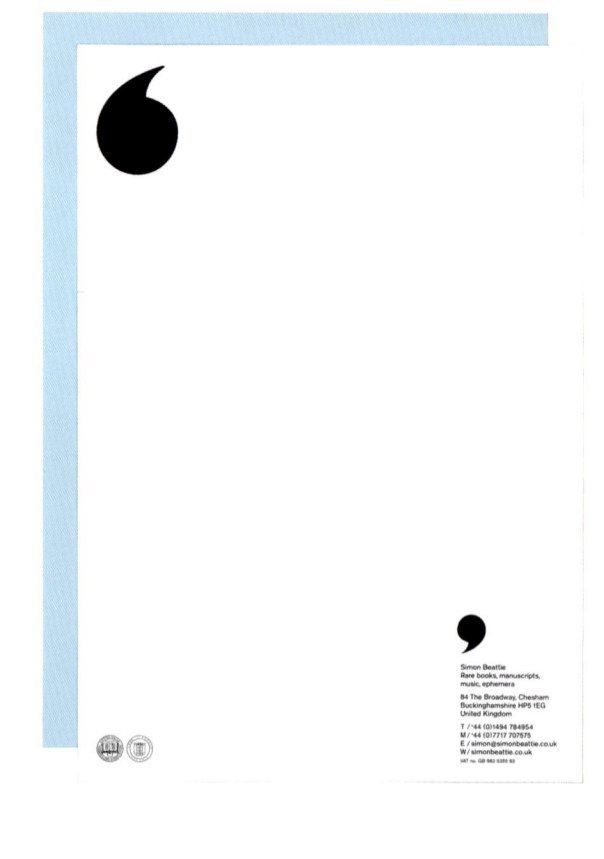

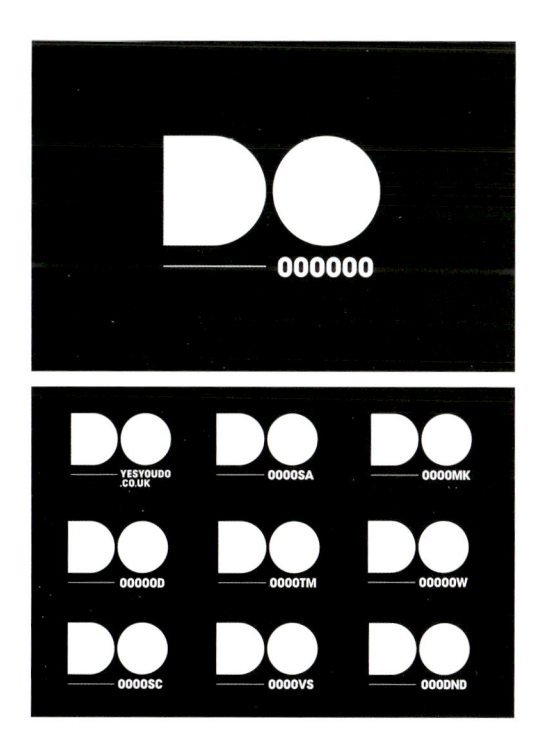

DO

Agency:
Red Design
Work Type:
Identity

Logo and identity for
UK based club promotion
company "Do". The
identity was applied over
stationery, a website,
posters and event.

BIZARRE

Agency:
Quinta-feira
Work Type:
Identity

Bizarre is a content and events production company from São Paulo.

The company takes part in different kinds of events, sometimes curating exhibitions, organizing lectures, setting music shows, etc. The visual identity is based on the schematic representation of these different activities by a group of abstract geometric forms. On the back of the card, the forms change their position to shape the company name.

KONTEXT ARCHITEKTUR
Designer:
Alexander Lis
Work Type:
Identity

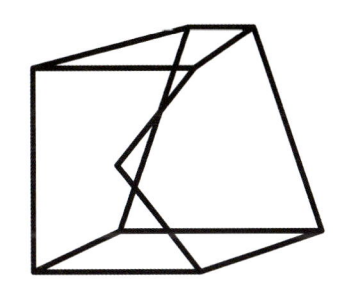

Corporate Design: three
dimensional buildable logo
and website concept for
Kontext Architektur in
Frankfurt (Main).

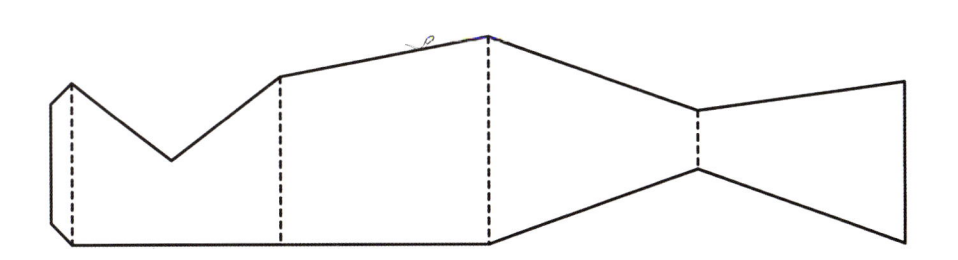

VALLILA INTERIOR

Agency:
Kokoro & Moi
Work Type:
Identity

Graphic identity for
Vallila Interior.

VALLILA
www.vallilainterior.fi
VALLILA
www.vallilainterior.fi
VALLILA
Deco House
VALLILA
Deco House
VALLILA
Deco House
VALLILA
Syksy
10
Hinnasto
VALLILA

DAY & NIGHT

Agency:
Kanella
Work Type:
Promotion

An object that captures the day's sun and at night reveals a cluster of starts that glow in the dark. May this ray of light mesmerize your senses and brighten up your world!

Day and night

An object that captures the day's sun
and at night reveals a cluster of stars
that glow in the dark.

May this ray of light mesmerize
your senses and brighten up your world.

END OF YEAR CARD

Agency:
Famous Visual Services
Work Type:
Greeting Card

This was a piece we made to wish our clients well for the new year. Balsa wood was screen printed with green phosphorus ink to reveal the message `C U IN 09' which becomes clear as night falls and the ink glows in the dark.

DAHL

Designer:
Bas Koopmans
Work Type:
Greeting Card

The Birth card for Dahl is printed on a real wooden plank of 3mm thick. A tree as symbol for growth and strength is the base of the card.

MVM

Designer:
Josep Román
Work Type:
Identity

Corporate identity for an engineer and industrial designer from Barcelona, who works between the two fields. The idea was to find a language that worked simultaneously for both of them, creating two different logotypes from one shape, showing the volume and technical view of the characters MVM. The plug is an easy way to produce all the stationery, and it allows to use various materials as support for the business cards, reflecting the variety of materials of an industrial designer.

INGENIERO &
DISEÑADOR INDUSTRIAL
VICENSME@GMAIL.COM
MVICENS.COM
TEL 622013382

BALTIC YOSHITOMO NARA

Agency:
Founded
Work Type:
Invitation

Various print and branding work for Baltic Centre for contemporary art.

YOSHITOMO
NARA+GRAF
A-Z Project

YOSHITOMO
NARA+GRAF
We are pleased to invite you to the preview event to celebrate the opening of BALTIC's new summer exhibition.
Wednesday 11 June 2008
BALTIC
Duvel
We are pleased to invite you to the VIP Laurent-Perrier Champagne reception to celebrate the opening of BALTIC's new summer exhibition.

1990–2010 TWENTY
YEARS OF FOURTH

Agency:
North
Work Type:
Promotion

From its inception in 1990, Fourth Floor has been a hairdressing studio that has done things differently. It's based in Clerkenwell, an area of London then considered somewhat outre, atop a 1930s industrial building; access is via a vintage goods lift.

To celebrate Fourth Floor's twentieth anniversary, owner Richard Stepney has collaborated with the design agency North to produce a 154-page limited edition cloth-bound book that encapsulates the Fourth Floor aesthetic. Curator and writer Andrew Renton analyses just what it is that makes Fourth Floor so different, so appealing; fellow clients Jon Snow and Nigel Slater provide, respectively, a psychogeographic guide to London WC1 (Fourth Floor's locale), and a selection of recipes based on the ingredients in the Fourth Floor product line. Photo essays document the creation of Fourth Floor's twentieth anniversary flag, designed by bespoke tailor Timothy Everest, and the Italian factories and cities where Fourth Floor's meticulously-crafted shampoos and conditioners were researched and developed. Like Fourth Floor itself, the book combines utilitarian clarity with scrupulous attention to detail to create something unique and highly covetable.

PLEASE KEEP OFF
THE GRASS
BEWARE OF THE DOG
TRESPASSERS WILL
BE PROSECUTED
POLITE NOTICE

NEW YEAR CARD 2010
Agency:
smbetsmb
Designer:
Keita Shimbo & Misaco
Shimbo
Work Type:
Greeting Card

New Year Card 2010 designed
with the motif of Japanese
traditional New Year.

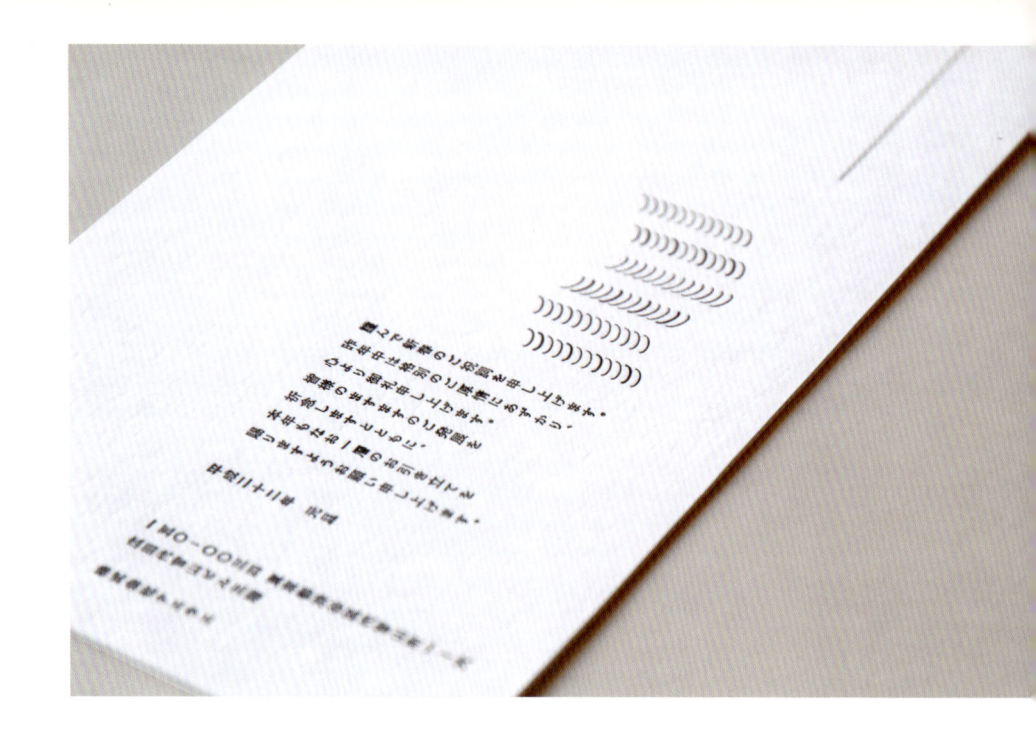

謹んで新春のご祝詞を申し上げます
昨年中は格別のご厚情にあずかり
心より御礼申し上げます
皆様のますますのご発展を
祈念しますとともに
本年もなお一層のお引き立てを
賜りますようお願い申し上げます

平成二十二年 元旦

株式会社ナラニ
東京都渋谷区代官山町一-六
代官山ビル三階
一五〇-〇〇三四

happy new year

DECOBOCO

Agency:
smbetsmb
Designer:
Keita Shimbo & Misaco Shimbo
Work Type:
Promotion

The work was exhibited at the exhibition of letterpress. The rubber plate for prints was carved by hand.

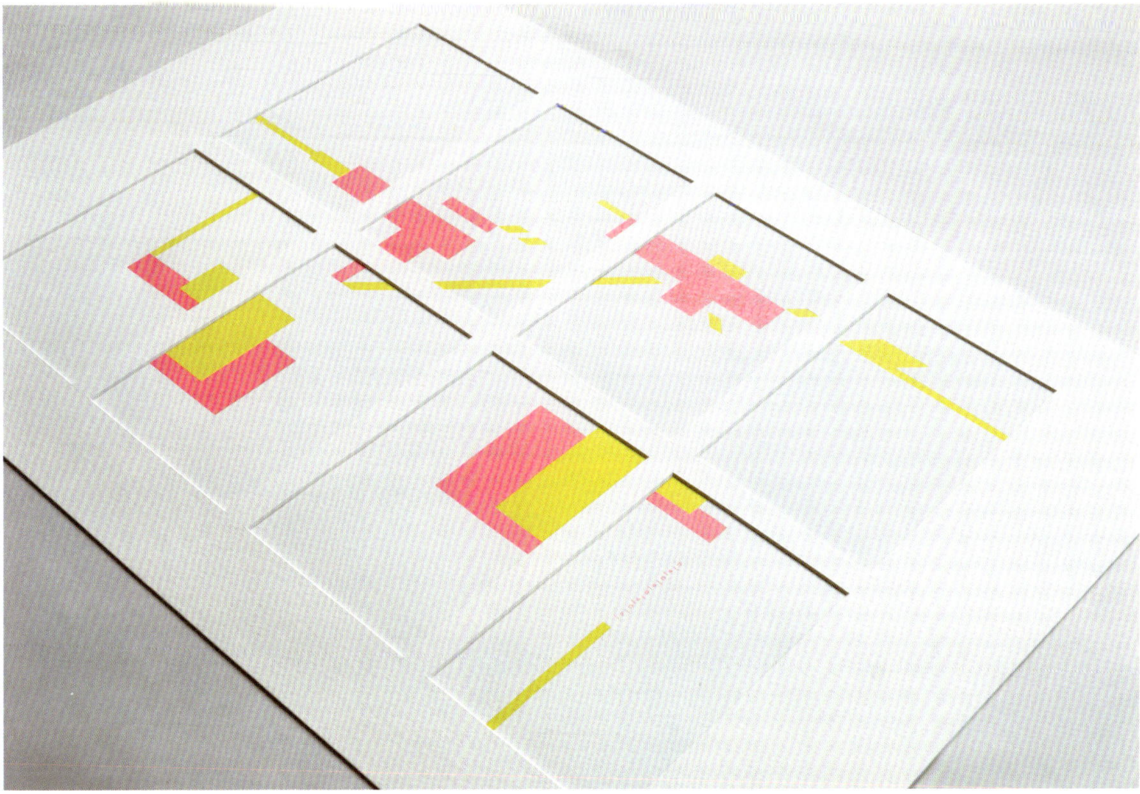

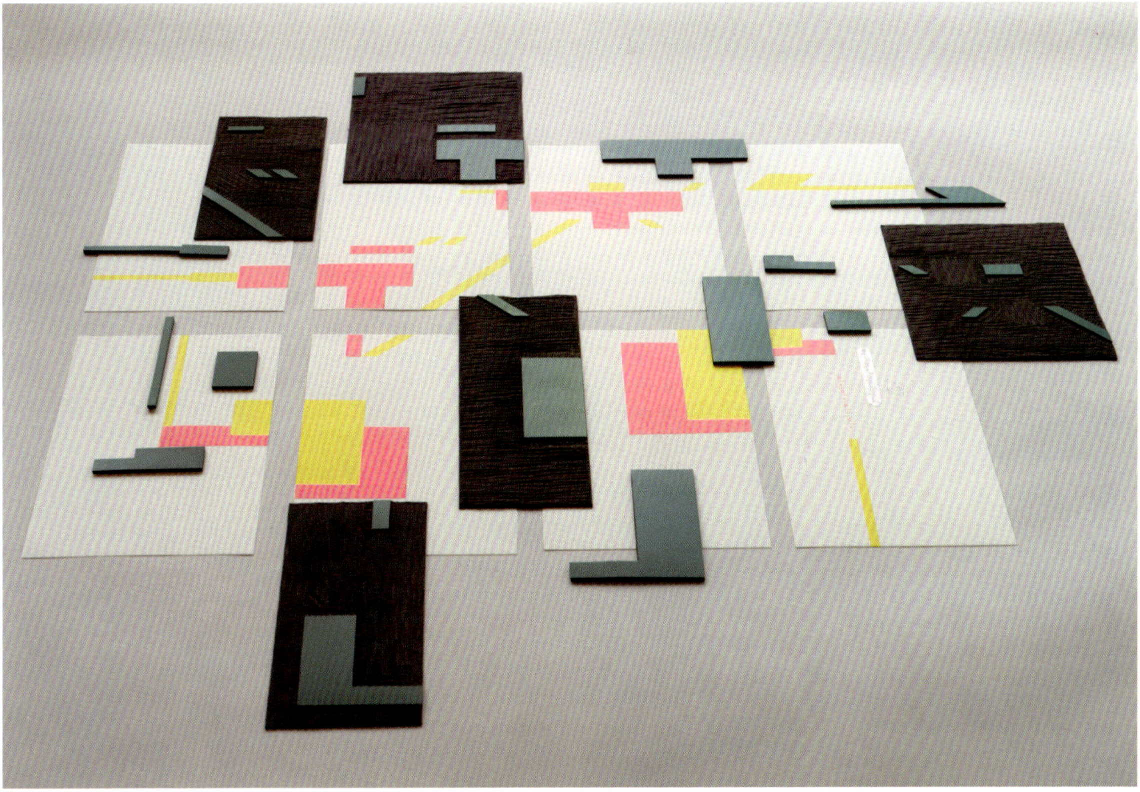

PRISM

Agency:
Njenworks

Work Type:
Identity

Gallery Branding and on-going Identity Program for Exhibitions. In the established L.A. gallery community, Prism set out to be a new kind of practice with diverse art programs that defy the typical classification of gallery types. The branding strategy for Prism is also based on the premise, that each exhibition will have its own unique identity. Overtime the collage of identities will manifest a rich, exuberant design program that mirrors the gallery's mission in pushing the boundary of art and design.

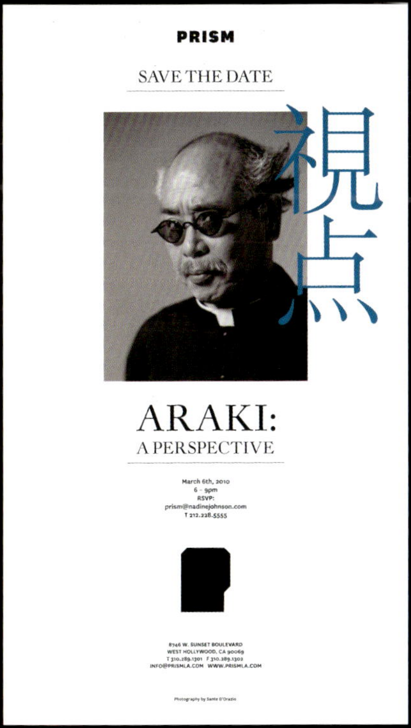

PRISM
SAVE THE DATE
視点
ARAKI:
A PERSPECTIVE
March 6th, 2010
6 - 9pm
RSVP:
prism@nadinejohnson.com
T 212.228.5555
8746 W. SUNSET BOULEVARD
WEST HOLLYWOOD, CA 90069
T 310.289.1301 F 310.289.1302
INFO@PRISMLA.COM WWW.PRISMLA.COM
Photography by Sante D'Orazio

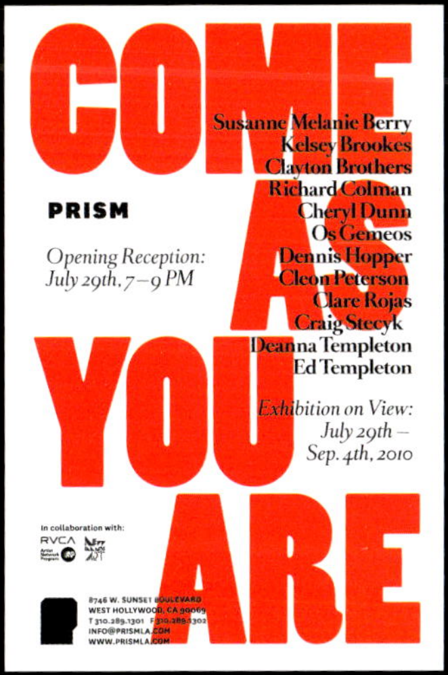

COME AS YOU ARE
PRISM
Opening Reception:
July 29th, 7–9 PM
Susanne Melanie Berry
Kelsey Brookes
Clayton Brothers
Richard Colman
Cheryl Dunn
Os Gemeos
Dennis Hopper
Cleon Peterson
Clare Rojas
Craig Stecyk
Deanna Templeton
Ed Templeton
Exhibition on View:
July 29th –
Sep. 4th, 2010
In collaboration with:
RVCA
8746 W. SUNSET BOULEVARD
WEST HOLLYWOOD, CA 90069
T 310.289.1301 F 310.289.1302
INFO@PRISMLA.COM
WWW.PRISMLA.COM

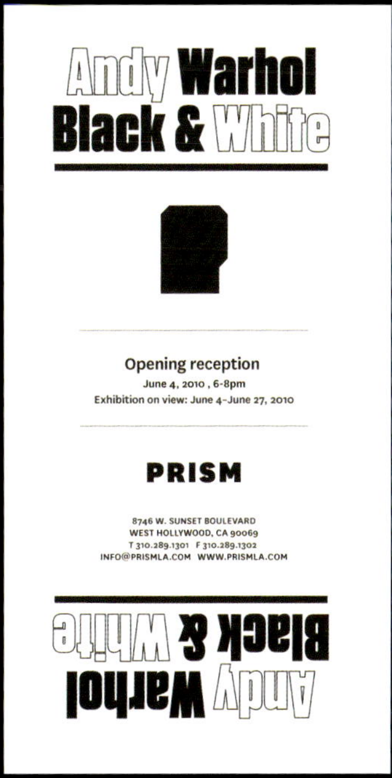

Andy Warhol
Black & White
Opening reception
June 4, 2010 , 6-8pm
Exhibition on view: June 4-June 27, 2010
PRISM
8746 W. SUNSET BOULEVARD
WEST HOLLYWOOD, CA 90069
T 310.289.1301 F 310.289.1302
INFO@PRISMLA.COM WWW.PRISMLA.COM
Andy Warhol
Black & White

PRISM
8746 W. SUNSET BOULEVARD
WEST HOLLYWOOD, CA 90069
ARAKI:
A PERSPECTIVE
March 6th, 2010
6 - 9pm
Please RSVP to 212.228.5555
or prism@nadinejohnson.com
PRISM
8746 W. SUNSET BOULEVARD
WEST HOLLYWOOD, CA 90069
T 310.289.1301 F 310.289.1302
INFO@PRISMLA.COM WWW.PRISMLA.COM

PRISM
8746 W. SUNSET BOULEVARD
WEST HOLLYWOOD, CA 90069
視点

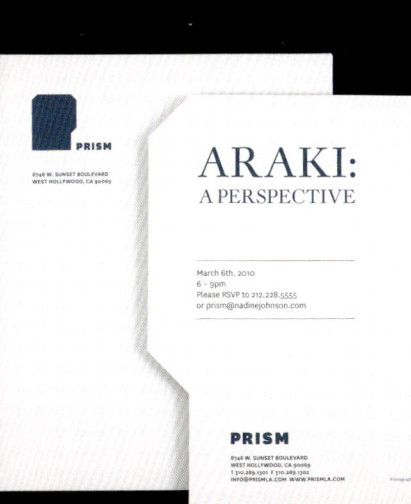

LATITUDE

Agency:
Studio Iknoki
Work Type:
Identity

Business cards and portfolio for Latitude, an experimental platform for urban research and design. Latitude has a very flexible structures, acting within different territories and social contexts around the globe; its visual identity is therefore continually negotiated. We have decided to work to a dynamic identity. Every Latitude's project communicate the whole organization by the signs which represent its spatial relations, that is to say the representation of the territory within which Latitude works. This representation is based around the idea of the territory as a complex system and uses four different layers of signs.

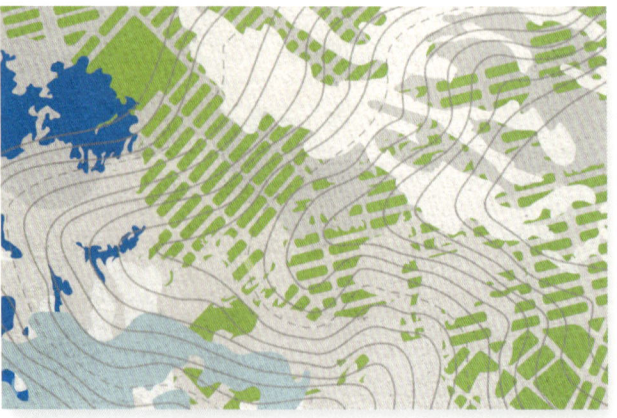

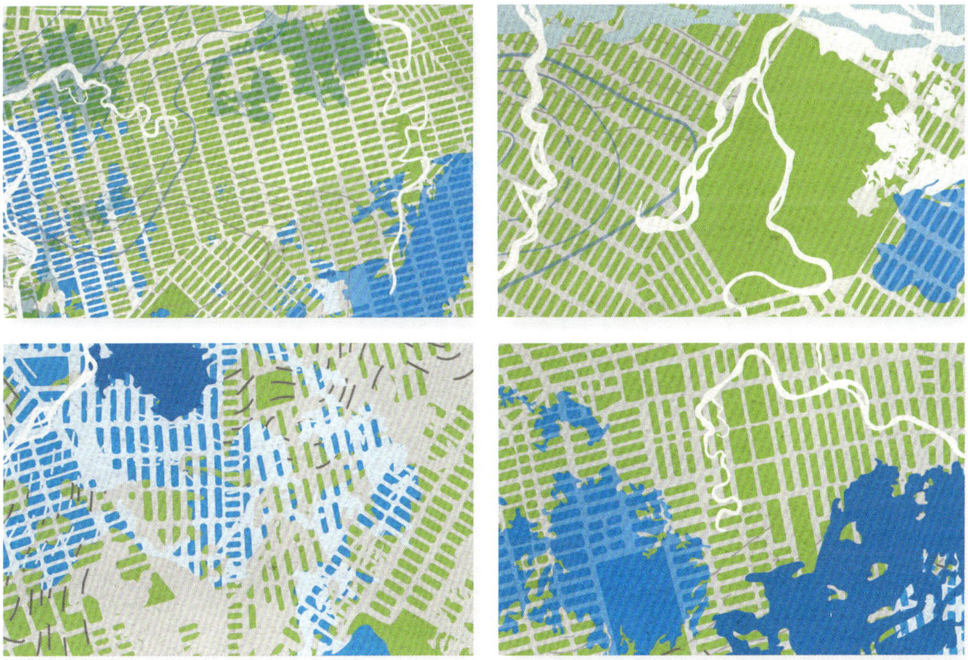

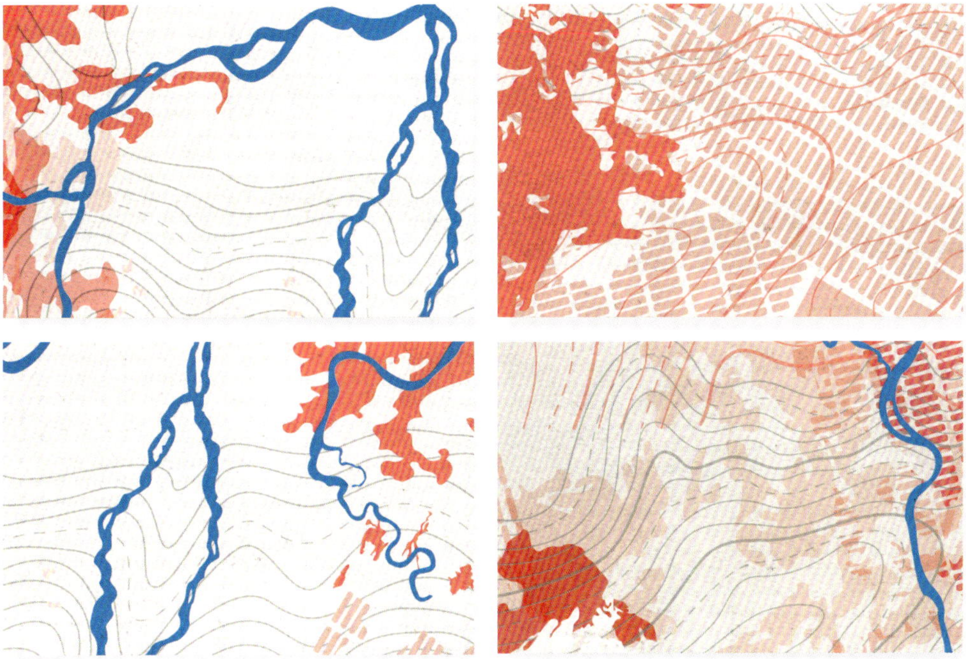

FRI ANTISMOKING PROGRAM

Agency:
Bleed
Work Type:
Identity

Conceptual rebranding of the FRI Antismoking program for the elementary schools in Norway. The program has turned so successful amongst students and teachers that we were instead asked to make some additional graphic artwork for new posters and postcards to be printed as supplements.

NEWS

SE FRE E
LV T E
G VELKOMMEN N
I R
D A
I

SEESAW CARDS

Agency:
Seesaw
Work Type:
Identity

The cards were designed to showcase the idea of balance. Each card has a 'business' side and a 'personal' side with each staff member choosing imagery representing two opposing aspects of their personality. In terms of the finish, a gold foil was utilized together with an off white textured stock.

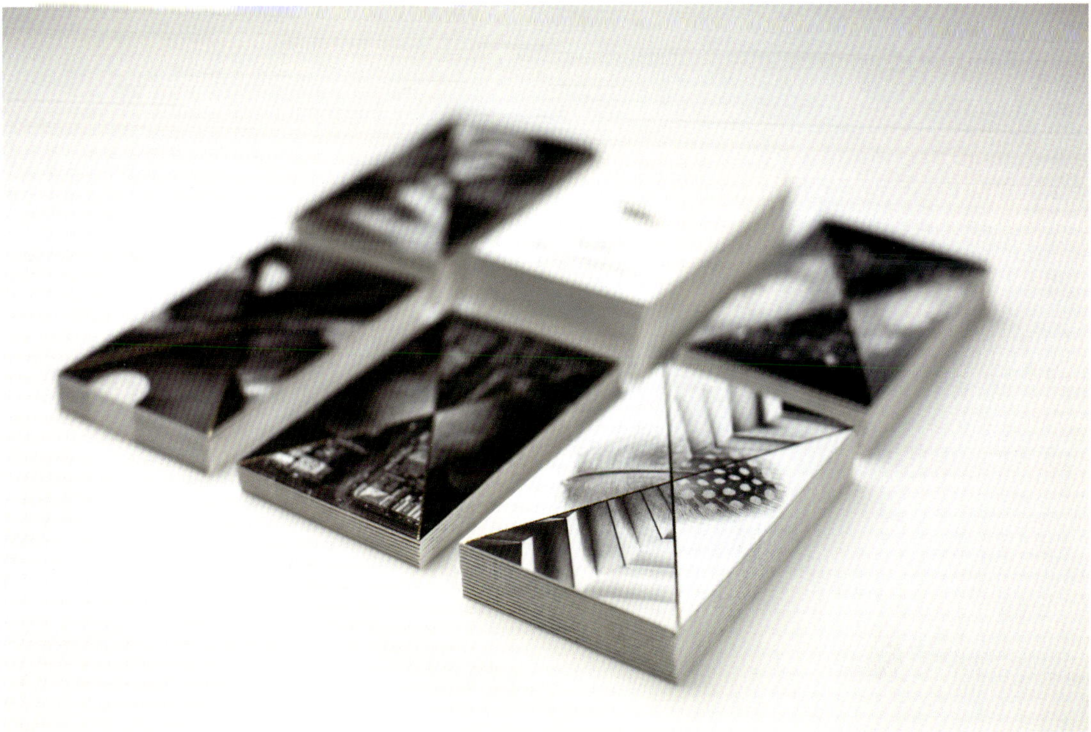

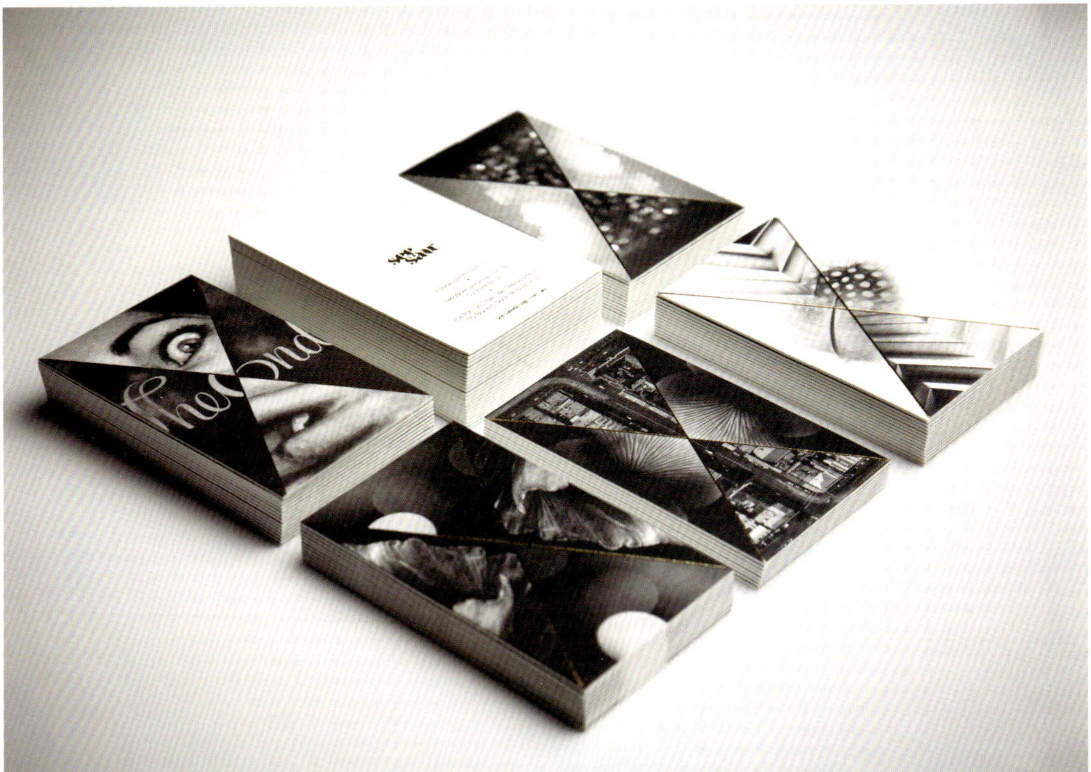

MYSPACE

Agency:
Bleed
Work Type:
Identity

Brief from MySpace to Bleed: "Lead the rebranding efforts for MySpace. We have a new logo and entirely new site and are very ready to design out the rest of our identity system."

Myspace is a shared experience around global culture that gives curators, tastemakers and consumers the tools to discover, publish, and connect based on common interests.

The revitalized brand is fresh, designed as a vessel that leverages MySpace brand equity and core culture allowing it to mature into the most satisfying and engaging social entertainment entity.

Visually mixing interests and personalities of the users, we communicate MySpace as the place where everyone can be whoever they want to be.

Giving the brand experience room to grow we use simple typography and the usage of the logo for different corporate illustrations.

The strong type and material is the base, the visuals can be random from users of MySpace or generated by professionals.

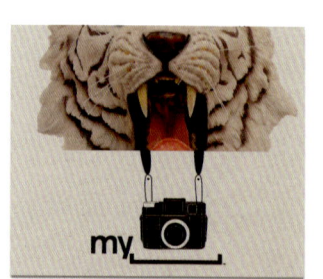

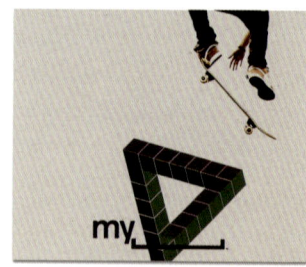

my
my 
my 

CREATE
my

celebrate
my

my

my
my  
my

HAND-MADE BUSINESS
CARDS

Agency:
TNOP™ DESIGN
Work Type:
Identity

There are our limited
quantity hand-made business
cards. We wanted to
experiment with the home
silk-screen printing kit
(print gocco) and the hand-
held embosser. The home-
screen printed kit has a
limited printing area of
6"x4", so we laid 4 cards
up in one sheet then trim
every card by hands.

TNOP W.
DESIGNER
+1.312.
235.0170
1440 S. MICHIGAN
AVE. #322 CHICAGO
TNOP@
TNOP.COM
HTTP://WWW.TNOP.COM

CUTTER & SAVAGE

Agency:
Cutter & Savage
Work Type:
Identity

We wanted the look and feel of our business cards to reflect the ethos and identity of Cutter & Savage. Victorian style with a hand made quality and attention to detail. The designs themselves were illustrated by hand and then cut into brass plates. These were then put through antique letterpress engines on 100% cotton paper.

Terry Whidborne esq.
CREATIVE DIRECTOR

mrwhidborne@cutterandsavage...
+61 (0)417 645 051

CUTTERANDSAVAGE.COM

Jon Groom esq.
CREATIVE DIRECTOR

mrgroom@cutterandsavage.com
07734 592 699

CUTTERANDSAVAGE.COM

Mr Mat Sunderland
HEAD OF PRODUCTION

mrsunderland@cutterandsavage.com

PLAYLAB

Agency:
Mind Design
Work Type:
Identity

Identity and stationery for Playlab, a workshop space aimed to be a creative playground for stressed adults. The illustrations used are a mixture of scientific elements and random fun images. The stationery is printed in fluorescent Pantone colours while the actual logo is just blind embossed. The address details are filled in using a rubber stamp.

232

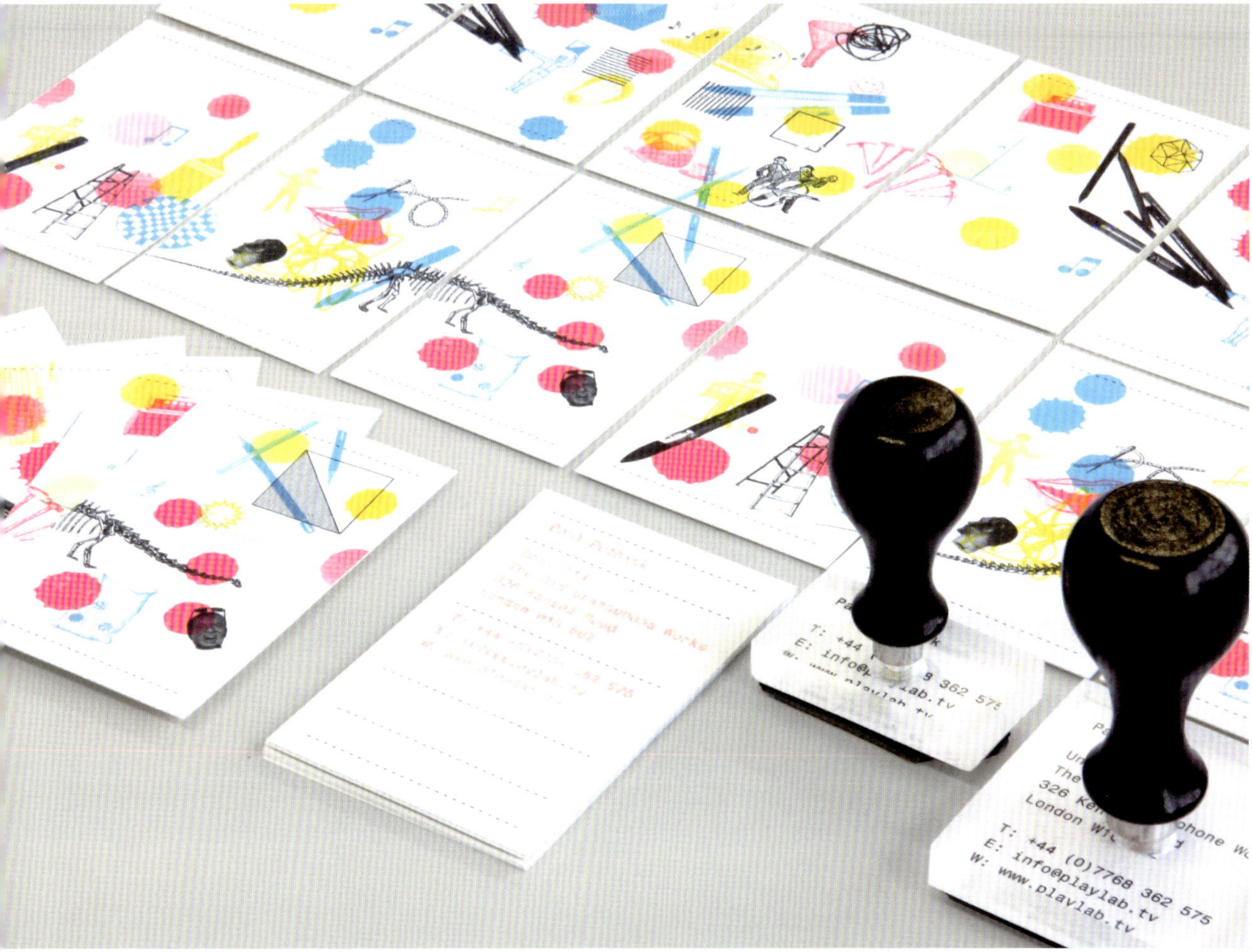
T: +44 (0)7768 362 575
E: info@playlab.tv
W: www.playlab.tv

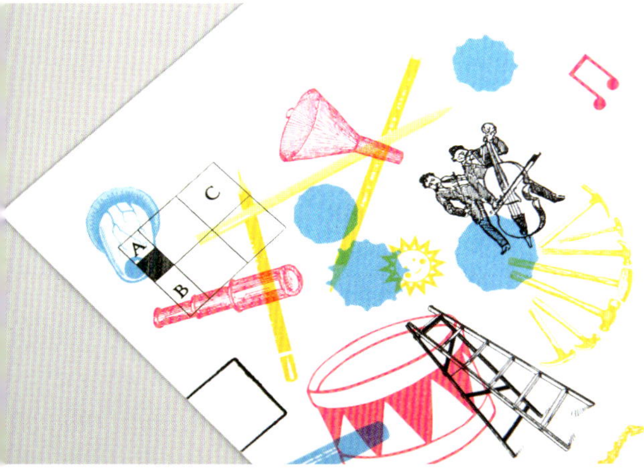
A
B
C

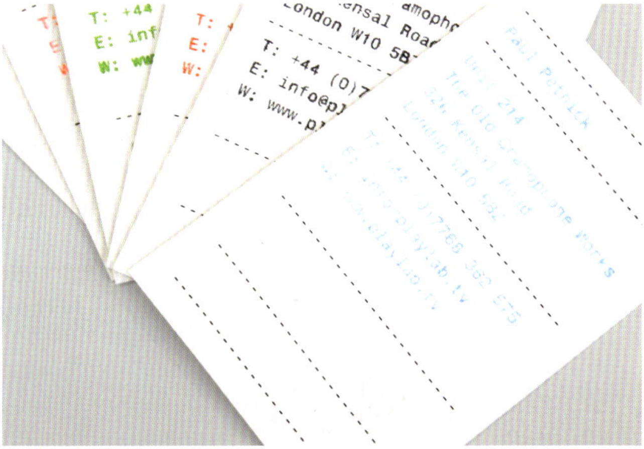

KERRY PHELAN DESIGN OFFICE (K.P.D.O.)
Agency:
Fabio Ongatato Design
Work Type:
Identity

K.P.D.O. is a new identity designed for Kerry Phelan Design Office, a newly formed, but well-established interior design studio in Melbourne. Kerry Phelan is one of the most respected and awarded interior designers in Australia. Kerry left Hecker Phelan & Guthrie in December 2009 to pursue individual creative pursuits. It gave Kerry Phelan the opportunity to focus more on the personal qualities of her business. The focus is on the purity of design, a personable nature and a more inclusive based studio.

Moving from a brand to become a personable identity, we took an oldschool atelier / studio approach to reflect the purist, humble and approachable qualities of the studio. The idea is based in subtleties that count, allowing the work to speak for itself and not hide behind corporate branding. The result is a pure, simple, intelligent piece of design, with an element of surprise. The non-designed aesthetic is contrasted by the subtle use of colour and the reveal of a modern take on old-school envelope security patterns. The juxtaposition between old and new and the calm strength with reveal/surprise capture the essence of the brand and the personal nature of the identity.

K.P.D.O.
K.P.D.O.
KERRY PHELAN
DIRECTOR
KERRY PHELAN DESIGN OFFICE
61 LITTLE COLLINS ST. MELBOURNE
VICTORIA AUSTRALIA 3000
T: 03 8102 3142
M: 0400 180 955
KERRY@KERRYPHELAN.COM.AU
WWW.KERRYPHELAN.COM.AU

SANDRA BOILS

Agency:
Estudio Menta
Work Type:
Identity

This business card was created for a Jazz Vocalist from Valencia (Spain): Sandra Boils. She needed something simple and elegant, so we proposed a monochromatic design with simple graphics and typography.

BRIGITTE RECHSTEINER

Designer:
Dominic Rechsteiner
Work Type:
Identity

Brigitte Rechsteiner is an artist, who creates sculptures, bowls, cups and various other everyday objects out of clay and plaster. Concept: design of a business card. With their abstract and cubic-linear forms, the sculptures inspired to develop a self designed font. The use of recycled paper (carton) adds a natural look to the geometric elements.

WEMOTION

Agency:
Catalogue
Work Type:
Identity

Communication and identity cards for a motion design studio called "Wemotion".

Offset sliver print on 380 skin black paper.

Original logo created by Antoine Eckart.

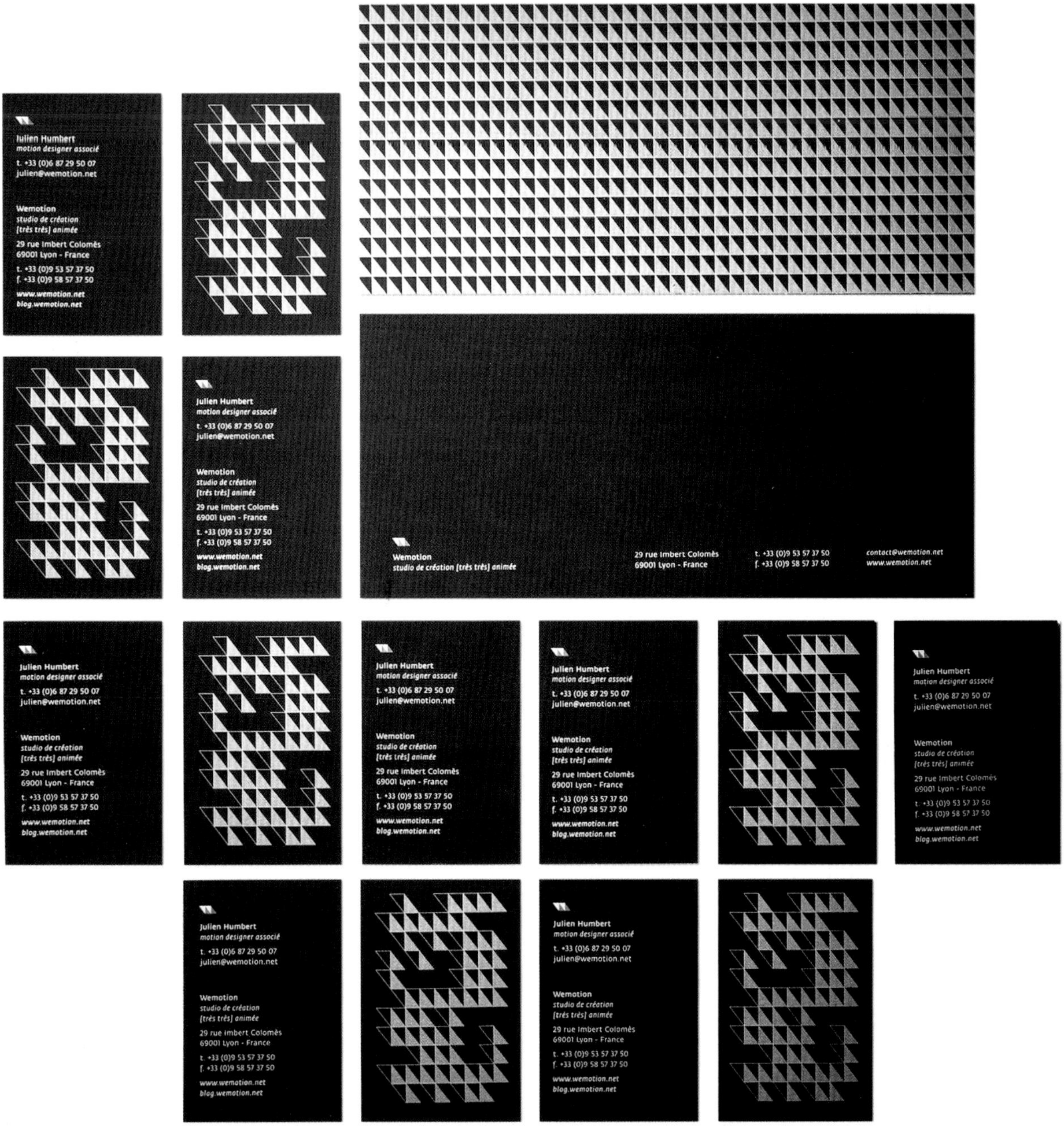
Julien Humbert
motion designer associé
t. +33 (0)6 87 29 50 07
julien@wemotion.net
Wemotion
studio de création
[très très] animée
29 rue Imbert Colomès
69001 Lyon - France
t. +33 (0)9 53 57 37 50
f. +33 (0)9 58 57 37 50
www.wemotion.net
blog.wemotion.net
Wemotion
studio de création [très très] animée
29 rue Imbert Colomès
69001 Lyon - France
t. +33 (0)9 53 57 37 50
f. +33 (0)9 58 57 37 50
contact@wemotion.net
www.wemotion.net

TADAS KARPAVICIUS

Designer:
Tadas Karpavicius
Work Type:
Identity

Personal limited edition triangle business card screen printed on black/white paper. The main idea was to create a different size card and to avoid standards.

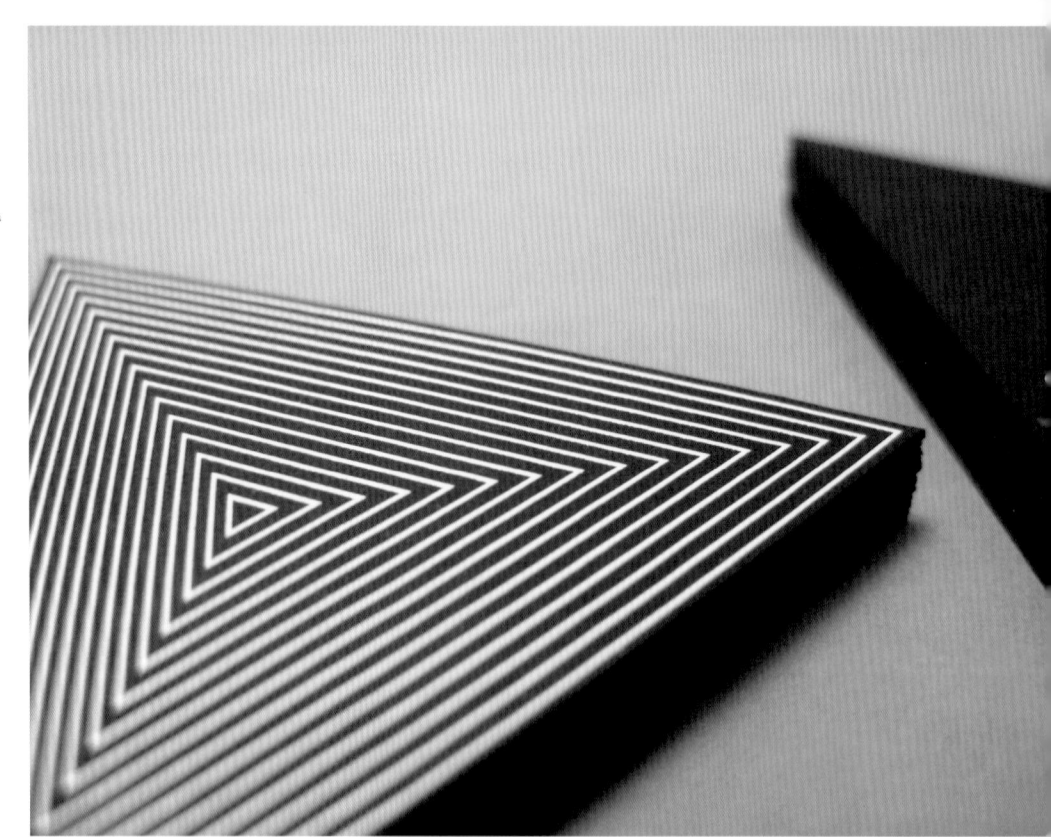

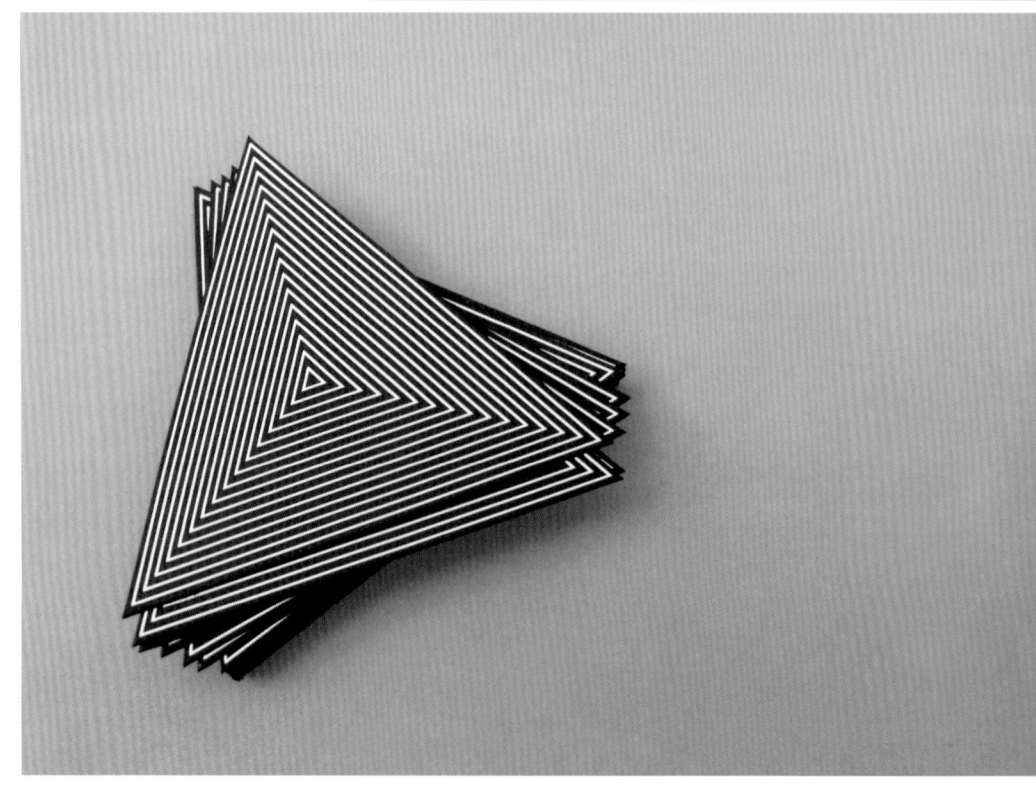

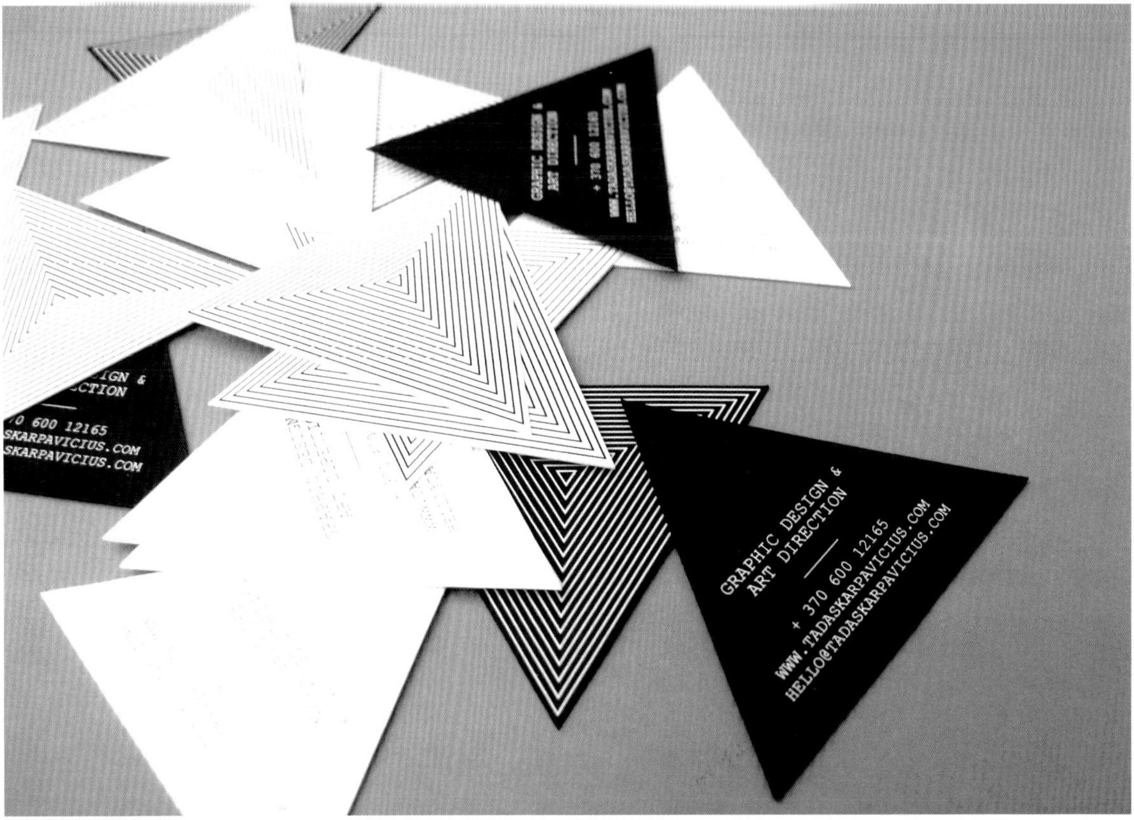
GRAPHIC DESIGN &
ART DIRECTION
+ 370 600 12165
WWW.TADASKARPAVICIUS.COM
HELLO@TADASKARPAVICIUS.COM

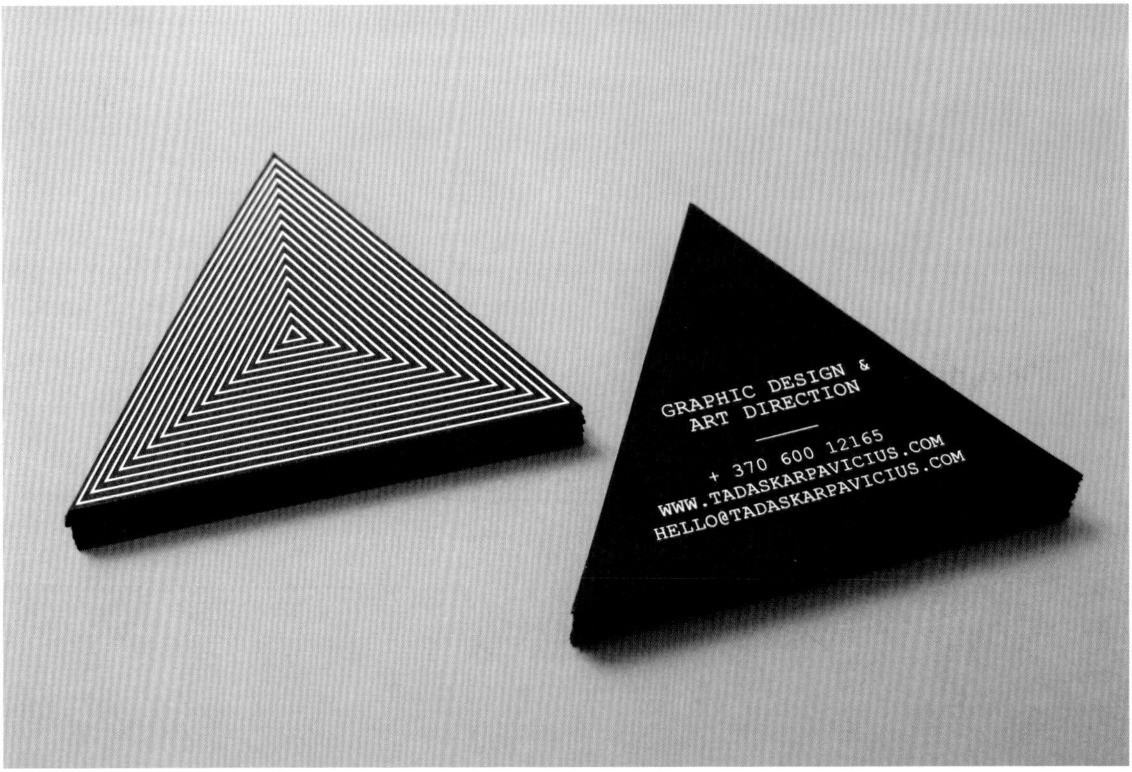
GRAPHIC DESIGN &
ART DIRECTION
+ 370 600 12165
WWW.TADASKARPAVICIUS.COM
HELLO@TADASKARPAVICIUS.COM

A HUNDRED A DAY
Agency:
Bianca Wendt Studio
Work Type:
Identity

An identity for a London / Bonn based fashion label set up by Central Saint Martins graduates Nina Andersson and Agnes Korn. This consists of a logotype and a series of changeable triangular logos representing the letter A. For the business cards, a large custom designed pattern is cut down to give ten different variations on the back of the cards.

A HUNDRED A DAY

CUTS FROM ABOVE

Designer:
Ivan Khmelevsk
Work Type:
Identity

Hairdresser Peter Sokolov needed business cards so I created a name and a logo for him as well as the cards. He is a very tall guy, so I came up with "Cuts from above" name, which really suits him and what he does. All cards are hand screen-printed with silver on black and black on white, hand cut and hand perforated myself. Perforation makes the cards breakable in 2 separate tall cards that emphasize hairdresser's height. The one with Peter's phone number and logo goes to the customer, the second one is kept by Peter as a kind of

Rolodex card. It has 4 empty fields for the customer's name, phone number, haircut style and appointment time, so Peter could easily manage his clients.

CUTS
FROM ABOVE
Петр
+7 926 341 09 31
Имя: Анна
Время: 19:00
Работа:
Тел.:

CUTS
FROM
Петр

RANDOM

Designer:
Carlos Bermúdez & Mau Morgó
Work Type:
Identity

Identity for a furniture company which is totally based around the concept of randomness.

P·P·O·W

Agency:
Project Projects
Work Type:
Identity

Project Projects designed the identity system, printed matter, and publications for P·P·O·W gallery, which was founded in 1983 by Wendy Olsoff and Penny Pilkington in the first wave of the East Village Art Scene in New York City in 1983. In 1988 the gallery moved to Soho and in 2002 moved to Chelsea. P·P·O·W maintains a diverse roster of national and international artists.

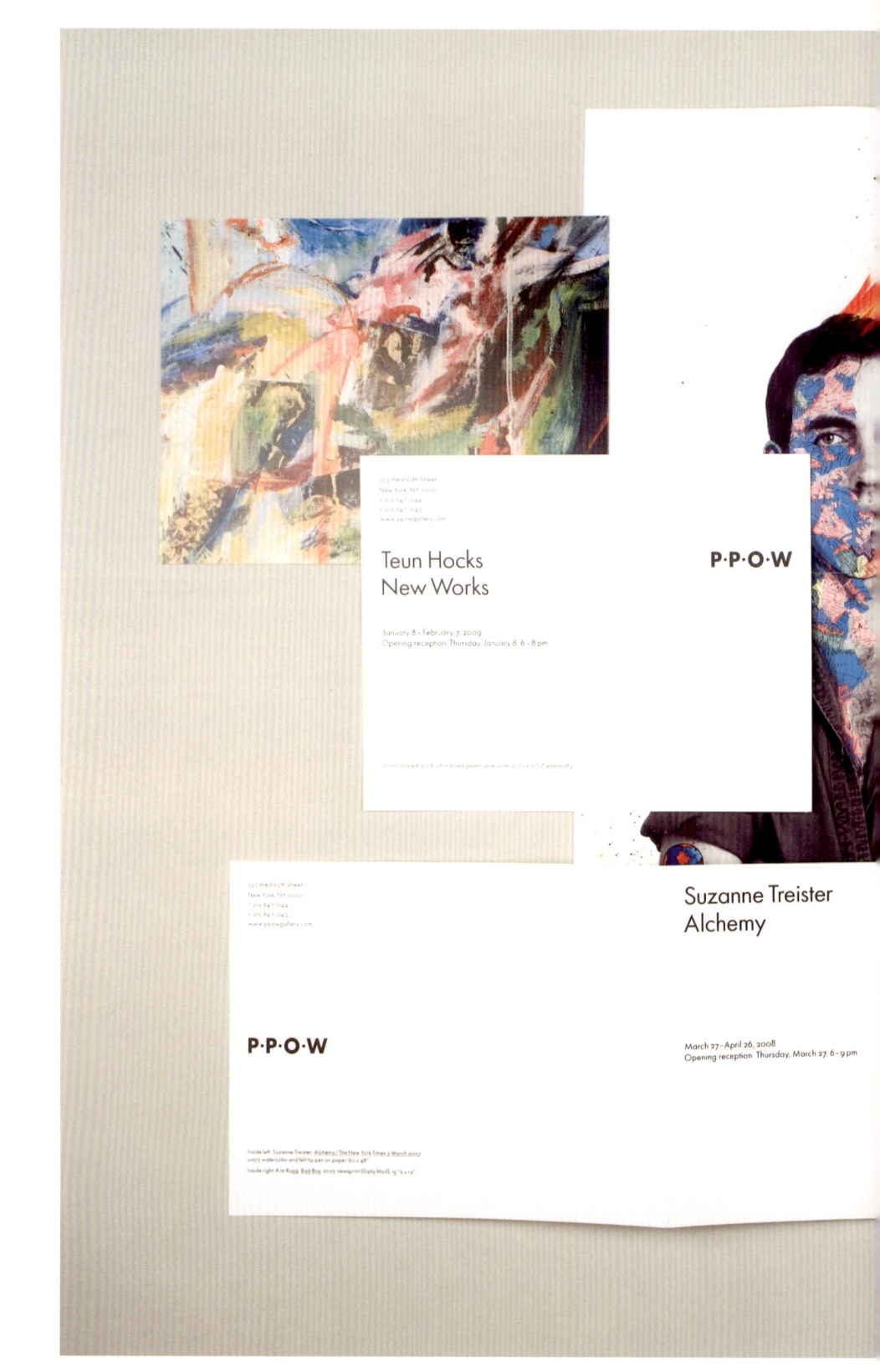

248

Walter Martin
& Paloma Muñoz

Islands

January 10–February 9, 2008
Opening reception: Thursday, January 10, 6–8 pm
Color catalog available

LAST DANCE
Designer:
Andrés Requena
Work Type:
Identity

Poster for the 25th anniversary and dadabar's farewell, a 90's indie emblematic place.

Some hypothetical vandals have struck the event in opposition to the closure of the only decent music bar in Viladecans.

BRAVISIMO

Designer:
Andrés Requena
Work Type:
Identity

Bravísimos is a concert and dj sets night held for a long time in dadabar. The name plays on the duality of meaning. The graphic design of the first three months revolves around the bravery of dubious characters who historically had.

FASHION SHOW KABK
2009

Agency:
Drawswords
Designer:
Rob van den Nieuwenhuizen &
Barbara Hennequin
Work Type:
Identity

Graphic identity for the
Royal Academy of Art's
fashion graduates show
of 2009. The main design
element is a cross-like
typographic shape that
refers to the white plastic
church built especially
for the catwalk show. Each
item has a silkscreened
UV Spot varnish layer on
top, as a metaphor for the
photographic flash lights at
the end of the catwalk.

MODE SHOW KABK
11 JUNI 2009
ENTREE KAART
MODE SHOW KABK
SHOW TIME
18.00 20.00 22.00
UITNODIGING
MODESHOW
Koninklijke Academie van Beeldende Kunsten, Den Haag
11 juni 2009
TIJDEN
18.00 / 20.00 / 22.00

UITNODIGING
MODE SHOW KABK
11 JUNI 2009
MODESHOW
OP DE AFGELOPEN MODEFABRIEK WERDEN ZIJ NOG GEPRESENTEERD ALS MOST PROMISING 3RD YEAR BACHELOR VAN 2008 EN NU DOEN ZIJ EINDEXAMEN!
DE EINDEXAMENSTUDENTEN VAN DE KONINKLIJKE ACADEMIE VAN BEELDENDE KUNSTEN PRESENTEREN, SAMEN MET DE STUDENTEN UIT DE ANDERE STUDIEJAREN, HUN BIJZONDERE EN HEDENDAAGSE VISIE OP MODEONTWERPEN.
DE STUDENTEN LATEN OP EEN INSPIRERENDE LOCATIE VOL OVERTUIGING ZIEN DAT ZIJ HET EXPERIMENT AAN DURVEN GAAN.
ENTREE KAART
MODE SHOW KABK
SHOW TIME
18.00 20.00 22.00
11 JUNI 2009

CULT DEALER ENZO

Agency:
Drawswords
Designer:
Rob van den Nieuwenhuizen &
Barbara Hennequin
Work Type:
Identity

Identity for Cult Dealer Enzo, an event and workshop place in one of the storage yards in the centre of Utrecht, the Netherlands.

Cult Dealer Enzo has three counterparts: Cult, an experimental lab for creative talent in Utrecht. Dealer, as a dealer for concepts, formats and dreams. And Enzo, which is a surprise everytime, for all parties involved. Each counterpart is paired up with its own cult-like icon and can be used separately or in any preferred combination.

This was a design collaboration between Rob van den Nieuwenhuizen (Drawswords) and Barbara Hennequin.

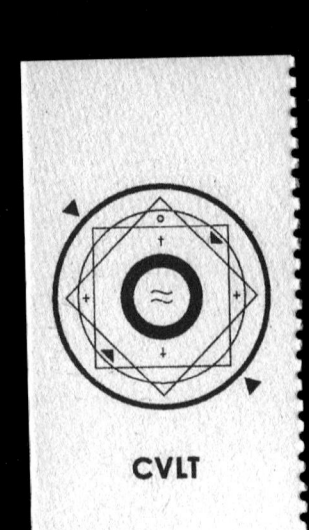

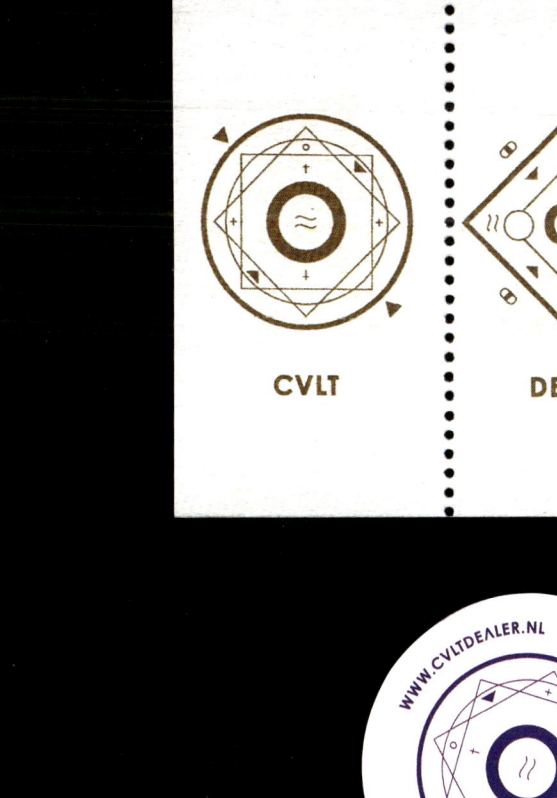

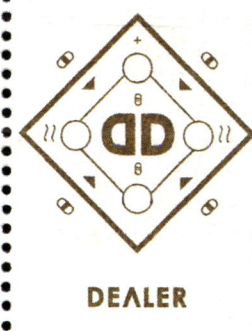

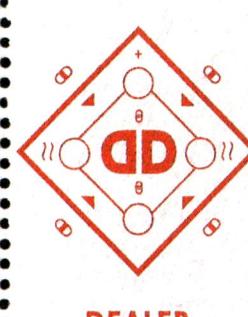

CVLT DEALER ENZO

CVLT DEALER ENZO

PLAYFUL

Agency:
Plenty
Work Type:
Identity

One of my faces is my business cards, used at every meeting. So my idea was to make a good impression. So I choose:

2 Papers. 350grs Black Paper and 350grs Mate Illustration White Paper.

1 Cliche. to bas-relief and stamping.

9 Stampings foils. Mate and brilliant Gold, Mate and brilliant Silver, Iridicent Silver, Black, Red, Violet and Blue.

playful
Pablo Altieri
Graphic Design
(5411) 15 5481 3857
pablo@pabloaltieri.com
www.pabloaltieri.com

playful
Pablo Altieri
Graphic Design
(5411) 15 5481 3857

LIQUORICE STUDIO

Agency:
Liquorice Studio
Work Type:
Identity

In June 2011, Liquorice Studio refreshed their brand identity with the addition of a set of colour swatches inspired by liquorice allsorts. The brief for the business cards was to use these swatches, while experimenting with print and production processes, to create a talking point. The triplex cards feature a coloured layer sandwiched between two layers of black—like a liquorice allsort—while the text and logo have been screen-printed to produce a tactile finish.

LIQUORICE

Scott Bonanno
Director
Liquorice Studio
Level 1, 184 Brunswick Street
Fitzroy, Victoria 3065
Phone +61 3 9023 5767
Mobile +61 402 442 939
scott@liquoricestudio.com
www.liquoricestudio.com

LIQUORICE
LIQUORICE
Anna Gowers
Liquorice Studio
Level 1, 184 Brunswick Street
Fitzroy, Victoria 3065
Phone +61 3 9023 5767
anna@liquoricestudio.com
www.liquoricestudio.com
Scott Bonanno
Director
Liquorice Studio
LIQUORICE
LIQUORICE

HELSINKI DAY
Designer:
Tuukka Koivisto
Work Type:
Invitation

Every year the city of
Helsinki organizes a
Helsinki Week happening.
At the last day of this
week there is a party held
for the crem de la crem of
Helsinki. This invitation
was made for that party.

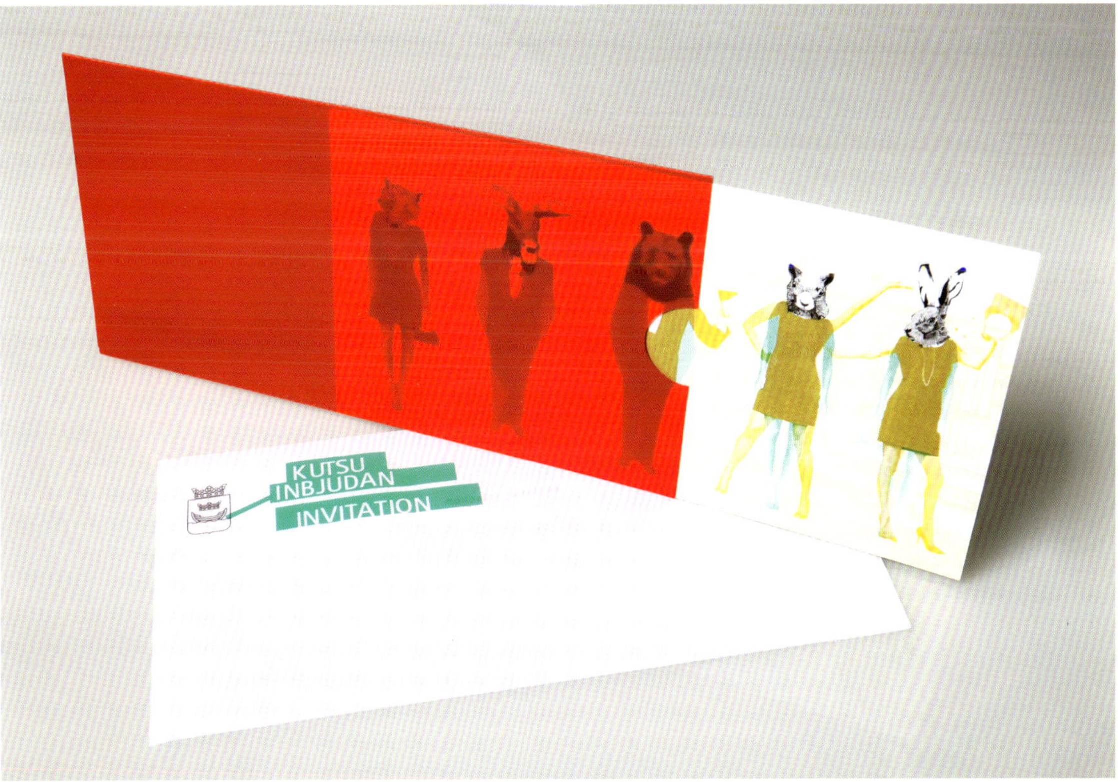
KUTSU
INBJUDAN
INVITATION

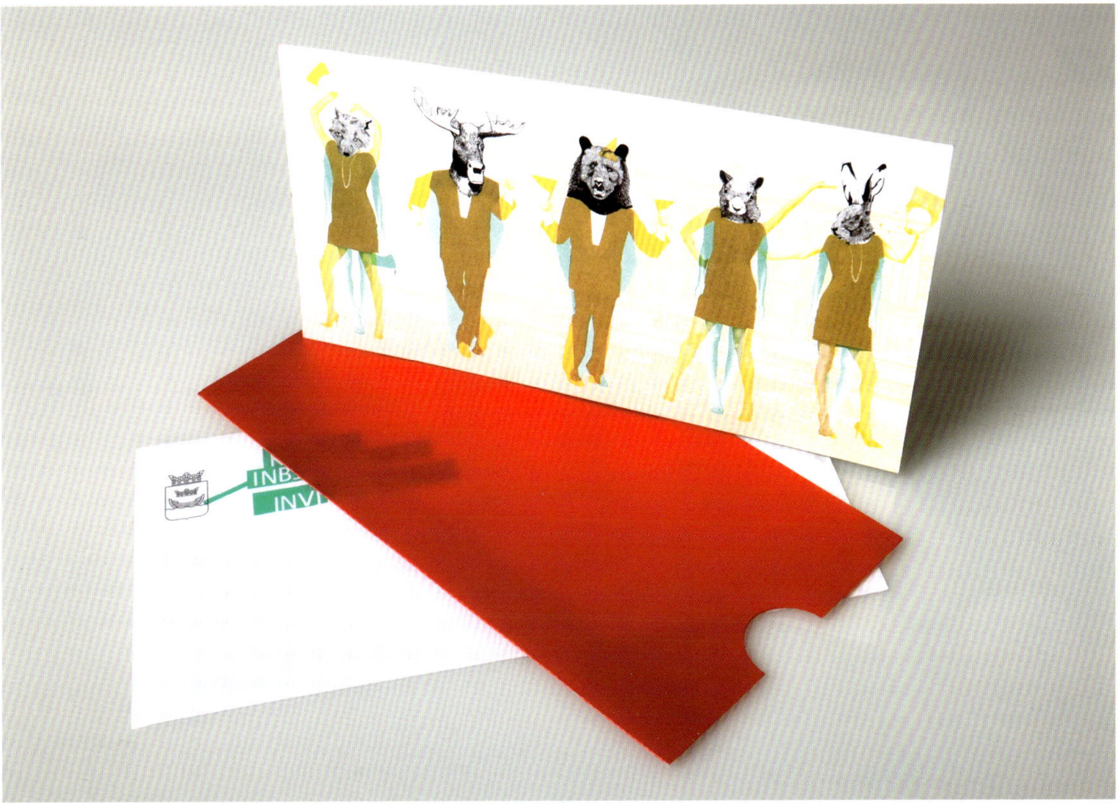

DANIELA GREGIS
EXHIBITION

Agency:
Fujimoto Gumi
Work Type:
Promotion

Flier for Daniela Gregis
Exhibition where item of 25
becomes complete.

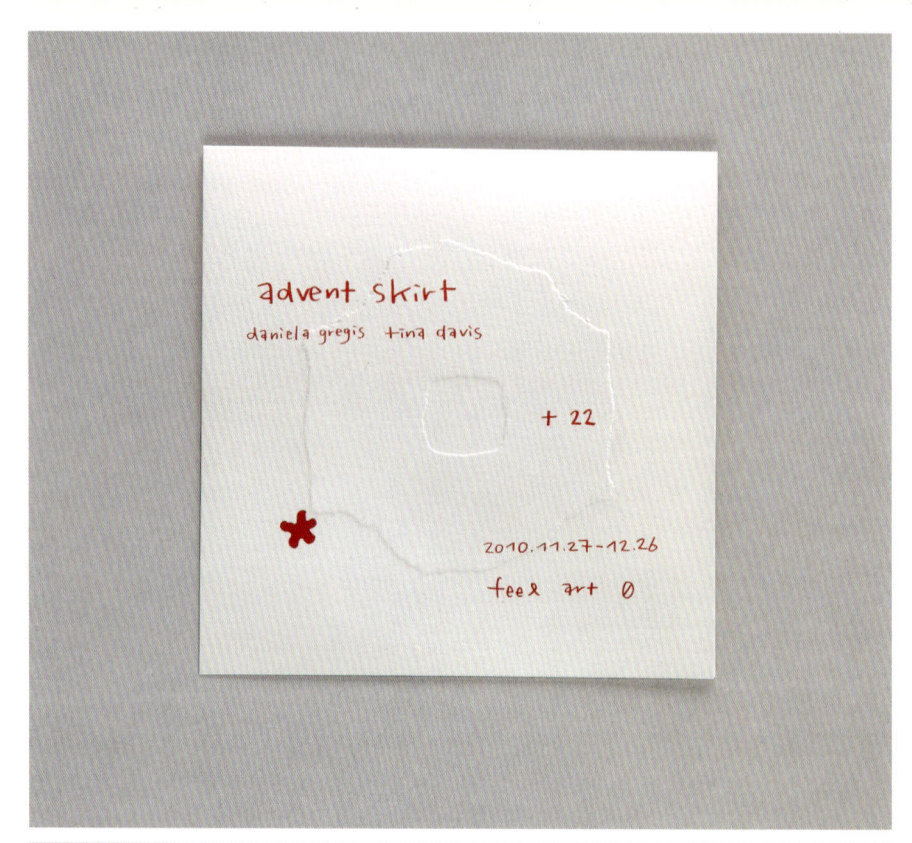

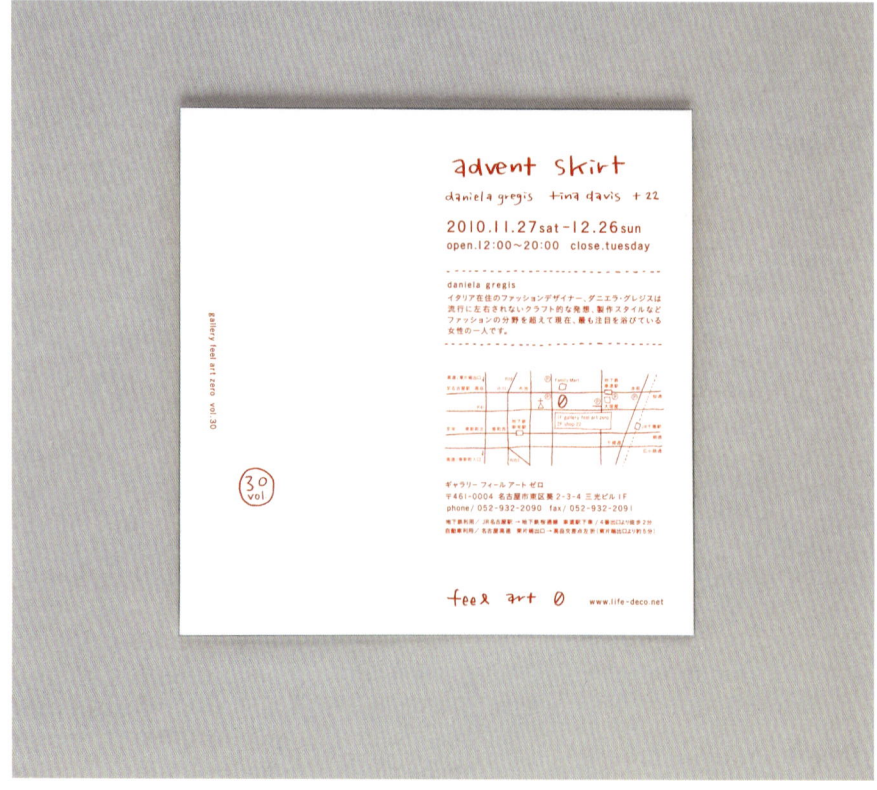

262

dec. 20 10

0 1 2 3 4

5 6 7 8 9 10 11

12 13 14 15 16 17 18

19 20 21 22 23 24 25
items

+ advent skirt

advent skirt daniela gregis with tina davis for [children action] +25 items

今回はダニエラ・グレジスが2008年に子供の絵本のデザイナーであるティナ・デービスと製作したクリスマスのアドベントスカートのオークションが行われます。この取り組みはダニエラが毎年クリスマスに、子供たちのためのチャリティーとして友人のアーティストたちと共に続けている大切なもので、収益はすべてスイスのチルドレンアクションアソシエーションの活動に贈られています。

http://www.childrenaction.org

XMAS CARD 2010

Agency:
Bob Foundation
Work Type:
Greeting Card

This is our greeting card for 2010 Christmas and 2011 New Year. We organize a paper brand `Number 62', and there are always waste papers when the cards are produced. We considered those waste papers to re-use in some way without any process. The design was thought about both of the season (Christmas) and the shape of waste papers.

HAVE
A
SWEET
XMAS
AND
HAPPY
NEW
YEAR!
去年からのまさかの恒例化!!
2010年 Bob Foundation 3大ニュース
どうでも良すぎる話題!
STUDIO&OFFICE
このカードは Number62 のカード断裁の際に出る切れ端を
そのまま使用したので長いんです。

HAVE
A
SWEET
XMAS
AND
HAPPY
NEW
YEAR!
去年からのまさかの恒例化!!
2010年 Bob Foundation 3大ニュース
どうでも良すぎる話題!
STUDIO&OFFICE
このカードは Number62 のカード断裁の際に出る切れ端を
そのまま使用したので長いんです。

HAVE
A
SWEET
XMAS
AND
HAPPY
NEW
YEAR!
去年からのまさかの恒例化!!
2010年 Bob Foundation 3大ニュース
どうでも良すぎる話題!
STUDIO&OFFICE
このカードは Number62 のカード断裁の際に出る切れ端を
そのまま使用したので長いんです。

HAVE
A
SWEET
XMAS
AND
HAPPY
NEW
YEAR!
去年からのまさかの恒例化!!
2010年 Bob Foundation 3大ニュース
どうでも良すぎる話題!
STUDIO&OFFICE
このカードは Number62 のカード断裁の際に出る切れ端を
そのまま使用したので長いんです。

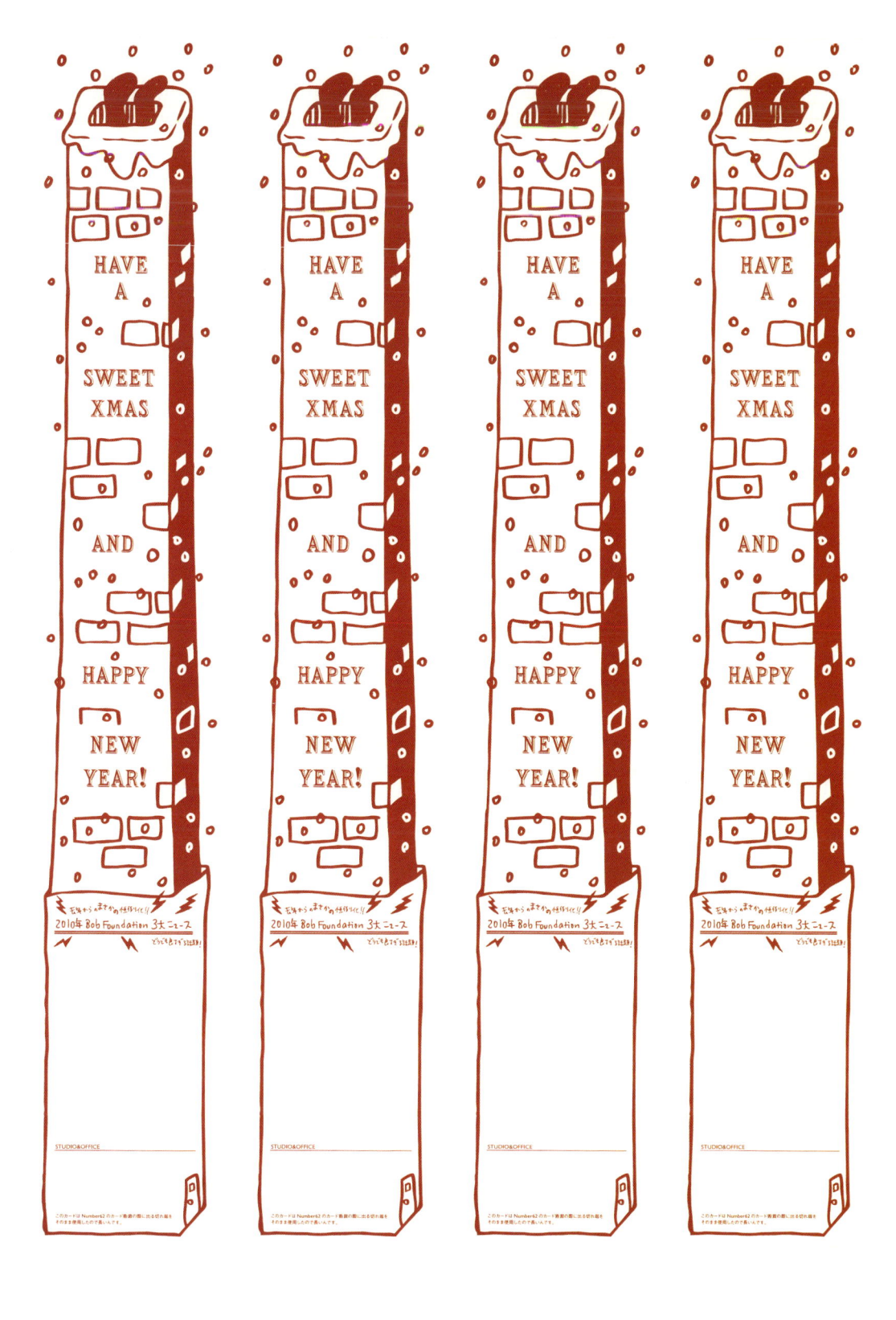

ONDA DESIGN
Agency:
6D
Designer:
Shogo Kishino
Work Type:
Identity

Identity design for Onda Design.

SALHAUS

Agency:
6D
Designer:
Shogo Kishino
Work Type:
Identity

Identity design for Salhaus
Architects.

SALON L

Designer:
Celia Leung & Agnes Wong
Work Type:
Identity

Salon L is a new trend hair salon in Hong Kong. The client commissioned us to create an identity, indoor graphics and signages for their new salon that could reflect their brand essence -- creative, contemporary, unique, diversified, and tasteful. We achieved the goal by creating a distinctive, bold yet delicate collage-like logo and geometrical graphic elements for the identity. The blind embossing effect for the business and invitation cards added a sensational touch to the whole system.

SALON L

ICE LIU
Management
Co-ordinator
Tuesday off
M. +852 9669 3839

香港尖沙咀漆咸道南79號中國五礦大廈地庫
B/F China Minmetals Tower, 79 Chatham Road S,
Tsim Sha Tsui, Hong Kong
T. +852 2369 0666 F. +852 2369 6077
info@salon-l.com

SEPTEMBER

Agency:
The Chase Creative
Consultants
Work Type:
Identity

The unusual combination of a ground floor hairdressers and first floor seafood restaurant lend a surreal quality to this unusual stationery.

SEPTEMBER
Brasserie
15-17 Queen Street Blackpool
Lancashire England FY1 1PU
Telephone 01253 23282
SEPTEMBER
Brasserie
15-17 Queen Street Blackpool Lancashire England FY1 1PU
Telephone 01253 23282
Michael Golowicz
SEPTEMBER
Hair Studio
15-17 Queen Street Blackpool Lancashire England FY1 1PU
Telephone 01253 28394
Pat Wood
SEPTEMBER
Hair Studio
15-17 Queen Street Blackpool
Lancashire England FY1 1PU
Telephone 01253 28394
SEPTEMBER
Hair Studio
15-17 Queen Street Blackpool
Lancashire England FY1 1PU
Telephone 01253 28394
Vat No. 401 187 490

BUILDING BLOC ARCHITECTS

Agency:
Kawakong Designworks
Work Type:
Identity

The idea was to "build" the identity with type, from the information given without unnecessary graphics.

The website and the company's name were highlighted in bigger font size because we want people to view their works and see what they are capable of. The hand creased lines on the name card were inspired by the architect, when we noticed that everytime we were having meetings, he has a habit of "folding little paper".

And we thought, perhaps those who are interested in "folding papers", can join them too.

www.BUILDING-BLOC.COM/

M +6 012 6755 441

E wen@building-bloc.com

/ WEN HSIA ANG

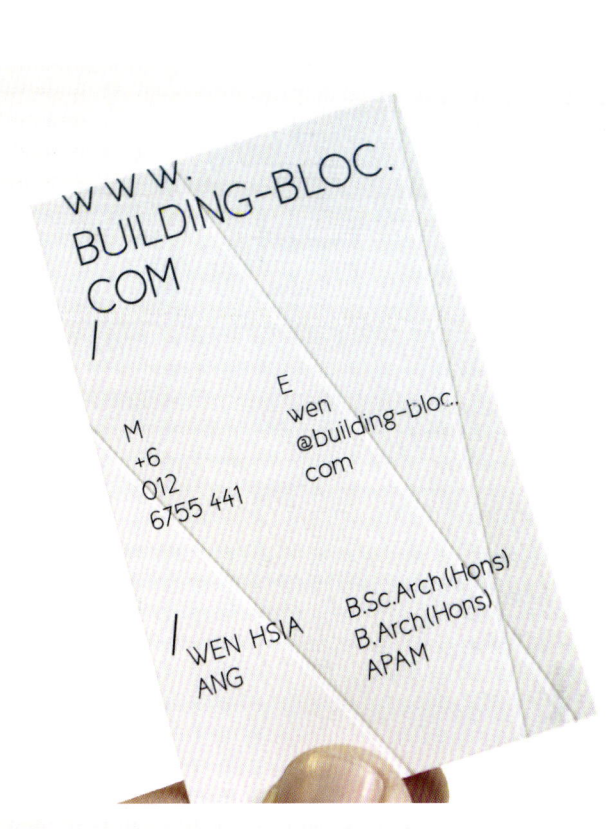

B.Sc.Arch (Hons)
B.Arch (Hons)
APAM

BUILDING BLOC ARCHITECTS

P/B3

T +6 03 7960 6960

F +6 03 7960 5960

11, Jalan 11/6A, Sec.11
46200 Petaling Jaya
Selangor, Malaysia

UMA/DESIGN FARM
Agency:
UMA/design farm
Designer:
Yuma Harada
Photography:
Takumi Ota
Work Type:
Identity

Business card for UMA/
design farm.

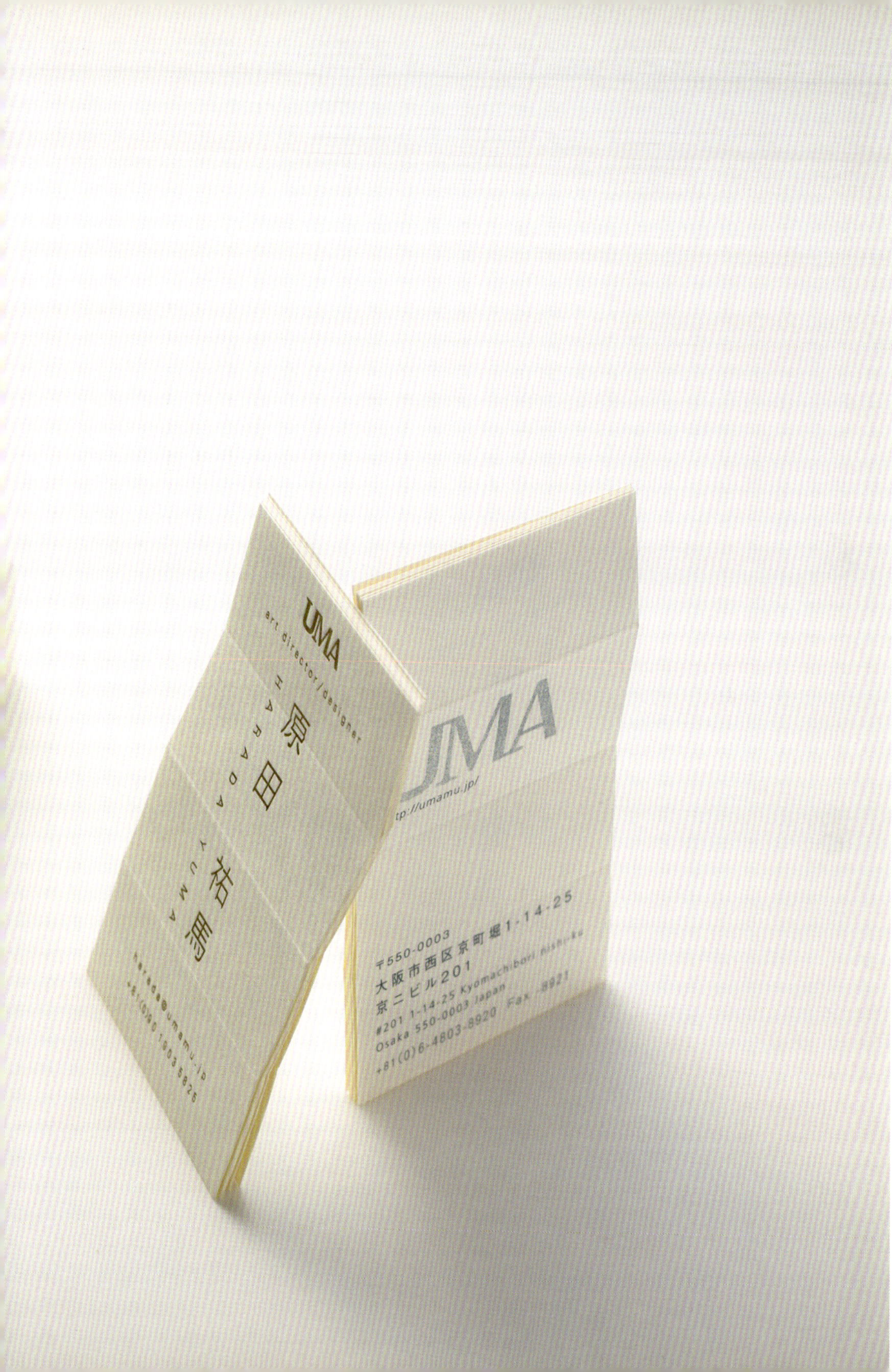
UMA
art director/designer
原田 祐馬
HARADA YUMA
harada@umamu.jp
UMA
tp://umamu.jp/
〒550-0003
大阪市西区京町堀1-14-25
京二ビル201
#201 1-14-25 Kyomachibori Nishi-ku
Osaka 550-0003 Japan
+81(0)6-4803-8920 Fax -8921

MODULAR BUSINESS
CARDS

Designer:
Pharaon Siraj
Photography:
Wendy Chua
Work Type:
Identity

Personal business cards of a freelance graphic designer and copywriter. These modular cards interlock to form various polyhedra, giving reference to the humble name card's ability to connect people. Each card is standard size with a score line and two slits, and can be used as a template to connect other name cards.

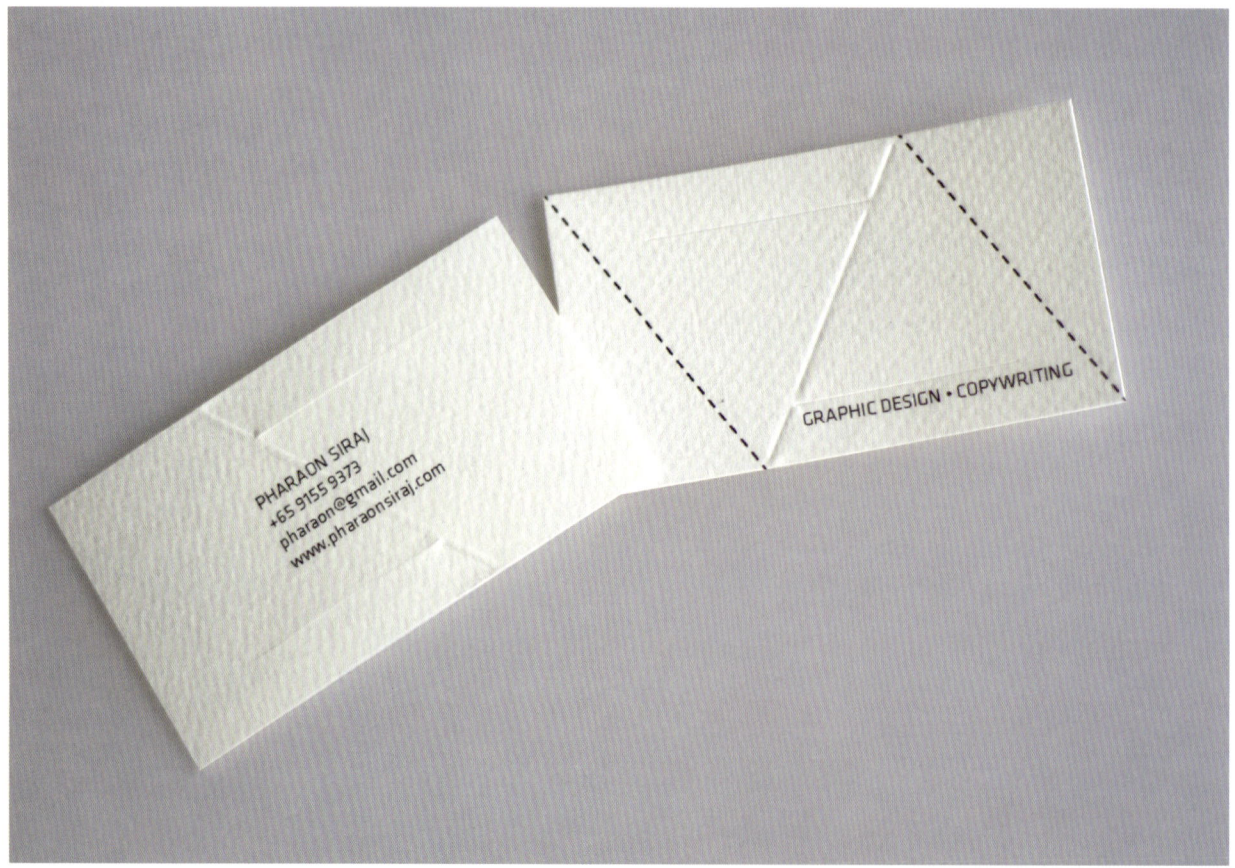

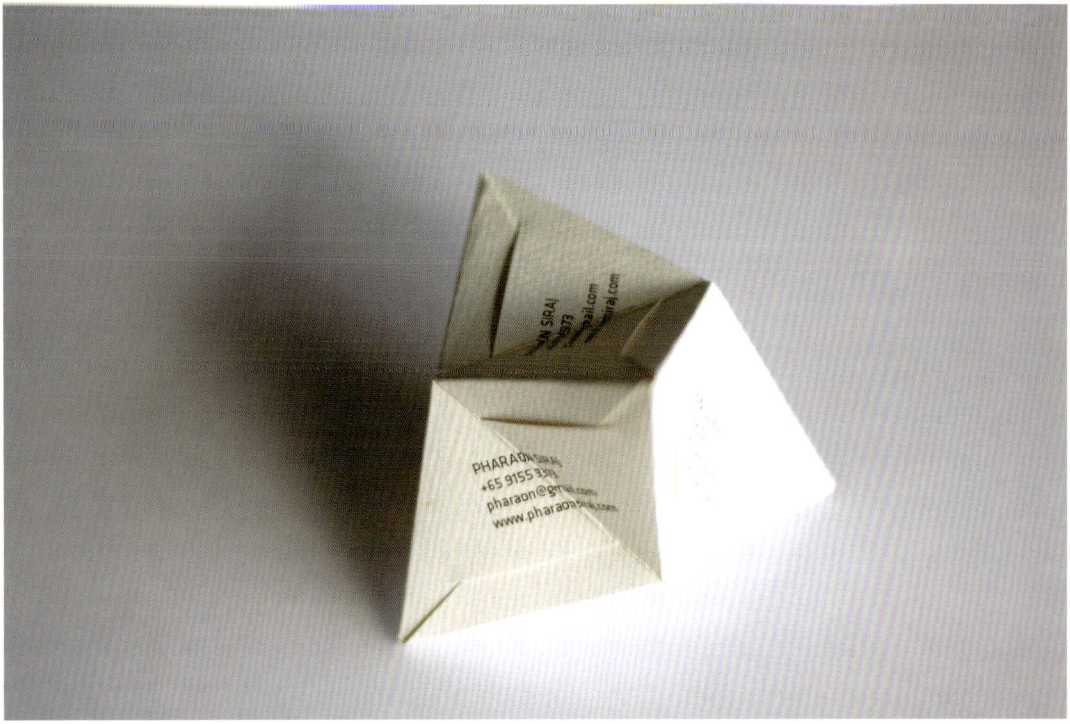

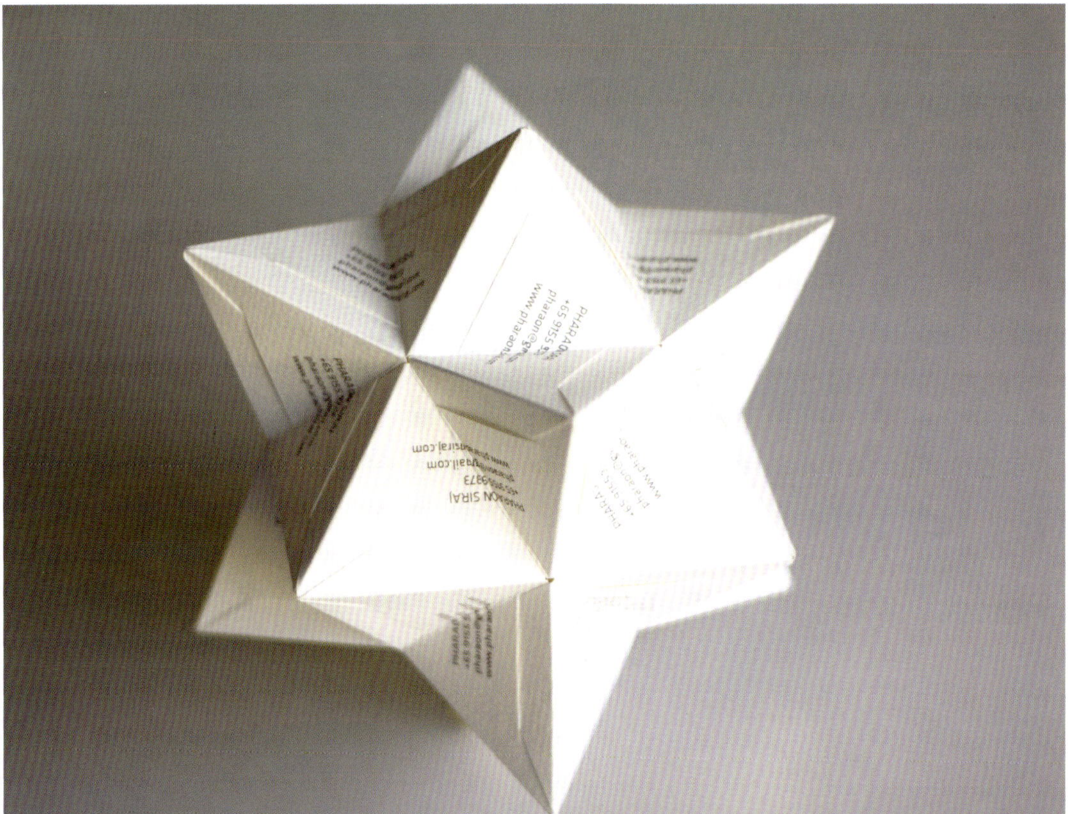

BELL RUNE
Agency:
R&D
Work Type:
Identity

Business card for artist
Bella Rune on the occasion
of her residence in Tokyo.

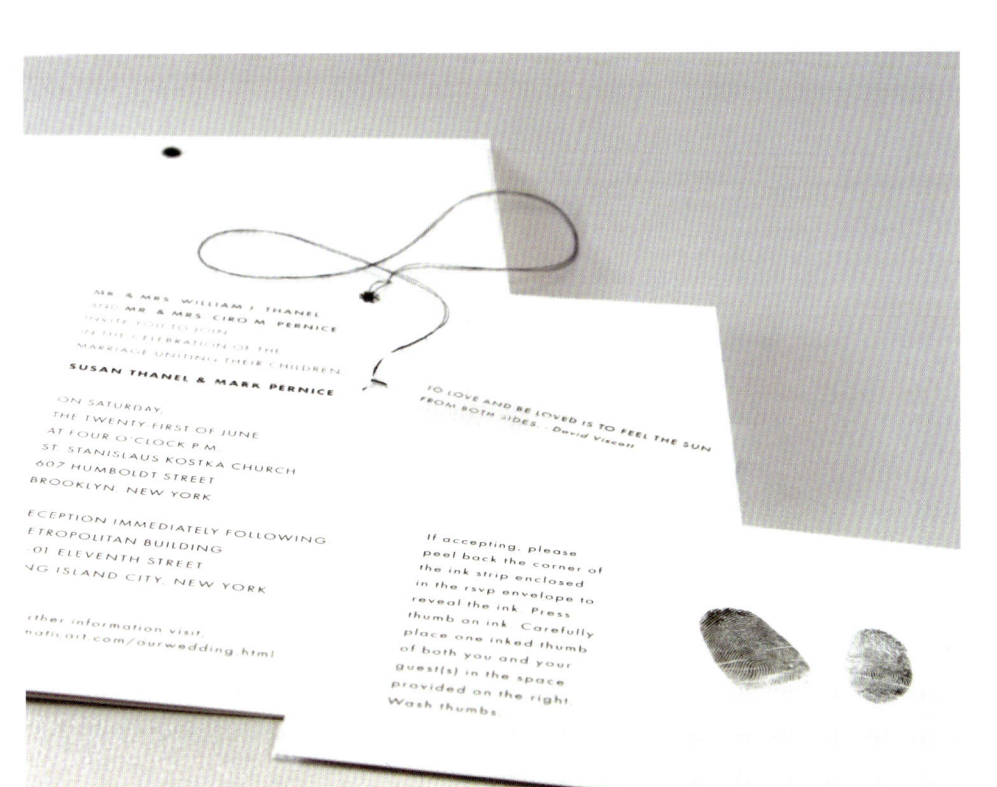

WEDDING INVITE

Agency:
Mark Pernice / Matic
Work Type:
Invitation

Two pieces of cardstock, blind embossed on one side and gold foil stamped on the other then riveted together. In the middle is a piece of thread that falls out and hangs to reveal a message. "To love and to be loved is to feel the sun from both sides." Also, included was an ink strip. Invitees were asked to include their thumbprints and that of their guests. Later, each place card was individualized with a unique design made from the two. Some guests got creative including messages, toes, entire fingers and a cat's paw.

PETER CRAWLEY
Agency:
Studio Parris Wakefield
Illustration:
Hand stitched by Peter
Crawley
Work Type:
Identity

We were asked by up-and-
coming stitched artist Peter
Crawley to design a logo
for him that communicated
his craftsmanship, and
convey his contemporary
interpretation of a
traditional medium. We found
that Meta Serif italic, a
contemporary serif, has
an air of luxury, with a
phenomenal level of detail
and we thought that it
perfectly described Peter
Crawley's work too. The
Meta Serif italic logotype
is supported by Meta Roman
for all communications
which provides two
elements that can be
successfully combined yet
remain distinct. A simple
monochromatic palette
supports the work which is
consolidated by these solid
typographic foundations.

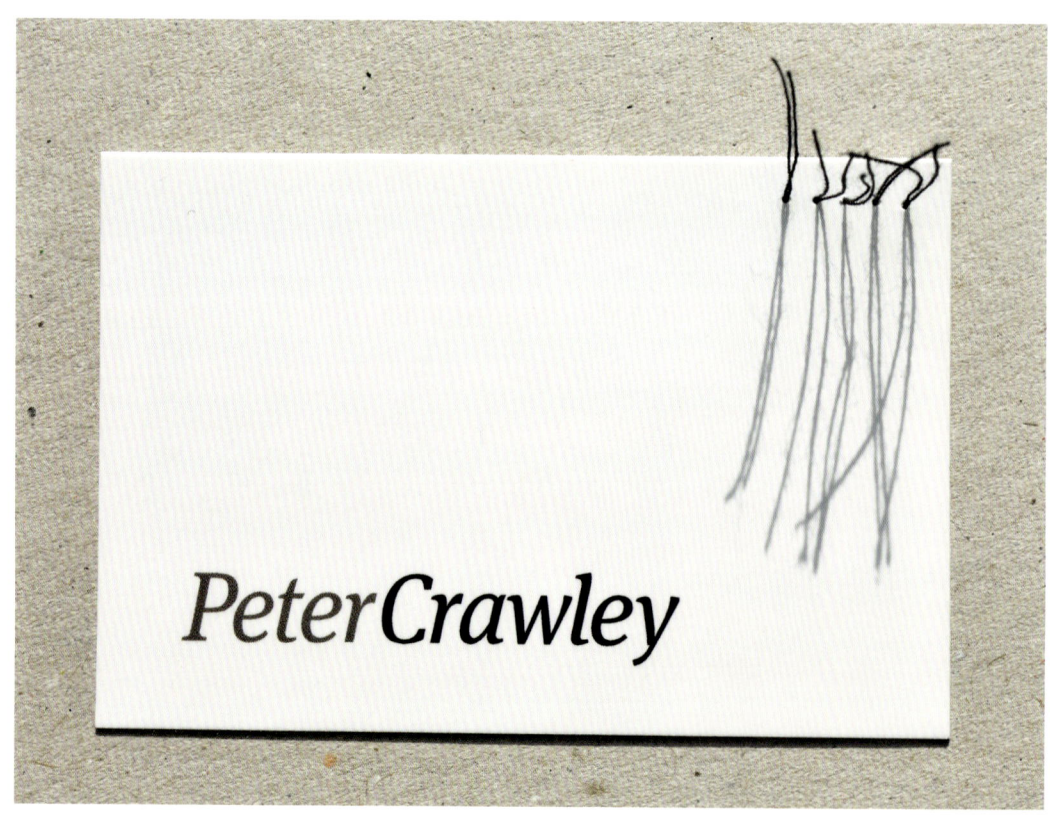

07932 9
hello@pe
www.peter
2 The Rickyar
Sherington
Buckinghamshir
PeterCrawley

PeterCrawley
2 The Rick
Sherington
Buckinghamshi

YEAR OPEN PARTY
Agency:
Liao Graphic Studio
Designer:
Wei Liao & Yurong Zhen
Work Type:
Invitation

It's a dinner invitation designed for Liao Graphic Studio. The concept is a fantastic dining experience. Through fresh vegetables and re-combined characters, you can imagine and construct a unique dining memory by yourself in pure space. Try to communicate the essence of something and wonderful experience of living. Enjoy it!

春酒
a function of spring
2011

春酒
a function of spring
2011 敬邀

2011/01/16 or 2011/01/29
SANYI , MIAOLI , TAIWAN (R.O.C)
苗栗縣 三義鄉雙湖村八鄰第20-6號

one person , one cooked

LiaoGraphix

MIZUKAGAMI
Designer:
Rikako Nagashima
Work Type:
Invitation

This is the invitation to my solo exhibition mizukagami.

At the exhibition, I showed an installation of a mirror in the shape of water (mizukagami in Japanese).

The invitation text is reversed, but can be read when reflected onto the mirrored part.

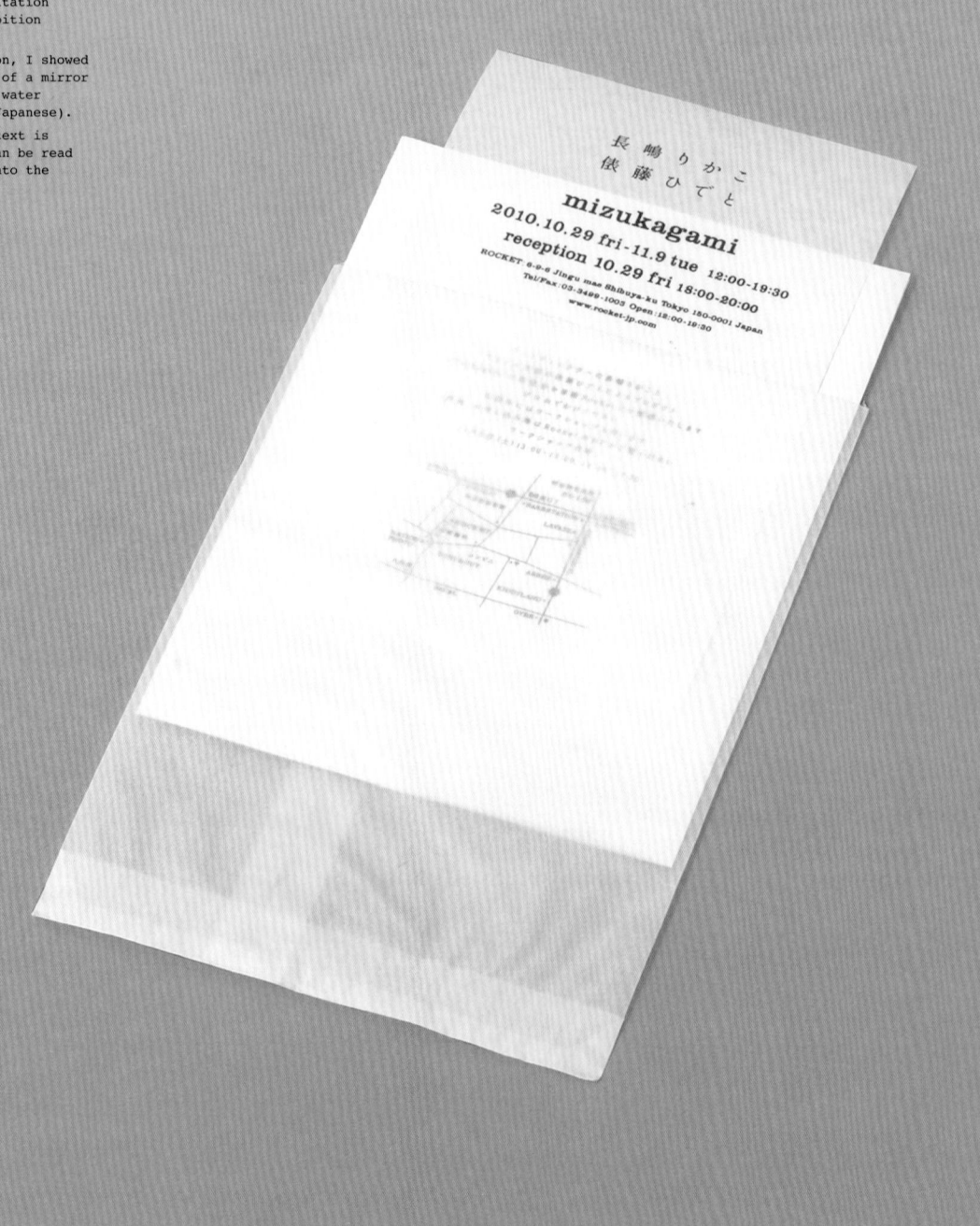

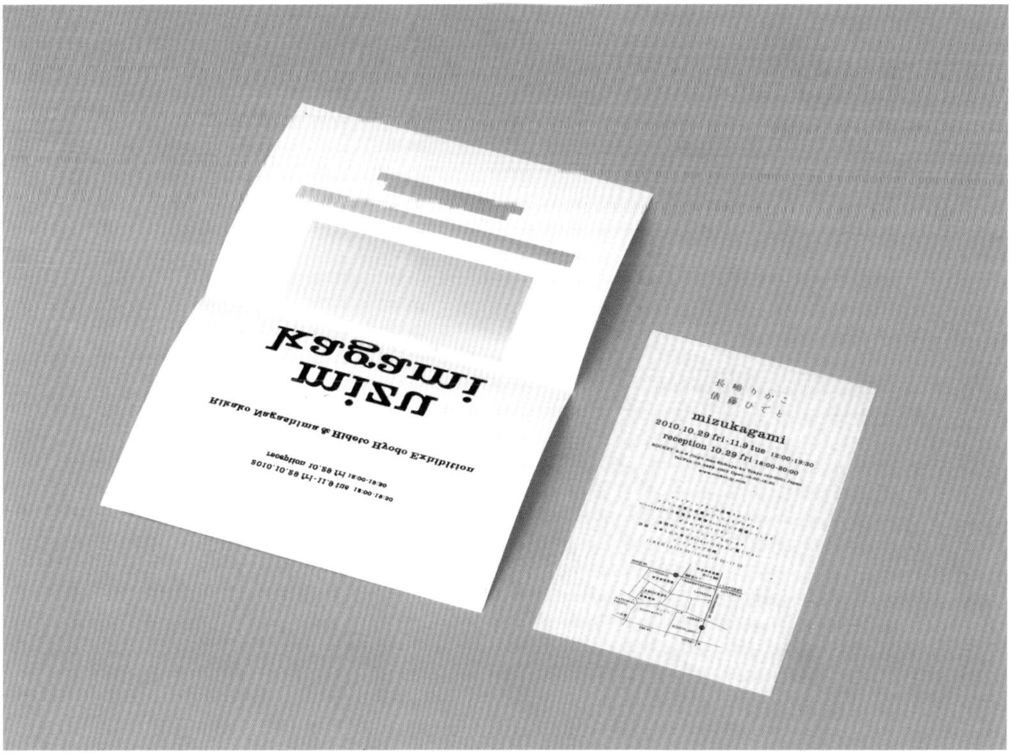
長嶋りかこ
俵藤ひでと
mizukagami
2010.10.29 fri - 11.9 tue 12:00-19:30
reception 10.29 fri 18:00-20:00

mizu
kagami
長嶋りかこ
俵藤ひでと
mizukagami
2010.10.29 fri - 11.9 tue 12:00-19:30
reception 10.29 fri 18:00-20:00

KIMITAKA KISAKI
Agency:
UMA/design farm
Designer:
Yuma Harada
Photography:
Takumi Ota
Work Type:
Identity

Business card for Kimitaka
Kisaki.

BAMBINI

Agency:
Studio Filippo Nostri
Work Type:
Invitation

Invite made of a DIN A4 sheet folded in half with colored paper glued on the inside and fold on cover to reveal it.

THE VIRIDI-ANNE
2011 SS COLLECTION
INVITATION

Agency:
NIGN Company Limited
Designer:
Kenichiro Ohara
Work Type:
Invitation

The Viridi-anne is a fashion brand, initiated and produced by Tomoaki Okaniwa. The brand holds two collections in Paris every year and 2011 Spring/Summer Collection's theme was blue period. The invitation card expressed the theme by allocating "moment" between a white card and thin blue paper.

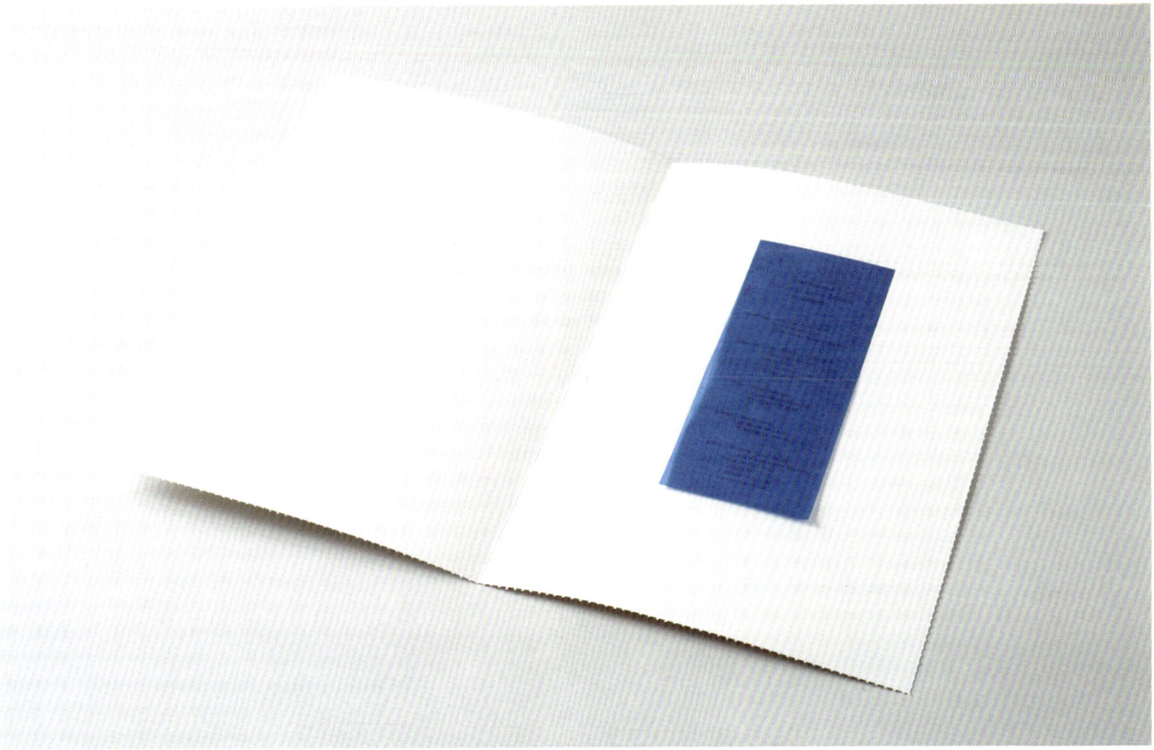

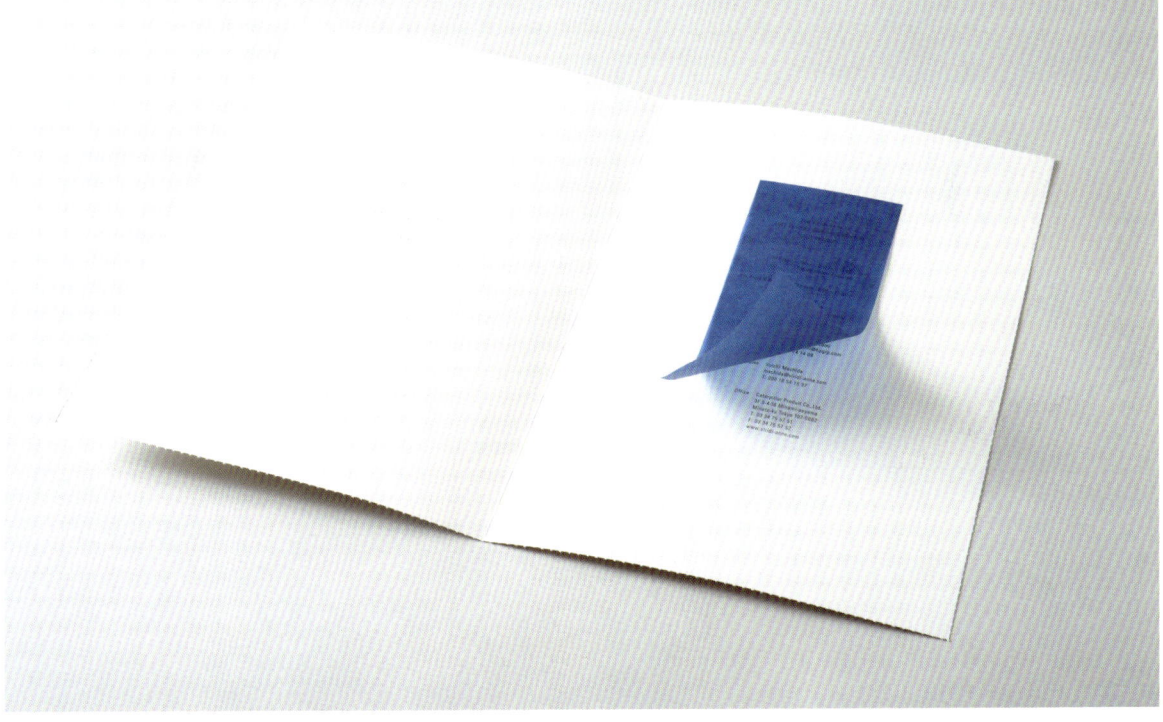

TRAPPED IN SUBURBIA

Agency:
Trapped in Suburbia
Work Type:
Identity

You'll probably recognize the following situation. You meet someone and that person introduces himself. When that person walks away, you are wondering what his or her name was. You only remember 'the guy with the black glasses' or 'the chick with that big haircut'. With this in mind we've made business cards without names, but with a description. For instance: "Je weet wel dat ontwerpburo met die moeilijke naam", meaning "You know, the design agency with the difficult name".

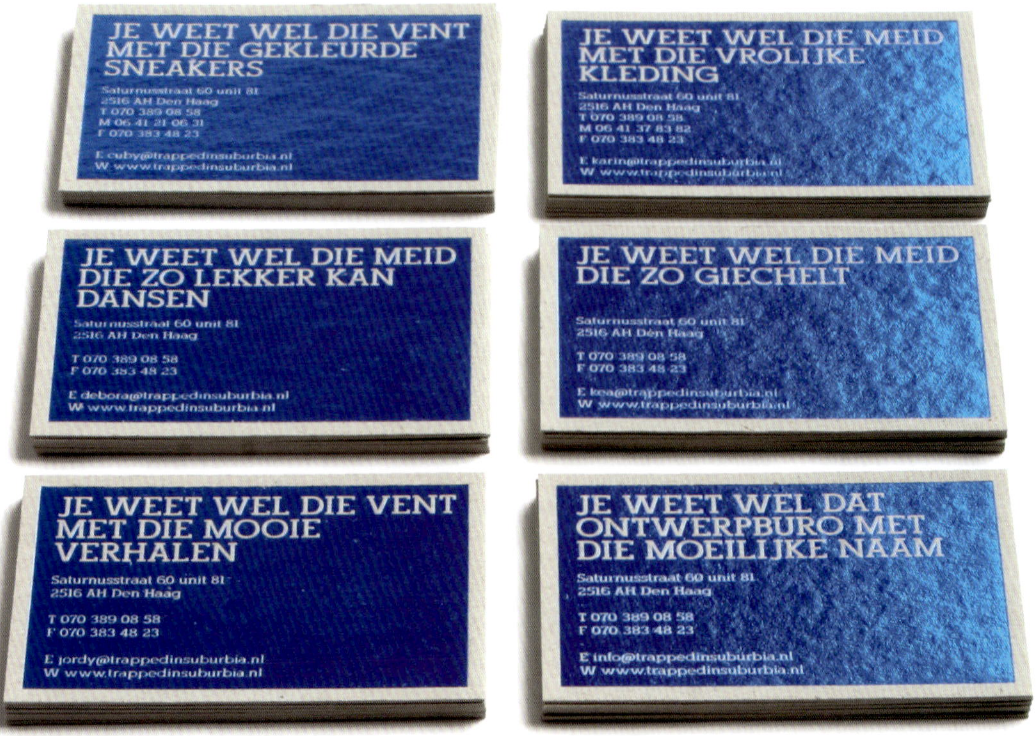

JE WEET WEL DIE VENT MET DIE GEKLEURDE SNEAKERS
JE WEET WEL DIE MEID DIE ZO LEKKER KAN DANSEN
Saturnusstraat 60 unit 81
2516 AH Den Haag
T 070 389 08 58
F 070 383 48 23
E debora@trappedinsuburbia.nl
W www.trappedinsuburbia.nl
JE WEET WEL DIE MEID DIE ZO GIECHELT
Saturnusstraat 60 unit 81
2516 AH Den Haag
T 070 389 08 58
F 070 383 48 23
E kea@trappedinsuburbia.nl
W www.trappedinsuburbia.nl
JE WEET WEL DIE VENT MET DIE MOOIE VERHALEN
Saturnusstraat 60 unit 81
2516 AH Den Haag
T 070 389 08 58
F 070 383 48 23
E jordy@trappedinsuburbia.nl
W www.trappedinsuburbia.nl
JE WEET WEL DAT ONTWERPBURO MET DIE MOEILIJKE NAAM
Saturnusstraat 60 unit 81
2516 AH Den Haag
T 070 389 08 58
F 070 383 48 23
E info@trappedinsuburbia.nl
W www.trappedinsuburbia.nl

Trapped in Suburbia
Trapped in Suburbia
Saturnusstraat 60 Unit 81
2516 AH Den Haag

HELLO JOHN IDENTITY

Agency:
Alva
Work Type:
Identity

John is our friend,
and we love to support
our friends. He is a
very gifted young movie
director.

We've made his identity and
business cards -- original
typography, printed in
various hot foil colours.

JOHN FILIPE
& GRAPHIC
HELLOJOHN.NET
HELLO JOHN

FILM & GRAPHIC
JOHN FILIPE
HELLOJOHN.NET
91 07 06 213
HELLO JOHN
HELLO JOHN

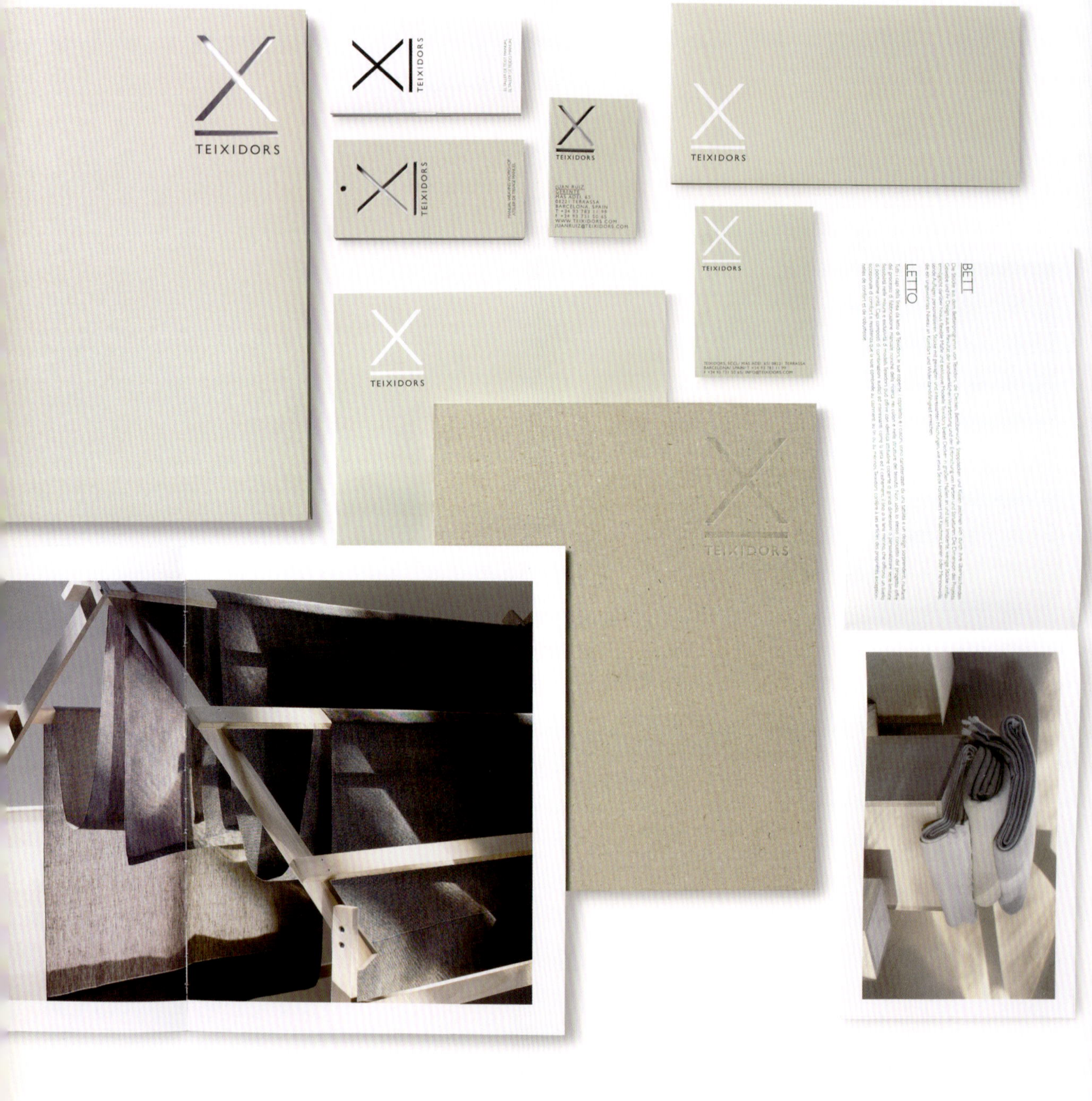
TEIXIDORS
BETT
LETTO

TEIXIDORS
Agency:
Clase bcn
Work Type:
Identity

A project for a very special cooperative, winner of the National Award for Craftwork 2008. The refined simplicity of the products provided the inspiration for our approach to the design. Clear forms, warm and simple colours and a very clean and fine typeface. The logotype, formed of an underscored x shape which refers to the basic component of weaving and also accents the most notable letter in the company's name. The art direction of the photographs show a wooden house which represents the house of Teixidors and the idea of Teixidors's products in a very abstract way: natural light, clean images and a very simple and abstract way of a house.We showed the range of handwoven blankets, pillows, courtains without using the common language appearing in decoration magazines etc. Everything is very simple but at the same time unique.

VERA XANE

Agency:
Toben
Work Type:
Identity

"A prayer for the wild at heart, kept in cages." (Tennessee Williams)

Vera Xane is a new jewellery brand with great inspiration and an exciting first range to launch later in 2011.

Toben was involved in the design of its visual identity, identity concepts, logo mark, and its first applications.

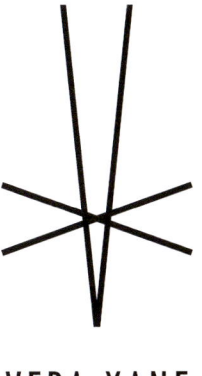

VERA XANE

VERA XANE

VERA XANE

THE FRINGE HAIR
LOUNGE

Agency:
Packofwolv.es
Designer:
Nicholas Hawker
Work Type:
Identity

The Fringe Hair Lounge identity was designed to reflect the style and attitude of a contemporary hair salon. The idea of the 'haircut' was translated in to a triangular shape which is consistent throughout the overall design. Foil on the business card was chosen to display the diverse light spectrums which relate to the individuality of ones hairstyle.

the FRINGE hair lounge
the CLIENT list
name
phone
mobile
email
address
date
colour information
stylist intl
notes
the PRICE list
cut and blow dry
women from
men
shave from
$70
$45
$15
re–style
women
men
$85
$55
hair–up
hair–up
$70
bridal parties
price on request
blow dry
set
short
medium
long from
$48
$45
$55
$60
children
boys 10–18
girls 10–18 from
tints
regrowth
short
medium
long
foils
the FRINGE hair lounge
next visit
contact
03 9853 7477
address
shop 2/4–14
walpole st.
kew 3101

TRICOLETTE BRANDING

Agency:
KentLyons
Work Type:
Identity

KentLyons developed Tricolette's brand, signage, packaging, stationery, business cards and flyers, store signage and website. The retail store is located in London, NW8.

KentLyons were asked to avoid tired associations with knitting, a more modern approach was needed appealing to both new / young as well as experienced knitters.

Tricolette's brand logo is made from a bespoke logotype created using 3 parallel lines. This is both a response to the name Tricolette and also as a reflection of the intricacy of wool and yarn. A fresh colour palette was created using a three colours; pistachio, amethyst and fushia. Copper foil adds a flourish to stationery and the shop fascia.

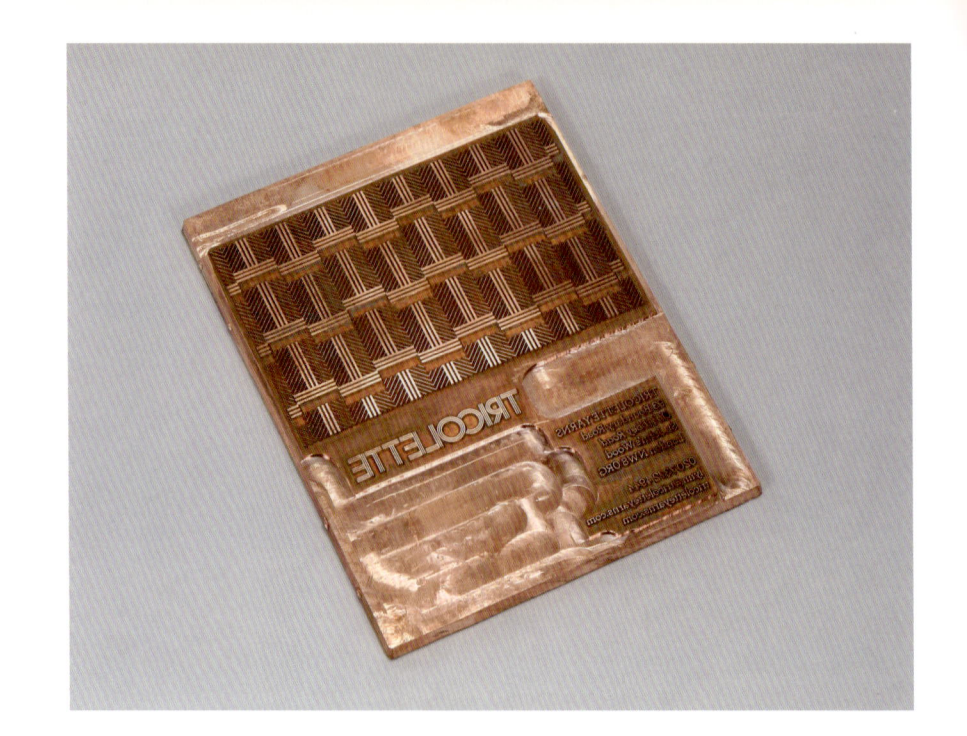

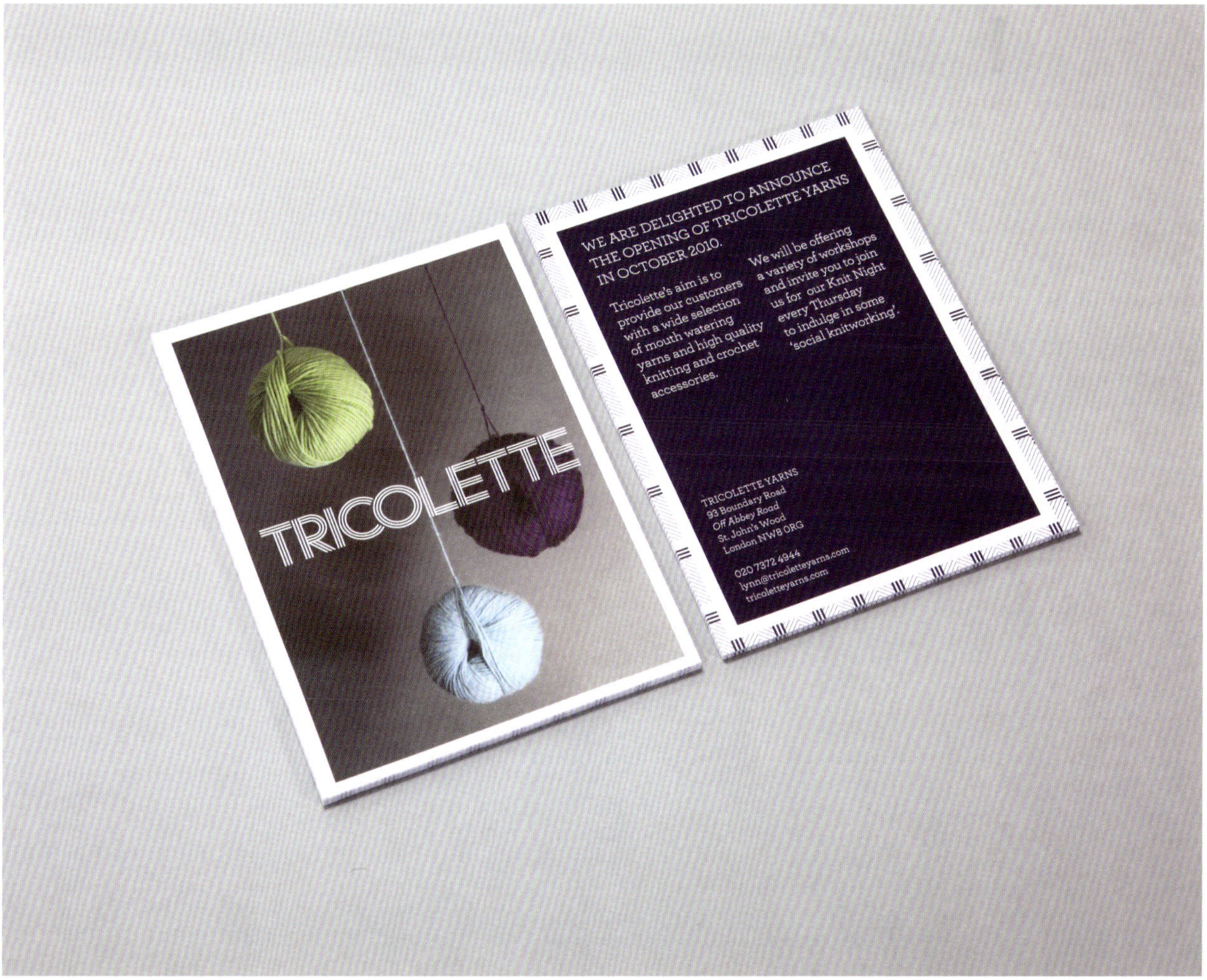
TRICOLETTE
WE ARE DELIGHTED TO ANNOUNCE THE OPENING OF TRICOLETTE YARNS IN OCTOBER 2010.
Tricolette's aim is to provide our customers with a wide selection of mouth watering yarns and high quality knitting and crochet accessories.
We will be offering a variety of workshops and invite you to join us for our Knit Night every Thursday to indulge in some 'social knitworking'.
TRICOLETTE YARNS
93 Boundary Road
Off Abbey Road
St. John's Wood
London NW8 0RG
020 7372 4944
lynn@tricoletteyarns.com
tricoletteyarns.com

LUXE CARDS

Agency:
Seesaw
Work Type:
Identity

Luxe is a Melbourne based make-up artistry service. A custom pattern was created to represent the soft hues of a eye-shadow palette. When designing the business cards, a gloss silver foil was used to contrast against this delicate yardage.

TRIGGER SOLUTIONS

Agency:
Pupilpeople
Work Type:
Identity

Logo and namecard design for a local painting company.

Instead of traditional colour-printing methods to reflect the vibrancy of the palette offered, we applied a rainbow foil to the "brush" as a more eye-catching representation of the nature of the business. This treatment also appealed to their target market of young home makers.

NICOLAS LE MOIGNE
Agency:
Ultra:studio
Work Type:
Identity

Nicolas Le Moigne is an industrial designer in Switzerland.

The slash is like the letter "L" of Nicolas Le Moigne.

There is also a reference to the acronym limited edition (example: 1/100).

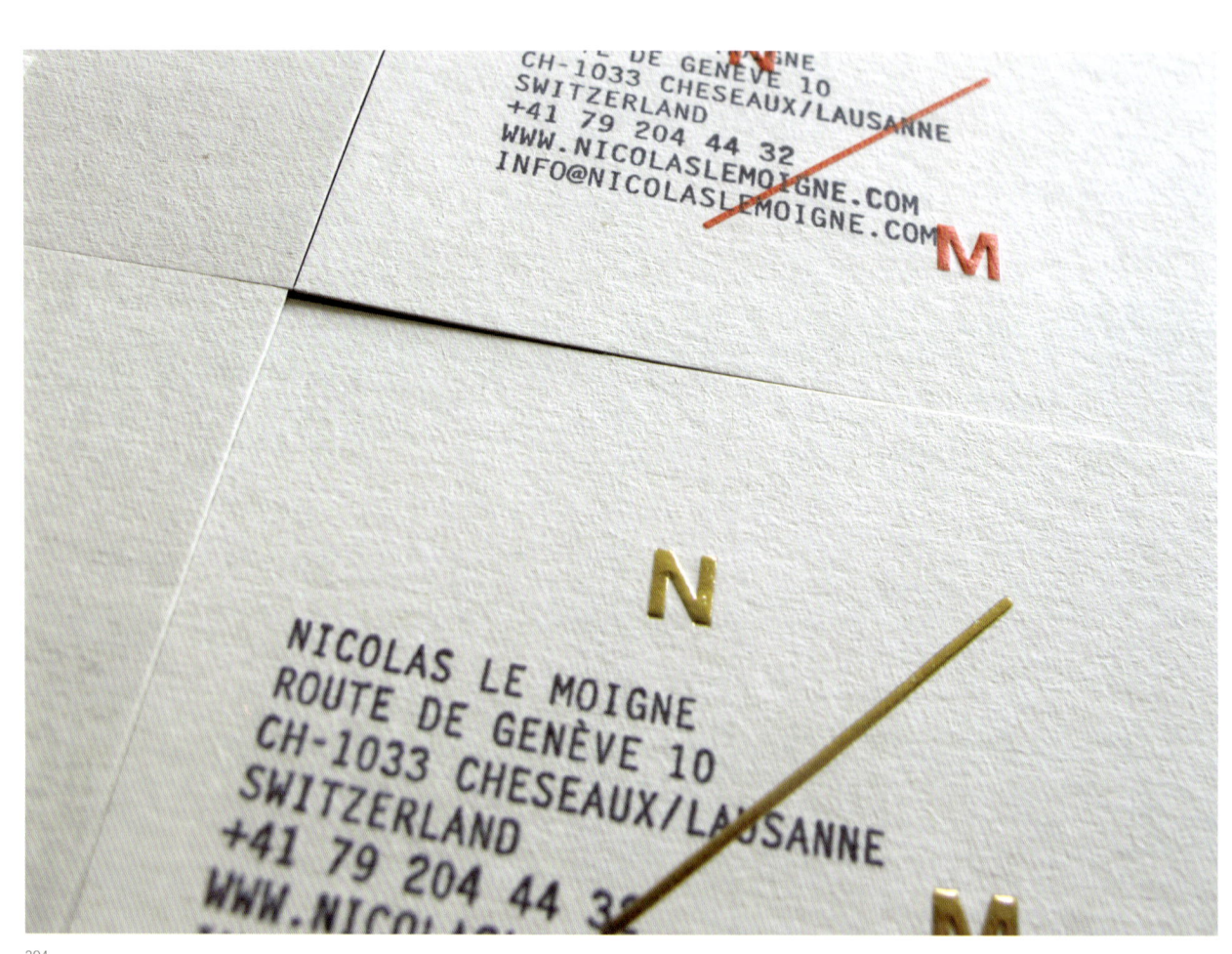

DAYNIGHT FOR MAMASTUDIO

Agency:
Mamastudio
Work Type:
Invitation

The Mamastudio Picnic is a well-established brand on Warsaw's culture scene. Every year Mamastudio celebrates the birthday of their studio with the people of Warsaw. The 2011 event was the studio's 10th anniversary and required something special. The event's theme was titled DayNight and a bat was chosen as the mascot. He appears in a range of promotional materials in two versions: for day and for night. The bat was awake or asleep depending which way you turned the invitation, flyer or poster. The 2011 Mamastudio Picnic broke all previous records, continuing for twenty hours, and attracting over 3,000 guests.

BESPOKE BRANDING

Agency:
KentLyons
Work Type:
Identity

KentLyons created an identity, membership card and website for Bespoke, a membership programme run by Manhattan Loft Corporation (MLC) for their residents. MLC collaborate with a number of companies to offer special deals and services, which are listed on the website and accessible using the Bespoke membership card.

0500
Manhattan Loft Corporation
BE
SP
OK
E

0400
0399
0398
0397
0396
0395

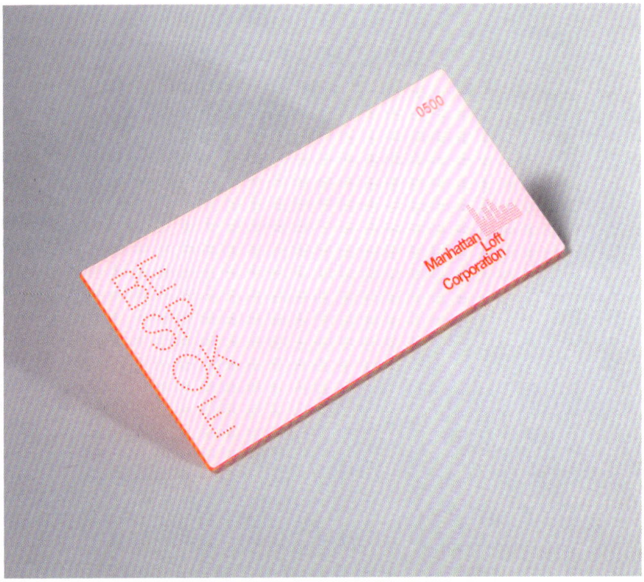
0500
Manhattan Loft Corporation
BE
SP
OK
E

SAMIA KHAN LONDON

Agency:
Hello
Work Type:
Identity

Samia Khan London is a unique boutique PR agency, specializing in fashion and lifestyle. The agency builds and promotes brands via music, design the arts and fashion, while also delivering bespoke personal campaigns within the retail, wholesale and press platforms. Hello created an identity that captured the spirit and character of the founder and echoed the unique `boutique' elements of the service, through innovative triplexing, foil blocking and chisel die-cut techniques.

ERKA INTERIOR DESIGN
Agency:
Seven25. Design &
Typography. Inc.
Work Type:
Identity

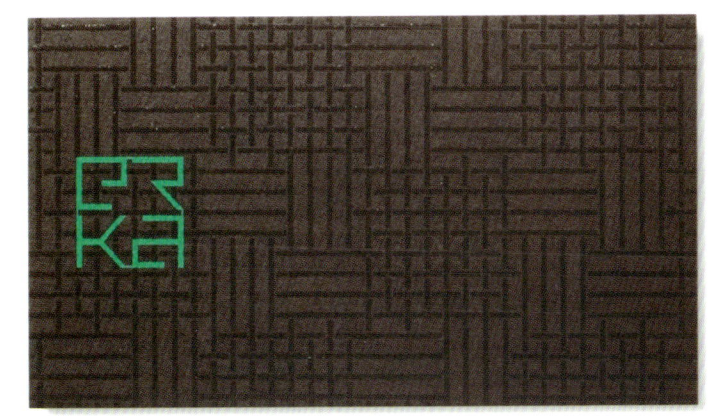

ERKA Interior Design
approached us to create
an identity for their
new firm. We devised a
visual language that is
clear about the company's
activities and showcases
the rich textures and
materials found in its
creations.

CONTACT

Agency:
MURMURE
Work Type:
Identity

Contact is a series of business cards whose heat-sensitive ink changes its appearance when it comes into contact with body heat. The project consists of three sets of cards on a common theme: the urban culture. The first two include graffiti, and the third is based on light-graff portraits where the graffiti on the wall completes the model. The business card is totally black at first, a feature that calls, for it goes against the desire to transmit information. But once in hand, the image appears along with information on the back of the card, the same way the portrait is revealed in the light. It is not only a medium of information anymore but it becomes an object to manipulate, playful and sensual.

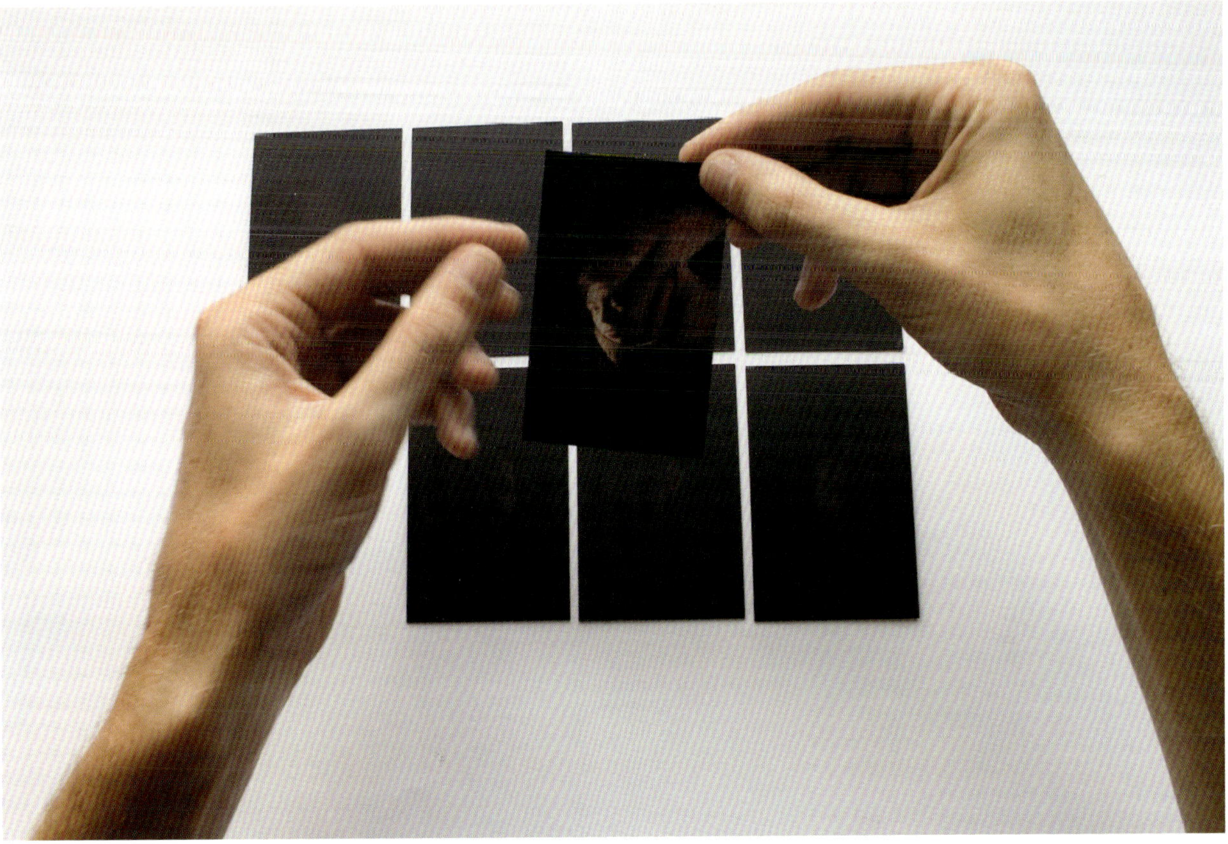

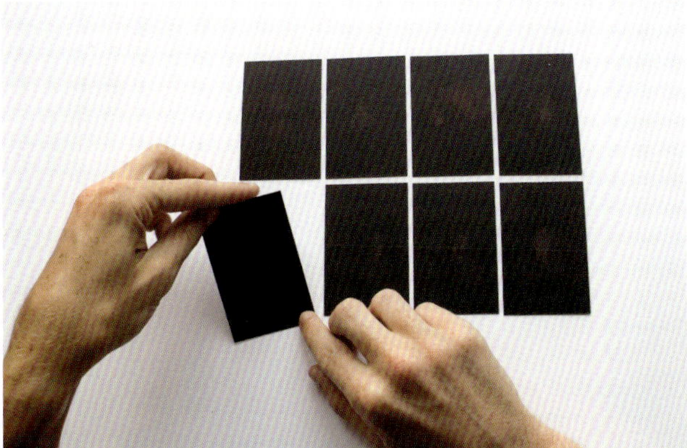

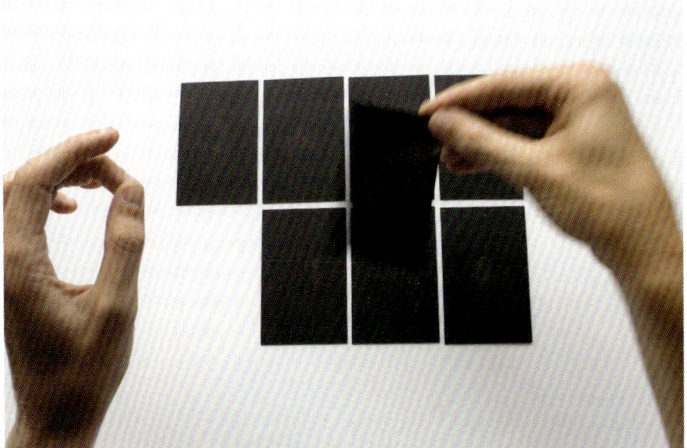

SUITE DISCOUNT CARD
Agency:
LSDK
Work Type:
Promotion

For the famous Stuttgart Bar Suite 212, LSDK has developed a discount card, showing only pictograms, printed negative on the smoked plastique. All additional content is written with hot foil onto the carrying flyer using only majuscule. The card was intended to be given to all neighbours of the bar, stimulating them to visit the bar more often.

312

INFLATABLE
ARCHITECTURE INVITE

Designer:
Gareth Procter
Photography:
Stephen Robertson
Work Type:
Invitation

Experiential Design agency E2 were holding an event and talk about Inflatable Architecture. To publicise and promote the event, I created an inflatable invite in the form of a balloon that was sent out to all guests, to reveal all the event details. Various applications including invites, posters and a stop frame animation created a holistic identity for the event.

FRANK Q

Agency:
Walnut
Work Type:
Invitation

Fashion fair invitations for Frank Q.

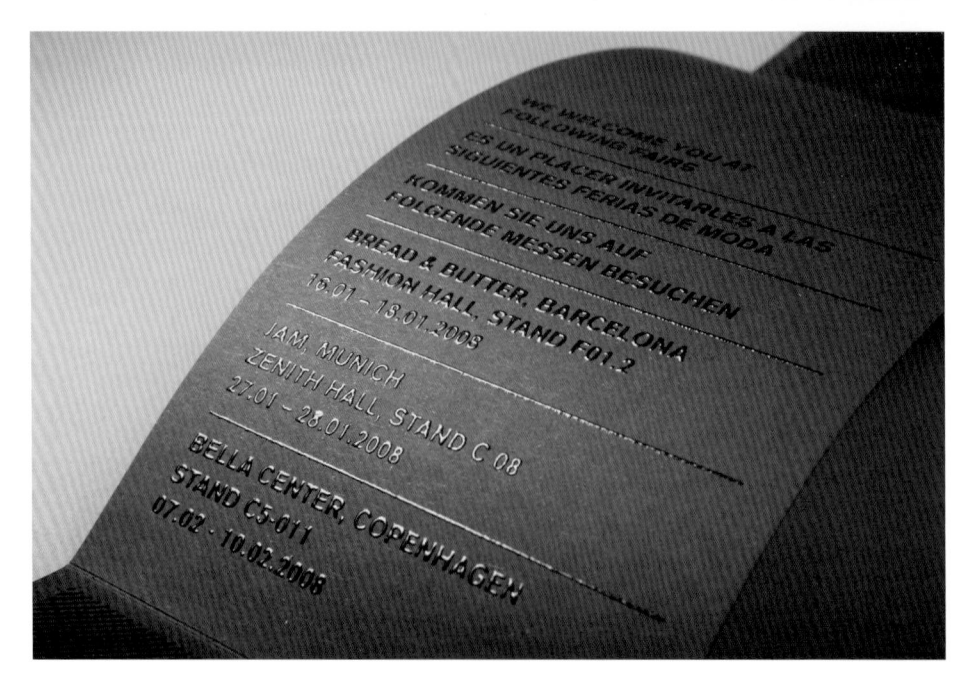

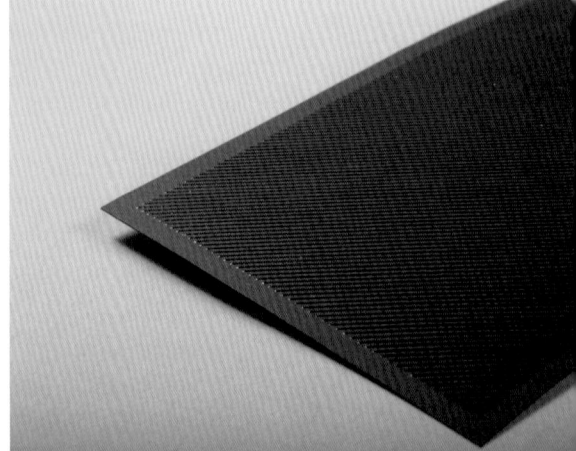

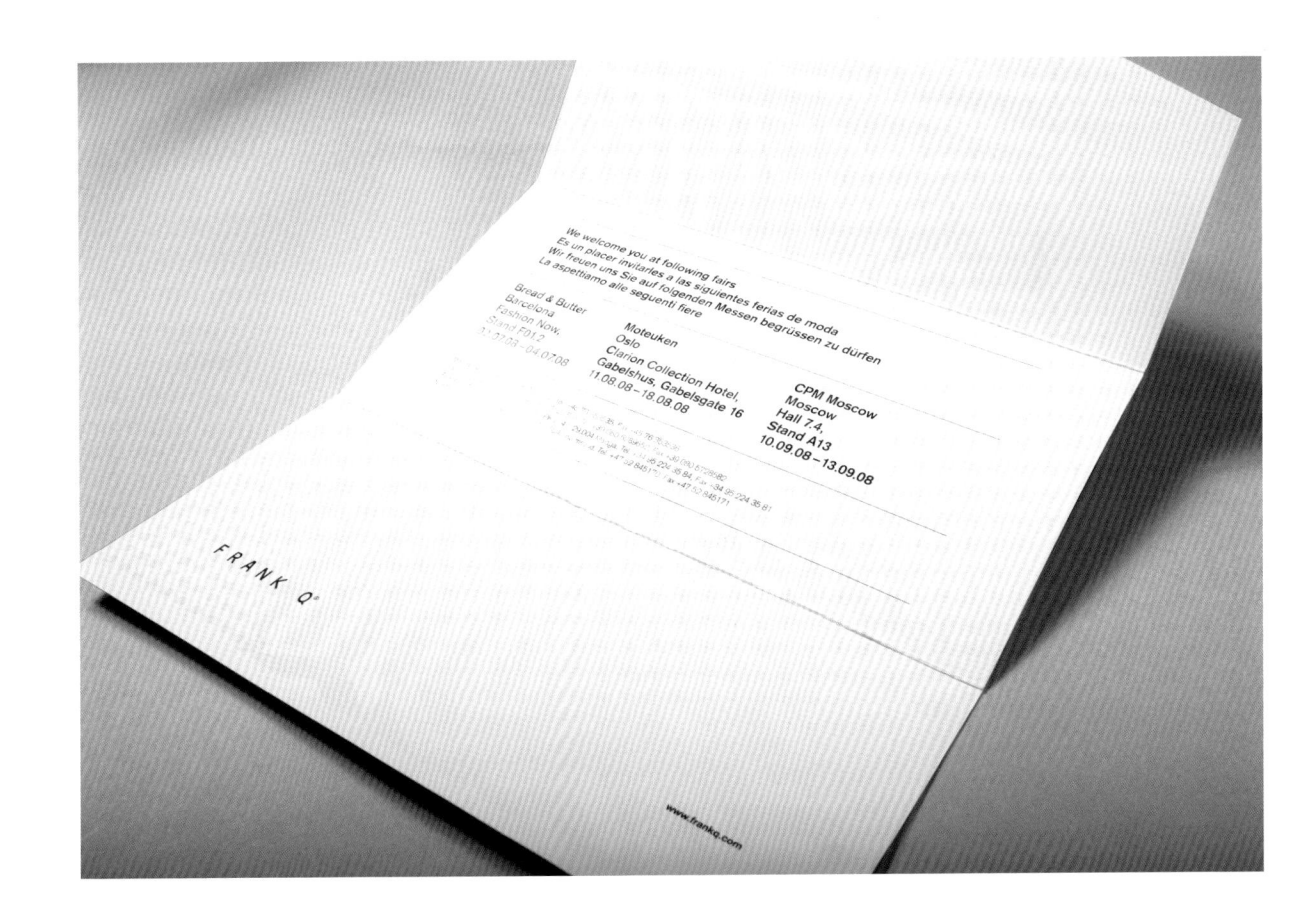

We welcome you at following fairs
Es un placer invitarles a las siguientes ferias de moda
Wir freuen uns Sie auf folgenden Messen begrüssen zu dürfen
La aspettiamo alle seguenti fiere

Bread & Butter
Barcelona
Fashion Now,
Stand F012
02.07.08 – 04.07.08

Moteuken
Oslo
Clarion Collection Hotel,
Gabelshus, Gabelsgate 16
11.08.08 – 18.08.08

CPM Moscow
Moscow
Hall 7.4,
Stand A13
10.09.08 – 13.09.08

FRANK Q®

www.frankq.com

FILTHYMEDIA

Agency:
filthymedia
Work Type:
Identity

We strongly believe in the value of print, so as a print-based design studio, we feel it's important that our stationery is a showcase of what we can do within the medium. We created a bespoke logo that was then embossed across all of our stationery, creating a latex texture on uncoated paper. We used a color palette set in black & white, with a hint of turquoise to demonstrate the attention to detail we like to achieve with all of our projects.

All printing and finishing produced by Generation Press.

Josh White
filthymedia
Studio +44 (0)1273 683591
Mobile +44 (0)7846 557231
josh@filthymedia.com
filthymedia.com
29 Kensington Gardens
Brighton BN1 4AL
filthy

filthymedia
Studio +44 (0)1273 683591
studio@filthymedia.com
filthymedia.com
29 Kensington Gardens
Brighton BN1 4AL
filthy

Steve Gotts
filthymedia
Josh White
filthymedia
Studio +44 (0)1273 683591
Mobile +44 (0)7846 557231
josh@filthymedia.com
filthymedia.com
29 Kensington Gardens
Brighton BN1 4AL
Joe Pilbeam
filthymedia
Studio +44 (0)1273 683591
Mobile +44 (0)7838 124737
joe@filthymedia.com
filthymedia.com
29 Kensington Gardens
Brighton BN1 4AL

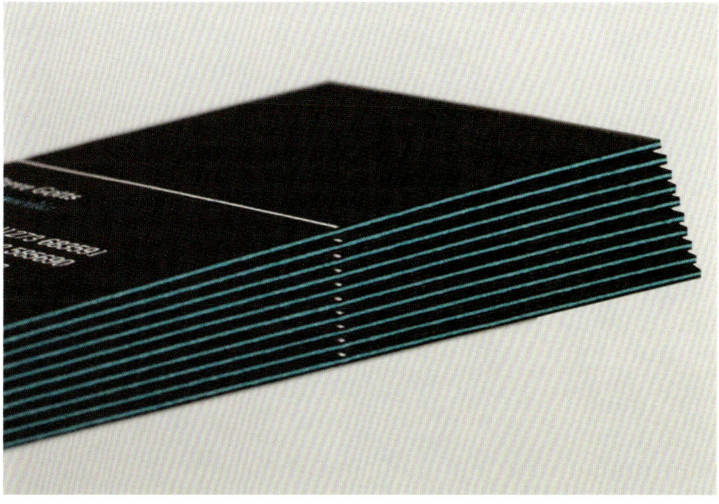

EINE

Agency:
ROOT
Work Type:
Identity

Ben Eine is one of London's most prolific and original street artists who specialises in the central element of all graffiti - letter forms. Eine has now built an outstanding worldwide reputation and wanted a brand that could translate across all platforms appealing to his collectors and the world's greatest galleries.

Our solution was to combine the black paint drips that Eine uses on the edges of his unique canvases with one of Eine's signature typefaces, the Circus font, in the form of an embossed `E'. Applying the identity to a stationery range we achieved an outstanding result by mixing several processes; screen printing onto duplexed card and applying UV to achieve the gloss finish we required.

EINE
Einesigns Limited
1 Cloudesley Road St Leonards on Sea East Sussex TN37 6JN
T +44 (0)7738 856 770 E bens1977@me.com W einesigns.co.uk
EINE
Einesigns Limited
1 Cloudesley Road St Leonards on Sea East Sussex TN37 6JN
T +44 (0)7738 856 770 E bens1977@me.com W einesigns.co.uk
EINE

JAMES PRUNEAN PAINTER CARDS

Designer:
James Prunean
Work Type:
Identity

Swatch business card designed for Ovi Prunean, a professional painter. A relatively basic design direction but with powerful results. Printed on a 220lb cotton paper stock with letterpress applied on "painter" in the corresponding swatch color for each card.

PAINTER

OVI PRUNEAN
T 519.569.9894
E OPRUNEAN@HOTMAIL.COM

INTERIOR · EXTERIOR · RENOVATIONS

MATTHEW DEL DEGAN

Designer:
Tyler Adam Smith
Work Type:
Identity

As an industrial designer looking for a business card and identity, materiality and objects were of the highest importance for Matthew. In order to speak immediately to the fact that at its core, what he does is making things, we opted to skip the ink and make the card itself the object by simply blind embossing the details on a beautiful, thick cardstock.

TAKUMI & KAEKO
WEDDING PARTY
Agency:
Yanagawa Design
Work Type:
Invitation

Invitation design for wedding party of Takumi & Kaeko.

TIMOTHY TAYLOR
GALLERY

Designer:
Stefi Orazi
Work Type:
Invitation

A selection of invitations and other print for art gallery in Mayfair.

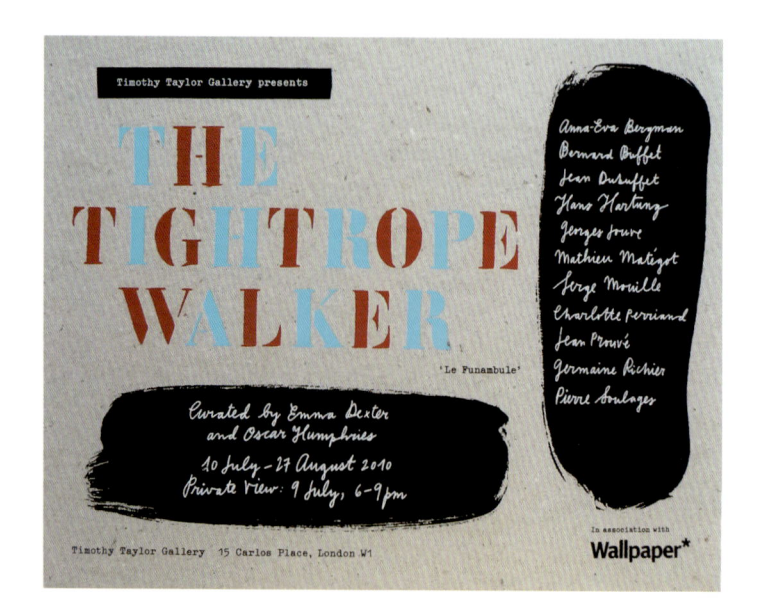

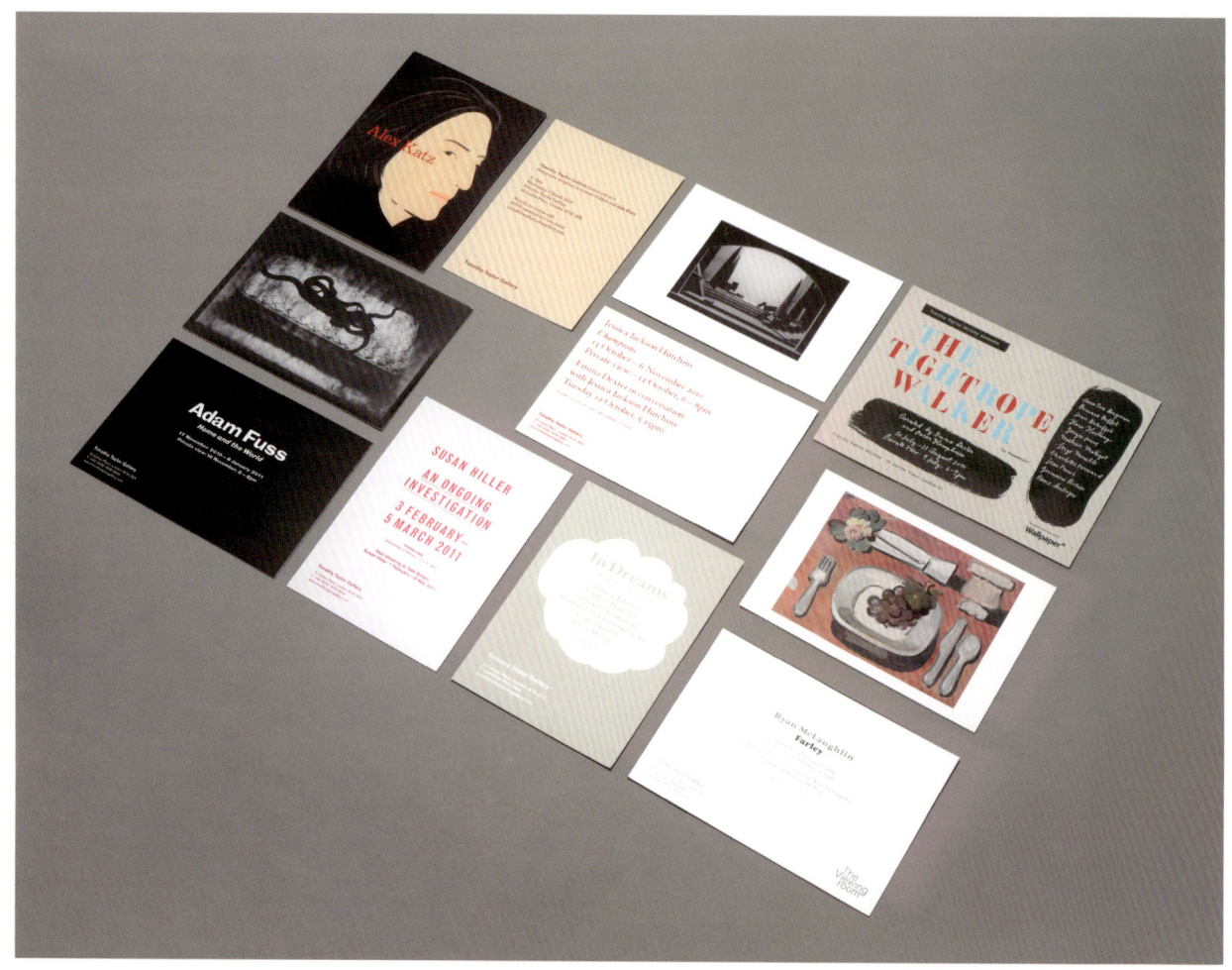

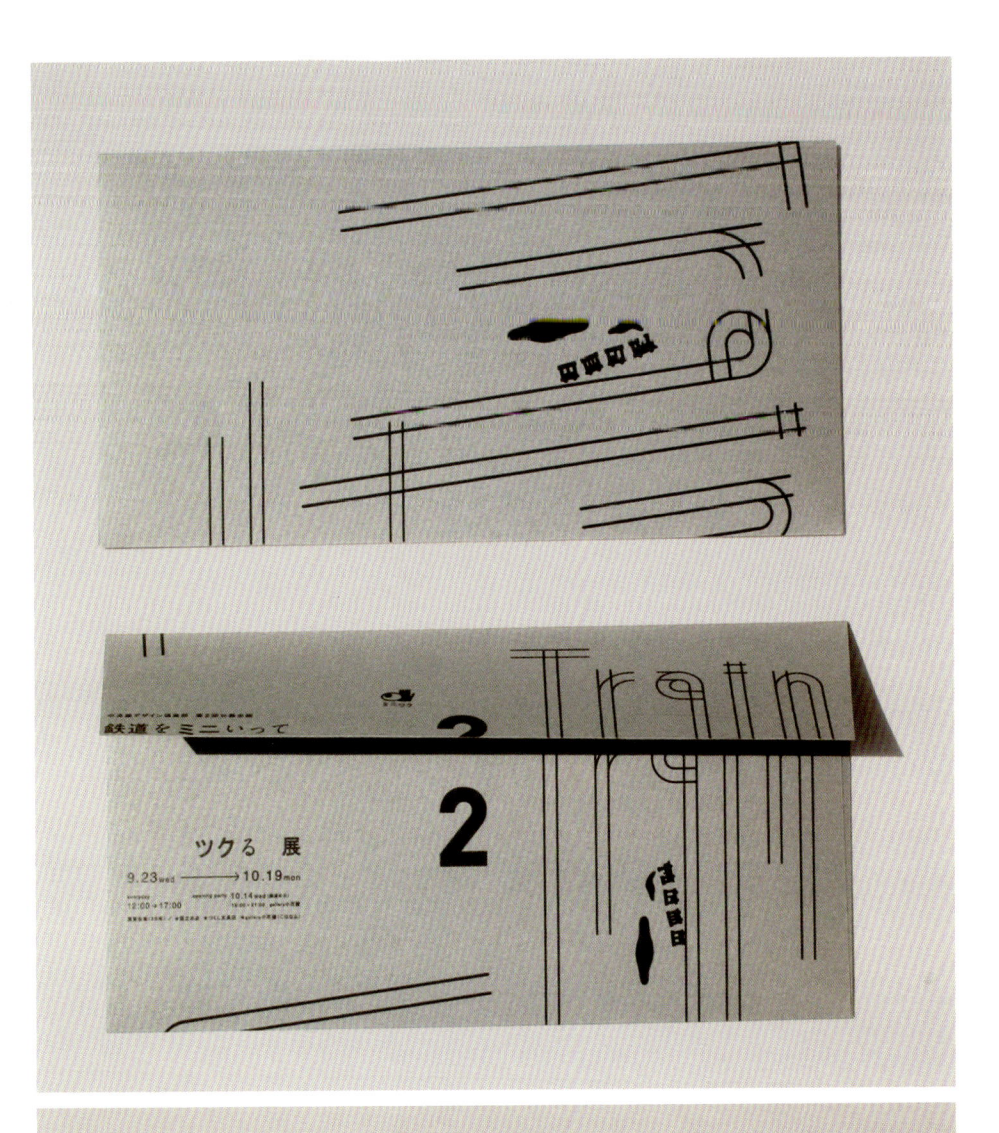

CENTRAL LINE DESIGN
CLUB

Agency:
K.M. design
Work Type:
Invitation

It is a public advertisement special exhibition of the Central Line Design Club.

The showplace and the place near each station are specified. The made thing is exhibited feeling it because it goes there, and it sees. It is scheduled to hold it once every year, and 32 station conquest is a project with a long breath to which it takes 32 years.

A4 PAPER FESTIVAL
V.I.P OPENING NIGHT
EVENT

Agency:
Peachy Flamingo
Designer:
Kylie McIntyre
Work Type:
Invitation

Invitation designed for
the A4 Paper Festival
V.I.P Opening Night Event.
The invite was designed
to represent the idea
of the paper festival;
being tactility, play
and expression through
handcrafted paper
creations. The invitation
invites the recipient to
get hands on and experience
these ideas.

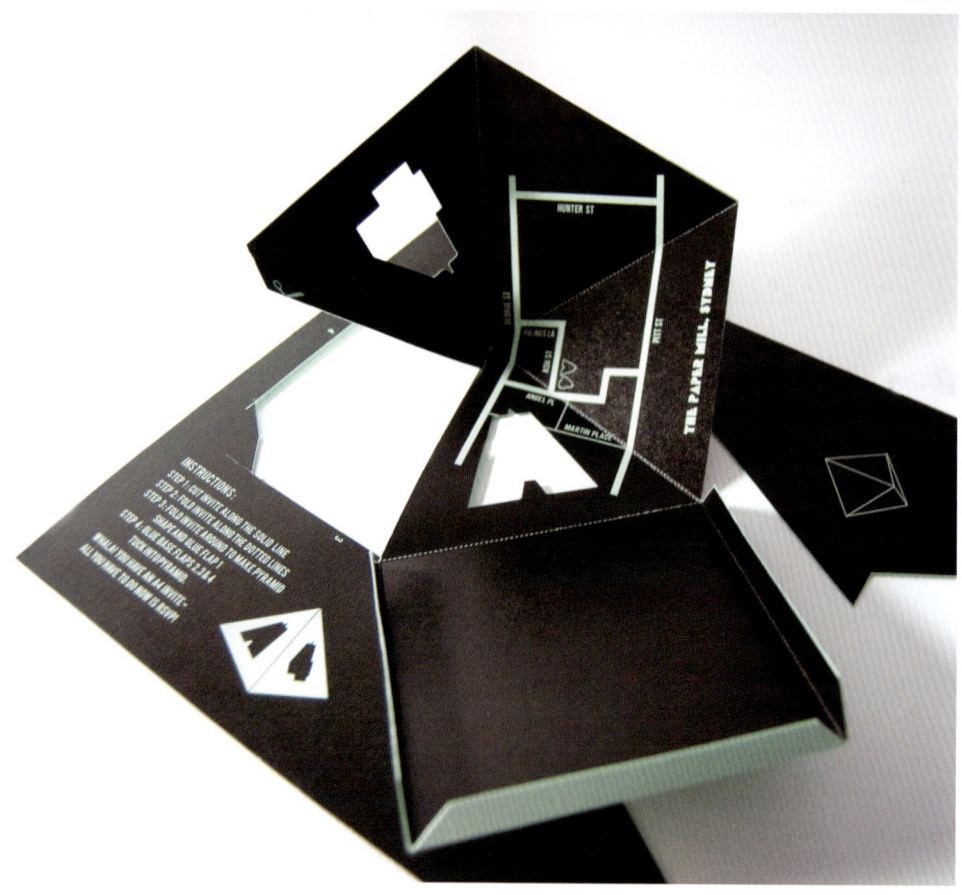

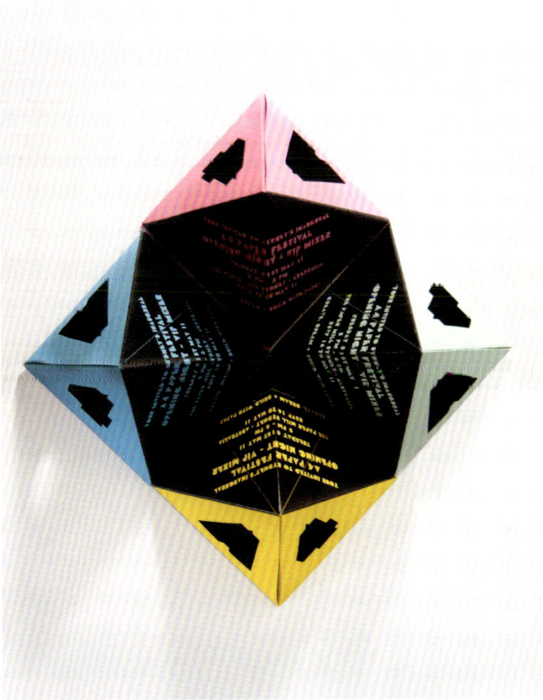

PRESENTED BY:
PAPER CONVENTION COLLECTIVE
THE PAPER MILL
ASHST, SHOP2, 1ANGEL PL.
SYDNEY 2000
AUSTRALIA
RSVP TO:
HELLO@PAPERCONVENTION.COM
MORE INFO VISIT:
PAPERCONVENTION.COM
SPONSORS, VENUE & MEDIA PARTNERS:
K.W.DOGGETT Fine Paper
digitalpress
CREATE, DREAM + BUILD WITH PAPER

XMAS CARDS 09
Designer:
Nicholas Jeeves
Work Type:
Greeting Card

Having decided not to waste by only ever reusing found materials for his Christmas cards, the designer collected and pressed a variety of autumn leaves, and individually stamped and numbered them. They were then sealed in clear recycled polybags.

ANDREW MALABRE
Designer:
Tyler Adam Smith
Work Type:
Identity

Andrew approached me as the Toronto International Film Festival was gearing up. Looking for a "snappy little business card" that would set him apart from the sea of people in the industry. We very much liked the notion of working with the obsessive-chain-smoking-writer-locked-up-in-a-bell-tower-somewhere.

Ultimately, we wanted to create a little narrative in the card.

330

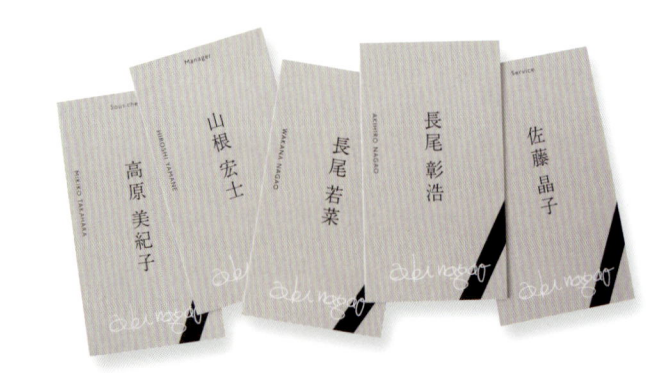

THINK BIG, DO SMALL

Great life isn't about huge things; great idea isn't about grand manifestations; it's all about small things that make a difference. There are always people who believe life is full of adventures and surprises, and they are willing to take risks as one man band or as a team. As conversations are carried out with six independent designers and studios, we will see how they break the convention and make a difference. What ever "mini" is in their eyes, the world allows for diversity.

Transwhite Studio   HANGZHOU, CHINA
Bond   HELSINKI, FINLAND
Casper Chan   LONDON, UK
Commune   SAPPORO, JAPAN
Prinz & Prinz   STOCKHOLM, SWEDEN
Neo Neo   GENEVA, SWITZERLAND

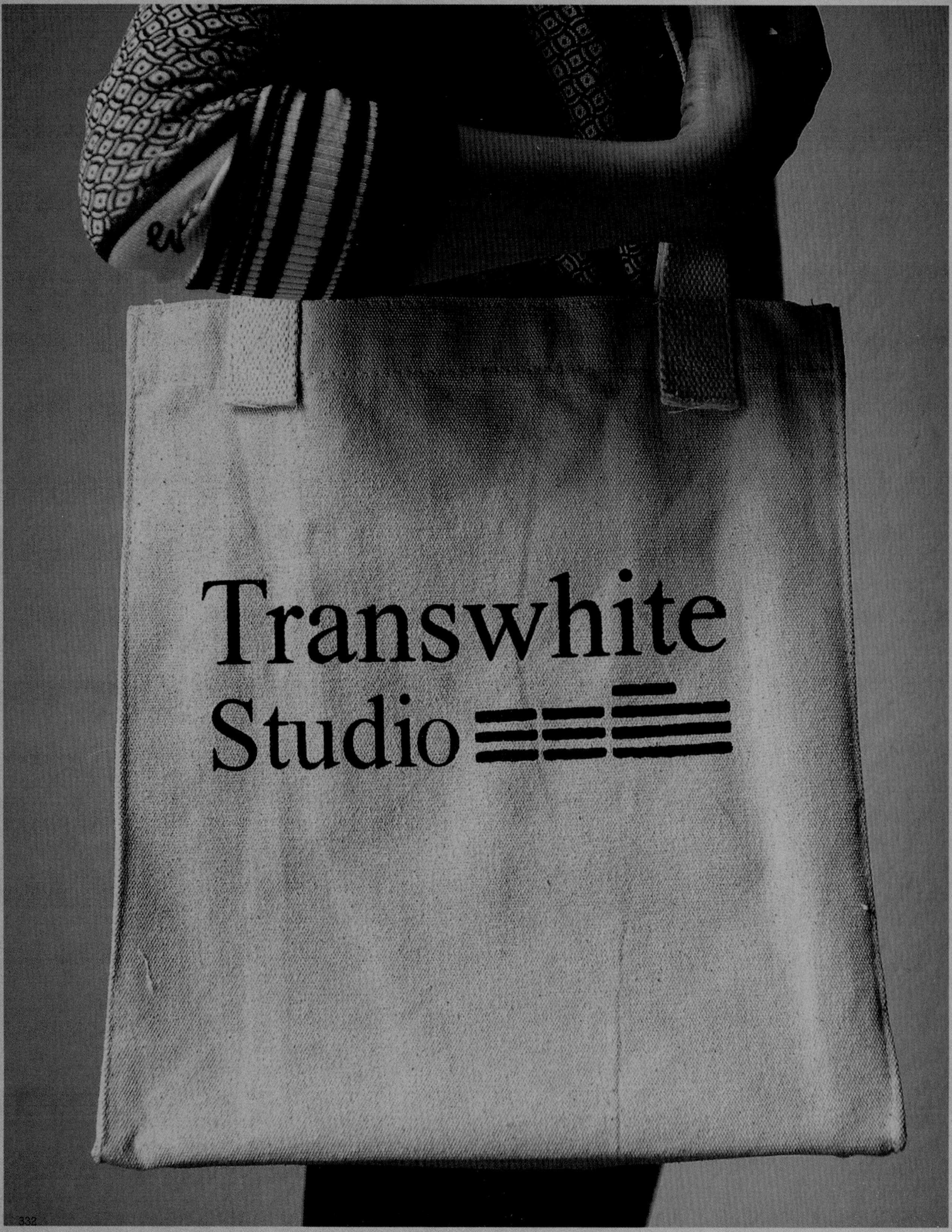
Transwhite
Studio

What do you usually get inspiration? Take the visual identity of YISI Space as an example.
Daily design inspiration comes mainly from my concerns on some things. For example "YISI Space" design was inspired by visiting the antique and flea market. During the weekends when I was in London, I often went to museums or antique markets. Therefore, you can find many design elements of "YISI Space" related to those experiences.

You have designed very smart name cards, stickers and invitation for YISI Space. Do you think those "mini" designs are "big" enough to communicate your ideas?
I think "mini graphic" is a "mini", but it can convey all information and design ideas, thus, they have no direct relationship. Small carriers, like name cards, stickers and invitations, also communicate big ideas of designers.

What distinguishes your work from that of your contemporaries?
In my opinion, the difference of my design work is because of my study and life experience. Both Chinese and Western art have a direct impact on my designs. I think mine is more like western design: free, bold and diverse.

As a designer, how do you understand "mini"? Please list 5 items which you think are "mini".
I think "mini" is a form. "Mini graphic" is expressing ideas and concepts through a number of smaller carriers. I believe that "less is more" should be able to explain the meaning of the word "mini" here.
Mini items are brochure, invitation, sticker and stamp, etc.

Have you seen any "mini" design works lately? Please describe them.
Recently I have been researching Chinese graphic designs in the early 20th century. Take matchbox label design as an example, designers of that age paid great attentions to the relationships between fonts, graphics and colors. They are very strict in how to use the graphic language perfectly.

What do you think are the key elements in making a difference with "mini" graphic works?
Idea, concept, design form and printing technology.

❛ "Less is more" should be able to explain the meaning of the word "mini" here. ❜

Interview With:
Transwhite Studio

Qiongjie Yu, founder of Transwhite Studio, is a graphic designer and book artist. She is now also a teacher of Zhejiang Gongshang University.

Qiongjie went to Camberwell College of Arts in University of the Arts London for further study in 2007. She'd majored in graphic design and book arts and achieved double master's degree in 2010. After graduation, she's back to China again and successfully founded Transwhite Studio in Hangzhou in 2011.

In addition to graphic design, Qiongjie is particularly keen on book arts. A number of her works have been collected by Tate Gallery, Leeds University Library, University of the Arts London, Camberwell College of Arts, University of Coventry, and so on. She'd also participated in many artist book fairs in Leeds, Glasgow, Warsaw, London and other cities.

TRANSWHITE STUDIO

Agency:
Transwhite Studio
Designer:
Qiongjie Yu
Work Type:
Identity

Culture of young people needs creativity. "Transwhite Studio" is young designers' practice of rethink and retranslates white. The designer would like to avadavat an attitude that be able to tolerance everything in art design and daily life. The reflection in graphic design is that different combination between classical English letters and abstract Chinese characters. The logo with horizontal lines and trace of brush in the seal is applied to different prints of the studio to present the taste of Transwhite.-- Simple but elegant.

Transwhite
Studio

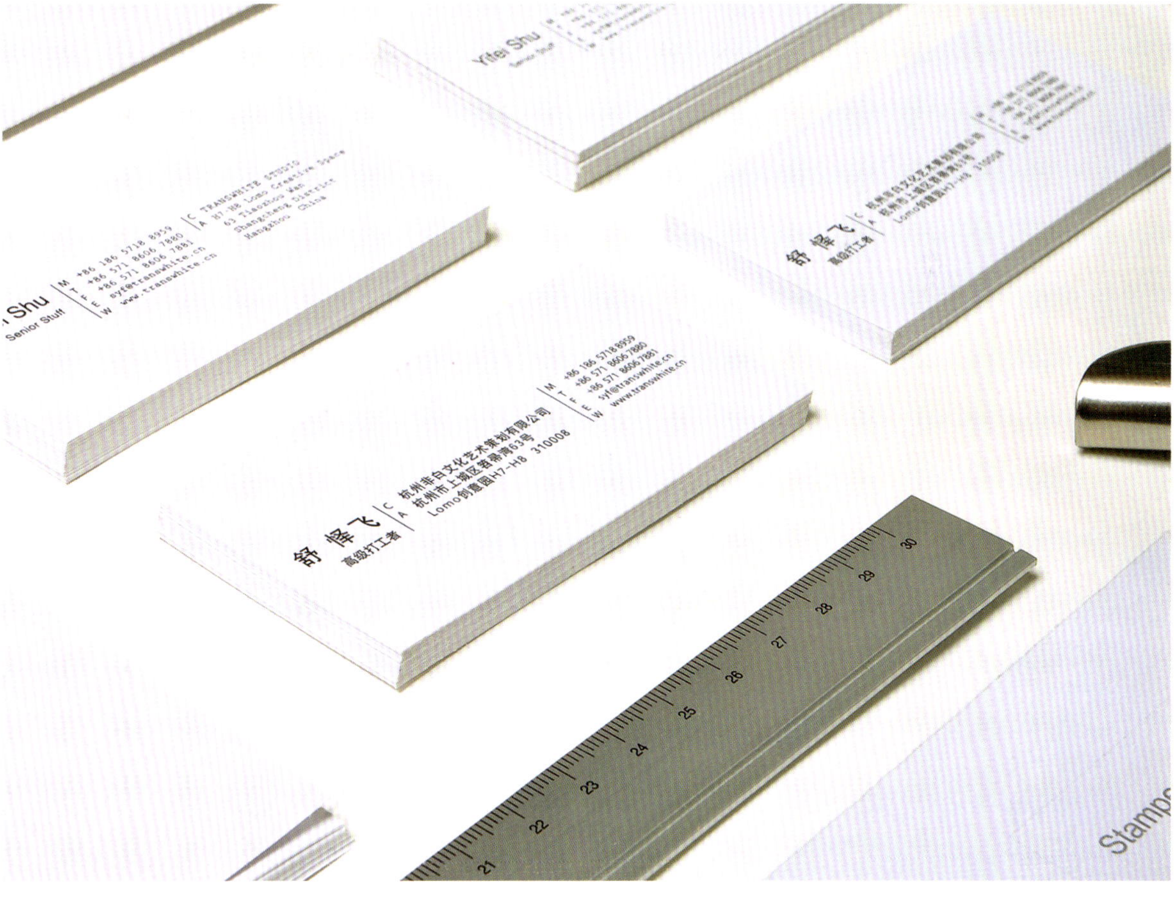
Yifei Shu
Senior Stuff
Shu
Senior Stuff
M +86 186 5718 8959
T +86 571 8606 7880
F +86 571 8606 7881
E syf@transwhite.cn
W www.transwhite.cn
C TRANSWHITE STUDIO
A H7-H8 Lomo Creative Space
63 Tiaozhou Wan
Shangcheng District
Hangzhou China
舒怿飞
高级打工者
C 杭州非白文化艺术策划有限公司
A 杭州市上城区茗帚湾63号
Lomo创意园H7-H8 310008
M +86 186 5718 8959
T +86 571 8606 7880
F +86 571 8606 7881
E syf@transwhite.cn
W www.transwhite.cn
21
22
23
24
25
26
27
28
29
30

YISI SPACE

Agency:
Transwhite Studio
Designer:
Qiongjie Yu
Work Type:
Identity

The antique store seated alongside Westlake. They hope to bring special and pleased art journey for customers. Those antique furniture from Europe, paintings from Russia, silver products and exclusive jewelry let people wander between classic and modern. It will give you a surprise whenever you take a breath. The logo is perfectly integrated the geometry patter into European print illustration to obtain modern art visual image. The design tries to meet the collision between classical and modern. This is also the culture atmosphere that the store attempts to show the public.

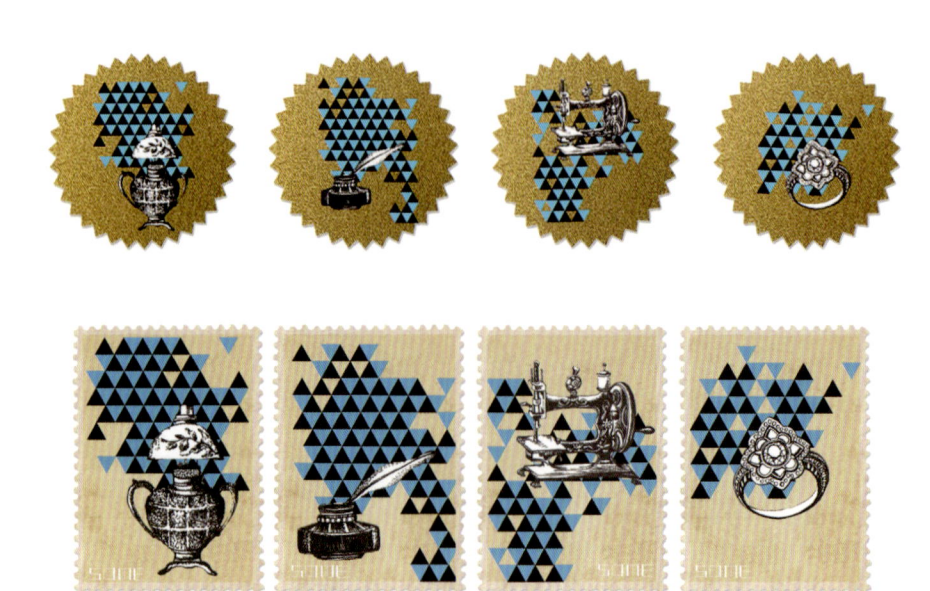

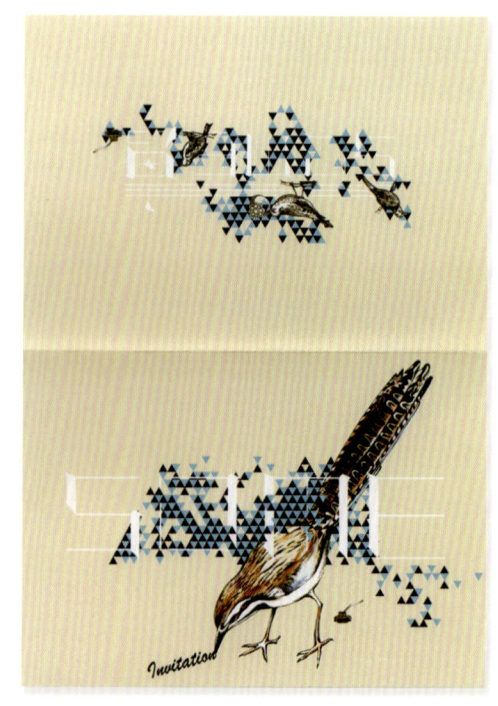

Vintage Collection
古董收藏

Vintage Jewellery
古董瑰宝

Class Watches
腕表展示

About us
关于我们

Contact Us

"YISI" Space

World's Paintings
世界画派

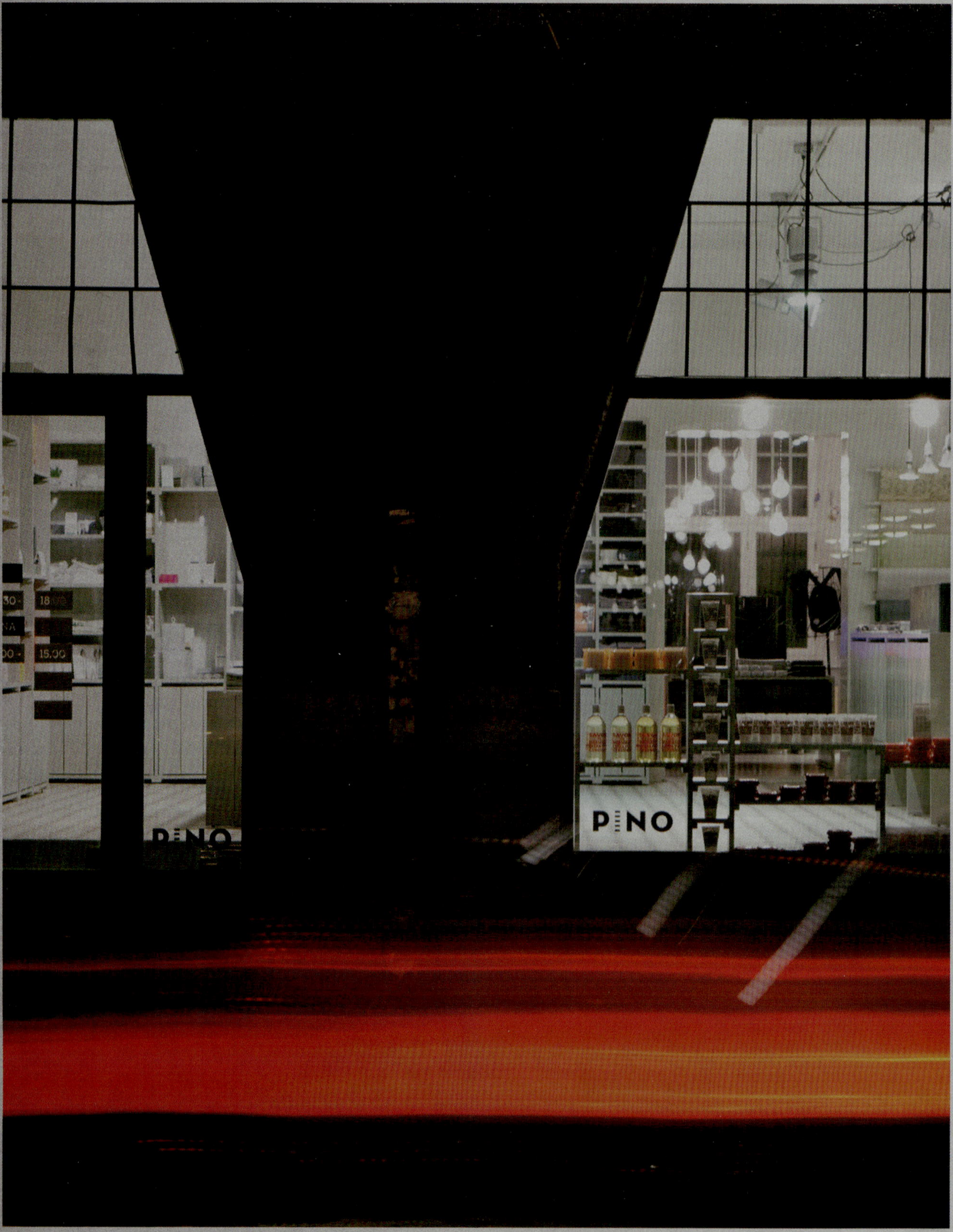
PINO

Take the project "Kesko" as an example, what did the client want from you when they first approached you?
Actually, Kesko isn't at all what you would consider a "mini" client, it's one of the largest listed companies in Finland. On the other hand, our approach to design doesn't differentiate the size of the client. All clients face basically similar challenges in their brand communication in creative sense.
The Kesko's preceding identity fore mostly needed updating and modernizing to current times. The brief from Kesko was to communicate the brand attributes driven by their brand strategy.

What inspired you to design such a colorful and simplified identity?
Kesko has a number of brands of it's own in food, home & speciality goods, home improvement and in machinery trades. We wanted to present Kesko as a house of brands, but without showing the actual products or logos. It had to be something more abstract, something that could stand up for a long time. The range of colors reflect the vast range of products and services that Kesko offers. Also the image of a desirable employer is very important to Kesko, so it was thought that the colorful identity would add a little extra to the life at the Kesko's offices. People at Kesko have now the option to choose the color of their stationery items or mix the colors as they like.

As a designer, how do you understand "mini"? Please list 5 items which you think are "mini".
Pragmatically I see "mini" connected to small batches of applications, custom made work and handcrafted stuff. These are often the benefits of small scale projects; when the number of items to be produced is small, they can be handcrafted and made special just for that purpose. I think people really understand the value in there, it's the kind of stuff you would save rather than throw away.

Have you seen any "mini" design works lately? Please describe them.
In Helsinki, there are many small teashops that package the tea on the spot depending on what the customer wants. It is as much about service as it is about the look and feel of the shop. On the same lines, there are many bicycle repair shops with very simple designs and great service focusing on quality work.

What do you think are the key elements in making a difference with "mini" graphic works?
Simplified approach in general. Getting straight to the point. Simple applications, simple layouts, the number of messages to communicate is small. Keeping things simple should be the way to go in larger projects as well, but it isn't always possible.

' Pragmatically I see "mini" connected to small batches of applications, custom made work and handcrafted stuff. '

Interview With:
Bond

Bond is a creative agency focused on branding and design. They create and renew brands. Bond is founded and run by designers. They work for clients who value creative and practical ideas. They demonstrate their expertise through their work rather than talking, because design is, first and foremost, a craft for them.

They design, visualize and define brands in a way that help companies differentiate themselves from the competition. This can mean creating brand identities, branded environments, packaging, experiential web services or advertising.

They are agile and designer-driven. Their clients appreciate working directly with the designers.

PINO

Agency:
Bond
Work Type:
Identity

The store concept for interior decoration shop Pino is based on its name, which means a `pile' or a `stack' in Finnish. That is taken visually into the new logo and the design of the shop fixtures. The interior design concept, with its subtle palette, works as a neutral background for the fresh, colourful visual identity and products.

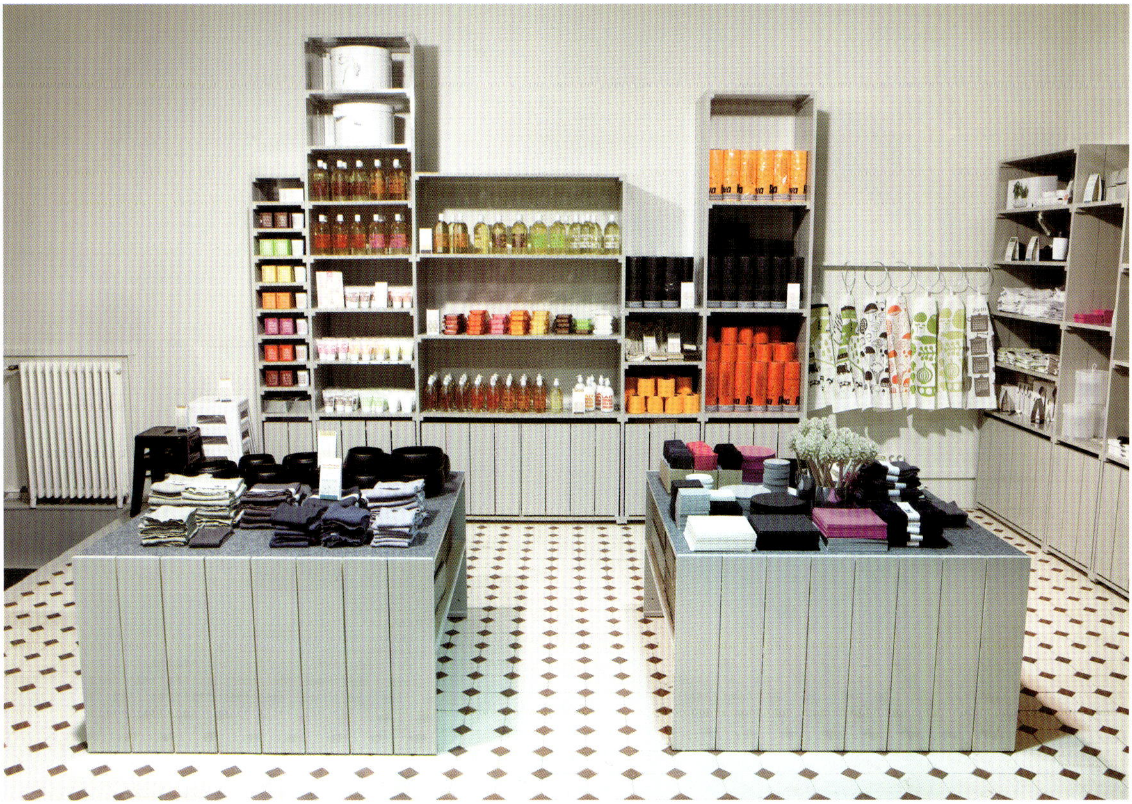

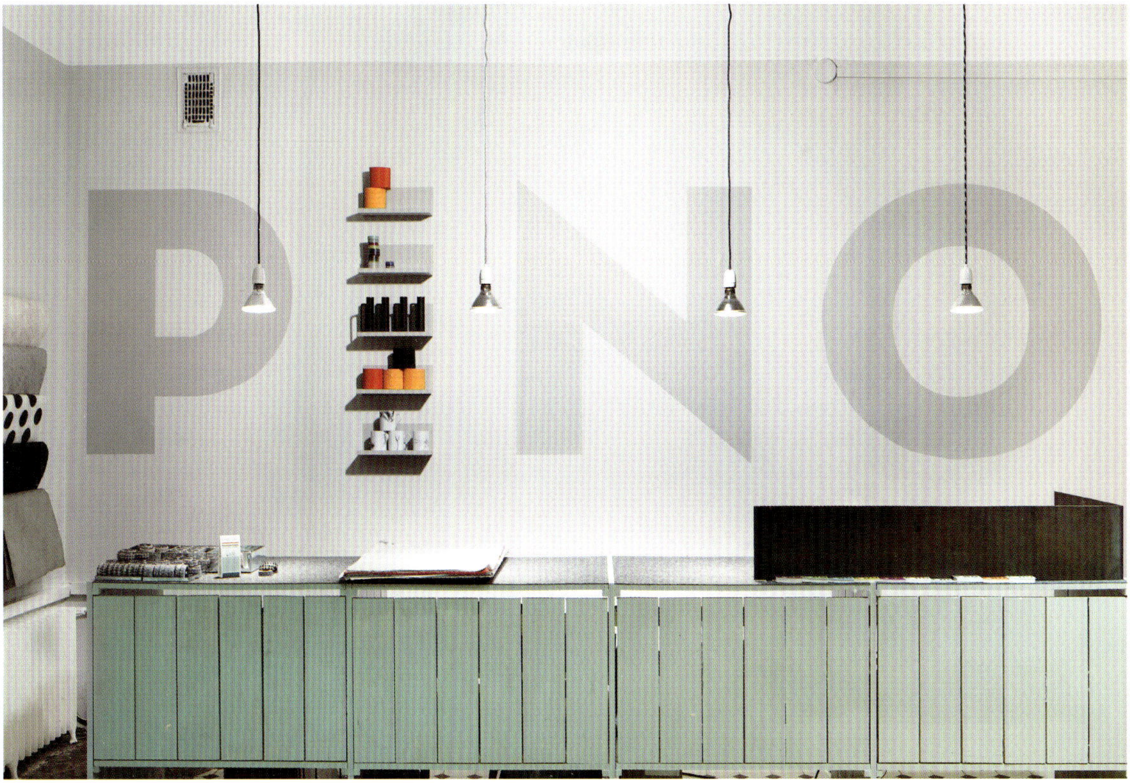

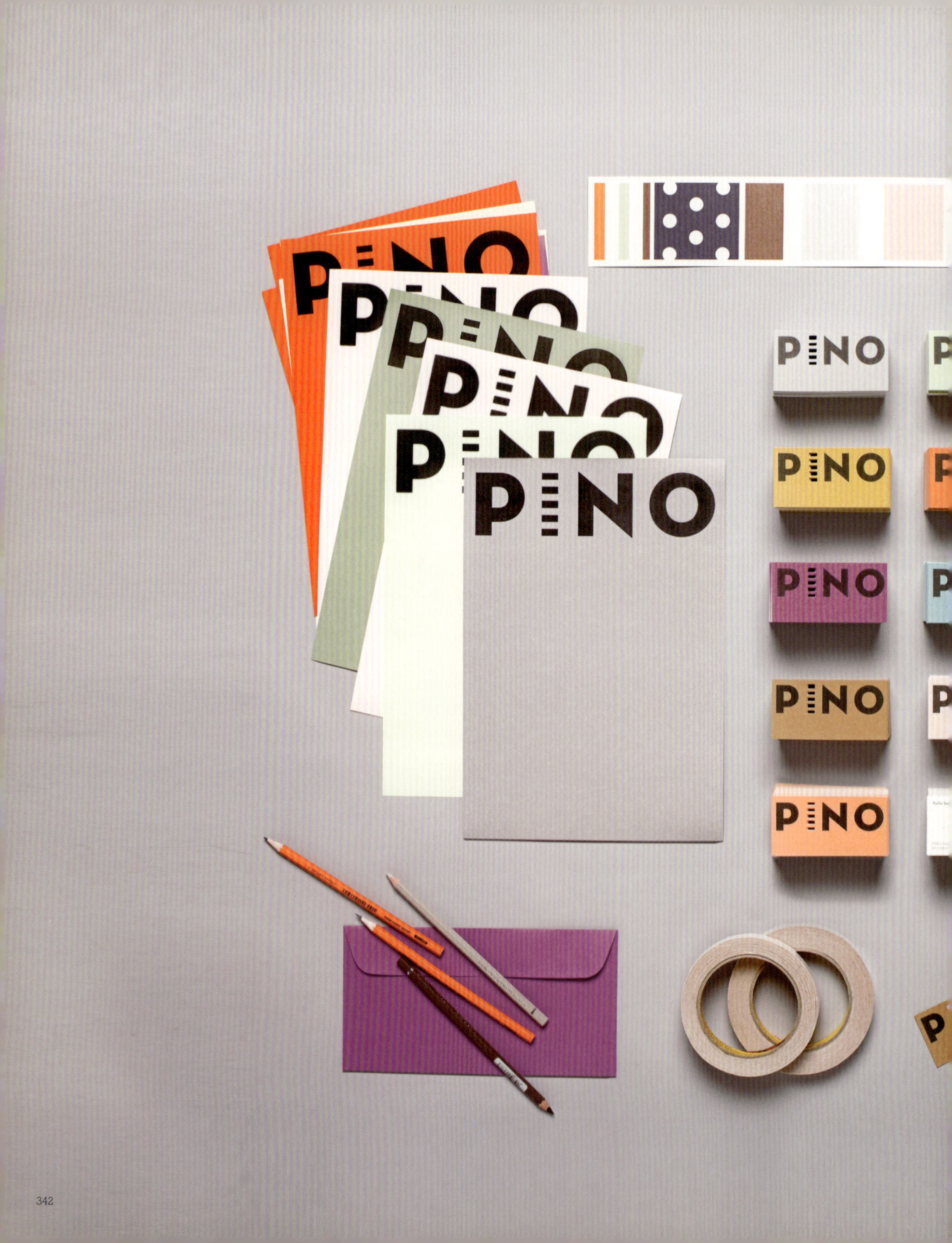
PINO

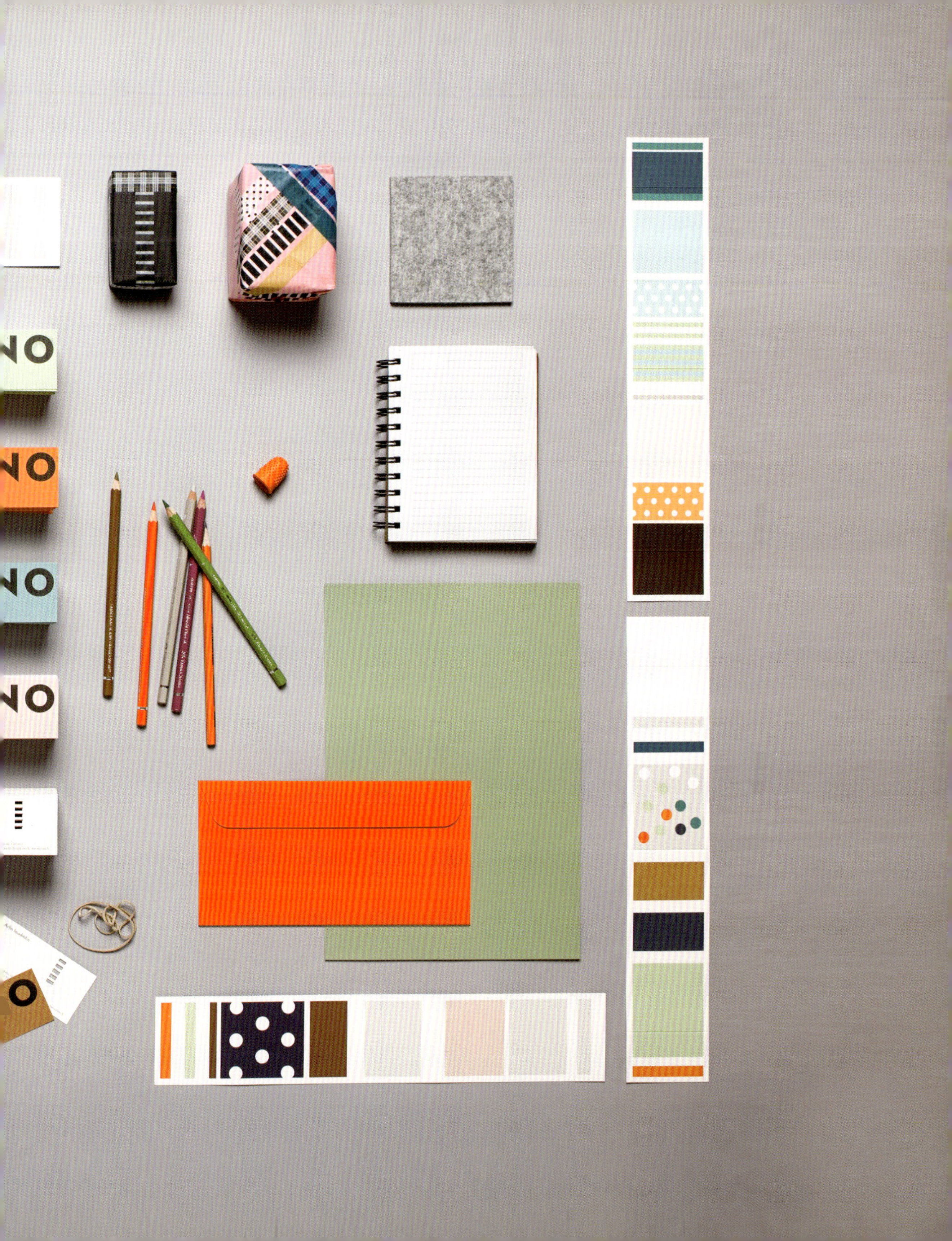

KESKO

Agency:
Bond
Work Type:
Identity

Kesko is a leading provider of trading sector services. The updated identity is colorful, simplified and positively happy. The elements are simple and time-resistant. As part of the identity update the corporate logo is modernized delicately. The colorful identity reflects corporation's entrepreneurial culture and its versatile brands and services.

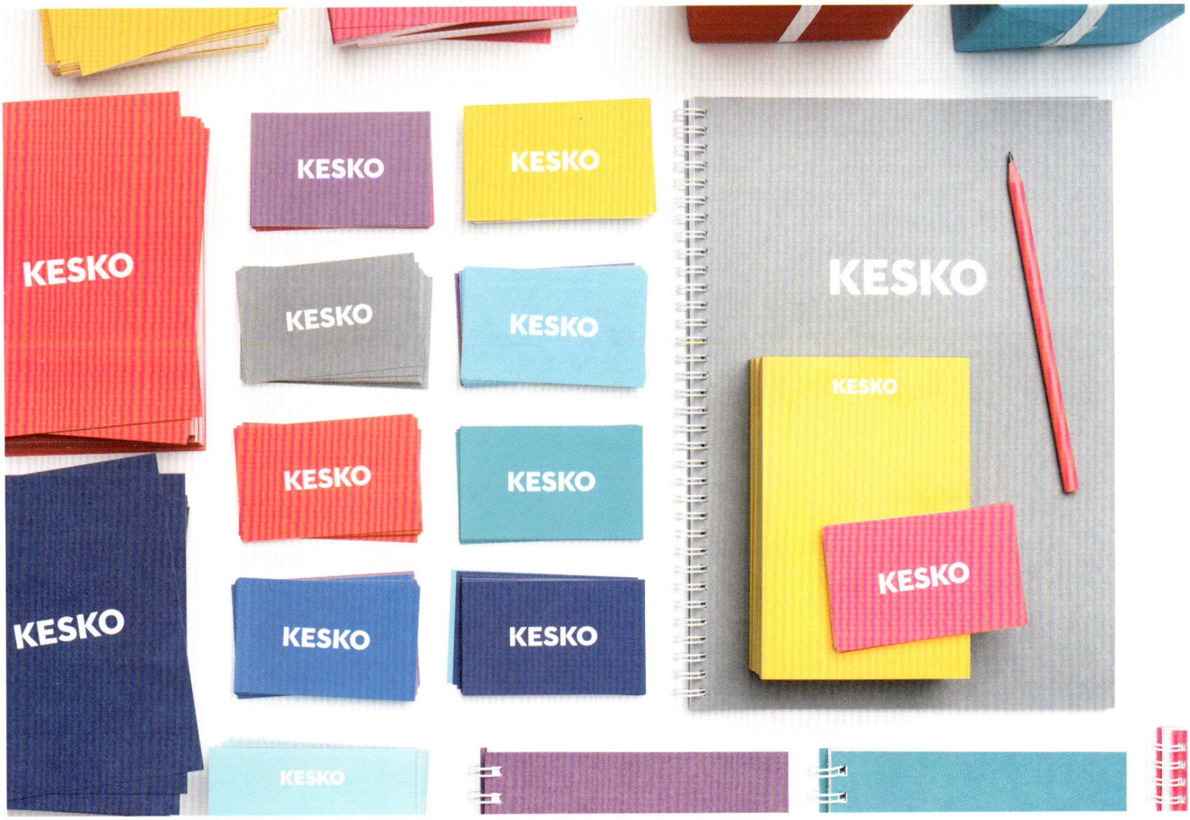
KESKO

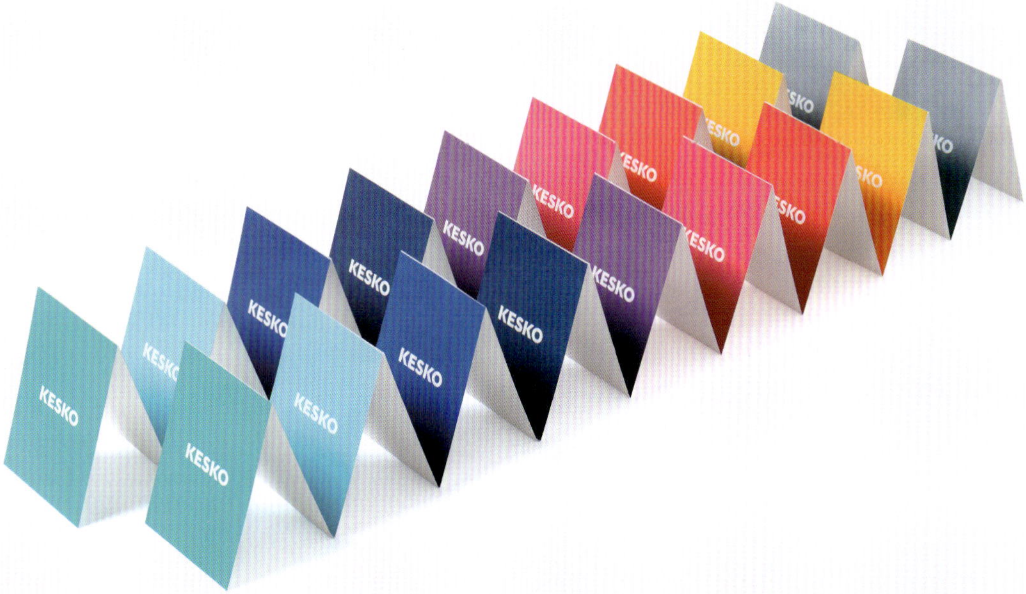
KESKO

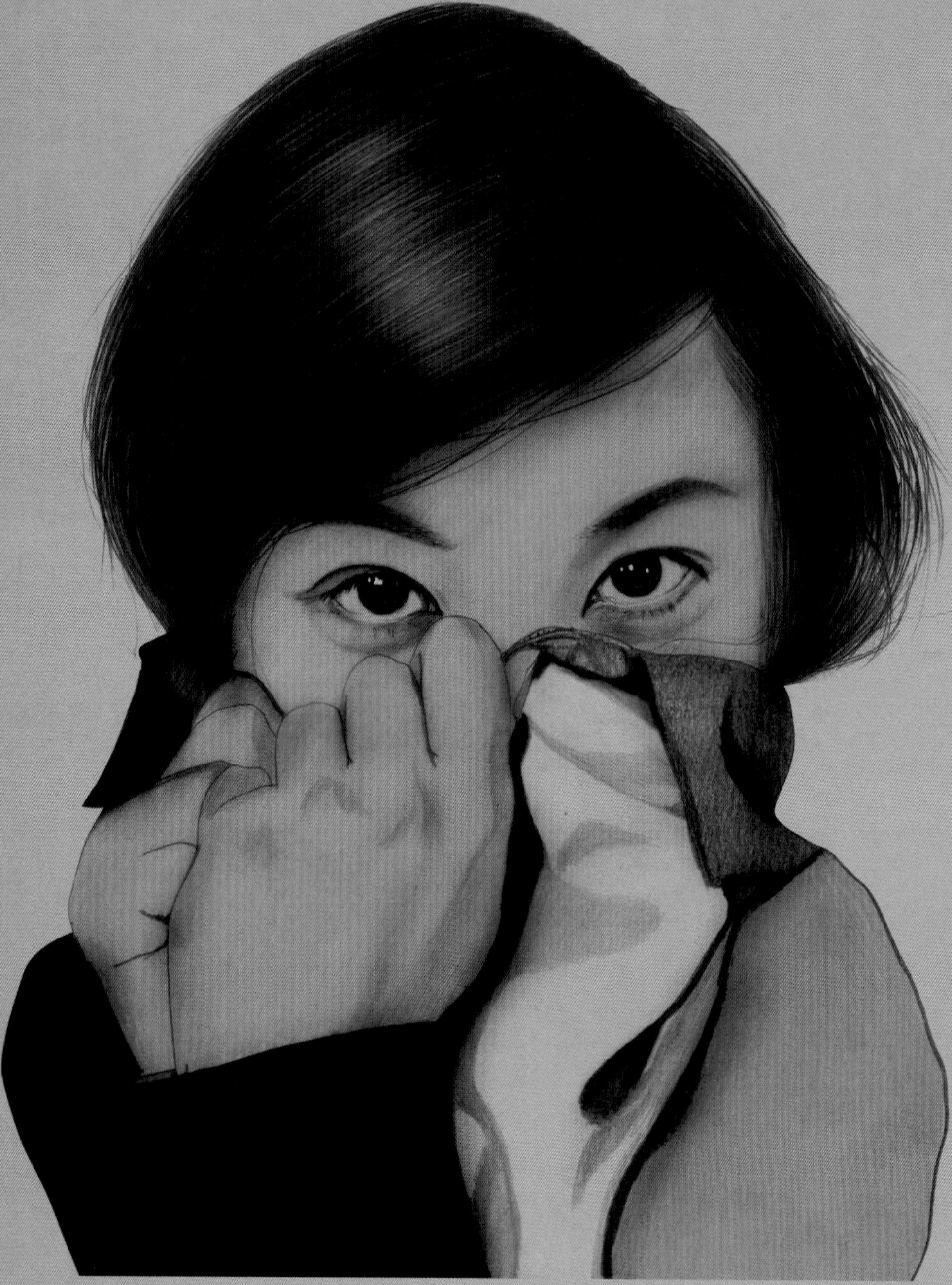

Four of your selected projects here are cards. Do you think those "mini" designs are "big" enough to communicate your ideas?

Design needs boundary; we need to design under certain frameworks, for example, a book is limited by its page numbers, an animation is limited by time duration etc. Hence, size can be one of the interesting parameters in creative process. Sometimes, design needs to achieve its purpose, for those selected projects in "Mini Graphics 2", they serve and act as the first medium to communicate with people who have never seen my work before. So, its lightness, smallness, and accessibility are all very crucial factors. I think my projects achieved in two purposes — "mini" and communicative approach.

What do you usually do for inspiration? Take Fabricated Body Postcard as an example.

Fashion, gender and visual representation are the three inspirations for my body of work. Fabricated Body postcard is designed for my MA graphic design show aimed to propose a question — "How can we explore the visual representation of male and female with reference of the two powerful fashion magazines — Vogue and GQ?" It proposes a position to use visual to illustrate a different perspective in evaluating the existing subject. It aims to hybridize and appreciate the body image of men and women. We, as designers, are group of people who are responsible to bring new evaluation in existing norms and values. Our mission is not only to solve existing problems but also bare the responsibilities to reveal the problem itself. In another way, it is to expose the fact for counter arguments and hopefully by this platform, we shape a better future of our living. This project offers an opportunity to explore novel representation in visual persuasion and aesthetical appreciation by challenging an intangible social value through graphic design practice. All in all, I wish that through my work of art and design; people see curiosity, if not, to arise their curiosity.

What has been repeatedly used in your artwork?

I have always been amused by multidisciplinary design expression specialized in the field of fashion and image processing. As a graphic designer, I am trying to seek for a linkage between inspirational approach to represent visual and identity in our society. A close weaved of visual and dynamic typography can always be found in my works.

What distinguishes your work from that of your contemporaries?

I don't have a specific style or personal preference when creating a piece of work. However, it is very interesting to note that many audiences and fellow designers think I was a female designer. I guess these observations suggested a sense of softness, fluidity and androgynous feeling, which these attributes offer me the flexibility to create, recreate and generate a novel analysis to ordinary subject and finally create a work with a new point of view.

As a designer, how do you understand "mini"? Please list 5 items which you think are "mini".

"Mini" doesn't necessarily link to items that are extremely small in size; however, it has to offer an ease to carry from one place to another. It is a co-relation between size and weight. "Mini" also suggested a sense that in a minimal size but conveys the most. It is all about information propagation and transmission.
A namecard, a postcard, a ring, a necklace and a love letter.

Have you seen any "mini" design works lately? Please describe them.

It is a postcard designed by Southbank Centre, London, named as Disturbia for a BBC Concert orchestra. They use a simple visual illusion to project a sense of dizziness and vibrant atmosphere. It offers you a glimpse of excitement for the show.

What do you think are the key elements in making a difference with "mini" graphic works?

From my personal observation, "mini" graphic works mostly bounded or restricted by their sizes and functions. Taking an invitation card as an example, it is very often that people tend to discard and trash these deliverables when they have arrived at the venue or have attended the event. However, if we are able to transform these "mini" products not only become a communication tool, but also as part of a memorable and interesting souvenir, collectable or premium artifacts. We can make these "mini" artifacts extended their life span and inject a second meaning from their original function.

> ❛ All in all, I wish that through my work of art and design; people see curiosity, if not, to arise their curiosity. ❜

Interview With:
Casper Chan

Graphic designer, illustrator and stylist based in London. His portfolio diversely synthesizes typography, illustration and fashion styling. His clients include LOVE magazine, Wallpaper* magazine, McCann Erickson, Lane Crawford and Richard James.

In 2009, he was awarded the British council 60th anniversary scholarship in contribution toward a MA Graphic Design in London College of Communication.

In 2011, he formed Studio 247 with Monkey Leung with a vision of "24 hours a day, 7 days a week, is never our motto".

TOPAZ LEUNG

Agency:
disinlok
Designer:
Casper Chan
Work Type:
Identity

Freelance photographer, writer and stylist based in Hong Kong. To embank a unique and poetic allure of her name card. The self-portrait illustrated namecard expose the infinite creativity of Topaz and acts as a key visual to stand out from the crowd.

SOCIAL ETIQUETTE
NAMECARD

Agency:
dicinlok
Designer:
Casper Chan
Work Type:
Identity

To incorporate his signature imaginative visual with typographic treatment.

Casper designed this namecard for his special friends and clients. The surface was treated with UV vanish in a negative space of a capital letter "C" to show a simple yet elegant design.

BJÖRK NAMECARD

Agency:
disinlok
Designer:
Casper Chan
Work Type:
Identity

To incorporate his signature illustration with typographic treatment, Casper designed this namecard for his special friends and clients. The surface was treated with UV vanish in a negative space of a capital letter "C" to show a simple yet elegant design.

FABRICATED BODY
POSTCARD

Agency:
disinlok
Designer:
Casper Chan
Work Type:
Invitation

Postcard designed for Casper's personal work featuring in MA Graduation show, London college of Communication. This major project aimed to question the boundaries of visual persuasion and representation of male and female body images in fashion magazines. 'Fabricated body' proposes a platform to articulate an investigation between image of gender and visual identity.

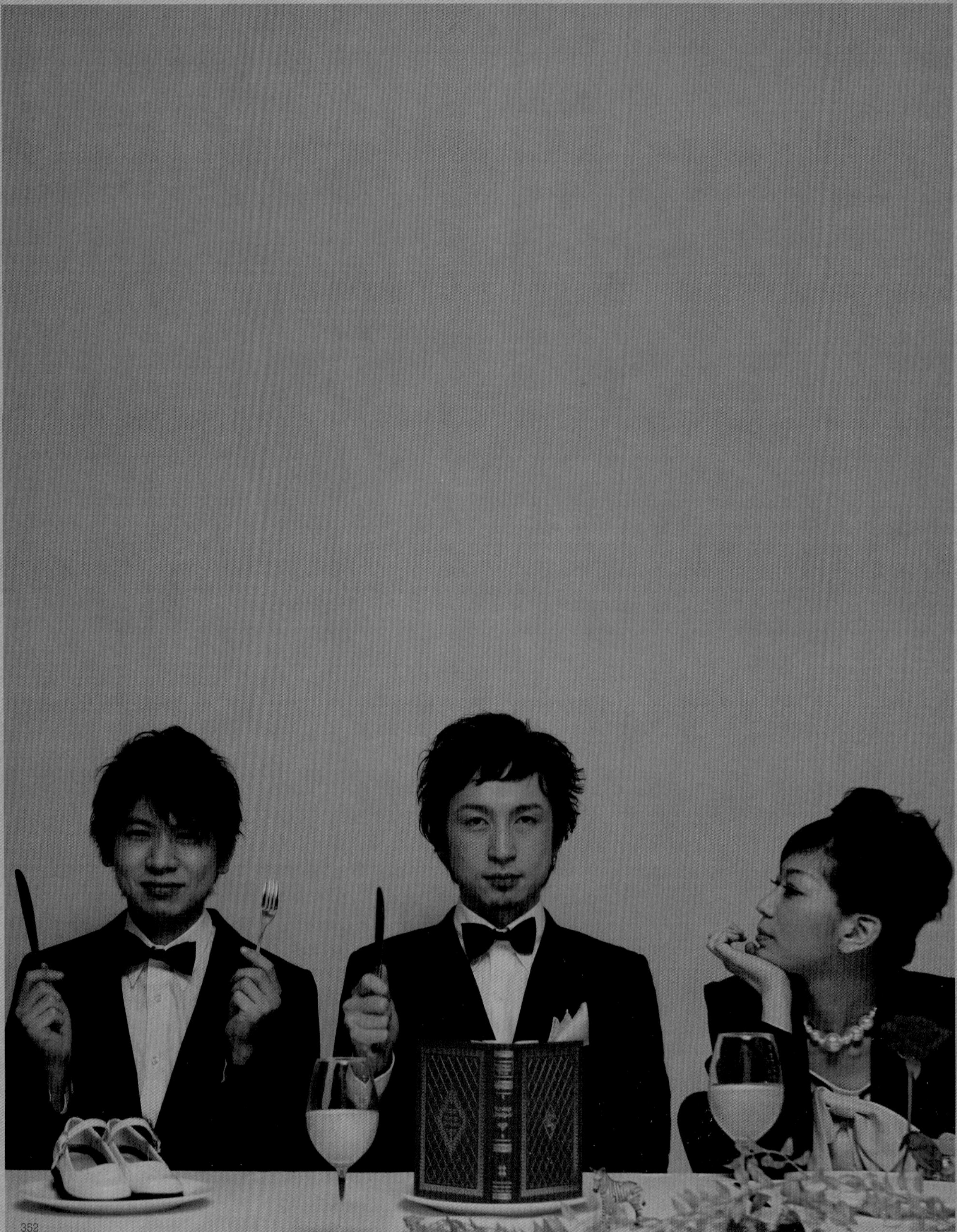

How did you choose 14 different Scandinavian symbolic icons for the identity of Piccolina? What inspired you?
Using 14 different Scandinavian symbols, each with their own history, we hoped to produce a logo that would communicate the owner's memories and stories about Scandinavia to their customers.
With the shop owner, as I myself have lived in Sweden, we picked the most famous 14 topics of which most people know only two or three, but not all 14. These 14 different icons are developed on a range of promotional products, such as shopping tags, each with a story on the back and a rubber stamp for a stamp card, and after customers have collected all 14 icons they received a special promotion from the various places. Each time Piccolina shoppers purchase something from the shop, they become more familiar with Scandinavian culture.

You have designed a range of smart name cards. Do you think those "mini" designs are "big" enough to communicate your ideas?
Those small tools called "mini graphics" differ from advertising media such as billboards, they are mini, producing a small ripple effect instead. However, this mini graphic is something that is picked up by each person, read and owned and due to this tangible nature, it is more powerful than the "larger graphics". I don't think that just because it is small that it is ineffective. Rather I believe that the beautiful "mini graphics" will prove to be even more powerful than impersonal larger ads.

What has been repeatedly used in your artwork?
Our ideas are produced based on the purpose and function of the work. So it is unlikely that we would use a piece of artwork in another project. However, if the idea bears a resemblance to another we could make an exception, and it is possible we would use visual elements that do not have a connection with the idea.

As a designer, how do you understand "mini"? Please list 5 items which you think are "mini".
"Mini" might be the true worth of Japanese graphics. In Japan, which is a small narrow country, it could be said that people have elevated the value of things by reducing and narrowing the size. For example, cell-phones, music players, cars, PCs, and home electronics, all of these have their own value despite their small sizes.

Have you seen any "mini" design works lately? Please describe them.
That will be the national flag of Japan, which we call "Hinomal." There have been a number of charity projects and activities all over the world since the great earthquake and tsunami hit the east coast of Honshu, Japan on March 11th. Most of the logo marks use the Hinomal as those motifs. I do not think the flag of Spain or Argentine would be used in the same way. For this reason, I am truly convinced that the simple red circle has come to strongly identify Japan as 'Hinomal'.

What do you think are the key elements in making a difference with "mini" graphic works?
In designing graphics, the details become the most important factor when it comes to the difference in the quality and weight of paper and the weight of typefaces. There are no particular key elements, but if I dare to choose one, it would be detail.

'Creation means thinking about achieving something better, for whatever the purpose.'

Interview With:
Commune

Commune is a creative team based in Sapporo, Japan, mainly has been active in graphic design. The theme of creation for us is to make something better. Inspired by the will to make something better, our design work may move people or it may make society work a little better. It's like giving a gift. We choose a gift with the idea of delighting that special someone. It's a pleasure for us to be able to present something the recipient doesn't expect and truly appreciates. At times, our creations take people by surprise, awaken their emotions, or even move them to tears. That's exactly what we're looking to create.

CHICKEN PECKER

Agency:
Commune
Work Type:
Identity

A chicken specialty restaurant, CHICKEN PECKER serves grilled dishes, deep fried chicken, hamburgers, and rice bowls. Meticulous in every aspect of the preparations -- from ingredients and recipes, to safety, and service, this restaurant is simple yet imbued with passion, establishing itself apart from chain restaurants. All visual elements -- the logo, signage and menu -- were redesigned to reflect its charm as a "Japanese countryside restaurant specializing in chicken."

テレフォンオーダー
お店に来る前に注文しておこう。

電話で予約注文 → ご来店 → てきたてをお渡し！

0120-298-908

全国発送
店頭かウェブサイトにてご注文ください。

看板メニューである「若鶏の炭火焼き」「若鶏のから揚げ」を真空パックで発送します。

商品代金		送料			
3人前	¥2,520	北海道	¥750	中部	¥1,270
4人前	¥3,400	北東北	¥960	関西	¥1,480
5人前	¥4,250	南東北	¥1,060	四国	¥1,590
6人前	¥5,100	関東	¥1,170	九州	¥1,800
7人前	¥5,950	信越	¥1,170	沖縄	¥1,900
8人前	¥6,800	北陸	¥1,270		
9人前	¥7,650				
10人前	¥8,500				

WWW.CHICKENPECKER.COM

CHICKEN PECKER

チキンペッカー
〒004-0052
北海道札幌市厚別区厚別中央2条4丁目11-39
TEL 011-894-2989 FAX 011-894-1389
営業時間 10:00AM-8:00PM 年中無休

PICCOLINA

Agency:
Commune
Work Type:
Identity

Piccolina is a Scandinavian antique shop that offers a variety of collectibles. One of the reasons why antiques are so appealing is that they preserve an aspect of the values or culture from people living in a different period. Each antique item tells customers something about Scandinavian history or culture. 14 different Scandinavian icons are used to form the shop logo, which could be used on a range of promotional tools, such as wrapping paper, direct mailings and Sapporo shop signage. Each of the icons is of important history and it can all be found at Piccolina.

KATSUYA ISHIDA

Agency:
Commune
Work Type:
Identity

This is a business card for Mr.Ishida who is a visual producer using space and communications. The card's concept was to leave a persistence of vision to the recipient. Visual is information through light and time. Storage light become luminescent in dark place and keep memory to the recipient.

AKI NAGAO

Agency:
Commune
Work Type:
Identity

French restaurant Aki Nagao, named after its head chef and owner, opened in Sapporo, Japan, in 2010.

Head chef Aki Nagao's cooking style is directly influenced by his personal background and experiences. This very individual character is expressed with the use of the DNA motif and his signature logotype. The restaurant itself is brand new with a predominantly white theme, but antique objects and old wood are used as key elements of the interior décor to suggest the fusion of new and old. The "Everyday French cuisine" slogan was integrated into the overall branding design to make the restaurant more inviting to customers.

Manager
山根 宏士
HIROSHI YAMANE
Sous chef
高原 美紀子
MIKIKO TAKAHARA
長尾 若菜
WAKANA NAGAO
長尾 彰浩
AKIHIRO NAGAO
Service
佐藤 晶子
aki nagao

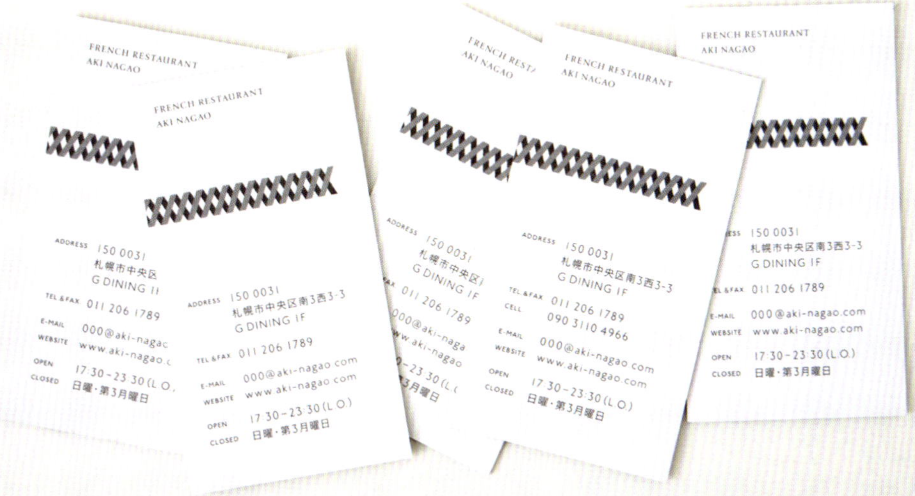
FRENCH RESTAURANT
AKI NAGAO
ADDRESS 150 0031
札幌市中央区南3西3-3
G DINING 1F
TEL & FAX 011 206 1789
CELL 090 3110 4966
E-MAIL 000@aki-nagao.com
WEBSITE www.aki-nagao.com
OPEN 17:30-23:30 (L.O.)
CLOSED 日曜・第3月曜日

HAPPY TREE

Agency:
Commune
Work Type:
Identity

Commune's task was to turn the company's name "Happy Tree" into their identity. The client wished to have a tree stand in everybody's happiness. So "tree of happiness" is the motif.

The form of happy tree comes up to surface by not drawing tree itself or its shadow. The logo stands up in the business card and this concept has been embodied. Happy Tree is mainly in the cleaning business, so white and clean image was used for its identity.

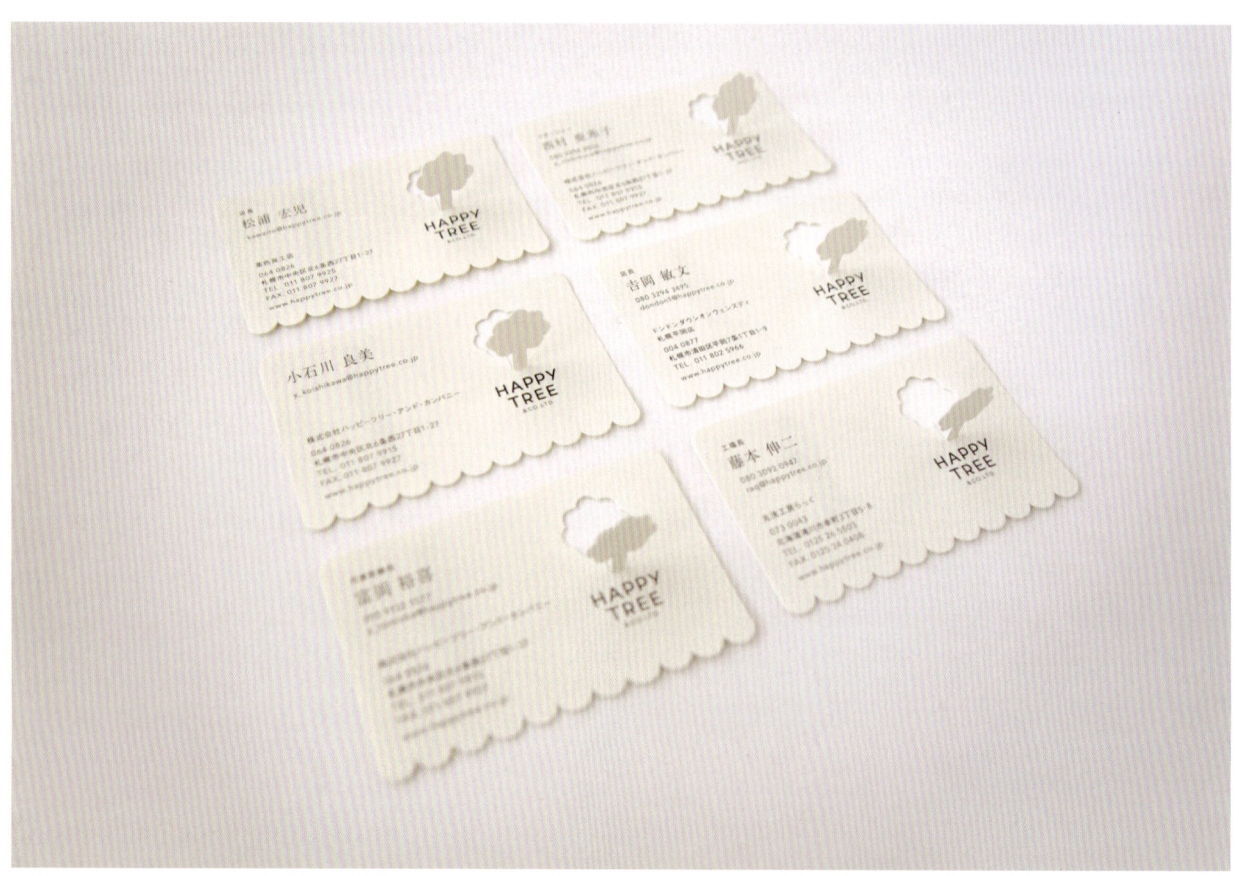

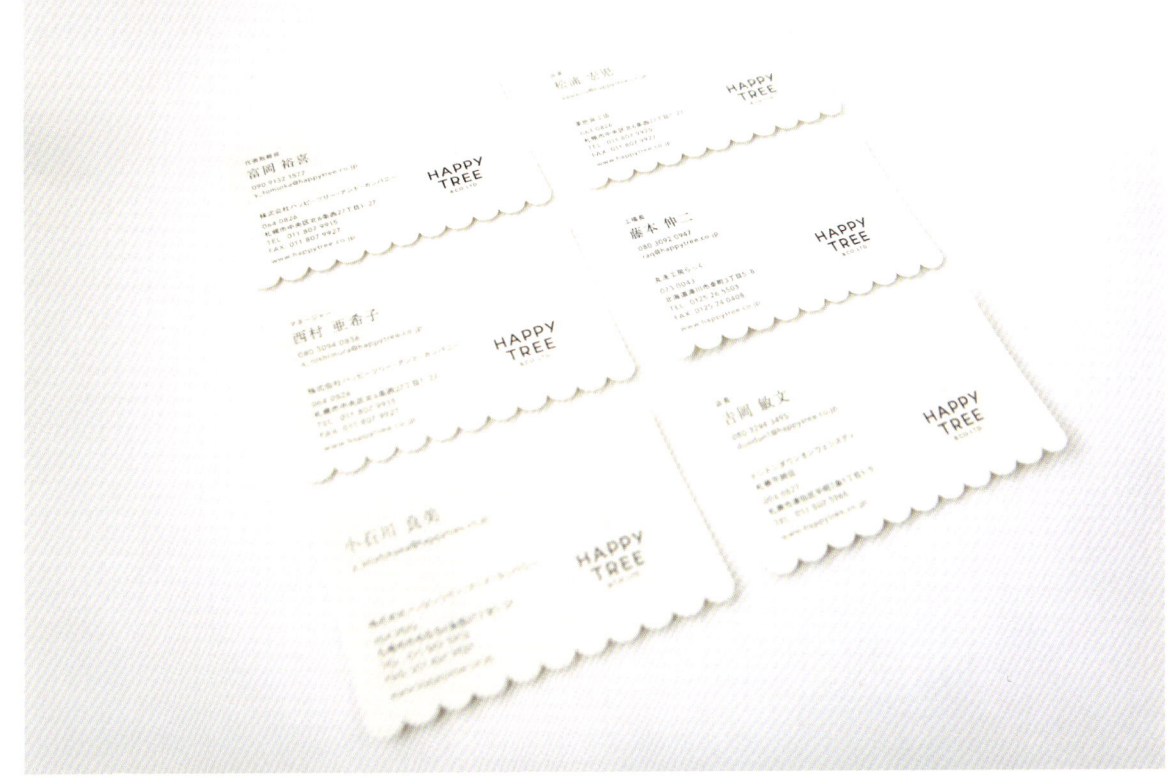

362

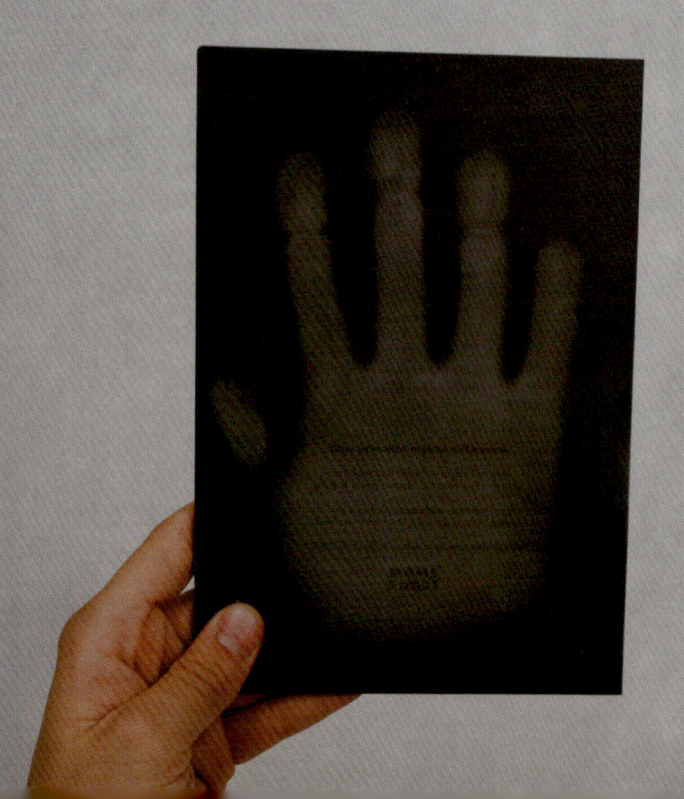

What inspired the project Moms & Dads on the Street?
When we were about five years old we had a toy car that changed color when you held it in your hands. Twenty years later we thought that it would be a cool color to use in a print — especially when the message is all about the presence.

Exploring a material is an unfailing source of creativity and discovery. The sensitive material used in this project is a good way of showing participation, so what else materials do you find interesting?
Both of us are fascinated and read a lot about nanotechnology, the future of all material. Let's give one example. Aerogel "Frozen Smoke" is the world's lightest and solidest material, it can also protect you against heat from a blowtorch at more than 1300 °C. Maybe every home in the future will be built in this new type of glass?

How did your audiences react to this design when they received it? Did the design attract more people to join the activity?
Since it was just a small DM for a small brand we'd never done any case study on this project. But the overall responses have been over expectations.

Have you recently received any invitation from friends? What are they about?
The last invitation from a friend was to an in real life theater experience.

As a designer, how do you understand "mini"? Please list 5 items which you think are "mini".
Nanotechnology. Micro typography. Words. Material. Perfection.

Have you seen any "mini" design works lately? Please describe them.
Not lately. Mini design was more common in the past when typography and material was crafted in a different sense. The work was supported by time and perfection. Today everything is going too fast and most of the stuff we see today is made without any passion at all.

❛ (Five mini items in our eyes are) nanotechnology, micro typography, words, material and perfection. ❜

Interview With:
Prinz & Prinz

Prinz & Prinz is a multidisciplinary creative studio from Stockholm. It was founded in 2009 by the two brothers Petter Prinz and Kaspar Prinz. Their work is a mix between art and science and they do everything from film to inventions. At the moment they are based in London as a part of Google Creative Lab.

MOMS & DADS ON THE STREET
Agency:
Prinz & Prinz
Designer:
Petter Prinz
Work Type:
Invitation

The brief was to visualize the message "Your presence makes difference." The organization's purpose is to maintain a calm evening out on the street, just by acting as a parent or adult. The postcard is performed with a warm sensitive color. It gets transparent from the heat of a human hand. While it is transparent you can read the message "Your presence makes difference."

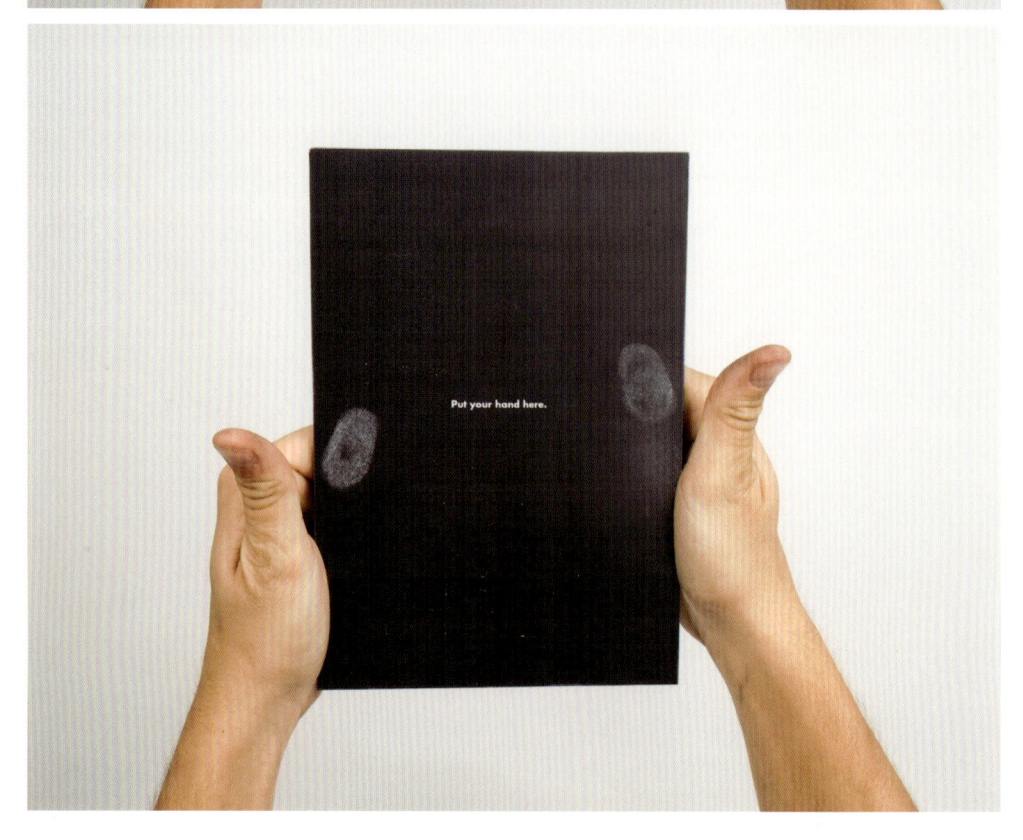

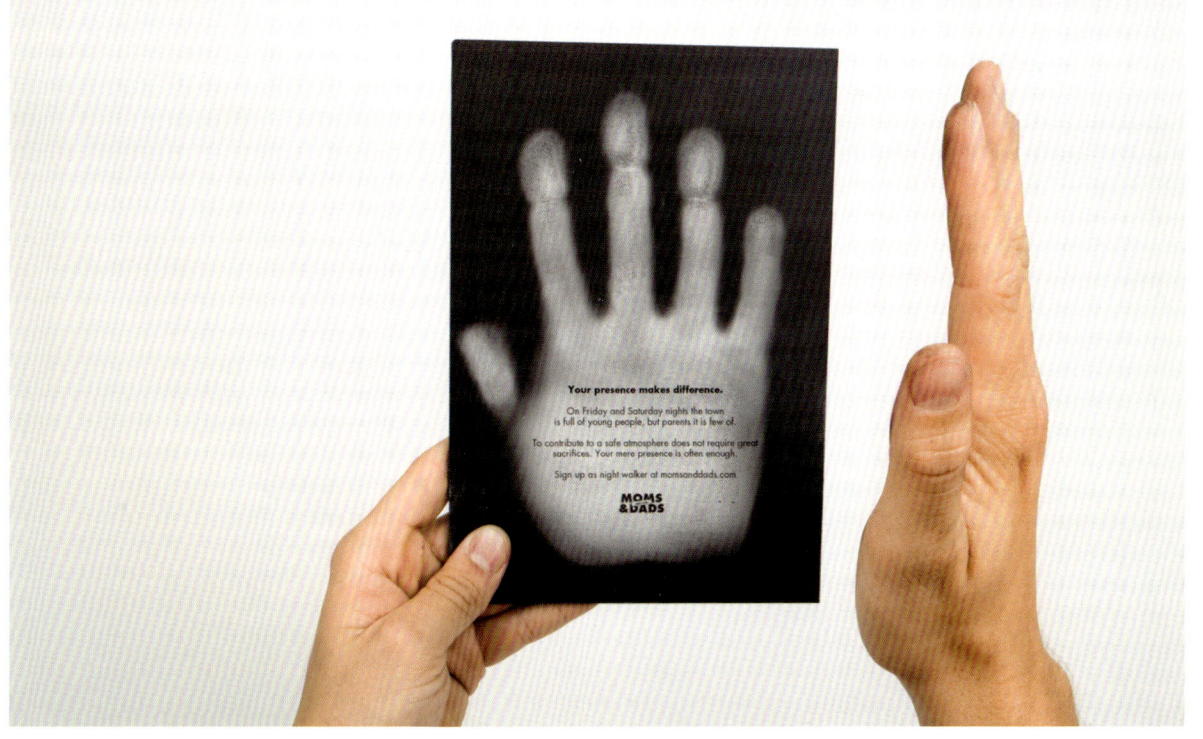

Your presence makes difference.

On Friday and Saturday nights the town
is full of young people, but parents it is few of.

To contribute to a safe atmosphere does not require great
sacrifices. Your mere presence is often enough.

Sign up as night walker at momsanddads.com

MOMS &DADS

WWF DIRECT MAIL

Agency:
Prinz & Prinz
Designer:
Kaspar Prinz
Work Type:
Promotion

A polar bear made of carbonic acid ice is kept in a styrofoam box. The ice bear will slowly melt away during the whole work day of 8 hours.

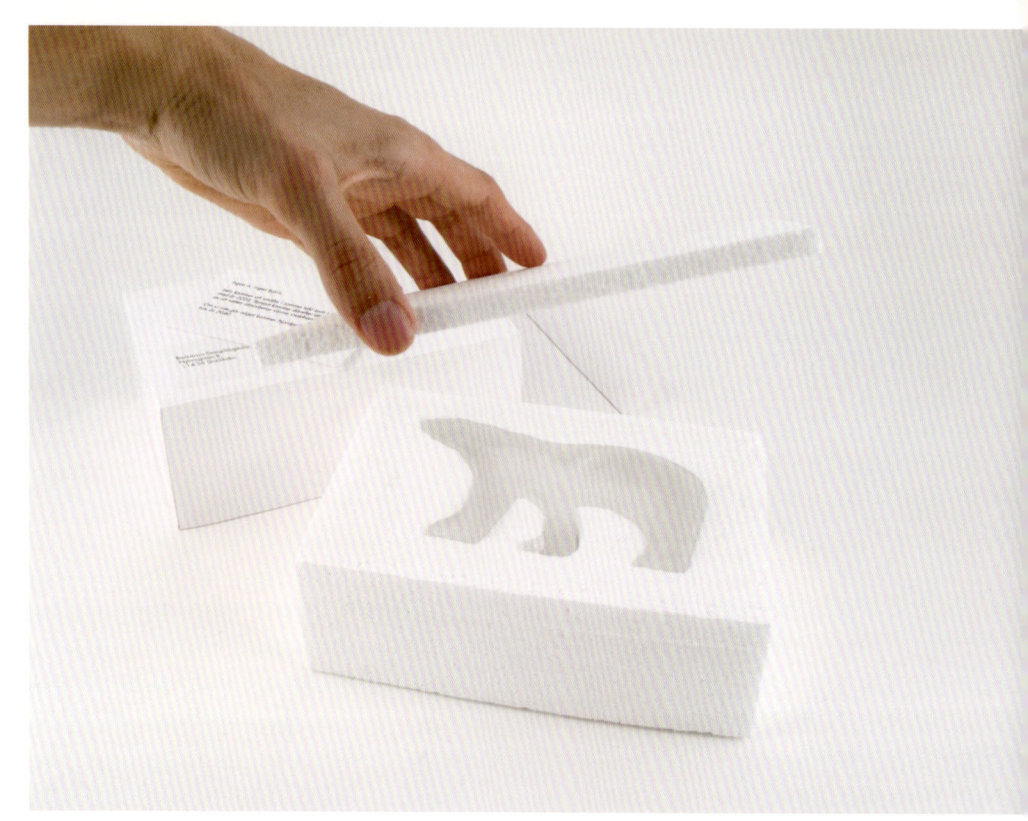

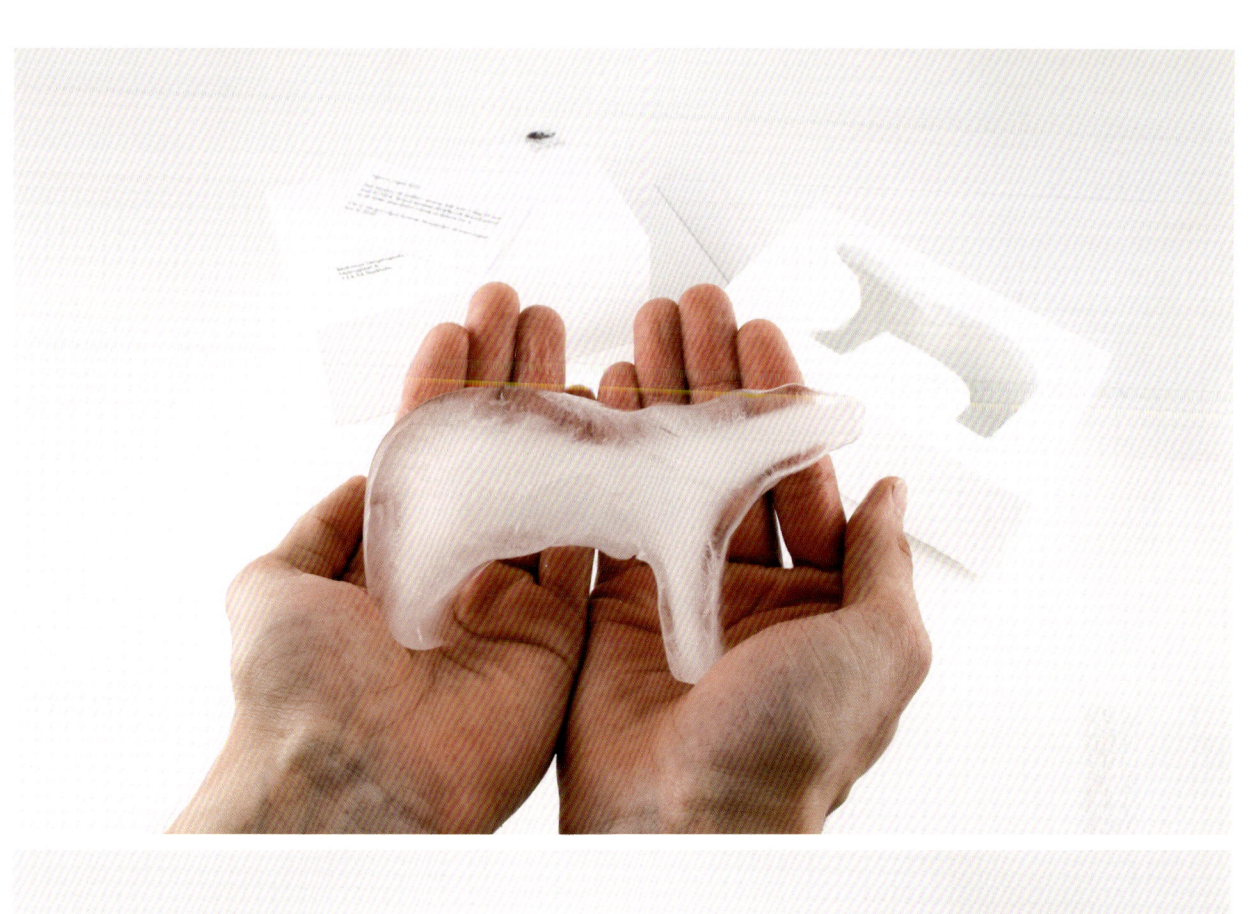

Beckmans Designhögskola
Nybrogatan 8
114 34 Stockholm

WWF

KUNSTKAMMER
MANYSTUFF
POSTER 1
MANŒUVRES GRAPHIQUES
DÉTOURNEMENT ET
SUBVERSION
IMPRESSUM
SOMMAIRE
12
1

Tet 2011-Cosunam is quite an eye-catching invitation. Do you think those "mini" designs are "big" enough to communicate your ideas?
It depends what you need to communicate. The size of the format is normally chosen considering the distance between the information support and the reader. Often small formats are used to communicate a small amount of information, like business cards, so they don't need to be bigger.

What do you usually do for inspiration? Take different invitations for Vitnamese New Year Eve as an example.
Before working on a new project, we always spend some time on searching in our library and on the web for similar kind of projects. It's giving ideas and it also helps to know what you can't do because it has already been done too much. It's quite impossible to be completely innovative today.
In the case of Tet cosunam, it was quite clear for us. We wanted to work with illustration so we had a look at typical Asian cats drawings and tried to mix it with Swiss modernist typography. It was our way to promote a Vietnamese party in Switzerland.

What has been repeatedly used in your artwork?
Like a lot of other designers, and particularly Swiss designers, we pay much attention on typography. So you can see it takes an important part of our designs. It happens often that we use typography as the only image in our artworks.

As a designer, how do you understand "mini"? Please list 5 items which you think are "mini".
Anything could be mini, even a poster or a book. In our graphic designer habits, we first think of business cards, brochures, invitations. And then to Hobbits and Dwarves…

Have you seen any "mini" design works lately? Please describe them.
The first idea coming to our mind when thinking of mini graphics is Bulb Graphix Mini illustration lopporello Books: 3.5 x 4.5 cm. The tiniest books we've seen.
http://www.bulbfactory.ch/comix/collection.php?c=1

What do you think are the key elements in making a difference with "mini" graphic works?
It's probably when the use of a small format fits perfectly with the concept of the project. In French we say:" la forme doit refléter le fond".

> ❝ In our graphic designer habits, we first think of business cards, brochures, invitations. And then to Hobbits and Dwarves… ❞

Interview With:
Neo Neo

Neo Neo is a Geneva based graphic design studio, founded in 2010 by Thuy-An Hoang and Xavier Emi. They mostly work for cultural clients and try to propose contemporary solutions, giving importance to details, emphasis typography and direct messages.

MUDAC

Agency:
Neo Neo
Work Type:
Invitation

Invitations to Mudac workshops (Museum of Design and Applied Arts, Lausanne). The workshops are connected with the exhibitions of the museum. The invitations are screen printed on 1000g/m2 cardboard.

FIL ROUGE

Agency:
Neo Neo
Work Type:
Identity

We created the new identity of Fil Rouge, a Geneva based communication agency. The stationery is offset printed with a varnish on cyclus offset paper.

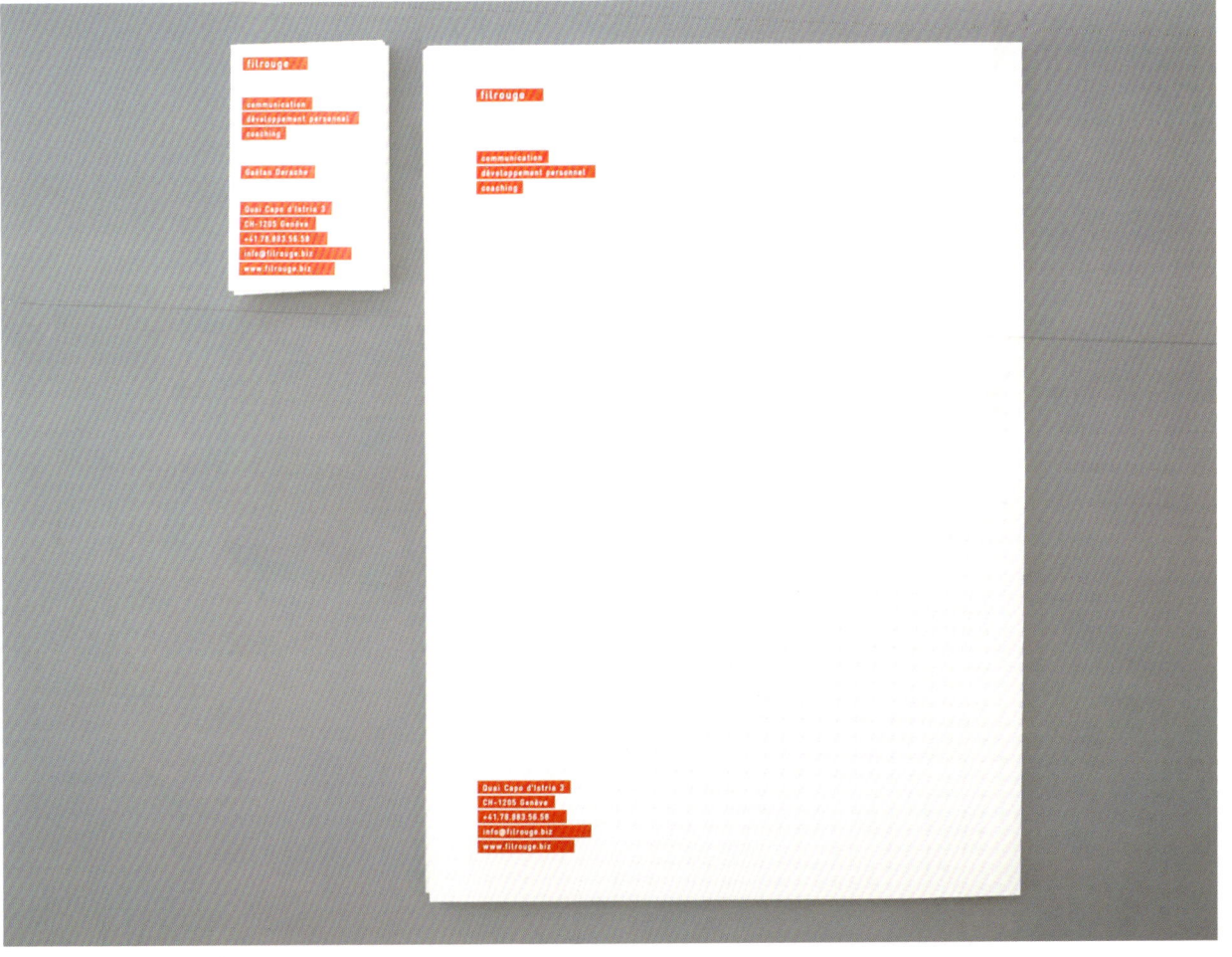

TET 2011 – COSUNAM
Agency:
Neo Neo
Work Type:
Invitation

Each year we are responsible of the communication of the Vietnamese Near Year Eve in Geneva. 2011 was the year of the cat. Offset print (Gold + Red Pantone) on folded A4 cardboard.

Biography

6D
6D, founded by Shogo Kishino, is a design agency based in Japan.

p266-267

A BEAUTIFUL DESIGN
Beautiful is about looking at things differently.

It's about perception. It's about beauty in imperfection, beauty in the ordinary, beauty in everything. Most of all, it's about finding silver linings, living a happy life.

p172-173

AGUSTIN ZEA
Agustin Zea is graphic designer, with a lot of publication in books and newspaper.

p191

ALBERTO HERNANDEZ
Alberto Hernandez is a London-based Spanish graphic designer with a Degree from Escuela de Arte numero 10 and a Masters from the London College of Communication. His main interests are designing for print and typography but Alberto's work is diverse.

Paying attention to every title detail and being extremely hard working had won him several work placements at renowned studios including Spin and Proud Creative (London). Alberto has been nominated for awards such as grafic design awards: Best Newcomer (2010) and Chaumont Poster Festival (2009) and he has showed his work at various collective exhibitions such as Imaginary Friends (London, 2011), De l'Ombre et du Reve (Tours, 2010) and Basurama: 2x1 (Madrid/Gipuzkoa, 2006).

p196-197

ALEKSANDAR SAVIC
Aleksandar Savic is a freelance graphic designer, illustrator and animator from Bosnia and Herzegovina, currently living and working in Belgrade, Serbia. He'd recently graduated from Faculty of Arts and Design in Belgrade. His interests vary through many fields of graphic design, and he's not bounded by any particular style or graphic expression (because he thinks that limits his tendency to experiment with different materials, styles etc).

p030-031

ALEX KETZER
The Cologne based designer Alex Ketzer is keen on printed matter and typography. He loves to fill blank pages in books and magazines with good typography, great pictures and gripping white space. And if there's no more paper, he works in the field of website and e-zines…

p018-019, 100-101

ALEXANDER LIS
Alexander Lis is a freelance graphic designer / visual communicator currently based in Frankfurt Main / Germany. Since graduation communication design at University of Applied Sciences Darmstadt, he has worked at different places like Neubau (Berlin), Bergmannstudios (Frankfurt), Sara de Bondt Studio (London) and Pixelgarten (Frankfurt). He has also given talks and workshops at the Universities of Art and Design in Offenbach, Halle, Mainz and Darmstadt. At "Typography Summer School" (London) and "Letter Press Workshop" (Darmstadt) he worked as an assistant for Fraser Muggeridge and Wolfgang Weingart. Alexander Lis is part of the self-initiated research project fourfiveX and a contributor at reform.lt.

p038, 201

ALVA
Alva is a multidisciplinary design studio based in Lisbon. Alva designs print and digital media. It operates as a small studio with a focused team, whose projects range from graphic design, art direction, identities and stationery, books, magazines, posters, typography, illustration, websites, motion and environmental design. Alva is composed of Diogo Potes and Ricardo Matos at the beginning of 2008. Alva believes in good ideas, good design and loves the details.

p186-187, 292-293

ANAGRAMA
Anagrama is a specialized brand development and positioning agency providing creative solutions for any type of project. Besides their history and experience with brand development, they are also experts in the design and development of objects, space and multimedia projects.

p146-147

ANDRÉS REQUENA
Andrés Requena is from Viladecans (Barcelona, Spain.). He believes in the shape's synthesis as a way of explicit/direct communication, avoiding needless visual elements. He always tries to add objectivity to his work facing the lack of REAL information and dissembled advertising that we are submitted every day.

p250-251

ANT GATT
Ant Gatt is a design director based in Auckland, New Zealand. He has worked extensively in the UK where he specialised in brand identity and design for the cultural and publishing sectors. Whilst in the UK his passion for typography and information design led him to complete a Masters in Book Design from Reading University. Since returning to New Zealand he has continued to develop his craft on projects for clients such as Pugeot, 3M, Z Energy, Westpac and Auckland Philharmonia Orchestra.

p192-193

BAS KOOPMANS
Bas Koopmans (1981) lives and works in Amsterdam. Originally from the north, Bas was raised in a period when different

music styles started to mix. Being raised on a mixed diet of punk rock and straight edge hardcore to hiphop to electronic dance music, this blend of styles can be seen in his work.

Beside a ton of personal work, Bas makes graphic stuff for clients. He does this with a pen, pencil or magic wand. And he rarely does it the easy way. As a collaborator, either artist or friend, Bas demands that you keep up with him.

p207

BEN JENNINGS

Ben Jennings is a Communication Designer based in Melbourne, Australia.

p078-079

BIANCA WENDT STUDIO

Bianca Wendt runs a small studio overlooking Smithfield market in London. She is a graphic designer and art director, working on a variety of projects for cultural, arts and fashion clients across different media including books, magazines, newspapers, identities, stationery, exhibition design and websites.

Bianca is the art director of The London Fashion Week Daily, Viewpoint magazine and Rubbish magazine. She is Creative in Residence at the Hospital Club, London, for 2011.

p242-243

BLEED

Bleed is a multi-disciplinary design consultancy based in Oslo, Norway, established in June 2000. They are working to challenge today's conventions around art, visual language, media and identity.

Bleed's work spans brand identity and development, art direction, packaging, printed matter, interactive design, art projects and exhibitions.

Both their client list and creative output has become diverse and impressive, and made them one of the most awarded agencies in Norway, with international and national acclaim.

Bleed believe in the power of visual language. Their work deals with long term brand-strategies as well as keeping it fresh by constantly challenging the boundaries of design and media.

Bleed for the revolution™.

p222-223, 226-227

BLOK DESIGN

Blok is a design studio specializing in brand identities and experiences, packaging, exhibit design, installations and editorial design. They also design and publish books and have produced a line of dishware.

Now here's what they really do: steep themselves in the world around them, seek out the normal, the abnormal, the mundane, the exciting, the current, the obsolete, the real, the fake, the inspiring, the disheartening, and then use what they see to find surprising, compelling ways to move people. And they do it by collaborating with highly talented thinkers from around the world, taking on initiatives that blend cultural awareness, a love of art and humanity to advance society and business alike.

p142-143

BLOW

Born in Hong Kong, Ken graduated from HKU SPACE Community College with Distinction in Higher Diploma in Visual Communication in 2005. In the same year, he won the Champion of "Design Student of The Year" presented by Hong Kong Designers Association.

He started working as a design internship in CoDesign Ltd. in 2004, and became a designer after graduation. He joined Alan Chan Design Company in 2006 and became a Senior Designer in 2007.

After leaving Alan Chan Design Company in 2010, Ken has started up his own design company, BLOW and launched his tote bag brand, luckipocki, aiming to spread out positive messages and share good luck with everyone around the world.

p022, 144

BOB FOUNDATION

Bob Foundation was established in 2002 by Mitsunori Asakura and Hiromi Asakura, both graduated from Central Saint Martins College of Art & design. They communicate, share and explore their interests with people through artwork, design, drawing, film, photography, text and anything else that present possibilities. They actively collaborate with overseas artists and designers and their works cover a wide range of fields. Bob Foundation also produces a paper brand 'Number 62' in 2007.

p264-265

BOND

Bond is a creative agency focused on branding and design. They create and renew brands. Bond is founded and run by designers. They work for clients who value creative and practical ideas. They demonstrate their expertise through their work rather than talking, because design is, first and foremost, a craft for them.

They design, visualize and define brands in a way that help companies differentiate themselves from the competition. This can mean creating brand identities, branded environments, packaging, experiential web services or advertising.

They are agile and designer-driven. Their clients appreciate working directly with the designers.

p338-345

BRAVO COMPANY

Bravo Company is a creatively led, independent design studio based in Singapore. They work with a variety of individuals and organizations to deliver considered and engaging design. Bravo Company specialize in identity & brand development, printed communications & art direction.

p166-167

BUNCH

Bunch is a leading creative design studio offering a diverse range of work, including identity, literature, editorial, digital and motion. Established in 2002 with an international reach, from London to Zagreb, Bunch has an in-house team of specialists to deliver intelligent and innovative cross-platform solutions of communication design. Over the years they have been commissioned by many blue chip companies as well as younger brands and artistic industries. They've built an impressive client base that covers many styles and disciplines, such as BBC, Nike, Diesel, Sony, Sky, Red Bull and others...

p034-035, 130-131

CARLOS BERMÚDEZ & MAU MORGÓ

Carlos Bermúdez and Mau Morgó had finished graphic design study at Eina School of Arts and Design in 2010. They are now working at the Barcelona based agency Mucho, and also running their personal project: www.wedieforbeauty.com

p246-247

CASPER CHAN

Graphic designer, illustrator and stylist based in London. His portfolio diversely synthesizes typography, illustration and fashion styling. His clients include LOVE magazine, Wallpaper* magazine, McCann Erickson, Lane Crawford and Richard James.

In 2009, he was awarded the British council 60th anniversary scholarship in contribution toward a MA Graphic Design in London College of Communication.

In 2011, he formed Studio 247 with Monkey Leung with a vision of "24 hours a day, 7 days a week, is never our motto".

p346-351

CATALOGUE

Catalogue is a pluridisciplinary graphic design studio based in Lyon, France. They provide visual identities, paper and web based communication, books and signage for cultural, institutional or industrial fields.

p238

CELIA LEUNG & AGNES WONG

Celia Leung and Agnes Wong are two young Hong Kong-based graphic designers. Celia graduated from San Francisco Academy of Art University with a Masters Degree in Graphic Design. Her work has been recognized by The DieLine, GDUSA Packaging Awards and Brand New Awards. Agnes graduated from Hong Kong Institute of Vocational Education (HKIVE). She is also an illustrator named Mcmary, who has published two story books — A Story about Santa and Walking with Slowman. Celia and Agnes specialize in identity, print, publication and websites designs. They both appreciate that real originality and creativity exits in hand and the head, but not the hard drive.

p268-269

CLASE BCN

Clase bcn is a graphic design and visual communication studio in Barcelona. It is made up of a team of ten young, international, multidisciplinary professionals whose work has won a number of awards.

The team work on all areas of design, but pay particular attention to typeface and the element of surprise. When they take a project on, they see to all phases of the strategic and creative process and come up with specific, innovative and distinctive languages following a coherent, exacting approach in accordance with the needs of each project. Claret Serrahima's professional career got under way in 1978 and, driven by her nonconformist, restless spirit, she set up Clase bcn in 2001 with two new partners: creative director Daniel Ayuso and managing director Sandra Parcet.

p090-091, 294-295

CLUTCH DESIGN

Clutch Design is a communication design company. The company offers a comprehensive service including development and implementation of branding, communication strategy, product concept, and execution. In addition, it also develops, produces, and sells design and original design goods such as advertisement, poster, graphic, logo, movie, and package.

p048-049

COBA & ASSOCIATES

Coba & Associates is a leading design and branding agency, based in Belgrade, Serbia. Their clients range from large multinational companies to small local producers. They believe in a culture of change. Change of attitudes, perceptions, meaning, understanding... Design is a language that can best explain and show all that.

p046-047

COMMUNE

Commune, a creative team based in Sapporo, Japan, has been mainly active in graphic design. The theme of creation for them is to make something better. Inspired by the will to make something better, their design work may move people or it may make society work a little better. It's like giving a gift. They choose a gift with the idea of delighting that is specially for someone. They feel very pleasant that recipient truly appreciate them when receiving something hasn't been expected. At times, Commune's creations take people by surprise, awaken their emotions, or even move them to tears. That's exactly what they're looking to create.

p352-361

CORPORATION POP

Corporation Pop is a design and communications agency based in Manchester, UK. Their team of expert designers, project managers and developers create solutions for print, branding, websites, virtual worlds, mobile applications and motion graphics. Corporation Pop provides first class customer service together with creative solutions that stand out for their clients. They always deliver eye-catching, original and above all effective results whatever the brief or target market is.

p183

CUE

Where strategy is transformed into tangible expression, you'll find Cue. Navigating from strategy to creative expression requires grounded thinking, intuition and understanding. But more than that, it requires taking ownership of a meaningful idea in the name of a brand.

p032-033

CUTTER & SAVAGE

Cutter & Savage is a full service agency dedicated to creating stories. Stories are about brands, products and people.

A good story can hook everyone's attention, without the unpleasantness of using actual hooks.

p230-231

DALSTON CREATIVE

Dalston provide creative direction, art direction, branding and design for commercial and editorial clients within the lifestyle, fashion, retail, culture and arts world.

Dalston want to "challenge, simplify and surprise". Dalston love a challenge and work in all forms of media. Among their projects you can find a selection of art direction for fashion, interiors and entertainment brands, visual communication for packaging, magazines, brand identities, digital applications and exhibitions.

Within their established network of creatives they can tailor complete and unique workgroups for most projects and client needs. This helps them be flexible, and gives each and every project a unique outcome.

p104-105

DAVID YANG

As Creative Director of Beijing Woowe Design Co., ltd, David Yang is a graphic designer and photography as well. He is a member of Capital Corporation Image Institution (ccii) and International Council of Graphic Design Associations (icograda).

p016-017

DESEGNO LTD

Haruhiko Tainuchi, born in 1979, had established his design company desegno ltd. in Tokyo in 2007. He works in the graphic design, typography, printing, drawing, web design, programming, image advertising, and branding for clients at home and abroad. The name of the company, desegno, means "design" in Esperanto, representing Tainuchi's idea that the power of visual expression can create new forms of universal languages like Esperanto, not limited by linguistic constraints to communicate. His work translates intangibles, concepts, and ideologies into a visual language to create new and efficient methods of universal communication.

p176-177

DESIGNLIGA

Designliga is an office for visual communication and interior design. Founded in Munich in 2001 by product designer Saša Stanojcic and communication designer Andreas Döhring, the office has grown into a strong team of 10 experienced designers, consultants and interior designers. Their clients include companies such as Adidas, Bayerischer Rundfunk, Cartier, IWC Schaffhausen, Marc O'Polo and Officine Panerai.

p068-069

DEUTSCHE & JAPANER

DEUTSCHE & JAPANER studio was initiated in 2008 and offers expertise in various disciplines, such as graphic design, product design, interior design, illustration and scenography as well as conceptual creation and strategic brand escort.

The studio focuses on communication, regardless of its physical condition, environmental, haptical or visual, but always in regard of sustainable experiences.

p112-113

DOMINIC RECHSTEINER

In 2008, Dominic Rechsteiner graduated at the University of Basel with the Bachelor of Arts in visual communication. He's currently working as a self-employed and freelance graphic designer.

Together with some friends he founded the studio "Bureau Collective" in 2009. It is mainly a design studio for graphical solutions, a place where they share ideas and work on their own projects. Throughout the past years Dominic has worked together with various clients, for instance the St.Gall Theatre, EAU-DC, SONST and more.

p145, 182, 237

DRAWSWORDS

Amsterdam-based design studio Drawswords was founded by graphic designer and concept developer Rob van den Nieuwenhuizen. The studio's work is characterized by visually strong, clear and refreshing content-based typographic solutions.

Barbara Hennequin is an Amsterdam-based independent graphic and type designer focused on structured typographic design projects. She also holds an MA in Communication Studies.

Van den Nieuwenhuizen and Hennequin sometimes work collaboratively on specific projects.

p252-255

EDWARD DESSASO

idiolalia represents Edward Dessaso's continuing immersion into the world of multi-disciplinary graphic design. Edward had studied Graphic Design at Brighton University. His other interests include living an active lifestyle, comics and a growing pursuit into textile design.

p025

ESTUDIO MENTA

Menta is a multidisciplinary design studio and communication agency specialized in various fields related with publicity and design. A profile that covers from the consulting and coordination of corporate identity projects to the production of catalogues, including web design projects, space design, signage, editorial design, as well as production of video adapted to the new channels of content distribution.

p236

EXPOSURE

Exposure is a creative agency working with brands to generate good solid ideas. They believe in sparking conversations. Conversations that are shared. With offices in New York, San Francisco and London they work across a wide range of media and disciplines to deliver the good news. They are always glad to provide a point of view.

p045, 185

FABIO ONGARATO DESIGN

Founded in 1992 by partners Fabio Ongarato and Ronnen Goren, based in Melbourne, Fabio Ongarato Design is renowned for the diversity of its work. The studio takes an open approach to graphic design, operating across a variety of graphic disciplines, from print to exhibitions to advertising. FOD's approach to design reflects their passion for architecture, photography and contemporary art. They work across a variety of fields such as fashion, corporate, arts and architecture deliberately crossing the boundaries between them.

p162-163, 234-235

FACETOFACEDESIGN

FACETOFACEDESIGN is a multidisciplinary graphic design studio based in Brussels, Belgium. They appreciate that each project comes with its own set of singularities, demanding a different, project-specific approach at each time.

p158-159

FAMOUS VISUAL SERVICES

Established in 2003 and directed by Dominic Forde, Famous Visual Services is a graphic design studio based in Melbourne. At Famous they approach each project with a process of enquiry, strategy and collaboration. They only give form to a project once they have a thorough understanding of it's content and objectives. By emphasizing the importance of communicating an idea in their work they aim to produce a body of work that is respectful to their clients' needs whilst displaying a level of inventativeness that makes each project memorable and unique.

p206

FILTHYMEDIA

filthymedia opened its doors in 2004, setting out to create an independent graphic design studio in the heart of Brighton. The company was conceived through a joint passion for all things design, music and fashion. Their belief is that effective design is engaging and attention grabbing.

filthymedia, like their work, stands out from the crowd and they aspire to turn their passion for design into commercial success with a creative edge for their clients.

p150-151, 316-317

FOUNDED

Founded is a Newcastle based design studio, working across a wide range of sectors and media creating stand out brand imagery with effective returns.

p210-211

FUJIMOTO GUMI

Fujimoto Gumi is a design agency based in Japan.

p262-263

GARDENS&CO.

Gardens&co. is a small independent graphic house. The team members mainly come from 3 areas: graphics, visual merchandising & web design. Every project undertaken is crafted with passion. They build partnerships with the clients to understand their communication challenges. Applying their design thinking to develop thought-provoking solutions to address commercial needs, they provide a one-stop service from enhancing corporate brand image to customers' shopping experience.

p124-125, 168-171

GARETH PROCTER

Gareth Procter is a freelance graphic designer living and working in both London and Sydney. He works primarily in the fields of brand identity, graphic design and art direction. The focus of all of his work is always strong and unique ideas and this is then followed by immaculate execution.

p313

GHAZAAL VOJDANI

Ghazaal Vojdani is an Iranian graphic designer born in London, 1986. She has experienced both cultures, having lived in Tehran for 11 years. After graduation from the BA Graphic Design course at Central Saint Martins College of Art and Design, she is currently on the MFA program at Yale School of Art.

p084-085, 088

GLASFURD & WALKER

Established in early 2007, Glasfurd & Walker offer multi-disciplinary, conceptual and design services and innovative brand communication and design solutions. With each project presenting new challenges and demanding unique outcomes, strategic, idea driven design is key to their approach. The studio services include, but are not limited to: identity and brand design, art direction and design for print and online communication, signage & installation, exhibition design and packaging.

p028

GRAPHITICA

Kazunori Gamo began working as a graphic designer for a clothing brand and has since delved into other fields and media, including fashion magazines, advertising and website production.

He further expanded his range of activities after setting up the "GRAPHITICA" design office in 2008.

He is a member of "Japan Graphic Designers Association / JAGDA".

p128-129, 153

HEINE/LENZ/ZIZKA

The design agency Heine/Lenz/Zizka focuses on visual communication. They help their clients to define the core of their brand in order to communicate successfully — analog and digital. At their offices in Frankfurt and Berlin, about 25 employees create products, corporate images and communication concepts that bring brands to life. The agency was founded in 1989 by Achim Heine, Michael Lenz and Peter Zizka. For several years Heine/Lenz/Zizka has been among the top 10 in the ranking of creative design agencies in Germany.

p054

HELLO

Hello was formed in 2002 by Creative Director Jamie Gallagher. Hello employ a fresh, instinctive approach to branding; working with their clients to forge beautiful, dynamic brands that have relevance and deliver real results.

They shy away from using formulaic, structured processes and believe that trusting in their experience and instinct leads to a braver, stronger and more unique body of work across a range of design disciplines: from books, brochures and point of sale, to packaging, signage, websites and stationery. They enjoy working collaboratively with their clients, large and small — sharing knowledge and vision to create brands that are confident, innovative and unique; brands that transform businesses.

p308

HUARONG CHEN

Huarong Chen was born in Jiangmen, Guangdong Province, China. He'd graduated from department of fine art of Xijiang University. He is now living and working in Dongguan.

p071

HYPERLOCALDESIGN

Hyperlocaldesign is a creation positioning which is founded on design — as its key tool in the exclusive brand building. A wise and multi-cellular design proposal, holding both the physical and digital world. A process from essence to the final result. A new way to look at the creation job, valuing the techno-biological symbiosis, through a flexible and unlimited way.

p154-155

INTERABANG

Interabang is a new London design agency, founded by Adam Giles and Ian McLean. Since setting up a year ago they've been working with clients such as Royal Mail, British Heart Foundation and Jimmy's Iced Coffee — creating brand identities, moving image, communication materials and picking up design awards along the way.

p092-093

IVAN KHMELEVSKY

Ivan Khmelevsky is a graphic designer from Moscow, Russia. He studied in UK, worked in London, but currently resides in Moscow, where he runs his small independent design studio The Bakery. His clients include both local and international businesses from small companies to big corporate clients.

p244-245

J. KENNETH ROTHERMICH

J. Kenneth Rothermich is a graphic designer who lives in Brooklyn, New York. He currently works as Design Director at The O Group, as well as independently as a freelance designer and art director. A Midwestern upbringing and a BFA in Graphic Design from Miami University in Oxford, Ohio keep him grounded. In his spare time, Ken has been known to make art, write music, play guitar in punk rock bands and travel the world.

p157, 160-161

JAMES PRUNEAN

James Prunean is a graphic designer based out of Waterloo, Ontario, Canada. He designs with the goal of developing unique products that combine aesthetic strength, with honest simplicity and a heightened sensitivity to user needs. The creative he designs ranges from web to traditional print and entire brand identities.

p320-321

JOSEP ROMÁN BARRI

Josep Román Barri was born in Barcelona in 1986. He chose the technical specialty in high school and after he studied Technical Engineering in Industrial Design at Elisava Design School in Barcelona, which he finished in 2009, there he started to study a bachelor in graphic design, combining it with an exchange at Écal, university of arts and design of Lausanne, Switzerland.

Josep is currently living in Barcelona working on his final project. In his free time he works on commissioned projects, projects for friends, and personal projects. Most of the projects presented in his website are academic and they show his knowledge and progression. His favourite fields are editorial design, art direction, typography, illustration, corporate identity and website. He feels comfortable with the printed matter but he's also interested in digital media, always working from the concept to the shape.

p208-209

JOYN:VISCOM

JOYN:VISCOM is an independent, multi-disciplinary design studio and communication consultancy based in Beijing, China. The studio aims to create experiences, whether they're commissioned client-work or self-initiated projects. By working across diverse disciplines, the studio consistently delivers exclusive, creative and easy-going solutions.

In addition, JOYN:VISCOM produces a wide range of independent projects, including exhibitions, lectures, publications, and events. All efforts the collective has been making are to devote itself to exploring all facets of contemporary visual culture and communications.

p044

JUAN AREIZAGA

Juan Areizaga is an independent graphic designer based in Barcelona, focusing on editorial design, web design, and corporate identity. "I explore the experimental, but I admire the rational. I care about details, but I investigate through errors. Contemporary vision and classic touch. Friend of the concept and lover of the form. And more contradictions…"

p164-165

K.M. DESIGN

Kenji Miyauchi is an art director and designer in Japan. He had won prizes in Tokyo ADC 2009, Graphic Design in Japan 2009/2010 and Tokyo TDC 2009/2010.

p325

KAMIKENE

Kamikene is a graphic designer/art director based in Tokyo. He is a member of the multi-talented collective team, Hatos.

He has been doing design for the magazine "+81" for 38 issues now since coming onboard since Vol.15.

He has encountered and created graphics for clients with heart from the underground all the way to the majors, including to SPANOVA, Kuniyuki Takahashi, DJ KRUSH, and THE NORTH FACE.

p126-127

KANELLA ARAPOGLOU

Kanella Arapoglou studied Graphic Design at TEI, in Athens, and later received an MA in Communication Design from Central Saint Martins, in London. During her stay in London, Kanella worked for a number of prestigious design agencies, including the publishing and music industry. The long client list include names such as The Rolling Stones, Elton John, Jimmy Hendrix, Sallivan's Punk. Book, Penguin Books and more. Having spent 7 years in the British capital, she moved back to Athens where she filled the position of the Art Director at various creative groups. Kanella is currently teaching at TEI, in Athens (where she started her life in Graphic Design), is doing projects under her own name (www.kanella.com) and collaborating with offices in Greece and abroad.

p204-205

KAPIL BHIMEKAR

Kapil Bhimekar had graduated in Applied Arts in Mumbai. Extreme passion for design and ideas brought him in to the business.

He pours his heart and soul into every piece of work. His painstaking attention to the smallest details creates work that offers something new every time you look at it.

While his extreme sense of humor is reflected in his designs, Kapil is nonetheless very serious about his work. His intimate approach and sincere thoughtfulness elevate his designs.

In his 7-year long career span, Kapil's work has been recognized at several award shows including Cannes lions, One Show, New York festivals, London International awards, Adfest Asia Pacific, Dubai Lynx, etc.

p178-181

KARIM CHARLEBOIS-ZARIFFA

Karim Charlebois-Zariffa is an accomplished graphic designer and director. Working mainly with objects, installations and photography when working with stills. In his director side, he works with stop-motion and video effects to do commercials, TV openings and music videos. He has worked for clients such as the New York Times Magazine, STM and Stefan Sagmeister. His work is all based on craft work.

p094-095

KAWAKONG DESIGNWORKS

Formed in September 1999, by Chung and Ming, pursuing their dream to become graphic designers. Like the others, they have vision too. First, to design for their client, Second, to design for themselves, and their mission is to make the gap closer each and everyday. Gratefully, they have completed their studies from the Malaysian Institute of Art, and Curtin University of Technology. Largely of their time were divided to what they do best, which is graphic and identity design. Not to forget, they love illustration too. The other part of their time were reserved for a self initiative project that they name it the B-sides project, where they either work together or separately. B-sides began naturally from unexpected doodling process to working on larger sheet of papers, and then, to various surface and for now, stitches on fabrics. For now or future, their only wish was to be able to find ways to invent happiness in their work.

p272-273

KENTLYONS

We are a design agency

We are visual communicators

We are digital specialists

We are brand consultants

We are an advertising agency

We are KentLyons

KentLyons creates communications that are beautiful and useful without compromise.

They've created some interesting projects for some well-known companies such as Channel 4, the BBC, Macmillan, the D&AD, Sky, the Design Museum, LV=, Swiss Re, Film London, ITV, Westfield, Foster + Partners, and many others.

p040-041, 300-301, 306-307

KISSMIKLOS

kissmiklos is a Hungarian designer and artist. He works on a range of projects in architecture, fine art, design, graphic design and typography.

p062-063

KOKORO & MOI

Kokoro & Moi, founded in 2001 by designers Teemu Suviala and Antti Hinkula, is a multidisciplinary design consultancy specialized in brand identity and development, creative direction, visual communication and interaction. Their clients represent commercial players from multinationals to start-ups, as well as various cultural and public institutions, all searching for better concepts and ideas for the future.

They work on a broad range of assignments, from development of brand identity systems or new service concepts to orchestration of complex design projects for print, screen, products and environments.

They love asking questions, challenging accepted explanations and inferring possible new worlds.

p202-203

KYLIE MCINTYRE

Peachy Flamingo is Kylie McIntyre, Graphic Designer in Sydney, Australia. Born an Artsy Fartsy creative type, Kylie couldn't imagine herself doing anything but be creative. Not only is Kylie a Graphic Designer, she is also a Jewellery Maker, Illustrator, Photographer and Crafter. Kylie is still a young gun in the creative world, and with her willingness to experiment and push the boundaries in her work, things can only get 'peachy' from here on in.

p326-327

LA CAJA DE TIPOS

La caja de tipos is a graphic design studio formed by Maria Saez and Ander Sanchez, located in Leioa, a town near Bilbao, Spain. After graduation, they'd worked separately in several studios and they decided to start their own in 2008. They love what they do and what most matters in their projects is to convey concepts through the correct choice of colors, typographies, and graphics resources. They design branding projects for companies, posters for music festivals, invitations for events and editorial design, among other things.

p060-061

LARISSA KASPER

Larissa Kasper is currently studying Visual Communication at the Zurich University of the Arts. Besides he often collaborates with St.Gallen based graphic designer Rosario Florio for several commissioned projects. They share a small studio called Bureau Collective with some friends in St.Gallen.

p066

LIQUORICE STUDIO

Liquorice Studio is a multi-disciplinary communication design agency, formed in 2009 by director Scott Bonanno. Based in Melbourne, Australia, Liquorice Studio is a small team of diverse individuals who specialise in brand and identity design for print and web. The studio's current portfolio features a wide scope of clients ranging from large corporations to medium and small businesses, and their output includes publication design, art direction, website design, exhibition design, signage and brand identity.

p258-259

LSDK

Specialised in conceptual design, creation and communication design, LSDK was founded in 2009 by Christian Vögtlin and Sergej Grusdew. Based in Stuttgart, the agency stands for a holistic principle which brings the clients with their ideas, desires and views into the focus. The main ambition is to create authentic concepts and individual designs. Being convinced that the haptic experience is a key factor in the transmission of emotions, LSDK always consider possible supporting materials when designing. In the end of the progress they want to create a project with which the client is not only comfortable but can identify himself as well.

p312

LUCAS RAMPAZZO

Lucas Rampazzo is a graphic designer and he's recently completed an artistic residency in Rotterdam/NL at Hommes Gallery.

As a graphic designer, Lucas develops works into various segments such as editorial, fashion, video, music, package, visual identity, print, among others.

He often uses patterns and repetitions of shapes as the main subject of his works, but he also engages in the opposite approach, one that is more abstract and organic.

Music is also a passion of his and he seeks to combine these concept in the minimal and atmospheric pieces he composes.

As an introspective observer, Lucas tries to transcend the music, purity, beauty and simplicity into inspiration.

He's open to partnerships with clients and design studios all around the world.

p103

LUCI EVERETT

Luci Everett is a freelance illustrator and graphic designer in Melbourne, Australia. She began creating artwork for musicians as a design student, and has since developed her distinctive visual style. She favours a handmade approach — designs will always begin in watercolour, collage, paint and pencil before being scanned into digital form. Her approach is intuitive and her aesthetic can be described as eclectic, whimsical, warm, tactile and light. Alongside her freelance projects Luci is also in the midst of planning an artists book/journal publication with her friend and photographer Olga Bennett.

p102

LUNDGREN+LINDQVIST

Lundgren+Lindqvist is a Sweden based design & development bureau offering services within branding, design for print, digital, illustration & art direction.

They believe that good design is more than ink or pixels on a surface; it is understanding how a message is received and experienced. By identifying the essence of that experience, they can create efficient and interesting communication that uniquely conceived for each project. They embrace the constantly evolving possibilities of digital design, and approach web design with the same attention to detail as they do in print.

Lundgren+Lindqvist has a wide base of national and international clients that include a variety of corporations, media and cultural institutions.

p042-043

MAMASTUDIO

Mamastudio is an award winning independent design studio specializing in creating coherent and emotionally engaging visual communications for brands, companies, places, people, products and organizations. Based in the heart of Warsaw, Mamastudio bases its approach to design and brand development on three pillars: creativity, knowledge and commitment.

Through a process that incorporates strategy, analysis and innovative design, Mamastudio examines the broader context of a brand and the role it has on social and consumer activity. The effect is a result driven foundation for creative decision-making, both for work in the commercial realm, as well as for arts-inspired cultural projects.

p305

MARISSA RIVERA

Marissa Rivera creates compositions that are often simply in design yet complex in the way she constructs unity though variety. By enlisting an array of materials to enhance the aesthetics of the design, Marissa simultaneously creates visual intrigue. She views the design process from the artists' perspective. This has developed her interest in designing for those who also create. She embraces the challenge of designing for fellow creatives because she then has the opportunity to figure out how her aesthetic will compliment their vision. She finds this to be the most rewarding result of the entire design process.

p077

MARK PERNICE / MATIC

Mark Pernice / Matic is a graphic design and illustration studio in Brooklyn NY.

A New York native and School of Visual Arts alumnus, he advanced from early work in movie poster design to designing for a variety of clients including The New York Times, Bloomberg View, Anthropologie, The Urban Green Council, Virgin Mobile, The Boston Globe, and The Lincoln Center for the Performing Arts.

Pernice spent part of 2008 working with world renowned graphic designer Stenfan Sagmeister and Paula Scher in 2010. Recently Pernice's "Photo Booth Mask" gained viral attention with over 1.5 million image hits in it's first 3 months.

p098-099, 279

MATHIAS MARTIN

Mathias Martin is a freelance graphic designer. He's a photographer as well.

He chooses to let his economic career follow his real passion: typography and identity.

He designs identities for restaurants and public places. Some of his work are regularly published in design books.

p191

MATÍAS FIORI

Matías Fiori is a young and fresh Graphic Designer from Uruguay, with clients all around the world, including Barcelona, England, Brazil and many others. He is the Founder of Re-Robot studio, based in Montevideo Uruguay.

p194-195

MATTSON CREATIVE

Mattson Creative is an award-winning graphic design studio based in Southern California.

They create visual language for vibrant brands.

p024

MESSY DESIGN

Messy Design is a multifaceted branding and design studio, focused on delivering innovative work through creative form and precise function. They are defined by their versatility and purpose-built design solutions. With clients covering a broad spectrum, Messy constantly evolves and adapts its approach to suit each individual project — always delivering quality executions that get results.

p058-059

MIND DESIGN

Mind Design is an independent London based graphic design studio founded in 1999 by RCA graduate Holger Jacobs. Mind Design focuses on integrated design which combines corporate identity, print, web and interior design. They work for a wide range of clients across various sectors; from startups to established companies.

Mind Design's philosophy and approach is based on a passion for craftsmanship and typography. They offer practical and friendly design solutions and believe that content and form are inseparable. It is important for them to work in close collaboration with clients, ideally right from the start. Every project is seen as a new challenge and they never follow an already established graphic house style.

p232-233

MOTHERBIRD

Motherbird is a Melbourne based creative outfit consisting of 3 young designers, Jack Mussett, Chris Murphy & Dan Evans. They have worked with a variety of clients including: Qantas, Warner Music, ABC, Billy Blue School of Design and Positive Posters. Motherbird specialise in brand identity, print design, image making, packaging and environmental signage. In 2010 they were awarded the nation-wide 'Spirit of Youth Award' (SOYA) as well as being on the Australian Graphic Design Association (AGDA) council.

p096

MURMURE

Created in December 2009, Murmure is a communication, design, web and art agency. It is composed of four members: Julien Alirol, graphic designer, photographer and web designer; Simon Roche, CTO and illustrator; Paul Ressencourt, artistic director; Cyril Baekelandt, programmer, SEO. It includes a set of skills allowing to achieve full graphic identities. Its headquarters are located in Caen and its web pole in Lille. Shattering the boundaries between art and communication, the agency is specialized in print communications, Internet, street marketing, creative and conceptual research. Their work achievements include graphic identities, editing, photography, design, packaging, business cards, web sites and they are open to further requests.

p120-121,188-189,310-311

MUSAWORKLAB

Musa is a design project of Portuguese designers Raquel Viana, Paulo Lima and Ricardo Alexandre formed in October 2003.

The project started with Musabook with the main objective to publish a book showcasing the best Portuguese designers, the first Portuguese emergent graphic design book ever compiled published by idN Hong Kong.

The work developed by the name of MusaWorkLab (the studio) put the Portuguese design scene on a higher stage of international visibility. MusaWorkLab is a design studio of graphic experiments that aim for the innovation and search of excellence that decided to join several artists/designers in order to promote the new Portuguese talented and emergent young visual culture.

Musa is working on their own projects like exhibitions, books, toys, participations with international designers and projects, and working on their commercial projects like fashion and trendy clients like Bombay Sappire, Moet&Chandon, Lisbon Fashion Week and many others Portuguese and international brands.

Musa work as many aspects of design as possible, from artistic/experimental to commercial.

p050-051, 055-056, 74

NATHAN HINZ

Nathan Hinz tells stories and solves problems. Based in Minneapolis, Minnesota USA, his identity & branding work spans print, packaging, and interactive mediums. His work has been recognized in many major American and International competitions, such as AIGA, Communication Arts, The One Show, London International Awards, and Cannes; for clients such as BMW, The Bahamas, The Children's Theatre Company, and Jack Daniel's.

p032-033

NEO NEO

Neo Neo is a Geneva based graphic design studio, founded in 2010 by Thuy-An Hoang and Xavier Emi. They mostly work for cultural clients and try to propose contemporary solutions, giving importance to details, emphasis typography and direct messages.

p368-372

NEUE DESIGN STUDIO

Neue Design Studio has since its establishment in 2008 created visual communication with the belief that insight and creativity are equally dependent in the process toward creating engaging, long-lived concepts. Working from their 6th-floor studio with its overview of Oslo, they develop strategies, make editorial design, brand identities, packaging and illustration for both print and screen.

p029

NICHOLAS JEEVES

Nicholas Jeeves left Cambridge School of Art in 1994 with a degree in graphic arts and illustration. He began his career designing some of the UK's earliest commercial websites, as well as print projects for clients including The Royal Albert Hall and Virgin Publishing.

After five years as an active independent designer, he was invited by Cambridge School of Art to return as a visiting lecturer, and has continued there since. His graphic design, made under the company name 'Public', has been widely published and internationally acknowledged, with projects for clients including The Living Wage Foundation, Frank PR, Ellesse, Saatchi & Saatchi, Blackberry and the UK Film Council. Nicholas has also helped to develop D&AD's Student Awards briefs, and served on its jury. A major contributor to the Thames and Hudson book 'Graphic Design School', he has also tutored young designers at Milan's Accademia di Comunicazione and Ankara's Baskent University.

As of 10th December 2010, Nicholas has retired the name 'Public' and now works under his own name. His design practice will incorporate more experimental projects in 2011, while continuing to make clear, intelligent and finely-crafted works for a select list of clients.

p328

NIGN COMPANY LIMITED

Kenichiro Ohara is Art Director and Graphic designer in NIGN Company Limited.

Kenichiro Ohara was born in Hyogo in 1973. After graduating from an industrial high school, Kenichiro has self-taught the discipline of design throughout a wide range of his professional careers. In 2000, he became a freelance designer and in 2006, he founded his own design firm, NIGN. NIGN has been a gateway to an extensive field of design services, including CI, branding, book design, fashion, and packaging. Kenichiro is a member of Tokyo Type Directors Club and Japan Graphic Designers Association.

p108-109, 110-111, 132-137, 288-289

NJENWORKS

Njenworks is a design studio based in New York with a global outlook. The studio was founded by Natasha Jen in 2010. Prior to founding Njenworks, Natasha held art director and senior designer positions at 2x4 Inc and Base Design for several years.

Njenworks' practice does not specialize by media nor industry, but rather it explores the notion of identity and its propagation across media, industries, culture and scale.

Njenworks is involved in projects at a wide spectrum of scales, ranging from the new identity for MIT Architecture, a video project for artist Doug Aitken, a map project for the Sharjah Biennial in the U.A.E., to an urban intervention project that will take place in Beijing, New York, and London.

p218-219

NOMINA DESIGN

Nomina Design is a studio that focuses mainly on people and brand identity, and uses its expertise in this area to build brands, create identities, plan businesses, design stores, communicate in retail, study trends and come up with products for industries. They're also specialized in analyzing and designing store concepts that are sure to achieve success with clients and customers alike. Their professionals have solid backgrounds on design, architecture, fashion, culture and trends, which makes for unique ideas and solutions for both commercial and residential needs. The projects presented by Nomina Design comprehend not only interior design and visual merchandising aspects, but also cater for retail and communication strategies, stationery and packaging development, furniture design, among others.

p174-175

NORTH

North is an independent London-based design agency, founded in 1995.

They build identities and brands that achieve business success and have transformational effects on organisations.

Their clients include RAC, The Royal Mint, HSBC, First Direct, The Royal Mint, HSBC, Coca-Cola and the Barbican.

p212-213

PACKOFWOLV.ES

Packofwolv.es is the working title for freelance graphic designer – Nicholas Hawker.

Situated in Melbourne, Australia, Nicholas works with clients both locally and internationally.

His approach to design speaks of simplicity, originality and tailoring each project to the individual client.

p298-299

PAULO LOPES

Paulo Lopes Studio, an independent studio, is able to reach where others can't fit. He specializes in unique and innovative graphics, contemporary and content-driven visual communication.

He loves to work with cultural institutions, open-minded individuals, committed corporations, and collaborating with other studios he can share his ideas with.

p190

PHARAON SIRAJ

Pharaon Siraj is a graphic designer from Singapore. Previously trained as an engineer, he worked in various (non-engineering) positions before deciding to pursue his passion in design. For the past two years he has been in the Visual Communication graduate program at the School of the Art Institute of Chicago.

His practice spans various disciplines including identity, editorial, environmental and interactive design. He is especially interested in design for the arts, cultural institutions and social causes.

p276-277

PLANET CREATIVE

Brand management is the core strength of Planet Creative – whether it's about building a brand from the ground up, the positioning of an existing brand, or creating brand collateral such as presentations, etc. Planet Creative is a creative agency focused on graphic design, from strategy and concept to finished product.

p122-123

PLENTY

Pablo Alfieri is a graphic designer and illustrator from Buenos Aires, Argentina. After working as an art director in local studios, he decided to create his own place, "Playful", where he dedicates all his passion for graphic design, illustration and typography. Characterized by a constant quest for simplicity in geometrics shapes, a mix between analogous and digital, lead Pablo to captivate the interest of companies like Nike, MTV International and Latinamerica, Snickers, Chevrolet, Motorola and Nextel.

A year ago Pablo joined Gula's owner, Mariano Farias, (an experienced motion graphic designer) to created PLENTY, a new graphic and motion graphic design studio meant to be a reference in Argentina where he continues working with international brands as MTV, Discovery Channel, Fox, Johnnie Walker, Chandon, among others.

p256-257

PRINZ & PRINZ

Prinz & Prinz is a multidisciplinary creative studio from Stockholm. It was founded in 2009 by the two brothers Petter Prinz and Kaspar Prinz. Their work is a mix between art and science and they do everything from film to inventions. At the moment they are based in London as a part of Google Creative Lab.

p362-367

PROJECT PROJECTS

Project Projects is a design studio focusing on print, identity, exhibition, and interactive work with clients in art and architecture.

The studio was founded in 2004 by Prem Krishnamurthy and Adam Michaels; Rob Giampietro joined as a principal in 2010.

The studio has been a Finalist twice in the Cooper-Hewitt National Design Awards (2009 & 2011) and has received numerous distinctions including the ADC Bronze Medal, I.D. magazine's 2007 Design Distinction Award, the Art Directors Club Young Guns 5 Award, several Society of Publication Designers merit awards, and the AIGA 365 Award. In addition to client-based work, the studio initiates and produces independent curatorial and publishing projects.

p248-249

PUPILPEOPLE

Pupilpeople is a Singapore-based design studio formed in 2008. Their collective approach focuses on integrating their individual capabilities to produce current, coherent and unified work for a broad range of clients.

p303

PURPOSE

Purpose is a brand communications consultancy specializing in brand identity and marketing communications. Their strategic, design and production skills enable clients to communicate more effectively – to stand out, to connect, and to prosper. Purpose is over thirty strong – they are independent – and they are listed in the Design Week league table of Top 10 UK Creative Award winning agencies.

p198

QIONGJIE YU

Qiongjie Yu, founder of Transwhite Studio, is a graphic designer and book artist. She is now also a teacher of Zhejiang Gongshang University.

Qiongjie went to Camberwell College of Arts in University of the Arts London for further study in 2007. She'd majored in graphic design and book arts and achieved double master's degree in 2010. After graduation, she's back to China again and successfully founded Transwhite Studio in Hangzhou in 2011.

In addition to graphic design, Qiongjie is particularly keen on book arts. A number of her works have been collected by Tate Gallery, Leeds University Library, University of the Arts London, Camberwell College of Arts, University of Coventry, and so on. She'd also participated in many artist book fairs in Leeds, Glasgow, Warsaw, London and other cities.

p332-337

QUBE KONSTRUKT

Qube Konstrukt is a multi-disciplinary design practice, a studio in which inspiration, ideas and creativity are free to manifest themselves through different mediums. They work with confidence and ability across a broad range of disciplines encompassing identity and brand development, campaign, print and publication design, illustration and environmental graphics, as well as online, interactive and broadcast design. The creative diversity of the studio, both of its individual members and as a whole, is one of the studio's core strengths. A collaborative working process and time allowed for experimentation and play are vital components of their studio methodology.

p064-065

QUBE STUDIO

Qube Studio is a multi-disciplinary independent creative agency dedicated to enhancing their clients' communications and design. As specialists, they remain resolute in their appreciation of 'brand' as key to the success of any given service or product. Their strength comes from a solid team with over 20 years of global experience, served with loyalty, aptitude and professionalism. Their reputation is built on those of their discerning clients', who have grown and found success with the team.

p057

QUINTA-FEIRA

For a long time numbers no longer are used only to count and calculate but began to be appreciated by their own properties. Numbers exist independently of the palpable world and their study is not affected by the uncertainty of perception. Quinta-feira translates the natural world into numbers and back again to the natural world, ultimately trying to build worlds out of nature.

p070, 200

R&D

Research and Development Art Directors, based in Stockholm, Sweden, works in close collaboration with artists, curators, critics, collectors, directors, museums and cultural institutions.

p278

RED DESIGN

Established in 1996 and based in Brighton, UK, Red made its name by producing award winning graphic design for the music industry.

They now work across a range of diverse sectors delivering high quality still, moving and interactive design.

Their integrity and passion for beautiful and effective design is reflected in the work they do. They love and believe in what they do.

p199

RIKAKO NAGASHIMA

Rikako Nagashima, born in 1980, had graduated from Musashino Art University in 2003. And she joined Hakuhodo in the same year.

Her work includes advertising for Laforet Harajuku, a symbol of Japanese fashion; package design for the artisan Los Angeles chocolatier Yvan Valentin; art activities including the Takashi

Honma + Rikako Nagashima art book 'One of Them' (available at Utrecht); logo design for Artists Summit, which featured artists from around the world including Cai Guo-Qiang and Ryuichi Sakamoto. Rikako has recently established the art project Peace Shadow Project with modern artist Tatsuo Miyajima.

p067, 082, 152, 284-285

ROANDCO

RoAndCo is a multi-disciplinary design studio devoted to holistic branding that serves a range of fashion, art, and lifestyle clients. Led by award-winning Creative Director Roanne Adams, RoAndCo offers design, image, and branding capabilities across a variety of mediums, from print to moving image. By thoughtfully distilling a client's inspirations, ideas, and motivations, RoAndCo generates fresh, sincere, compelling brand messages that engage and resonate.

p072-073, 089, 114-119, 140-141

ROOT

ROOT is a London based multi-disciplinary design studio that has built a reputation for delivering innovative and effective solutions for a diverse, worldwide client base. At the heart of their approach is an informed, inspiring idea, brilliantly executed. Great ideas add value to business and they know how to make an impact across all media.

ROOT is constantly evolving to ensure they remain as relevant today as they were when they first opened their doors in 1990. They create on brief, on deadline and on budget, cutting through blandness and going beyond expectation.

p318-319

SAGE

Sage is an ideas-driven graphic design consultancy specialising in brand building. They deliver intelligent, engaging and relevant visual communication solutions that connect your brand with your audience.

They take time to understand your business' objectives and unique characteristics. They analyse your market, question, strategies, explore ideas, then arrive at a visual solution that is distinctive and personal.

p150-179

SAVVY STUDIO

Savvy is a multidisciplinary studio based in Monterrey Mexico dedicated to developing brand experiences that generate lasting bonds between the clients and their public.

The team is made up of specialists in Marketing, Communication, Graphic Design, Industrial Design, Creative Copywriting and Architecture.

They also work closely with international artists and designers, and they offer innovative creative solutions with a global competitive vision.

They work on each project meticulously through a creative process that is open, dynamic and clear, and they facilitate the participation of their clients at all times.

p052-053

SEESAW

The name of Seesaw communicates their ethos: they balance creative insights with company objectives to generate leading design solutions. And they wouldn't be Seesaw without a little fun in between.

Established in 2005, Seesaw is a close-knit collective of hard working creatives who understand the impact of brand and design on business. Design is a valuable commodity and when they create, they do so with long-term intent. Seesaw develops visual messages to inspire your audience to accept the strength and value of your brand. Through the art of design and words, they create visual definitions of your business, your products, and your services.

p086-087, 224-225, 302

SEVEN25. DESIGN & TYPOGRAPHY. INC.

Seven25's focus is to design for better. They collaborate with their clients and partners to uncover the stories that need telling and the ideas that will lead organizations in the right direction to a better future.

p156, 309

SMBETSMB

Keita Shimbo and Misaco Shimbo are running a design studio named "smbetsmb" in Tokyo, Japan. They design for companies, exhibitions and trade fairs. Their work includes information systems, books and posters.

p214-217

SMEL

Smel, founded in 2001 by Edgar Smaling and Carlo Elias, consists of a dynamic team of dedicated, multidisciplinary creative people. Smel designs strategic corporate identities, magazines, books, corporate identities and websites; illustrious design concepts which subtly unite quality and imagination.

Smel works for a variety of clients, public service, fashion, design, art and architecture.

p106-107

STEFI ORAZI STUDIO

Stefi Orazi Studio is a graphic design studio based in East London. Founded in 2006 by Stefi Orazi after 8 years as senior designer at acclaimed agency Graphic Thought Facility. The focus of their work is mainly in print and exhibition graphics.

Over the years Stefi Orazi Studio have built a strong relationship with clients in a number of cultural institutions such as galleries and museums as well as individuals. Their approach is to find design solutions through research, rational thinking and craft. Recent clients have included the Serpentine Gallery, Timothy Taylor Gallery and Phillips de Pury & Company.

p324

STUDIO EQUATOR

Studio Equator is a multidisciplinary design agency based in Melbourne, Australia. Their focus is on return on design investment, using a creative and strategic approach. They help grow their clients' business using engaging and memorable design and their dedicated team of designers bring a fresh and artistic approach to every project.

p080-081

STUDIO FILIPPO NOSTRI

Studio Filippo Nostri deals with graphic design.

With years of experience and working for important museums, institutions, galleries and publishers, the studio has developed a deep knowledge of the entire design process.

Relevance to the content, coherence in the structure and in the details, right typographic choices and optimization of materials are the guidelines for each project.

p039, 287

STUDIO IKNOKI

Studio Iknoki is a visual design and communication studio based in Brescia, Italy.

In 2008 Francesco D'Abbraccio, Francesco Greguol and Christian Jugovac, after having attended together the design courses at IUAV in Venice, had decided to join forces and start up the studio.

The studio is active within different fields of design, from the visual identity of institutions and companies, to the design of editorial projects and exhibitions.

Their approach tries to be as multidisciplinary as possible, working with various media and disciplines; research plays always a fundamental role in their method of definitions contextualization and resolutions of problems.

p220-221

STUDIO LIN

Studio Lin is the graphic design practice of Alex Lin. Their work process is founded on a desire to explore new territory through challenging collaborations with creative visionaries in the fields of architecture, industrial design, art and fashion. By combining the studio's analytical rigor with strong input from external forces, the resulting design is exponentially enhanced: 1 + 1 = 3. This formula also permits a fluid aesthetic to prevail.

p026-027

STUDIO PARRIS WAKEFIELD

Howard Wakefield and Sarah Parris both worked with Peter Saville as directors of Saville Associates and now run their own independent design studio Studio Parris Wakefield. The studio specialises in identity design and implementation as well as contemporary digital illustration. The Studio is passionate about their work and believe honesty in design is paramount.

p280-281

TADAS KARPAVICIUS

Tadas Karpavicius is a graphic artist from Lithuania currently living in London who specializes in the fields of illustration, typography, visual identity, publication design, moving image and photography. He works for various cultural and commercial projects.

p240-241

TAKT STUDIO

Takt Studio develops creative idea for new and existing brands. Specializing in branding and art direction they produce work that is engaging and direct in its communication allowing the strategy to dictate the most appropriate medium for each project.

p076

TEACAKE

Teacake is something quite essentially British, inventive and conscientious. They love visual organisation, people, places and the idea of creating a tangible interaction with those who see their work. This has subsequently led to them having a strong affiliation with design for print and a passion for typography inspired by time spent working and learning in Amsterdam. Teacake's partnership is based on a mutual love for all things creative and an ambition to be able to whistle while they work every day of the week!

p083

THE CHASE CREATIVE CONSULTANTS

The work of the Chase Creative Consultants has been described as "disarmingly simple". They like that. The Chase has always been about ideas that are carefully crafted. Since forming in 1986, they've stuck to a very simple philosophy, a little traveler's tale heard on the radio. It's this. There was once an old Indian craftsman who carved beautiful elephants from old blocks of timber. When asked how he did, the craftsman simply replied: "I just cut away the wood that doesn't look like an elephant". Absorb everything, interpret only the essential.

p270-271

THE GREENSPACE

Greenspace is a unique agency that believes passionately in the value of fresh ideas.

With a nimble team of senior staff, Greenspace delivers cross-discipline marketing programmes that include brand strategy and design — through to brand experience, marketing concepts, advertising and digital executions.

Working across all sectors, developing programmes for the likes of Nokia, Toyota and Heineken can be seen globally.

p148-149

THIS IS REAL ART

This is Real Art is an ideas business.

Ideas that have impact and change perceptions. Ideas that transform the way people think, act and make their choices.

For MTV this sort of thinking resulted in their highest ever spontaneous awareness. They helped put Make Poverty History in every mind, on every wrist and on the lips of Nelson Mandela.

Three of their campaigns have started debates in parliament. And for Sony, they helped launch their "like.no.other" branding across the world. The same year, they designed and launched the UK's largest recruitment website. It gained 2.5 million new users.

And they've just created a brand with Massive Attack, Kasabian and Robbie Williams.

They've won major global awards in advertising, film, digital and graphic design. And D&AD have awarded their work every year they've been in business.

p023

TIM WAN

Tim Wan is a Leeds (UK) based freelance graphic designer with a focus towards information driven design solutions predominantly for print based output. His design practice is very much about the process of solving a problem by pin pointing the core issue and message and delivering it with the attention to process, message, production and format. His passion lies within typographic driven design solutions for print and the conventions of publication designs.

p184

TNOP™ DESIGN

TNOP™ DESIGN is a design studio in Chicago founded by Tnop Wangsillapakun. Tnop is originally from Bangkok, Thailand and formerly worked as a senior designer with Carlos Segura at Segura, Inc. in Chicago. His unique work and experimental logo and graphic designs put him at the forefront of today's contemporary artists and designers.

p075, 228-229

TOBEN

Toben is a Sydney based studio for creative thought, art direction and design.

Toben was founded in 2010 by Katja Hartung and Thorsten Kulp. It started out with a passion to build a studio with creativity at its core and one that continues to challenge conventional approaches and processes.

p296-297

TRAPPED IN SUBURBIA

Trapped in Suburbia is a smart creative studio based in the Hague, the Netherlands. They enjoy working at the cutting edge, challenging themselves and those around them, looking further than the length of their nose. They create conceptually and strategically strong projects with clear, clever designs and solutions. They think before they act, but they act before they talk. They love telling stories and inspiring people, doing extensive research and pushing boundaries. To drink from a cup that's half empty and have fun. Next to the design agency they also run the contemporary graphic art gallery Ship of Fools.

p036-037, 290-291

TT:NT

TT:NT is established by the collaboration projects between Tithi Kutchamuch and Nutre Arayavanish. They both graduated from Royal College of Art in 2007, one in product design and the other one in jewellery design and making, one who develops ideas in her dreaming head and the other who develops by her hand, one who makes things in one piece and the other who puts hundreds pieces in one, one who would go for the most basic stuff and the other who would look for the most detailing work.

They share their difference in the projects under the name of TT:NT, seeking to design the product that response both design and craft needs, good concept and fine quality along with their uniqueness and of course, happiness.

p013-015

TUUKKA KOIVISTO

Tuukka Koivisto is a Helsinki based graphic designer. He has learnt more by doing than by paying attention at school. He does anything he gets his hands on. And he does it without hesitating and he does it big.

If Tuukka was wine, he would be vinegar. If Tuukka was a woman, he would be a man. If Tuukka was a vegetarian, he would feast on meat. If Tuukka was an animal, he would be a lion. He is more extreme than you are.

He is a nightmare to work with because you do not know what he does next, but you love to work with him for the same reason. And what he does next is something that saves your ass.

p260-261

TYLER ADAM SMITH

Tyler Adam Smith is a designer who currently calls Toronto home. He is a drinker of black coffee, and a maker of things. He bikes to the studio every day to work on brands large and small, crafting memorable and thoughtful identities and communications for an exciting variety of businesses. He believes that life is too short for mediocre communication, and ultimately aims to do great work for good people.

p322, 329

ULRIKE MEUTZNER

Ulrike Meutzner studied Graphic Design at the University of Applied Sciences Wiesbaden and after that, she worked as a freelancer for several agencies and magazines. At the moment she is employed at Peter Schmidt Group and wishes she had more time for personal projects.

p097

ULTRA:STUDIO

Created in 2004 by Ludovic Gerber, Ultra:studio is a Graphic Design studio based in Vevey, Switzerland.

Ultra:studio is characterized by simple and clever concepts based on typographic design and bold colours.

p304

UMA/DESIGN FARM

UMA/design farm is a design studio in Japan.

p274-275, 286

WALNUT

Walnut is a multidisciplinary design studio. They have a passion for design, art and communication. Their work span across a wide range of projects from illustrations and to web design and video. They have an eye for detail and a belief in idea-based design as the key to great solutions. Walnut is founded by Camilla S. Reenberg and Per S. Reenberg.

p314-315

WANG ZHI HONG

Born in 1975 in Taipei, Wang Zhi Hong is an award-winning graphic designer based in Taiwan. He'd graduated from department of advertisement design at Fu-hsin Trade and Arts School in 1995. He started his studio in 2000 and has been specializing in graphic design for books on various subjects and for fine art projects and events, ranging from architecture, film, to performing arts. In 2008 he launched his book publishing program insight with a trade publisher, featuring translated titles on art and design, such as the works by Kashiwa Sato, Araki Nobuyoshi, Kenya Hara, Yayoi Kusama, Taku Satoh and Otl Aicher.

Wang Zhi Hong is a five-time winner of Golden Butterfly Awards, Taiwan's highest honor for excellence in book design. He has received many international awards and recognitions, including Kaoru Kasai Choice Winner and bronze awards from HKDA Asia Design Awards, excellent work from Tokyo Type Directors Club Annual Awards.

p020-021

WEI LIAO

Wei Liao, born in 1983, has been working as Design Director in Liao Graphic. He designs typography, layout and printer matters, which had won the Golden Prize of Taiwan Poster, Taiwan International Design Competition 2009 and Young Award for Taiwan International Graphic Design Award 2011. His work was also chosen for Brno, Golden Bee, Lahti, Output, ADAA and GDC, etc. He has been invited to display his works in Nizio Gallery in Warsaw-Poland, the OCT Art & Design Gallery in Shenzhen, Eslite bookstore and so on.

p282-283

YANAGAWA

Yanagawa Design, established in 2008, is a design studio in Japan.

p323

Acknowledgements

We would like to thank all the designers for their kind permission to publish their works, as well as all the photographers who have generously granted us the rights to use their images. We are also very grateful to many other people whose names do not appear on the credits but who made specific contributions and provided support. Without them, we would not be able to share these great ideas and works with readers around the world.